RECONSTRUCTING SOLIDARITY

Work is widely thought to have become more precarious. Many people feel that unions represent the interests of protected workers in good jobs at the expense of workers with insecure employment, low pay, and less generous benefits. Reconstructing Solidarity: Labour Unions, Precarious Work, and the Politics of Institutional Change in Europe argues the opposite: that unions try to represent precarious workers using a variety of creative campaigning and organizing tactics.

Where unions can limit employers' ability to 'exit' labour market institutions and collective agreements, and build solidarity across different groups of workers, this results in a virtuous circle, establishing union control over the labour market. Where they fail to do so, it sets in motion a vicious circle of expanding precarity based on institutional evasion by employers. Reconstructing Solidarity examines how unions build, or fail to build, inclusive worker solidarity to challenge this vicious circle and to re-regulate increasingly precarious jobs. Comparative case studies from fourteen European countries describe the struggles of workers and unions in industries such as local government, retail, music, metalworking, chemicals, meat packing, and logistics. Their findings argue against the thesis that unions act primarily to protect labour market insiders at the expense of outsiders.

This volume was edited by **Virginia Doellgast**, Associate Professor of Comparative Employment Relations at the ILR School, Cornell University, USA; **Nathan Lillie**, Professor of Social and Public Policy at the Department of Social Sciences and Philosophy, University of Jyväskylä, Finland; and **Valeria Pulignano**, Professor of Sociology of Labour and Industrial Relations at the Centre for Sociological Research, KU Leuven, Belgium.

T0323433

Reconstructing Solidarity

Labour Unions, Precarious Work, and the Politics of Institutional Change in Europe

Edited by
VIRGINIA DOELLGAST,
NATHAN LILLIE,
and
VALERIA PULIGNANO

OXFORD
UNIVERSITY PRESS

Great Clarendon Street, Oxford, OX2 6DP,
United Kingdom

Oxford University Press is a department of the University of Oxford.
It furthers the University's objective of excellence in research, scholarship,
and education by publishing worldwide. Oxford is a registered trade mark of
Oxford University Press in the UK and in certain other countries

First published 2018
First published in paperback 2020

Published in the United States of America by Oxford University Press
198 Madison Avenue, New York, NY 10016, United States of America

British Library Cataloguing in Publication Data
Data available

Library of Congress Cataloging in Publication Data
Data available

ISBN 978-0-19-879184-3 (Hbk.)
ISBN 978-0-19-885355-8 (Pbk.)

Acknowledgements

The idea for this book came out of a series of meetings organized by Jan Drahokoupil at the European Trade Union Institute to discuss research on union responses to outsourcing in Europe. The editors and several of the contributors to *Reconstructing Solidarity* presented draft chapters, which were published in *The Outsourcing Challenge: Organizing Workers Across Fragmented Production Networks* (ETUI, 2015). That book was directed to an audience of unions, policymakers, and other practitioners concerned with how best to respond to declining pay and working conditions associated with vertical disintegration in different sectors and firms. We were struck by how complementary our research findings and arguments were, and thought a lot could be gained by working together on a second book project.

As academics who broadly self-identify as comparative employment relations researchers, we observed that our field is producing a large number of detailed industry case studies looking at how outsourcing, temporary agency work, and other forms of 'externalization' of jobs are reshaping employment and union power. A similarly impressive body of research compares union responses to migration and campaigns to fight precarious work. However, researchers in our field more often cite theory in other disciplines—particularly comparative political economy and sociology of work—than seek to build on the arguments and insights of employment relations colleagues working on the same empirical questions. Why is that? One reason might be that we are not particularly good at developing parsimonious theoretical frameworks, as researchers attuned to the complexities of workplace- and industry-level politics: it is more straightforward to poke holes in other simplifying theories or point to their lack of subtlety. Another is that we draw on so many different research traditions that the terms and theoretical concepts we use are difficult to reconcile. Our focus on particular industries, occupations, or countries can also make it difficult to generalize beyond these settings.

We see this book as one step towards developing a common framework for comparing the factors that drive growing precarity in labour markets or that support successful collective action necessary to combat precarious work. Our framework and arguments are grounded in the comparative employment relations tradition, but draw on and contribute to debates that have become common currency in our field: on institutional change in coordinated capitalisms from comparative political economy, and on processes of collective and individual worker identification from critical sociology. We draw most directly on the detailed empirical findings of the chapter authors, who collectively carried out many hundreds of interviews with workers, managers, worker representatives, and union activists across a wide array of workplaces, industries, and countries. Once we started using a common set of terms and concepts, it became much easier to see the patterns across these case studies concerning the sources of labour power and their impact on precarious work. This book is a product of that collective effort, and we hope it will inspire further work that builds on the arguments we advance here.

We developed this book collaboratively over several years, starting with our initial discussions at the ETUI in Brussels in 2014. We organized a chapter development workshop at Cornell University in June 2016, which was funded by the Pierce Memorial Conference Fund at the ILR School and the Cornell Institute for European Studies at the Mario Einaudi Center for International Studies. Chris Howell and Arne Kalleberg gave thoughtful summary discussant comments and contributed their critiques and insights throughout the workshop. Rose Batt, Alex Colvin, Shannon Gleeson, Chris Tilly, and Lowell Turner also contributed as discussants on different panels; while Stefanie Huertgen, Harry Katz, Nick Krachler, Andrew Morton, and Peter Turnbull participated in workshop discussions alongside the chapter authors.

Our respective home institutions and institutions that hosted us as visiting professors supported our work on this book over the past several years. These include Cornell University's ILR School; the Laboratoire d'Economie et de Sociologie du Travail (LEST); the Employment Relations Research Center (FAOS) at the University of Copenhagen; the Department of Social Sciences and Philosophy at the University of Jyväskylä; and the Centre for Sociological Research (CESO) and Faculty of Social Science at KU Leuven, in particular through the 'Solidarity Lecture Series' at CESO (2014–17). The editors were further supported by grants and fellowships from the Mario Einaudi Center for International Studies at Cornell University; the European Commission, DG Employment, Social Affairs and Inclusion; the Academy of Finland; the Fonds Wetenschappelijk Onderzoek (FWO) at the Flemish Research Council of Belgium; and the Bijzonder Onderzoekfonds (BOF) of the KU Leuven.

The most valuable contributions to this book came from the unionists, works councillors, and other labour organizers and activists who shared their time and insights, from discussant comments during the early ETUI workshops to interviews and informal discussions at international meetings and conferences. We hope some of these voices come through in our arguments and findings. These are the individuals and organizations who are working against difficult odds to build solidarity within and across an increasingly precarious workforce.

Contents

List of Figures

List of Tables

List of Contributors

Dominique Anxo is Professor of Economics at the Department of Economics and Statistics, Linnaeus University, Sweden, and Director of the Centre of Ageing and Lifecourse Studies. His research interests fall broadly into the areas of labour economics, industrial relations, and gender economics. He has during the last decades participated in multidisciplinary large European research projects and networks of excellence. Within this framework he has edited several books and scientific papers related to changing work patterns across the life course and cross-country comparisons of industrial relations systems, employment, and welfare state regimes.

Branko Bembič is a research assistant at the Faculty for Social Sciences, University of Ljubljana. He holds a PhD in sociology of culture from the Faculty of Arts, University of Ljubljana. He is involved in several international as well as national research projects. His research interests include critique of political economy, class analysis, and working class organizations.

Chiara Benassi is Senior Lecturer in Human Resource Management at King's Business School, King's College London. She holds a PhD from the London School of Economics. Her research is in the area of comparative human resource management and it investigates how national and local institutions as well as political and economic contingencies affect companies' human resource strategies in the areas of internal and external flexibility, training and human capital management. Her writing was published in, among others, British Journal of Industrial Relations, Socio-Economic Review, and the European Journal of Industrial Relations.

Carlotta Benvegnú is a Post-Doctoral Fellow at the CEPN (Economic Center of Paris Nord University) under the project PLUS (Platform Labour in Urban Spaces: Fairness, Welfare, Development). She holds a PhD in Sociology from the University Paris 8 Saint-Denis and the University of Padua. Her main research interests include labour market segmentation, labour mobility, logistics and digital platforms.

Erka Çaro is a Researcher and Lecturer at the Department of Geography, University of Tirana, Albania. She received her PhD in Population Studies from the University of Groningen in the Netherlands. She is a member of the executive board of the Western Balkans Migration Network and is the Principal Investigator of the Regional Research Promotion Program-funded project 'Industrial Citizenship and Labor Migration from Western Balkan, Cases of Albania and Kosovo Migration to Germany, Switzerland and Greece'. Her research interests include migration, labour mobility, trade union relationships with migrants, gender studies, and the Western Balkans.

Sonila Danaj is a Researcher at the European Centre for Social Welfare Policy and Research, Vienna, Austria in their Work and Welfare programme. She is also a

PhD candidate at the University of Jyvaskyla in Finland. Her doctoral research focuses on posted workers in the United Kingdom. Her research interests include labour migration, employment relations, the organization and mobilization of migrants, and organized labour responses to labour migration.

Virginia Doellgast is Associate Professor of Comparative Employment Relations at Cornell University's School of Industrial and Labor Relations. Her research focuses on the impact of collective bargaining and labour market institutions on inequality, job quality, and worker voice. Past projects include comparative studies of organizational and work restructuring in the European and US telecommunications and call centre industries. She is the author of *Disintegrating Democracy at Work: Labor Unions and the Future of Good Jobs in the Service Economy* (Cornell University Press, 2012).

Nadja Doerflinger is a Postdoctoral Researcher in the Research Group 'Employment Relations and Labour Markets' at the Centre for Sociological Research (CeSO) at KU Leuven (Belgium). Her research is mostly comparative, and focuses on contingent work, labour market segmentation and fragmentation, and flexibility and security in European labour markets.

Lisa Dorigatti is Assistant Professor at the Department of Social and Political Sciences at the University of Milan. Her research interests include trade union strategies, in particular towards precarious work, outsourcing and labour market segmentation, and comparative employment relations. She has published some of her work in the *British Journal of Industrial Relations*, in the *Industrial and Labor Relations Review* and in the *European Journal of Industrial Relations*.

Jérôme Gautié is Professor of Economics at the University Paris 1 Panthéon-Sorbonne. His fields of research are labour economics, industrial relations, and labour market and social policies. He has been involved in many international research programmes (funded by the ILO, the European Commission, and the Russell Sage Foundation). He has worked on the minimum wage, low-wage work, and job quality, in both the private and the public sectors. He is co-editor of *Low Wage Work in the Wealthy World* (Russell Sage Foundation, 2010).

Ian Greer is a Senior Research Associate at Cornell University's School of Industrial and Labor Relations. His research interests include trade union strategy and welfare policy, both within a line of questioning about the social effects of marketization. He has worked at Leeds and Greenwich universities in England and been a visiting researcher in Aix-en-Provence, Berlin, Chemnitz, Cologne, Jena, Paris, and Sydney. He is co-author of *The Marketization of Employment Services: Dilemmas of Europe's Work-First Welfare States* (Oxford University Press, 2017). Prior to entering academia he worked in the US trade union movement.

Damian Grimshaw is Professor of Employment Studies at King's College London. His published work covers international comparisons of low-wage labour markets, outsourcing and HRM, precarious work and gender inequality. Recent publications include Making Work More Equal (Manchester University Press, 2017) and "Market exposure and the labour process: The contradictory dynamics in managing subcontracted services" in Work, Employment and Society (2019). He was previously Director of the Research department at the International Labour Organisation, Geneva.

Bettina Haidinger is a Senior Researcher with the Working Life Research Centre in Vienna. Her main research fields cover work, migration and gender relations, and feminist economics, as well as industrial relations and global value chains.

Jane Holgate is Professor of Work and Employment Relations at Leeds University Business School. Her research interests include trade unions and the development of organizing and recruitment strategies, particularly as they relate to under-represented groups in the union movement; gender and industrial relations; the labour market position of migrants and black and minority ethnic groups; new geographies of labour; and the politics of intersectionality.

Kairit Kall is a PhD student at Tallinn University and at the University of Jyväskylä. She is also a project researcher at both universities and lecturer in sociology at Tallinn University. Her current research includes innovation within trade unions, transnational cooperation among unions, intra-EU labour migration, and platform labour.

Nathan Lillie is Professor of Social and Public Policy at the University of Jyväskylä, Finland. He has been a Fellow at the Helsinki Collegium for Advanced Studies, and Associate Professor of International Business at the University of Groningen, in the Netherlands. His current research relates to migration and posted work, free movement in the European Union, and trade union strategies. In his current project, *Protecting Mobility through Improving Labour Rights Enforcement in Europe*, he is working together with stakeholders on improving labour protection and access to industrial democracy for posted workers.

Małgorzata Maciejewska holds a PhD in Sociology from the University of Wrocław. Her work is focused on feminist theories, the socio-economic history of Polish transition after 1989, and industrial relations in Central and Eastern Europe. Most recently she has worked as a Research Fellow at the Institute of Sociology, University of Wrocław (Poland) under the project PRECARIR: 'The Rise of the Dual Labour Market: Fighting Precarious Employment in the New Member States through Industrial Relations'.

Laura Mankki is a PhD candidate at the Department of Social Sciences and Philosophy, University of Jyväskylä, Finland. She has been a guest researcher at the REMESO migration institute in Sweden. Her PhD research concentrates on life stories of labour migrants in Finland. She has co-authored articles in the Finnish labour issues journal, as well as in anthologies dealing with gender and labour market issues. Before her graduate studies, she worked as an assistant to a member of the Finnish parliament. She is a board member of the local researchers and teachers trade union.

Stefania Marino is Senior Lecturer in Employment Studies at the Alliance Manchester Business School and member of the Work and Equalities Institute of the University of Manchester. Stefania's research interests are in the field of labour sociology, international migration and industrial relations, with a particular focus on international and comparative analysis. Recent contributions include *The Politics of Social Inclusion and Labor Representation: Immigrants and Trade Unions in the European Context* (Cornell University Press, 2019) with Heather Connolly and Miguel Martinez Lucio and *Trade Union and Migrant Workers: New Context and Challenges in Europe* (Edward Elgar-ILO, 2017) with Judith Roosblad and Rinus Penninx.

Adam Mrozowicki is Associate Professor at the Institute of Sociology, University of Wrocław. His main research areas include comparative industrial relations, precarity, and the social agency of socially disadvantaged groups. He has published his work in *Work, Employment and Society*, the *British Journal of Industrial Relations*, and *Transfer*; and he authored the book *Coping with Social Change: Life Strategies of Workers in Poland's Late Capitalism* (Leuven University Press, 2011). He is currently involved in biographical research on young precarious workers in Poland and Germany within the NCN-DFG-funded project PREWORK.

László Neumann is a Senior Research Fellow at the Institute for Political Science, Hungarian Academy of Sciences. He was formerly at the Research Institute of Labour and its successor institutions. His earlier studies focused on shop-floor wage/effort bargaining and privatization of former state-owned enterprises. His current research interests are in the areas of industrial relations and labour market policy, including decentralized collective bargaining, employment practices and labour relations at foreign-owned companies, and social dialogue at various levels. He used to be an adviser to an independent union federation (LIGA), and gives lectures in industrial relations at ELTE University, Budapest.

Valeria Pulignano is Professor of Sociology of Labour and Industrial Relations and Chair of the Centre for Sociological Research (CESO), KU Leuven, Belgium. She is an Associate Fellow at IRRU (University of Warwick) and co-researcher at CRIMT (University of Montreal). She has worked extensively on comparative European industrial (employment) relations and labour markets, particularly on employee representation systems, trade unions, collective bargaining, multinational companies, labour (market) flexibility and employment security, social change, dualization, and inequality. Some of her co-authored publications include *Employment Relations in an Era of Change* (ETUI, 2016) and *The Transformation of Employment Relations in Europe* (Routledge, 2013).

Bjarke Refslund is associate professor in Sociology at Aalborg University. He holds a Ph.D. degree in Political Science from Aalborg University. His main research areas include industrial relations, labour migration and labour market sociology and he has been working on collectivism and unions, organising migrant workers, precarious employment, public regulation and Europeanisation of labour markets amongst others. His research has feature in journals such as *European Journal of Industrial Relations*, *Economic and Industrial Democracy*, *Work, Employment & Society and Competition and Change*.

Devi Sacchetto is Associate Professor of Sociology of Labour at Padua University. His main research areas include labour and migration processes, precarity, and labour market segmentation. His research has been published in *Work,*

Employment and Society, Transfer, and *South Atlantic Quarterly.* Currently, he is leading a research project entitled 'From China to Europe: Migration and Gender in the Global Production Network', which investigates the ways in which 'Chinese' modes of production are impacting on work and employment relations in Europe.

Barbara Samaluk is a Leverhulme Trust Early Career Fellow at the Work and Employment Research Unit at the University of Greenwich Business School. She completed her PhD at the Centre for Research in Equality and Diversity at Queen Mary, University of London. Her research interests lie in the cultural political economy of European East–West relations, transnational employment relations, labour migration, and the effects of marketization on post-socialist societies and welfare states. Her current research project investigates the process of work transitions and the transnational mobility of young and precarious workers. Her articles have been published in *Work, Employment and Society* and *Industrial Relations Journal.*

Markku Sippola is a University Lecturer at the School of Social Sciences and Humanities, University of Tampere, Finland. His research interests include industrial relations, migration, and societal and labour processes in the Baltic, Nordic, and Russian contexts. His articles have been recently published in *Economic and Industrial Democracy, Employee Relations,* the *European Journal of Industrial Relations,* the *Journal of Baltic Studies,* and *Work, Employment and Society.*

Miroslav Stanojević is Professor of Industrial Relations and Comparative Industrial Relations at the Faculty of Social Sciences, University of Ljubljana. His research includes the sociology of work and industrial relations, the marketization of formerly state-regulated societies, and the transformation of industrial relations. He has published his recent research on weakening social dialogue in Slovenia and neoliberalism in Hungary and Slovenia in the *European Journal of Industrial Relations* and *Europe-Asia Studies.*

Maite Tapia is Assistant Professor at the School of Human Resources and Labor Relations at Michigan State University. Her research revolves around organizing and mobilizing strategies of trade unions, community organizations, and social movements in the US and Europe, as well as work, migration, and intersectional organizing. She is co-editor of *Mobilizing against Inequality: Unions, Immigrant Workers, and the Crisis of Capitalism* (Cornell University Press, 2014).

Charles Umney is a Lecturer in Work and Employment Relations at Leeds University Business School. His writing on employment in live music has been published in journals including *Work, Employment and Society, Human Relations,* and *Work and Occupations.* Aside from this, his research interests include trade union mobilization, the marketization of public service provision, and the consequences of so-called 'platform capitalism' for work and employment.

Steven P. Vallas is Professor of Sociology at Northeastern University in Boston. He has written numerous books and articles on various issues involving the changing structure and experience of work. He has written on the reciprocal relation between technologies and work organizations, the nature of team-based systems of workplace authority, racial and ethnic boundaries among employees, and the shifting contours of 'knowledge work' in science-intensive fields. Most recently he has been studying the cultural meaning of career advice books and the cultural pressures currently reshaping employee identity. He is the author of *Work: A Critique* (Polity, 2012) and co-editor of *The SAGE Handbook of Resistance* (SAGE, 2016) with David Courpasson.

Ines Wagner is Senior Research Fellow at the Institute for Social Research in Oslo. Her research focuses on EU labor mobility, industrial relations and gender. She has published her work, amongst others, in the *British Journal of Industrial Relations, the Journal of Common Market Studies, Socio-Economic Review, Journal of Ethnic and Migration Studies* and Cornell University Press.

Claudia Weinkopf is Associate Director of IAQ at the University of Duisburg-Essen. Her research interests include minimum wages, trade union strategies towards precarious work, outsourcing and labour market segmentation, and employment relations. She has published some of her work in *Work and Occupations* and in the *European Journal of Industrial Relations*.

1

From Dualization to Solidarity

Halting the Cycle of Precarity

Virginia Doellgast, Nathan Lillie, and Valeria Pulignano

1.1. INTRODUCTION

Employment is becoming less secure. In the wealthy economies of the Global North, the traditional permanent job from which a worker could expect to earn a living wage over years or decades has become scarce, while short-term, unpredictable, and poorly paid positions have proliferated. Labelled as precarious work, these jobs are widely viewed as either symptoms or causes of rising inequality, poverty, and reduced economic and social mobility. Precarity is often associated with non-standard employment contracts. However, non-standard contracts are not necessarily precarious, and not all standard jobs are secure. We are concerned with *employment precarity*, characterized by a high degree of worker insecurity and instability in an employment relationship or labour market.

This is a book about efforts by workers and labour unions to contest the expansion of precarious work. Labour unions once regulated employment in ways they no longer effectively do for most people. Many scholars diagnose unions as more a part of the problem than a part of the solution, arguing that they often promote the job security of their 'insider' core members at the expense of 'outsiders' (e.g. Hassel 2014; Rueda 2014). We recognize that unions sometimes accede to employer demands to shift jobs to precarious contracts and deregulate labour markets, or neglect the interests of precarious workers. However, these exclusive strategies are rarely sustainable in the long term. Where core workers do not show solidarity with vulnerable workers, they often undermine their own bargaining power through creating lower-cost competition. Ensuring equal treatment for all workers, particularly those in unstable work, is essential to the long-term viability of the labour movement. The chapters in this volume show that labour unions increasingly seek to regulate precarious work and represent precarious workers, both to protect their members from low-cost competition and following from broader commitments to equity and social justice. Our central concern is to better understand the conditions under which they succeed in these objectives.

The empirical focus of this book is European industries and workplaces. In the post-World War II decades, Western European unions and social democratic political parties established a high degree of solidaristic and encompassing employment regulation supported by a diverse range of national and sectoral institutions. In Central and Eastern Europe, state socialist regimes also ensured widespread stable employment through central planning and a political commitment to full employment. In recent decades, changes in technology and skills, the integration of markets, and the collapse of state socialist systems have freed capital from dependence on national labour markets and broadened its access to cheap labour, weakening unions' bargaining power in their traditional strongholds. A free market ideology of policymaking in Europe has driven a shift away from traditions of social regulation and towards neoliberal employment deregulation and austerity. The chapters demonstrate that these factors are associated with expanding options for employers to use precarious work in a range of industries, and with declining labour power to contest these measures and their negative effects on the core workforce. In this sense, there is no distinct precariat as a class in itself (as, for example, Standing 2011, would assert), as the condition of precariousness is increasingly one shared to greater or lesser degrees by workers generally.

In this introduction, we develop an original framework to explain why unions are more or less successful in containing the spread of precarious work. We argue that employment precarity is both an outcome of and a central contributing factor to a mutually reinforcing feedback relationship between labour market, welfare state, and collective bargaining institutions; worker identity and identification; and employer and union strategies. Where employers are better able to exploit institutional exit options and divisions in the workforce, they are likely to seek cost containment and control via precarious employment relationships. The most compelling and consistent finding from the case studies examined in this book is that unions' success in responding to these challenges depends on mobilizing power resources derived from inclusive institutions and inclusive forms of worker solidarity.

The framework we develop builds on academic discussions of institutional change, dualism, and precarious work from three broad research traditions: comparative political economy, critical sociology, and comparative employment relations. We review this literature, outline our framework, and then discuss the chapter findings with reference to the framework.

1.2. PAST RESEARCH ON PRECARIOUS WORK: THREE TRADITIONS

1.2.1. Comparative Political Economy Debates: Dualism and Liberalization

The first perspective we draw on is the comparative political economy (CPE) literature, particularly the recent debates on institutional change and dualism in coordinated models of capitalism. This literature treats nations as coherent political-economic systems, which can be systematically categorized based on their economic structures and institutional characteristics.

In the CPE literature on national models of capitalism, the European social model was held out as the standard-bearer of a region with well-functioning non-market institutions that appeared to balance equity with efficiency, containing trends towards expanding inequality evident elsewhere in the post-Bretton Woods global economy. CPE scholars seeking to explain Europe's relative success at normalizing economic equity and social solidarity typically start with national archetypes formed from the 1950s through the 1980s. 'Neocorporatist' systems, such as Germany, Switzerland, Austria, and the Benelux and Nordic countries, were characterized by centralized, tripartite bargaining that supported competitiveness through promoting wage restraint (Schmitter and Lehmbruch 1979; Katzenstein 1985) and labour cooperation in industrial adjustment (Zysman 1983).

The varieties of capitalism (VoC) literature adapted these arguments to explain why employers continued to benefit from different institutional arrangements under intensified globalization in the late 1990s and early 2000s (Hall and Soskice 2001). Liberal market economies like the US generated high levels of precarity, due to employers' reliance on highly flexible labour markets, short-term capital investment, and market-based skill provision; while coordinated market economies (CMEs) such as Germany and the Nordic countries enjoyed less precarity due to lead firms' reliance on long-term labour cooperation, 'patient' capital, and high levels of industry- and employer-specific skills. Under coordinated capitalism, not all employers and investors supported inclusive institutions, but at least they did not fight collectively against these arrangements as long as they derived some benefits, for example through labour cooperation.

Since at least the early 2010s, CPE scholars have largely retreated from claims that European social institutions are stable and resistant to trends of market liberalization observed elsewhere in the world. In broad terms, the current CPE literature views the expansion of precarious work in the coordinated economies of Western Europe as a symptom of the declining coverage of coordinating institutions. However, scholars disagree on whether these trends result in the general liberalization and weakening of labour market and collective bargaining institutions (Baccaro and Howell 2011; Streeck 2009, 2016; Paster 2013) or in their sharp dualization (Rueda 2007, 2014; Palier and Thelen 2010). The former dynamic increases uncertainty for all workers, while the second protects the security of labour market insiders at the expense of outsiders, who bear increasingly high levels of economic risk.

The dualism thesis shows continuity with the VoC framework. Dual labour market arguments assume that the institutions of CMEs continue to support competitive advantage with high pay and job security—although only for a decreasing circle of firms and workers in high-value-added production. Those workers and firms have built productivity alliances, which shelter the position of the core workforce in stable jobs at the expense of precarious and unemployed workers. This drives a process of dualization, whereby policies 'increasingly differentiate rights, entitlements, and services provided to different categories of recipients'—allowing insiders to maintain good terms and conditions, while existing and new categories of outsiders experience declining pay and security (Emmenegger et al. 2012: 10). Unions are often implicated in dualizing strategies: they cooperate with employers and social democratic political parties to preserve the status of insiders, who are more likely to be union members, while permitting the deregulation of institutions and bargaining arrangements that used to protect workers in service jobs, at subcontractors, and on non-standard contracts (Rueda 2007). These close ties between employers and unions often support the global competitiveness of large firms in export sectors by reducing the cost of low-skill activities in the production chain (Hassel 2014; Palier and Thelen 2010; Thelen 2012).

In contrast, CPE scholars associated with the liberalization thesis view dualism (where it occurs) as a temporary state or 'way station' on a general trajectory towards convergence on market liberalization—accompanied by a more general decline in labour power and union influence (Baccaro and Howell 2017). Their arguments draw more heavily on the power resources school of the CPE literature typically associated with Korpi (1983), which traces Europe's coordinating institutions to capital's historic compromises with strong and militant labour movements rather than to employer interests. As globalization frees capital from its dependence on labour or the nation state, 'unruly' employers grow increasingly aggressive and creative in 'relentlessly whacking away at social rules'—even in the high-skilled core sectors of the economy (Streeck 2009: 241).

We can draw useful insights from both recent veins of the CPE literature. Their comparative research findings demonstrate common trends of institutional change and expanding precarity across Europe, including in post-communist Central and Eastern European (CEE) countries (Bohle and Greskovits 2012). They document the insider–outsider political dynamics associated with the shrinking scope of the core workforce, particularly in manufacturing sectors in Germany and other Bismarkian welfare states; which increasingly rely on cheap labour to support competitive exports, even in high-value-added market segments (Baccaro and Benassi 2016). This helps explain the distinctive challenges unions face in expanding their representation domain to new groups in these countries.

CPE scholars also provide differentiated analyses of how national collective bargaining systems and the structure of welfare states influence insider–outsider political dynamics. One set of arguments in the dualism literature holds that the spread of precarious work is more likely to be contained where institutions are encompassing across, and support coalitions between, lower-productivity, lower-wage service or non-traded sectors and high-productivity tradable or high-value-added sectors (Thelen 2014, Martin and Swank 2012). CPE researchers broadly agree that these conditions have been most stable in (at least some of) the Nordic countries, resulting in greater continuity in policies and union strategies promoting social solidarity and reducing inequality (Emmenegger et al. 2012). According to scholars associated with the liberalization thesis, this may be traced to residual (if ultimately declining) union power (Baccaro and Howell 2011) or to more balanced 'growth models' in these countries that depend on the export of knowledge-intensive goods and services (Baccaro and Pontusson 2016).

However, the CPE literature has fewer tools to analyse the reasons why unions choose more or less encompassing strategies towards labour market outsiders as their core workforce shrinks. The CPE literature's focus on lead industries and national political coalitions means that it has less sensitivity towards (or fewer empirical tools to evaluate) strategic interactions between labour and employers at the firm or industry level, particularly as regards the expansion of precarious work. Its methodological nationalism leads to the neglect of trans- and supra-national actors and institutions, such as multinational companies (MNCs) and the European Union. CPE also assumes that labour is national in outlook and organization—in that the challenges as well as resources for pursuing collective action are conceptualized in national terms. This gives the CPE literature few tools to analyse the institutions and interests promoting dualism, liberalization, or, alternatively, worker solidarity and reregulation, that emerge within or between national systems.

1.2.2. Critical Sociology Literature: Identity, Subjectivity, and Solidarity

CPE scholars typically approach dualization and liberalization from a standpoint of mechanical institutionalism and economic rationality, with no systematic analysis of how the interests of different groups are constructed. They typically only mention in passing the overlap between labour market segments and identity-based categories, such as ethnicity, gender, nationality, immigration status, and class. The analysis of social identity and social boundaries, and how these reinforce labour market boundaries, is more centrally the focus of the critical sociology literature. In many ways this literature provides a mirror of the strengths and weaknesses of the CPE dualism debates, producing more differentiated analyses rooted in the experiences of precarious workers within workplaces and industries, but with less developed theorization of how these experiences are embedded within, or influenced by, political-economic institutions. Because critical sociology is a large and diverse field, we focus on two related streams of research, the first on labour market segmentation and resistance and the second on the social construction of precarious employment.

The analysis of how social boundaries between groups are constructed and maintained has been a central concern of critical sociologists studying labour market segmentation or dualism. One influential framework is Bonacich's (1973) 'split labour market' hypothesis, which addresses social boundaries that derive from ethnic antagonism, and in which both employers and 'insiders' are of one race or ethnicity while 'outsiders' are of another. Research in this tradition has shown that labour markets are not only split into core and periphery, but also segmented in complex configurations between groups with differentiated access to various jobs (McCollum and Findlay 2015), which may cut across geographical regions (Paret 2016; Wagner 2015). One set of findings concerns how groups reinforce and protect their own access to certain labour market segments through ethnic or gendered ties, and reinforce employer perceptions that groups of workers belonging to a certain nationality, ethnicity, or gender are suitable for certain kinds of work. For example, MacKenzie and Forde (2009) describe how employers come to regard workers in more vulnerable labour market segments as 'good workers' mainly because they will accept lower pay and are more readily exploitable. Workers may become participants in their own exploitation, and even strategically leverage these perceptions for market advantage (Piore 1979; Berntsen 2016).

A split labour market based on ethnic differences may benefit insiders at a moment in time, but splits are fragile. Outsider groups may undermine the insiders as competitors and strike breakers, or they may take the political approach of social protest. Research has shown that segmentation and the ethnic divisions behind it can serve as the basis for mobilization by precarious workers (Milkman 2015; Berntsen 2016). Agarwala (2014), for example, compares the organizing efforts of precarious workers in eight developing and developed countries, and argues that some of the more successful informal workers' movements are based on building bridges between identity-based social movements and labour movements. In their introduction to a special journal issue on precarious work, Mosoetsa et al. (2016) document creative forms of collective action by precarious worker groups in South Africa, Mexico, the United States, China, and India, often led through civil society organizations, non-governmental organizations (NGOs), and advocacy groups. These often involve tactics that mobilize 'symbolic politics' associated with appeals to culture, values, and social justice (Chun 2009). In the European context, a more central focus has been on established unions, and their efforts to bridge divides between ethnic groups or workforce segments (Adler et al. 2013). For example, Virdee (2000) charts unions' progress in the UK, from attempts to exclude ethnic minority workers from labour markets to more inclusive strategies that embrace multiculturalism.

A second stream of the critical sociology literature focuses on the social construction of precarious employment. Research in this tradition has analysed the cultural and ideological frames that legitimize precarity (Vallas 2015) as well as the subjective experience of precarious work. Vallas and Prener (2012) describe a complex interplay between structural and discursive influences that shape the ways in which workers think about and experience the employment relationship. Precarious work reflects not only the workplace, but also the larger society: cultural and ideological processes affect public views concerning which working arrangements or conditions are accepted or not. Hatton (2011) shows how the US temporary staffing industry successfully used 'cultural representations' in their campaigns to legitimize agency work. Thus, groups of outsiders in precarious jobs internalize the employers' value systems and become self-disciplining—for example, via discourses praising 'self-entrepreneurship' (Murgia and Pulignano 2016). A related set of studies examine the construction of precarious conditions as normal or standard in certain forms of highly skilled and creative employment, such as musicians (Cornfield 2015; Umney and Kretsos 2015) or high-tech workers (Lane 2011)—with workers coming to view themselves as entrepreneurs responsible for marketing their skills and talents.

The critical sociology literature provides distinctive tools for analysing the factors driving the expansion of precarious work, as well as the role of precarious workers in reinforcing or combatting this expansion. It provides a useful lens for distinguishing forms of precarity that show continuity with the past—particularly in the Global South as well as on the margins of the Global North—from dynamics associated with the emergence of new forms of precarious work. Across global regions and time periods, broader societal divides by ethnicity and gender are found to exacerbate the interest-based dynamics of insider politics. Critical sociology also provides concepts that are useful for analysing the basis for collective action in segmented labour markets. It suggests that constructing (or reconstructing) solidarity between protected and precarious groups not only requires common interests, but also often requires overcoming ethnic divides within split labour markets or entrenched forms of particularistic worker identity to establish a more collectivist group identity.

This literature also has limitations, particularly in application to comparative research. Most studies in this tradition are based on in-depth case studies of a particular group of precarious workers, from which general propositions or arguments are derived. This gives good detail on local context, but less insight on the interaction between the institutions of the political economy and the strategies of actors and organized interests within different institutional systems. While the CPE literature is centrally concerned with how institutions construct interests and power relations between groups, these relationships receive less attention in critical sociology. There is thus little guidance concerning the conditions under which employers would seek to cooperate with their core workforce or exploit segmented labour markets; or when unions are more or less likely to adopt inclusive strategies. Researchers instead posit different configurations of outcomes (employers may exploit outsiders or use them to undermine core conditions; minority ethnic groups may serve as strike breakers or form broader social movements) without specifying the contextual conditions under which different outcomes are expected. This is because researchers often view hegemonic hierarchies of power relationships among the social classes of a society as the key explanatory variable. Thus, power is embedded in class position, ethnic group privilege, or hegemonic discourse, rather than following concretely from institutions in the political economy—unions, labour laws, and collective bargaining and welfare state institutions.

1.2.3. Comparative Employment Relations

The comparative employment relations literature can be placed between the CPE and critical sociology traditions, with researchers drawing on theories derived from both literatures to analyse different aspects of precarious work. In common with CPE, and in contrast with the critical sociology literature, comparative employment relations is centrally concerned with how institutions influence patterns of inequality and precarity. The focus, however, is on the employment relationship rather than national models or state–society relations. This has led scholars to analyse the local dynamics of interest (and at times identity) construction, which are central concerns of critical sociologists. Power relations at the industry or workplace levels are also more directly the focus of empirical study compared to either of the other traditions. These are manifested in micro-relations that are generally influenced by societal conditions, but which can also be determined by a wide range of specific contingencies, such as the actions of organizations and individuals. Agency comes to the fore more frequently, as decisions on human resource policy, firm and union strategy, and collective bargaining play crucial roles in the outcomes of specific cases. Compared to CPE, comparative employment relations has a more differentiated analysis of sector-, firm-, and shop floor-level developments, with a focus on the strategies and power resources of employers and unions (Bechter et al. 2012). In addition, these scholars increasingly take an international frame for analysing multi-level relationships between industrial relations actors—in the case of Europe, integrating attention to EU-level institutions and processes (Marginson and Sisson 2004).[1]

We can identify two main areas of empirical focus in the comparative employment relations literature on precarious work: the analysis of employer strategies to exploit different forms of precarious work via organizational restructuring and strategic benchmarking; and the analysis of union strategies to respond to this increasing fragmentation of the workforce through alternative patterns of action.

First, employment relations researchers have analysed the impact of employers' strategies on collective bargaining institutions—and on union power within those institutions. At the national level, employers and their associations may publicly lobby for the deregulation of non-standard contracts or collective bargaining rules (Kinderman 2005, 2016). At the sectoral level, employers' associations introduce alternative membership forms that do not bind their members to collective agreements, and provide advice and legal resources that allow them to adopt non-standard contractual arrangements (Andersen and Arnholtz 2016; Haipeter 2011). At the firm level, employers increase their use of outsourcing, subsidiaries, and temporary agency work, with the common effect of undermining solidaristic bargaining structures by intensifying worker-to-worker and inter-firm competition across new market-mediated boundaries (Greer and Doellgast 2017; Marchington et al. 2005). These relationships have been analysed across a wide range of industries, including (as just a few examples) auto manufacturing (Greer and Hauptmeier 2016), telecommunications (Holst 2014), call centres (Batt et al. 2009; Taylor and Bain 2004), and privatized service industries (Hermann and Flecker 2013; Grimshaw et al. 2015b).

A second area of research focus has been union strategies towards precarious work, including their response to employers' restructuring strategies. As in the CPE dualism literature, some research finds unions drawing their circle of insiders ever tighter as they come under pressure from employers, introducing two-tier agreements and temporary work, and agreeing to lower wages and conditions for 'outsiders' (Lillie 2012). However, this exclusionary strategy is not the predominate one (Heery 2004; Gumbrell-McCormick 2011). Case studies examine how unions overcome divides and rebuild encompassing bargaining (Turner 2009; Benassi and Dorigatti 2015), adapt traditional channels of social dialogue to ally with diverse civil society organizations and public agencies (Grimshaw et al. 2016: 311), or seek to restructure their own organizations to promote greater strategic coordination in campaigns targeting core and peripheral employers (Holtgrewe and Doellgast 2012).

Comparative employment relations' most significant contribution to understanding precarious work is to provide detailed and differentiated analyses of the micro-politics associated with the expanding or contracting precarity of employment contracts. At the national or sectoral level, findings suggest the importance of inclusive institutions, deriving from some combination of labour and state power to extend institutional protections from stronger to weaker groups of workers: including uniform minimum wages, state action to extend collective

---

[1] This is most comprehensively exemplified by Marginson and Sisson 2004, although the introduction of multi-level elements has now become common.

agreements from well-organized to less well-organized sectors and workplaces, and universal welfare state protections that are redistributive and that raise the social wage (Bosch et al. 2010; Hermann and Flecker 2013).

At the firm or workplace level, researchers have also mapped combinations of power resources worker representatives employ as they respond to pressures for labour market segmentation. Studies in MNCs have shown that local unions' structural power (rooted in firm and workplace structures, market conditions, and technology) and associational power (rooted in the resources and capabilities unions develop through collective organization) can explain differences in concession bargaining or flexibility–security trade-offs in different national settings (Pulignano and Keune 2014; Pulignano et al. 2016). At the same time, local actors must also have the capacity to use the available power resources, or deploy them in a particular bargaining context (Pulignano and Signoretti 2016; Lévesque and Murray 2013; Fairbrother et al. 2013). Thus, there is an iterative feedback relationship between power and strategy. Marginson (2016: 1048) argues that this is associated with significant subnational variation in protective institutions, or a 'patchwork of various forms of regulation, whose contours reflect the outcome of contestation between a range of actors in which power resources are differentially distributed'.

Employment relations scholars tend to place less emphasis than the CPE literature on how configurations of national institutions are established or sustained— for example, through coalitions bringing together different configurations of state actors, representatives of capital, and major labour unions. However, they have a more sophisticated understanding of how capital and labour interacts below or beyond the national level. This results in more differentiated analyses of the conditions under which unions and employers oppose or reproduce dual labour markets, and of employers' expanding capacity to evade formal regulations. While CPE emphasizes the (potential) compatibility between employer collective interests and those of certain unions and state actors, comparative employment relations is more sceptical, usually regarding labour–management cooperation as directly tied to industry- and firm-specific union capacities. Dualization is viewed as a temporary state, as unions either devise strategies for organizing and representing precarious workers, or fail to do so and eventually lose influence entirely as precarity expands. This critique shares much in common with the recent liberalization vein of the CPE literature, but is more optimistic that unions can access or build alternative power resources outside of its traditional coalitions with segments of capital at national level.

Much of the comparative employment relations literature is in the structuralist institutional tradition, and thus it has less developed frameworks for analysing worker identity and identification compared to critical sociology. Many scholars do attempt to grapple with the role of ideas, ideology, and identity (Hauptmeier and Heery 2014; Tapia et al. 2015)—particularly in explaining how unions develop alternative approaches to organizing precarious workers. For example, researchers have explained the inclusive strategies of unions in southern European or Nordic countries (compared to more insider-focused strategies in Central Europe) with reference to their stronger class- or society-based ideologies (Hyman 2001; Benassi and Vlandas 2016), or as resulting from the intersection between union identity and their members' interests (Dorigatti 2017). Research on international union campaigns describes 'identity work' as important in building solidarity among labour representatives in MNCs or within global unions (Greer and Hauptmeier 2012). Recently, comparative employment relations has given more attention to the subjective experience of precarious work—how attitudes towards unions among different groups of workers, for example, are shaped by their past experiences and interactions (Berntsen 2016; Mrozowicki et al. 2016; Alberti et al. 2013). However, this is still a developing area of research, and somewhat outside of the mainstream of employment relations scholarship.

The comparative employment relations literature's sensitivity to the multi-level relationships between institutional context, power, and actor strategies also means it has been less successful than CPE and (at least some) critical sociologists at generating parsimonious arguments. Most research is based on empirically rich matched case studies, within one or several industries, which can limit generalizability. The diversity of forms of precarity studied, and factors found to contribute to it, make it difficult for inductive analysis to draw out common trends across countries and sectors. Scholars have tended to cobble together theoretical propositions from other literatures to explain heterogeneous patterns of empirical findings, or to poke holes in their simplifying propositions or frameworks without proposing alternatives.

In sum, comparative employment relations research cumulatively provides significant insight into the conditions under which unions are more or less successful in sustaining or rebuilding the collective, solidaristic institutions capable of reducing precarity in labour markets. However, there is a need to condense these insights into a more easily generalizable framework, to provide an alternative to those from CPE or critical sociology.

1.3. OUR FRAMEWORK

In the following sections, we develop an original framework for analysing the factors associated with the expansion and collective regulation of precarious work. This framework draws on the insights from the three literatures discussed in Section 1.2. We also seek to overcome their major limitations, with the aim of producing a robust set of propositions concerning the conditions under which collective action aimed at containing or contesting precarity can occur and be successful. Our focus is on labour unions but extends to other worker representatives, such as works councils or collectives. Our main units of analysis are industries and organizations, though we assume that institutions and actor strategies at these levels are significantly embedded in and influenced by national and (within Europe) European Union (EU)-level institutions.

Our central concern is with how labour's power resources to represent precarious worker interests are generated and deployed. We argue that two key variables support labour power: first, inclusive institutions that encourage coordinated bargaining and constrain employers' ability to shift work to precarious contracts or employment relationships; and second, forms of worker identity and identification promoting inclusive solidarity among different segments of the workforce. This connection between macro-institutions and micro processes of worker solidarity distinguishes us from the national focus in the CPE literature. It also gives us a distinct perspective on the political dynamics associated with restructuring and product market changes across countries, sectors, and firms. We seek to develop a more cohesive and parsimonious framework to make sense of these relationships, with two objectives. First, our framework provides a roadmap to communicate the insights from comparative employment relations research to a broader audience—including CPE and critical sociologists. Second, it provides an original organizing model to guide future research on precarity and institutional change—including, but not limited to, the employment relations field.

In the following sections, we develop our original framework, breaking our analysis down into two parts. The first part, presented in Section 1.3.1, addresses the problem of explaining how differences in the regulation of precarious work, once established, are sustained over time. This draws on past literature from the three traditions discussed in Section 1.2. Here we model two ideal types, which we label a 'virtuous circle' characterized by high and expanding employment stability and security across an economy or industry, and a 'vicious circle' characterized by high and expanding precarity.

The second part of our analysis, presented in Section 1.4, seeks to explain how economies or industries move from a situation of low to high precarity and vice versa. This analysis draws on the chapter findings from this book. Here we introduce factors outside of our ideal type models that encourage a shift in their component parts, emphasizing the dynamic relationship between institutions and actor strategies.

Through presenting both a relatively static and a more dynamic version of our framework, we seek to do justice to the ways in which institutional and market structures constrain power and shape action, as well as the conditions under which labour can challenge these structures through developing and accessing new power resources.

1.3.1. Two Models: Low Precarity and High Precarity

The first problem we address concerns how differences in the regulation of precarious work, once established, are sustained. Put another way, we seek to explain why similar kinds of jobs, with roughly equivalent skill levels and technology, are characterized by different patterns of employment precarity or stability—either across countries and industries or at different points in time. We model these outcomes as following from alternative 'ideal type' sets of conditions linking institutions (inclusive vs. fragmented welfare state, labour market, and collective bargaining institutions), employer strategies (voice-oriented vs. exit-oriented), union strategies (inclusive vs. exclusive), and worker identification and identity (solidaristic vs. particularistic). These are linked in self-reinforcing positive feedback loops, in which each factor serves to reinforce the others through shaping the relative power resources of capital and labour. Precarious work itself is at the centre of the model, as a factor that can serve as a resource for employers to exploit; a wedge dividing groups of workers or encouraging exclusive union strategies; and a source of systematic inequalities in countries or industries undermining broad support for encompassing institutional arrangements. We view the expansion of precarious employment (and its contraction or reregulation) both as an outcome and as a factor that drives subsequent changes in institutions, actor strategies, and worker attitudes or identity.

We define *precarious work* as employment characterized by a high degree of insecurity and instability, encompassing variability of income, job security, social status, and career progression. Employment precarity is often associated with non-standard employment contracts, such as temporary or marginal part-time work, which can allow employers to bypass the job security provisions that protect the 'standard' workforce. However, highly skilled or unionized workers may enjoy security when working for temporary agencies or as self-employed workers, and 'standard' employment contracts can be insecure, depending on their regulation and associated social security rights (Vosko et al. 2009). Most definitions thus contextualize precarious work more broadly, as we do here. For example, Standing (2011) defines precarity as a social category in which seven forms of security are absent: labour market, employment, job, work, skill reproduction, income, and collective representation and voice. These conditions overlap with aspects of low-quality or 'bad' jobs—defined in opposition to high-quality jobs in increasingly polarized employment structures (Kalleberg 2011).

Precarious work also relates to a worker's subjective experience of insecurity. Kalleberg (2009: 1) defines precarious employment as work that is 'uncertain, unpredictable, unstable and risky *from the point of view of the worker*' (emphasis added). This suggests that precarious work is relational—relative to workers' expectations and past experience, or to the standard employment relationship in the worker's country, industry, or social milieu. Kalleberg and Hewison (2013) describe precarious work as a process rather than 'a binary state'—marked by a shift in power between labour and capital and mediated by the state and its policies. Seen in this way, precarious work reflects not only conditions in the workplace, but also those in the larger society: cultural and ideological processes affect public conceptions of work, and shape what is accepted and what is not. A major concern is not only the overall incidence of precarious work, but also the gap in conditions between standard and non-standard employment. These patterns of inequality can affect the subjective experience of insecurity for each group as well as the power resources each can use to resist further erosion of their terms and conditions.

Our first model presents a 'virtuous circle' in which four factors contribute to reducing precarious work in a mutually reinforcing feedback loop: inclusive institutions, inclusive worker solidarity, voice-oriented employer strategies, and inclusive union strategies (Figure 1.1).

We define *institutional inclusiveness*, following Bosch et al. (2010: 91), as the degree to which welfare state protections, labour market legislation, and collective agreements extend the pay and conditions secured by employees having relatively stronger bargaining power to those with weaker bargaining power. More inclusive welfare coverage is characterized by broader formal eligibility criteria and lighter obligations relating to eligibility (Berclaz et al. 2004). Comprehensive coverage of welfare state protections, such as unemployment insurance, health insurance, or income protection during retirement, can affect subjective insecurity (Carr and Chung 2014) as well as workers' dependence on employers (Korpi 1983). Encompassing labour market legislation takes such regulatory forms as high minimum

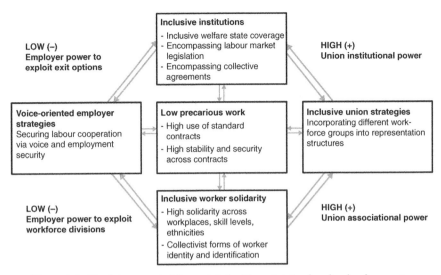

Figure 1.1. The 'virtuous circle' associated with sustaining low levels of precarity

wages, employment protection legislation, legal restrictions on the use of temporary staff, equal pay rules for temporary and part-time staff, and paid parental and sick leave. These measures improve job security, as well as pay levels and working conditions at the bottom of the labour market (Adams and Deakin 2014).

Encompassing collective agreements can substitute for or complement legislated protections. They extend the protective frameworks enjoyed by workers in strong labour market positions to those in weaker positions. The degree of inclusiveness of a collective agreement is typically assessed by bargaining coverage; as well as by bargaining coordination, or the extent to which to which 'minor players' (such as company-level managers or union representatives) adhere to agreements reached by 'major players' (such as peak associations) (Hall and Gingerich 2009). Coordination in bargaining can be an explicit goal of peak business and labour associations or the state, or it can be achieved through pattern agreements at large firms or in leading industries. Bargaining coverage and coordination are traditionally compared at industry and national level, but can also vary across firms' (increasingly vertically disintegrated) production chains (Benassi et al. 2016). Legal extension of collective agreements to cover entire industrial sectors is the primary mechanism in many countries for ensuring that collective agreements are encompassing, preventing firms from legally paying below wage rates in those agreements.

The second factor contributing to a virtuous circle is patterns of collective identification within the workforce that are conducive to *inclusive worker solidarity*. We define worker solidarity as the adherence to principles and patterns of behaviour that support mutual aid and collective action; particularly those that concern labour union strike and bargaining strategy. Solidarity can arise out of objective realities and pre-existing human relations, but can also be (strategically) (re)constructed; indeed, this is considered by many scholars as one of the major purposes of trade unions (Hyman 2001). Fantasia (1988) makes the point that the process of moving from having common interests to understanding them as common and acting on them is filled with contingency. In describing a wildcat strike that he observed, Fantasia (1988: 88) remarks, 'solidarity among the workers was not an a priori "fact", but grew out of the interactive processes among the workers in their confrontation with management'. Solidarity emerges in specific contexts, out of circumstances creating common interests or perceptions that norms have been violated, as well as frames and narratives that shape a common understanding of the appropriate remedial action to take.

We define solidarity as 'inclusive' if it is amenable to redefinition to include new groups of workers, particularly those in disadvantaged positions in terms of social rights and their position in the production process. Inclusive worker solidarity is grounded in broader forms of collective identification that involve forming common cause across groups holding diverse material interests and identities. Banting and Kymlicka (2017: 1) argue that 'the claims of solidarity require individuals to tolerate views and practices they dislike, to accept democratic decisions that go against their beliefs or interests, and to moderate the pursuit of their own economic self-interest to help the disadvantaged'. Inclusive solidarity requires workers not only to moderate their self-interest but also to recognize or establish common interests with other workers who hold more or less power in a labour market or production process.

A feeling of common identity and purpose is an important basis for solidarity, which is very much mixed up with class, but is not identical to it. Although embedded in various pre-existing sources of identity, there is also a strategic aspect to how unions construct identities and 'build solidarity' in ways that maximize leverage given existing political and economic opportunities. Workers are best served in terms of collective power by organizing into the kinds of structures most suitable for giving them leverage over employers. This logic is not always the same, and can even contradict the logic of solidarity arising from pre-existing identities (Lembcke 1988). For example, it has often been the case that when immigrants enter the labour market, unions have tried to exclude them from membership and have lost leverage as a result (Virdee 2000). Solidarity is thus a question of worker identity, ideology, and personal narratives, as much as it is one of organizations, interests, and institutions. Because pre-existing forms of identity may not be those best suited to exerting leverage over employers, unions often engage in identity work to build and rebuild solidarity (Greer and Hauptmeier 2012). The project of building inclusive solidarity to extend representation to precarious workers is frequently one of identity reconstruction.

Inclusive institutions and inclusive worker solidarity both serve as resources that *enhance union institutional and associational power*. Wright (2000) and Silver (2003) distinguish between associational power derived from workers' collective organization and structural power derived from workers' distinctive skills, tight labour markets, or location in a key industrial sector. We view *structural power* as an important constant or embedded condition within a given industry or labour market at a point in time. Indeed, the workers most vulnerable to precarity are those possessing systematically weaker structural power. *Associational power* follows more directly from distinctive conditions within a company, industry, or national political economy, as it derives from the resources and capabilities unions develop through collective organization.

One indicator of associational power is union density, but worker attitudes and union commitment are also crucial to mobilize workers for collective action. It is thus grounded most directly in worker solidarity. This is because power in collective negotiations depends on the capacity to strike, and the economic leverage of the strike 'weapon'. This is the case even where the strike weapon is rarely used: it nonetheless hangs as a threat over every collective negotiation, and determines the power relationship between actors (Hicks 1932). This leverage, in turn, depends to a large extent on the degree of solidarity among workers, who they include as members of their community of fate, and what norms justify or mandate their collective responses. Inclusive forms of worker solidarity based on more collectivist forms of identification provide associational power at a broader scale than the workplace or identity group (e.g. industry, national, or across a production chain). This serves the economic interests of workers, which in turn shores up the organizational stability of unions (Zhang and Lillie 2015).

Employment relations scholars, drawing on social movement theory, typically describe a further dimension of *institutional power*, which concerns unions' position within existing institutional arrangements that are themselves the product of historic power relationships, contestation, or coalitions (Brinkmann and Nachtwey 2010). Institutional power may be derived through participation in institutions such as sectoral or tripartite bargaining (Gumbrell-McCormick and Hyman 2013), or, more broadly, from labour market protections, welfare state support, and collective bargaining rights. Institutional power is strongest where institutions include unions in formal platforms that permit them to secure agreements and extend them to different groups in the labour market (e.g. tripartite agreements, sectoral agreements, company-level agreements). Encompassing bargaining is particularly important for institutional power, as it allows unions to negotiate these agreements with less fear of employer exit.

Strong institutional and associational power resources encourage more *inclusive union strategies* concerning approaches to represent and organize different groups of workers. These emphasize extending welfare state coverage and employment protections across the workforce, and/or pursuing solidaristic bargaining across groups of workers having different degrees of structural power (Schulten 2002). Unions may also be less likely to oppose the shift of work to non-standard contracts or employment relationships where these are regulated or employment conditions are protected due to encompassing welfare state protections and collective agreements. For example, in a comparison of local government outsourcing in four European countries, Grimshaw et al. (2015a) showed that unions were more willing to cooperate with outsourcing where workers in core and peripheral jobs were protected by strong labour market rules setting high wage floors and employment protections.

Institutions and solidarity intersect in shaping the broader alliances of cooperation that are forged across different unions and other worker representatives (such as works councils), between labour and civil society organizations, and across different worker groups (e.g. migrants and non-migrants, workers in standard and non-standard employment relationships). Where collective bargaining coverage is high and strongly coordinated, this provides a platform for cooperation among worker representatives in different (potentially competing) sectors and workplaces. Every industrial relations system has its own divides or competitive relationships within the labour movement, falling along industry and sector lines, or along ethnic, ideological, or craft divisions. Bargaining structures that include these groups within a common union or confederation—or with centralized coordination by strong unions—may more effectively bridge these potential divides (Thelen 2014; Oliver 2011; Gordon 2014). At the same time, workers themselves have to be willing to support 'solidaristic bargaining' within these structures, extending gains from core to peripheral workers. Research shows that unions' success in promoting the inclusion of migrants depends in part on the legitimacy they derive from the broader activism of the migrant rank and file (Marino 2015; Connolly et al. 2014), which may be best supported by decentralized bargaining and strong union presence in the workplace (Marino 2012). Institutional inclusion at industry level has been found to influence union strategy and success within countries in contesting precarious work. For example, Refslund (2016) compares four sectors in Denmark, and shows that unions were most successful in preventing segmentation based on migrant status in those sectors with high bargaining coverage.

Inclusive institutions and inclusive worker solidarity also *constrain employer power*. Inclusive institutions prevent employers from exploiting exit options to avoid or renegotiate internal employment relationships through shifting work to poorly regulated non-standard contracts or non-union subcontractors. Inclusive forms of worker solidarity have a related but distinct effect in reducing employer power to exploit divisions in the workforce—for example, based on occupation, workplace, ethnicity, or gender.

These constraints in turn encourage *voice-oriented employer strategies*. We assume that employers may pursue a range of potentially contradictory objectives (e.g. to reduce labour costs while securing worker commitment)—but typically they seek to secure labour cooperation in the production process (Edwards 2003). One way to secure cooperation is through real or threatened exit from internal employment relationships, via shifting production to non-union workers or those on precarious employment contracts. When they are constrained from shifting production, employers may instead seek to engage with labour through social partnership-oriented or corporatist channels of interest intermediation that rely on voice- rather than exit-based mechanisms (Hirschman 1970). This is consistent with early arguments by CPE scholars such as Streeck (1991), who described Germany's dual apprenticeship training system, occupational labour markets, and industry-wide collective bargaining as 'productive constraints' on employers, which allowed them to reconcile high wages and egalitarian social outcomes with (functional) flexibility and profitability. Along similar lines, Benassi et al. (2016) show that telecommunications employers adopted more cooperative approaches to restructuring, associated with less use of exit threats to gain concessions, in those European countries that had established encompassing collective bargaining and high inter-union cooperation.

The factors outlined in this section constitute a mutually reinforcing positive feedback loop. Inclusive institutions directly reduce the incidence of precarious work while constraining employers' ability to exploit exit options. These patterns of opportunities and constraints encourage inclusive union strategies and voice-oriented employer strategies. The strength and form of worker solidarity determines when unions have the associational power to enforce or defend existing encompassing institutions, to create new ones, or to undertake collective actions outside of institutional frameworks. Worker solidarity is stronger and more inclusive where there are more constrained possibilities for employers to exploit divides in the labour movement or among worker groups in the interest of reducing labour costs. These factors contribute to reducing the incidence of precarious working conditions and contracts. The contraction of precarity then further enhances worker solidarity, bolsters inclusive union strategies, closes off options for employers to segment work, and contributes to broad public support for encompassing legislation and welfare states.

This 'ideal type' model describes more or less the dynamics of labour regulation within contexts such as national sectoral bargaining. Some aspects of this 'virtuous circle' applied in most Western European welfare states in the post-World War II decades, when precarious work was less prevalent. The 'normal' worker in the core jobs of the industrial economy worked full-time hours, was paid sufficiently to keep a family in a decent standard of living, and, to a greater or lesser degree, was protected against capricious discharge. Relatively strong unions and encompassing labour market protections sustained these systems even after the economic and political crises in the 1970s, which were followed by several decades of deregulation and steady union decline in the US and the UK.

Western European labour markets were never completely free from precarious employment, with often significant segmentation by gender and ethnicity. However, low-paid, insecure work was the realm of young workers making their transitions into real jobs, women who would not normally be expected to support a family (Pfau-Effinger 1998), or immigrants and ethnic minorities (Castles and Kosack 1973). This suggests that worker solidarity was never all-encompassing, and always had exclusive elements. At the same time, it is noteworthy that particularistic identities were often recognized as a threat to sustaining social democracy, and challenged by labour unions and workers themselves. The Nordic countries were most successful in establishing inclusive welfare state protection and solidaristic bargaining structures that (at least superficially) overcame these divisions (Esping-Andersen 1990).

In pre-1989 CEE state socialist societies, a different set of dynamics occurred, but these are still partially consistent with our model. In these countries, the state unilaterally enforced inclusive institutions based on universal welfare coverage and employment security, and state-owned firms adopted strategies prefaced on full employment with reduced (but not eliminated) differentiation in pay or conditions by skill or industry. Union membership was semi-obligatory or obligatory, and unions were required to be inclusive of all groups, as the arm and 'transmission belts' of the Communist Party. Worker identification was assumed (and indeed required) to be broadly solidaristic—at least within the state socialist nation state or east of the Iron Curtain. The main differences between a virtuous circle in the CEE countries and in the Western capitalist welfare states were related to its sources, as a 'compromise' between capital and labour was impossible in the context of the top-down imposition of political and economic systems and the lack of autonomous interest representation of workers and employers. However, there was a similar effect of establishing strong and encompassing regulation, which maintained low levels of precarity—particularly in a relative sense as measured across groups of workers within industries and countries.

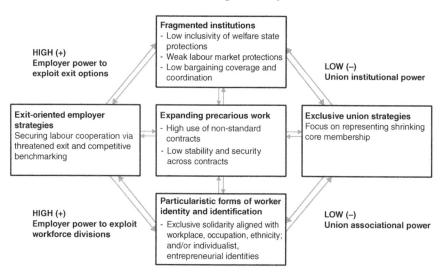

Figure 1.2. The 'vicious circle' associated with expanding precarity

The process of expanding precarity takes the opposite form, as a vicious circle (Figure 1.2).

Here, *fragmented institutions*, characterized by less inclusive welfare state protections, weak labour market protections, and low bargaining coverage and coordination, are associated with high or expanding precarity. Unlike the CPE dualism literature, we do not distinguish between more or less dualistic welfare states or collective agreements, based on their employment protections for different categories of workers. While these differences are relevant for patterns of inequality in the short term, we view declining coverage of these institutions as broadly contributing to a dynamic of expanding precarity within the workforce as a whole. Cross-national or industry-based comparative research shows that the deregulation of encompassing institutions is typically associated with higher incidence of precarious employment contracts or relationships (Vosko et al. 2009; Hipp et al. 2015). Gaps in institutional coverage also affect patterns of inequality based on gender or ethnicity. For example, gender inequality in welfare protection (e.g. discriminatory eligibility rules that exclude short hours part-time workers) has been found to contribute to gender inequality in pay bargaining and partly to explain women's over-representation in low-wage employment (Grimshaw et al. 2014).

Fragmented institutions produce a range of exit options, enhancing employer power to shift work to non-standard contracts or non-union subcontractors, or to leave collective bargaining arrangements altogether. These *exit-oriented employer strategies* take advantage of growing differences in pay and conditions across employee groups to leave internal employment relationships or renegotiate them under more flexible terms. These dynamics were extensively documented in a study of low-wage work in the US and five European countries: researchers found that pay and working conditions in matched occupations were strongly affected by employers' capacity to take advantage of different institutional exit options to bypass employment standards (Bosch et al. 2010). These varied not only at the national level, but also at the industry level, with existing exit options becoming increasingly accessible and attractive as employers faced intensifying price competition (Jaehrling and Méhaut 2012). Research has also shown that employers often copy successful practices used by similar employers to bypass collective regulation or introduce more precarious employment contracts (Holtgrewe 2001). As this process of institutional isomorphism progresses, the cost of exit further declines and the benefits of threatened exit increase due to the downward adjustment of demands by internal workers (Eichhorst and Marx 2011; Doellgast and Berg 2018). As such, employers play a key role in shaping the extent and character of precarious work, as well as the blurring of boundaries between protected and unprotected labour market segments (Grimshaw et al. 2017; Wagner 2014).

Staffing agencies and subcontractors are often particularly entrepreneurial in avoiding institutional constraints or exploiting gaps in regulations (Andrijasevic and Sacchetto 2016). Lillie (2012) documents the strategies of subcontractors in the construction and shipbuilding industries to exploit poor coordination between EU-level and national regulation of posted work, which allows employers to 'regime shop' around Europe to obtain the cheapest workers. Research in Europe and the US has shown that transnational staffing agencies take advantage of migrant workers' poor familiarity with local institutions and practices to tie them to short-term and exploitative jobs, often constraining their ability to challenge the illegality of their employment conditions or to organize collectively to improve them (Samaluk 2016a).

Fragmented institutions and exit-oriented employer strategies may also, at least initially, encourage more *exclusive union strategies*. The CPE dualization literature has shown that under conditions of declining institutional coverage, trade unions (and works councils, where these exist) may be pushed by their members to focus resources on defending their own conditions and status—often at the expense of a precarious workforce (Emmenegger et al. 2012). However, employment relations researchers argue that unions tend to enter these coalitions from a position of weakness, with findings showing that they typically serve to further exacerbate competition between labour market segments and thus expose both groups to increasingly precarious conditions (Benassi and Dorigatti 2015). Where workers focus on workplace- or firm-centric strategies to protect their jobs and conditions, this tends to result in further declines in union power across the sector or along the production chain.

Often what we might describe as exclusive union strategies are simply a result of unions focusing limited resources where they still enjoy some residual institutional or associational power (Frege and Kelly 2004). For example, Doellgast et al. (2016) showed that unions in European telecommunications firms more often agreed to large concessions on pay and conditions to insource work where they primarily or exclusively represented core workers, and where these workers enjoyed a significant wage premium relative to subcontractors. Where institutions were more inclusive, unions had a more credible route to focus on 'bringing up the bottom' through bargaining and campaigning across labour market segments. Exclusive union strategies that fall along lines of ethnicity, race, or nationality may be motivated by a narrow racism or chauvinism, but are often reactions to employer strategies aimed at exploiting these divisions. These exclusive strategies are also ultimately self-defeating: for example, the major German construction union initially sought to combat employer use of precarious migrant workers through sending representatives to construction sites to ask for worker papers, but this approach undermined efforts to build common cause with an exploited workforce while having no effect on the actual use of migrants (Lillie and Greer 2007).

Employers' segmentation strategies and exclusive union strategies together contribute to weakening existing or potential worker solidarity, particularly the more inclusive forms of solidarity built within and through encompassing collective bargaining. Instead, growing precarious work is accompanied by the expansion of more *particularistic forms of worker identity and identification*. One form of particularistic worker identification is based on narrow individual aspirations or more entrepreneurial identities. Another form is associated with exclusive forms of solidarity that are difficult to redefine in order to include new groups of workers. These may be based in strongly held shared interests and identities. For example, highly skilled professionals, or members of an ethnic or migrant group, may have strong solidarity within their groups, but not with non-members. Exclusive solidarity can be a formidable source of countervailing power, and mobilized by unions to achieve significant gains via strikes and collective bargaining. However, even dominant groups that are able to control the labour market at one point are vulnerable to employers introducing groups to the labour market to break their monopoly (Bonacich 1973). Exclusive practices and narratives create a path dependency that makes it difficult to change to inclusive solidarity when it becomes strategically necessary (Penninx and Roosblad 2000b).

One form of particularistic identification is along the lines of ethnicity, nationality, or migrant status. Research in the critical sociology tradition finds that ethnic groups in ethnically segmented labour markets become the 'good workers' they are expected to be, taking pride in their endurance of privation (Çaro et al. 2015), while new arrivals may strategically use positive views of their work ethic to access entry-level precarious jobs (Samaluk 2016b). Workers embrace the market-based 'exit' strategies open to them as outsiders, rejecting contestation and collectivism as ways to reregulate labour markets (Alberti 2014; Berntsen 2016). This 'normalization of precariousness' may take distinctive forms in post-socialist countries: for example, Mrozowicki (2016: 108) shows that young Polish workers have been reluctant to protest against the expansion of precarious employment due to broad internalization of 'market-individualistic discourses'. Across countries, particularistic identities may be associated with nationalism or anti-immigrant movements. The rise of support for far-right populist political parties and candidates in the US and much of Europe has been attributed by many to growing insecurity and inequality. According to this view, economically vulnerable groups or formerly privileged workers who see their former status threatened become susceptible to narrow forms of in-group solidarity (Bornschier 2010; Inglehart and Norris 2016).

These factors are linked in a negative feedback loop, whereby expanding precarity undermines the institutions and union strategies necessary to combat it, as employer power to exploit differences expands and union power to recollectivize risk declines. Dualization dynamics and benchmarking strategies by management can inhibit or undermine inclusive worker solidarity while fragmenting workers' pay and conditions across different national borders, and between industry and local levels. Employers are increasingly able to exploit divides in the workforce on the basis of race or migrant status to prevent successful collective action (Penninx and Roosblad 2000b). Unions seeking to organize precarious workers face the additional challenge of overcoming entrenched negative perceptions of collectivism or individualistic, entrepreneurial identities (Berntsen 2016). Particularistic identification may itself underlie exclusive union strategies, as unions face challenges in bridging segments of the workforce adopting narrow forms of solidarity focusing on an exclusionary form of nationalism, or oriented to their own workplace, profession, or ethnic group.

1.4. CHAPTER FINDINGS: EXPANDING PRECARITY AND RECONSTRUCTING SOLIDARITY

The two models outlined in Section 1.3.1 depict ideal-typical conditions that are only approximated in any given country or industry. They thus cannot do justice to the complex external and internal factors encouraging changes in institutions, actor strategies, and worker identities. Even the more pessimistic 'vicious circle' is inherently unstable: reframing of the narrative resulting as solidarity between core and periphery, enlightened self-interest within the core, and solidarity and self-organization among precarious workers are all important dynamics that can bring about change in employer and union strategies in significant ways—even where institutions are highly fragmented.

Thus, the second question we seek to answer is: What explains change over time in unions' capacity to establish and maintain encompassing regulation of precarious work? What factors undermined or are undermining the regulation of precarious work? To what extent do some aspects of a virtuous circle still apply in European countries, even under more challenging conditions? What are the possibilities for unions to challenge the loss of traditional institutional power resources, or to build new forms of worker solidarity where particularistic forms of worker identification prevail?

In the following sections, we draw on the case study findings from the chapters in this book to demonstrate the usefulness of the basic components of our framework for answering these questions—with the broader goal of explaining differences in union strategy and success in regulating precarious work. The chapters cover nine different industries and occupations, including metal, retail, manufacturing, chemical, cleaning, local government, freelance music, logistics, and slaughter-houses; and fourteen countries, representing the UK, Austria, Germany, Belgium, France, Italy, Greece, Finland, Denmark, Sweden, Poland, Estonia, Slovenia, and Hungary. Together, they show that most countries and industries fall somewhere between the two ideal types described in Section 1.3.1: while structure constrains action to a significant extent, unions can be entrepreneurial in building new institutional and associational resources to reconstruct solidarity under challenging conditions. Table 1.1 summarizes the chapters' empirical focus and comparative outcomes.

Table 1.1. Summary of the book chapters

Authors, sectors, countries	Main outcomes compared	Comparative findings
Chapter 2. Grimshaw, Marino, Anxo, Gautié, Neumann, and Weinkopf: local government in Sweden, Hungary, France, Germany, and the UK	Union success in: improving pay levels for lowest-paid standard workers; reducing pay inequality between standard and subcontracted workers	(1) Highest in Sweden; (2) moderate in France; (3) lowest in Germany, UK, Hungary (but with strong local variation in Germany and the UK)
Chapter 3. Wagner and Refslund: slaughterhouse sector in Denmark and Germany	Union success in: reducing inequality between standard and non-standard workers and migrants; resisting concessions in pay and conditions for standard workers; extending collective representation to non-standard workers	(1) Higher in Denmark; (2) lower in Germany
Chapter 4. Benvegnú, Haidinger, and Sacchetto: logistics sector in Italy (warehousing) and Austria (courier services)	Union and worker collective action success in: improving pay and conditions for non-standard workers; resisting exploitation and illegal practices; winning collective agreements	(1) Higher in Italy; (2) lower in Austria
Chapter 5. Pulignano and Doerflinger: metalworking and chemical sectors in Germany and Belgium (MNC focused)	Union success in: avoiding concessions for standard workers; reducing use of non-standard work; improving pay, benefits, security, and training for non-standard workers to reduce inequality with standard workers	(1) Highest in Belgian chemical and metal cases; (2) moderate in German metal case; (3) lowest in German chemical case
Chapter 6. Benassi and Dorigatti: metalworking sector in Italy and Germany	Union success in: improving agency worker wages, conditions, and prospects to be hired on permanent contracts; restricting employers' use of agency work	(1) Higher in Italy until mid-2000s; (2) improving in Germany (from 2008); (3) weakening in Italy (from 2003)
Chapter 7. Mrozowicki, Bembič, Kall, Maciejewska, and Stanojević: retail sector in Estonia, Poland, and Slovenia	Union success in: improving pay and conditions for all workers; reducing inequality between standard and non-standard workers	(1) Highest in Slovenia; (2) moderate in Poland; (3) weakest in Estonia
Chapter 8. Greer, Samaluk, and Umney: freelance musicians in London (UK), Paris (France), and Ljubljana (Slovenia)	Union/collective success in: providing collective goods that improve income and employment opportunities, reducing income insecurity, preventing exploitation (non-payment, requesting to play for free)	(1) Best access to welfare or protecting welfare support in Ljubljana and Paris; (2) best awareness of exploitative conditions at employers in London; (3) similar support for entrepreneurs via collectives in all
Chapter 9. Tapia and Holgate: migrant workers in the UK, Germany, and France	Union strategies to: organize and represent migrant workers in a more inclusive way	(1) Recognition of difference approach in UK; (2) republican assimilation in France; (3) institutional approach in Germany
Chapter 10. Danaj, Çaro, Mankki, Sippola, and Lillie: Estonian migrants in Finland and Albanian migrants in Italy and Greece	Migrant worker paths out of precarity; union success in protecting migrant workers; migrant union engagement	(1) Highest in Finland; (2) moderate in Italy; (3) lowest in Greece

The first set of findings discussed in the following sub-sections concern the factors the chapter authors identify that have driven the expansion of precarious work in their focal industries or countries. The second set of findings concern the conditions under which unions adopt more inclusive strategies across labour market segments and succeed in building countervailing power to challenge precarious employment.

1.4.1. Explaining the Expansion of Precarious Work and the Challenge for Solidarity

A number of factors can be identified that triggered a shift from a virtuous circle to a vicious circle in the European countries and industries discussed in this book. We focus on three here: the globalization of firms, product markets, and financial markets (associated most recently with financial crisis and austerity); EU market-making policies; and policies and practices associated with migration and labour mobility within and from outside of the EU.

The *globalization of firms, product markets, and financial markets* pressure employers to cut costs and also give them new exit options from formerly encompassing institutions. First, narrowing profit margins combined with in-creased focus on maximizing short-term returns lead employers to become more aggressive in pursuing labour cost reductions based on shifting risk to workers (Appelbaum and Batt 2014). These pressures are most intense in lower-productivity, lower-wage services and non-traded sectors. For example, the retail (Chapter 7) and logistics (Chapter 4) industries have experienced both intensifying competition and dramatic growth in precarious conditions, across traditionally 'core' as well as peripheral worker groups. However, higher-skilled manufacturing case studies similarly show that employers often use competitive pressures as an excuse to shift work to more precarious contracts, and to seek concessions for internal workers as a condition for job security or further investment at particular production sites (Chapters 5 and 6). Similar dynamics occur in the public sector, where economic crisis intensifies fiscal pressures. In their case studies of local government agencies, Grimshaw et al. (Chapter 2) show that public sector austerity encourages pay concessions and subcontract-ing, and also reduces union power to contest the erosion of conditions. In Pulignano and Doerflinger's case study 'Metal' (Chapter 5), the company's heavy reliance on public sector customers meant that austerity increased cost pressures, which in turn justified demands for increased labour flexibility.

Second, the globalization of production and distribution provides incentives and opportunities to segment work via outsourcing and value chain restructuring. In logistics, Benvegnú et al. (Chapter 4) show that the boundaries that previously differentiated sectors (e.g. postal, transportation), and were the reference point for collective agreements, are increasingly irrelevant. Value chain restructuring has resulted in higher levels of inter-organizational contracting across an array of multinationals specializing in different segments—often contracting across na-tional borders. In both the warehousing and courier segments of the industry, workers at the bottom of the supply chain predominantly have non-standard contracts resulting in unstable and insecure employment. In the slaughterhouse industry, MNCs increasingly locate similar meat processing jobs in different countries, allowing them to benchmark cost and performance and demand concessions (Chapter 3).

EU market-making policies undermine institutional inclusion by opening up employer exit options. While some EU policies aim to extend institutional protections and rebuild encompassing institutions, there is a deregulatory bias built into both the EU's normative underpinnings, as well as into its institutional decision rules (Höpner and Schäfer 2012; Jabko 2006). EU integration can also affect patterns of worker identity formation and union strategic orientation; for example, encouraging competitive cross-border benchmarking within MNCs or new forms of European-based transnational campaigns. Refslund and Wagner (Chapter 3) give the example of Danish Crown, an MNC in the meatpacking industry, which relocated thousands of jobs from Denmark to Germany in the mid-2000s. These relocated jobs did not go to Germans, but to posted workers from Eastern Europe, who were not protected by German minimum wages or collective agreements until recently. The company subsequently used benchmarking of labour costs with the workforce at the German facilities to try to gain concessions in higher-wage Denmark.

The chapters demonstrate the importance of the interaction between globalization and EU policies in encouraging both institutional fragmentation and exit-oriented employer policies. In the wake of the 2008 financial crisis, EU institutions have been central in directing European governments to adopt austerity policies and deregulate their labour markets. In Chapter 2, comparing restructuring in local municipalities across five countries, Grimshaw et al. illustrate how in the public sector, labour market deregulation, which followed the 2008 financial crisis, has led to a general degradation of pay and working conditions. This was less the case where existing encompassing institutions could mediate the effects of austerity. For example, local governments in Germany, Hungary, and the UK were under more fiscal pressure than Sweden and France. Strong fiscal pressure, in turn, was more likely to lead to a 'vicious circle' characterized by labour concessions, declining public sector pay, and increased precarity via outsourcing. On the other hand, Greer et al.'s (Chapter 8) comparison of freelance musicians shows that austerity pressures associated with crisis in the UK, France, and Slovenia resulted in reduced job opportunities and stability for freelance musicians in all three countries as state support for the arts declined.

Policies and practices associated with *migration within and from outside of the EU* is a third external factor providing employers with new resources to exploit divides in the labour force. Benvegnú et al. (Chapter 4) argue that Italian employers in the warehouse segment of the logistics industry use ethnic recruitment to undermine employment standards. Austrian courier firms exploit small ethnic businesses and self-employed migrant couriers. Refslund and Wagner (Chapter 3) show extensive use of migrant workers in lower-paid, subcontracted employment segments in the meatpacking industry, particularly via posted work in the German context (see also: Wagner and Refslund 2016). As a result of posting, there is now a transnationally mobile precarious workforce available to employers, who have low-wage expectations and do not have full social security or union representation rights in the host countries where they work (Lillie 2016).

Again, broader economic and policy changes form the backdrop for these employer strategies, which foster segmentation by reducing working conditions and challenging workers' solidarity. In Danaj et al.'s (Chapter 10) comparison of migrant worker experiences in Finland, Italy, and Greece, they find that the economic crisis and accompanying austerity were associated with increased precarity and informality among migrants in all three countries. However, these effects are most severe in Greece, where fiscal constraints and far-reaching labour market deregulation measures imposed by the Troika (European Central Bank, European Commission, and International Monetary Fund) form the backdrop for a significant expansion in informality among migrants. This weakened their interest in and access to unions, and undermined solidarity among migrants and native workers.

In sum, the chapters show that processes of industry and organizational restructuring, European integration, market liberalization, and dynamics of austerity have increased employers' power to shift risk to workers via precarious arrangements. In line with our framework, this takes two different, but related, forms. First, employers are able to exploit expanding exit options linked to increasingly fragmented institutions and the associated growing divides in pay and conditions between groups of workers. This either involves shifting work to more poorly regulated worker groups and firms, or demanding (and winning) concessions that increase precarity for their core workforce through benchmarking and exit threats. Second, employers exploit divides in the labour force associated with particularistic or individualistic forms of identity and identification. These divides can be across companies and occupations, or between the native and migrant workforce—with worker posting combining both of these forms. Another form of particularistic identity is self-exploitation of entrepreneurial or highly skilled professionals (e.g. freelance musicians) or migrants, which divides the workforce and reduces workers' solidarity—though at an individual rather than group level. These factors are closely linked: increasingly fragmented institutions make the work of building inclusive solidarity between the native and migrant workforce, between local and posted workers, or across entrepreneurial workers particularly challenging.

1.4.2. Reconstructing Solidarity: Conditions for Regulating Precarious Work

The chapters all show that precarious work has expanded across industries and countries, with their analyses pointing to some common causes. However, the central focus of this book is to explain the conditions under which unions are able to sustain regulation of precarious work or reverse trends of expanding precarity. In line with our framework, chapter findings show that union strategies to represent precarious workers derive from institutional conditions and the form and content of solidarity among workers. The central condition for unions' success is their willingness and ability to mobilize power resources to challenge employers' capacity to use precarious employment contracts to increase competition in the labour market.

1.4.2.1. Union Strategies to Represent Precarious Workers

If our primary objective is to understand the conditions under which unions are more or less successful in regulating precarious work, the first question concerns the enthusiasm with which they pursue this goal in the first place.

Findings from the chapters show that the extent of institutional inclusion and patterns of worker identity strongly influence union strategies. Benassi and Dorigatti's comparison in Chapter 6 of the German and Italian metal sector shows that encompassing regulation of temporary agency work (TAW) was a crucial support for inclusive union strategies. In Germany, changes to labour law and collective agreements significantly deregulated TAW contracts. As employers exploited these expanded exit options, plant-level works councils increasingly viewed their interests and identities as separate from each other and from precarious agency workers, undermining bargaining coordination and bargaining power. In Italy, conversely, stronger national regulation of agency work and more centralized and encompassing bargaining structures supported cooperation across unions, which continued jointly to pursue a more inclusive strategy for organizing and representing agency workers. Bridging ideological splits in the Italian labour movement was important for developing a successful, solidaristic response to regulating precarious work. When this approach came under pressure, CGIL (Confederazione Generale Italiana del Lavoro) was the only union confederation that continued to seek to maintain encompassing regulation of agency work and to organize these workers at the local level, due to its stronger ideological commitment to inclusive worker solidarity.

Benvegnú et al.'s findings (Chapter 4) similarly suggest that the ways in which unions define solidarity help explain different union responses to fragmenting institutions. As gaps opened up in collective bargaining coverage and legislative protections in the logistics industry, traditional Italian unions were slow to organize precarious workers in warehousing, due to their focus on better-organized industry segments. However, new rank-and-file unions like Si Cobas and Adl Cobas took up the militant Italian tradition to organize coordinated campaigns by cooperative workers based on direct action and grassroots mobilization, with the help of NGOs and other political activists. In Austria, there was less space to respond to increasing bargaining fragmentation with innovative grassroots approaches, as sectoral bargaining was dominated by ideologically conservative unions who used their shrinking institutional resources to protect core workers. Benvegnú et al. argue that the Austrian unions' strength in traditional, highly organized workplaces in logistics—for example, in the Austrian Post—led them to focus on preserving the conditions of these workers, rather than on organizing more precarious (mostly migrant) workers at the bottom of logistics supply chains. While these self-employed workers organized alternative forms of collective action, this had a limited impact on conditions due to the lack of bridging solidarity to unions and workers in core jobs.

Differences in the inclusiveness of institutions and worker solidarity also explain union approaches to migrant workers. Tapia and Holgate (Chapter 9) trace the shift from the 1970s in the migration policies of unions in the UK,

France, and Germany, from racist and exclusive to more inclusive. On the one hand, unions sought new members among migrant groups as their own membership declined. On the other hand, growing activism from members (some of them migrants) who opposed racist and exclusionary policies encouraged a shift in union positions. At the same time, these similar pro-migration macro-policies of the unions, when put into practice at a local level, result in different union strategies, which they trace to traditions concerning the appropriate sphere in which to build or rebuild solidarity as well as each union's institutional power resources. For example, the UK unions' focus on the workplace and historical emphasis on multiculturalism encouraged setting up separate structures to integrate migrant workers, as well as using government funds to establish learning initiatives for migrant workers, while the republican ethos in France led unions to organize workers at community level and target broader civil rights issues.

In Chapter 8 on freelance musicians, Greer et al. examine the challenges unions face in organizing and representing workers whose professional identity is highly individualistic. Institutional inclusiveness played some role in shaping union strategies: for example, stronger social security support for artists and public arts funding in France and (to a lesser extent) Slovenia encouraged unions to adopt strategies aimed at extending and defending this state support, or helping musicians to navigate it. However, they show that collective action by freelance musicians to fight anarchic conditions in the market was limited by workers' own artistic aspirations. Wages, working conditions, and job security had a lower priority than creative freedom; and musicians often accepted low or no payment to have the opportunity to have their music heard by a wider audience. 'Collectives' focusing on creating new spaces for making music controlled by the musicians themselves showed some success in replacing exploitative club owners and promoters. However, this only benefitted the narrow group of musicians that were members. This suggests that musicians' individualistic and entrepreneurial identities limited their capacity to mobilize any form of worker solidarity—frustrating union attempts to address precarity via traditional institutional routes.

Danaj et al. (Chapter 10) add the perspective of migrant workers to the discussion of worker identity and solidarity. Similar to Chapter 8, their chapter illustrates that the challenges to building inclusive worker solidarity are related to the nature and the composition of the workforce. Migrant workers come with very different life experiences than host country workers, and often feel that inclusive solidarity is irrelevant to them; this feeling lessens with host country integration, but is also affected by host country institutions. Overall, the migrants they interviewed were more likely to be union members and use union services if they were in standard jobs in highly unionized workplaces. However, among those migrant workers in the most precarious informal or non-standard jobs, unions differed in their efforts to adopt more inclusive strategies: while both Italian and Greek unions set up special structures for migrants, Greek unions showed broad disinterest in organizing the Albanians who were the focus of the study. In addition, the migrants in the most vulnerable, informal jobs were most likely to reference the negative experience of unionization under socialism as a reason for not joining a union (what they refer to as post-socialist quiescence).

1.4.2.2. Union Success in Regulating Precarious Work: Building and Accessing Power

The discussion so far shows that institutions and solidarity are jointly implicated in the strategies that unions adopt towards precarious work. This is an important starting point for understanding why unions may become trapped in exclusive strategies, or alternatively decide to pursue inclusive strategies aimed at organizing across labour market segments. At the same time, an inclusive strategy does not ensure inclusive outcomes. Our primary concern is to analyse the conditions under which unions are more or less successful in contesting or reducing precarity.

First, findings show that *more inclusive institutions constrain employers from exploiting exit options to increase precarity.* Conversely, employers take advantage of fragmented institutions to introduce more precarious employment contracts and relationships. Mrozowicki et al.'s (Chapter 7) retail sector case studies in Estonia, Poland, and Slovenia show this most starkly: in all three countries, minimum wages, employment protection legislation, and equal treatment provisions for non-standard workers in national laws were important in limiting the precarity of retail workers. Slovenia was the only country with sectoral bargaining in retail, extended by the state to all companies, and it also had the strongest legal provisions for equal treatment, established following tripartite negotiations. This led to better pay, stronger job security, and better conditions for non-standard workers compared to the other two countries—where unions faced more substantial battles simply getting weaker minimum treatment laws enforced in MNCs (Estonia) or across a dispersed atypical workforce in small and medium-sized enterprises and franchise stores (Poland). In Estonia, both standard and non-standard workers were precarious, while in Poland and Slovenia employers had various options for evading minimum standards. This influenced the form of precarious work employers chose to use. For example, in Slovenia students were excluded from coverage by the sectoral agreement, and so this became an employer exit strategy. In Poland, self-employed franchise owners were not regulated by the minimum wage or working-time and union representation rights covering other firms, and therefore workers at these firms had poor conditions and limited social security rights.

Several of the chapters show a spectrum where at one end institutions are so weak that all employees are precarious: this is the case with Estonian retail employers (Chapter 7) and Hungarian municipalities (Chapter 2). At the other end, encompassing regulation with high bargaining coverage reduces cost-based incentives for externalizing work, while also reducing precarity for all workers. This is seen in Slovenian retail (Chapter 7), Swedish municipalities (Chapter 2), and Danish slaughterhouses (Chapter 3).

In the middle, institutions reduce precarious conditions for the core workforce but provide significant opportunities to cut labour costs through non-standard working arrangements via, e.g., agency work, outsourcing, or self-employment. This helps to explain why the Polish retail sector has the highest incidence of temporary and self-employment of Mrozowicki et al.'s three national case studies (Chapter 7). Grimshaw et al. (Chapter 2) find the largest gaps in pay and union strength between municipalities and subcontractors in Germany and the UK, with the effect that municipalities in these countries faced the largest incentives to outsource. This, in turn, intensified pressure on public sector unions to develop creative responses that either reduced pay and conditions in-house to discourage subcontracting, or that used other scarce resources to fight against these strategies. Sweden's high bargaining coverage in both the public and private sectors reduced incentives for government outsourcing, but also meant that outsourcing did not result in increased precarity for affected workers.

Wagner and Refslund's (Chapter 3) comparison of union campaigns in German and Danish locations of the meatpacking MNC Danish Crown show how the more fragmented institutional coverage in Germany gave management its own power resources to contest union attempts at building more inclusive forms of worker solidarity. The majority of the MNC's employment in Germany was organized through subcontractors that used posted workers and were not covered by collective bargaining or minimum wages until recently. At one point, management withdrew orders from a subcontractor whose migrant workforce tried to organize a works council with union support. Conversely, more encompassing collective agreements in Denmark reduced incentives and opportunity for Danish Crown to use posted workers and agency work. Neither was allowed by the union and both were subject to more stringent equal treatment requirements in Denmark. At the same time, Danish Crown was still able to take advantage of Germany's less encompassing institutions by segmenting its workforce across national borders. This points to the limitation of sectoral agreements that are only encompassing up to the national border.

Second, unions relied on a combination of *institutional power, rooted in inclusive institutions*, and *associational power, derived from worker solidarity*, to fight the expansion of precarity at sector and workplace levels. Pulignano and Doerflinger (Chapter 5) argue that Belgium's stronger legislated equal pay provisions and more restricted possibilities for local deviation from central agreements together gave unions institutional power to resist concessions for their core workforce and improve conditions for the staff of agencies, contractors, and on-site subcontractors. In the Belgian chemical subsidiary, the union demanded and won improved job security for agency staff through the application of an inter-sectoral collective agreement affecting employee transfer to subcontractors. In the Belgian metal subsidiary, the union secured an agreement to extend voluntary benefits to tenured agency workers. In these MNCs' German subsidiaries, the regulatory and collective bargaining framework permitted larger differences between agency, permanent, and fixed-term staff. This led to concessions for the permanent workforce to prevent outsourcing (chemical case) and growing use of precarious agency work (metal case). At the same time, similar to Benassi and Dorigatti (Chapter 6), they observe a change in union strategy over time in the German metal industry, with unions demanding and securing numerical limits on the use of fixed-term and agency workers, as well as training investments for these workers. Both chapters show that the works councils benefitted from the 2012 metal sector agreement empowering them to conclude agreements on agency work.

The regulation of posted work is a particular challenge for countries and industries lacking legally established encompassing collective agreements or universal minimum wages, as the Court of Justice of the European Union (CJEU

2007, 2008) has ruled that non-universally applicable forms of collective bargaining and social standards in public procurement violate the free movement rights of contractors. While German unions have faced particularly steep challenges in responding to posted work, this is not an inevitable outcome: Grimshaw et al. (Chapter 2) give the example of a region in Germany where the local government introduced a pay clause in local contracts requiring subcontractors, including those using posting workers, to match minimum pay in collective agreements. This case showed adaptation to the legal limits imposed by the Rueffert decision, which was successfully defended before the CJEU. This demonstrates the heterogeneity of institutional 'power resources' across sectors and workplaces.

In contrast, in Wagner and Refslund's comparison of meatpacking plants (Chapter 3), the German union was unable to oppose the introduction of posted workers through foreign on-site contractors, while the Danish union succeeded in incorporating newer migrant workers under the same pay and conditions enjoyed by the established workforce. They argue that this was in part due to a stronger sectoral agreement in the Danish meatpacking industry, which prevented management from staging competition between production sites to gain concessions. At the same time, the Danish union enjoyed a favourable combination of high union density and strong local union representation. Union membership was a social norm, with migrant workers integrated into the union as members and activists. They argue that this integration promoted inclusive labour solidarity and reduced management's ability to segment the workforce. This gave the Danish union stronger bargaining power compared to the German union in the same industry and even the same MNC, Danish Crown. Thus, although encompassing sectoral bargaining in Denmark was historically an important power resource, unions relied on local mobilization to resist concessions. Mobilization was more difficult in Germany because of low union density combined with weaker capacity to coordinate across contracting firms with no union representation.

These examples all show that associational power is an important precondition for securing and sustaining institutional power. This can also be seen in Mrozowicki et al.'s retail case study (Chapter 7): Slovenian unions enjoyed the highest union density in retail of their three case study countries, but high density both depended on and helped to shore up strong and encompassing sectoral bargaining.

Grimshaw et al. (Chapter 2) give perhaps the most nuanced analysis of how institutional and associational power interact. They show that Swedish local government unions' high density and coordinated bargaining allowed them to win more sustained improvements in pay for core workers, as well as to secure more equitable pay structures in subcontracted workplaces. Despite their weaker institutional power, France, Germany, the UK, and Hungary also showed some examples of local union success in defending workers' pay or in making gains for low-wage workers—which they trace to local union strength and the strikes or campaigns this allowed. They also show the additional importance of transfer of undertakings rules and social clauses in procurement, as resources unions drew on to reduce precarity along the supply chain. For example, in Sweden, all municipality workers enjoyed the right to refuse to transfer to private sector contractors, while only civil servants had these rights in France, Germany, and Hungary (see also, Grimshaw et al. 2015a). At the same time, the extensive use of social clauses in Germany allowed unions to extend better pay and conditions to subcontractor workforces not covered by collective bargaining.

Even under more unfavourable conditions, unions could use strong localized member support to win patchwork gains. Benvegnú et al.'s logistic case studies (Chapter 4) show examples of successful mobilization based on organizing migrants outside established institutions. These were important for the workers affected, but limited to a small number of sites and vulnerable to management exit without integration into law or collective agreements.

High union density within sectors or firms also can encourage a strong norm for diverse groups to join unions—allowing them to mobilize potentially precarious workers more easily, and to incorporate their interests and demands into their bargaining agenda. Tapia and Holgate's German case study (Chapter 9) shows unions had most success in integrating migrants as union leaders where union density was already high. Danaj et al. (Chapter 10) show that high union density in Finland, combined with high bargaining coverage, normalized union membership and incorporated migrant Estonian workers into the union. This, in turn, shaped migrant worker attitudes towards unions, leading them to view unions more favourably and to engage in union campaigns. Their comparative findings suggest that only through these kinds of strongly enforced inclusive institutions, which did not depend on building solidarity among migrants themselves, was it possible to extend minimum labour regulation to this workforce.

Third, unions were most successful in fighting precarity where they were able *to build coordinated bargaining and coalitions within the labour movement and with other civil society groups*. Encompassing legislation and collective agreements both support and rely on strong cooperation between worker representatives at industry level, across firms' production chains, and in different labour market segments. Put another way, inclusive forms of solidarity among unions and other organizations representing workers was a central condition for building and sustaining inclusive institutions in the face of employer strategies that sought to escape or weaken those institutions. Divisions in the labour movement were difficult to overcome and undermined power in other areas.

Tapia and Holgate (Chapter 9) argue that the most effective strategies to organize migrants rely on coalitions, as a result of weakening associational and institutional power resources. For example, within France the Confédération Générale du Travail (CGT) led successful campaigns to reduce precarity among migrants in coalition with civil society and immigrant rights groups, including the 'Sans Papiers' campaign; while in the UK, the Justice for Cleaners campaign relied on joint work between Unite and a community organization, Citizens UK. In contrast, while German unions made some attempts at building broader coalitions—for example, IG BAU's (IG Bauen-Agrar-Umwelt) initiative to create the European Migrant Workers' Union (Greer et al. 2013)—they were least likely to organize joint campaigns outside of already organized workplaces.

Mrozowicki et al. (Chapter 7) show that Estonian unions accessed new resources for organizing retail workers through both cooperative campaigns among unions in different sectors and through international solidarity with Nordic unions through the Baltic Organising Academy. This allowed them to raise union density, improve monitoring of labour standards, and negotiate new collective agreements. In Poland, the retail branch of Solidarność benefited both from international support and from its location within the general union, which could shift resources from other sectors to retail organizing campaigns. In Slovenia, associational resources derived from inclusive solidarity and coordination within the labour movement: sectoral bargaining provided a platform for labour cooperation that did not exist in the other two countries.

The form and extent of labour cooperation is to some extent influenced by collective bargaining structure. In their comparative analyses, Refslund and Wagner (meatpacking, Chapter 3) as well as Pulignano and Doerflinger (chemical and metalworking, Chapter 5) find similar challenges to building or sustaining labour coordination across company- or workplace-level representatives associated with 'dual channel' representation in their German case studies. While this could be overcome by strong union leadership within well-coordinated sectoral bargaining (as in the German metal sector), both studies find that dual channel bargaining was associated with exacerbating competition between worker representatives at workplace or company level where bargaining was more fragmented. Benvegnú et al. (Chapter 4) show that despite high bargaining coverage overall in Austria, the large number of unions and agreements in the logistics industry and in the courier segment effectively prevented coordinated union responses to expanding precarity in a fragmented supply chain. This was made worse by the extensive use of self-employed workers who were not covered by these collective agreements, and who did not enjoy works council representation.

Unions' capacity to overcome divides to forge more solidaristic positions can change over time. Benassi and Dorigatti (Chapter 6), for example, illustrate that in the Italian metal sector, cooperation among the three Italian trade union confederations was underpinned by legislation that restricted the conditions under which agency workers could be used. Unions were able to negotiate even stronger sectoral agreements on top of this base with both agency and metal employers, investing in training and pay between assignments for agency workers, and limiting the proportion of and conditions for use of agency work. However, union cooperation unravelled as agency work was progressively liberalized after 2003 and as employers demanded an end to these arrangements. Deregulation of agency work in Germany initially had similar effects, opening divisions between plant-level works councils; but IG Metal was able to re-establish cooperation via a coordinated national campaign. This resulted in restricting agency work and improving conditions for agency workers via collective agreements, as well as supporting stronger legislation at national level (see also Chapter 5).

In sum, the chapters demonstrate that institutional structure can facilitate or inhibit inter-union cooperation—but also that a commitment to building more inclusive solidarity within the labour movement is a central condition for sustaining or building encompassing institutions capable of containing the spread of precarious employment.

In line with the analytical framework developed in Section 1.3.1, we have focused on institutional and associational power. We do not include *structural power* as a primary explanatory variable. Several of the chapters acknowledge that labour market conditions and structure and production processes can influence union willingness and ability to contest precarious work. For example, in Pulignano and Doerflinger's Belgian metal sector case study (Chapter 5), high local unemployment somewhat weakened unions' willingness to pursue tightened regulation of agency work. Poor labour market conditions after the financial crisis similarly contributed to the already steep challenges faced by retail unions in Slovenia, Poland, and Estonia (Chapter 7), exacerbated already highly competitive market conditions for musicians in the UK, France, and Slovenia (Chapter 8), and contributed to further weakening the fragile cooperation among Italian metal sector unions, leading to divisive concessions in sectoral bargaining (Chapter 6).

However, these labour market factors more typically explained common challenges rather than the differences in outcomes between cases. Similarly, while the chapters show that unions faced systematically high, often seemingly insurmountable, barriers in organizing migrant workers in the most precarious and informal jobs (Chapter 10), unions also drew on different sources of power to overcome these challenges. For example, grassroots unions in Italy mobilized precarious migrants in warehousing to negotiate collective agreements (Chapter 4), while traditional unions built coalitions to organize migrant cleaning workers and engage in successful campaigns to gain citizenship rights for undocumented migrants in diverse service industries (Chapter 9). Thus, while declining structural power undermines unions' ability to regulate precarious work, it does not determine outcomes: workers and unions can change the rules of the game, by reshaping the institutional environment and (re)building solidarity within a diverse workforce.

1.5. CONCLUSIONS

Recent research on precarious work has largely developed within disciplinary silos. CPE studies focus on macro- or national-level institutions and processes to analyse alternative patterns of labour market dualization and segmentation. Critical sociologists rely on ethnographies, case studies, and biographical interviews to analyse the interplay between different forms of power and ideology in exacerbating or legitimizing precarity. Comparative employment relations scholars have gone farthest in integrating theoretical insights from these disciplines, examining how institutions and (in some accounts) union identity shape union strategies towards precarious work, as well as their success at reducing precarity in a firm or labour market.

In this introduction, we have drawn on these three traditions to develop a new framework for analysing the conditions under which unions are successful at moderating or reducing precarity. This framework is most clearly grounded in the comparative employment relations literature, in focusing on the strategic interactions between unions and employers. It also incorporates insights from the CPE literature concerning how institutional structure shapes employer and union strategy towards precarious work, as well as those of critical sociologists concerning how worker identity and identification affect both employers' power to exploit divisions in the workforce and unions' ability to resist narrow or exclusive forms of worker identification. We model two alternative 'ideal type' sets of conditions. Under a 'virtuous circle', a low incidence of precarious work in the labour market both sustains and is supported by a positive feedback loop linking highly inclusive institutions, inclusive union strategies, inclusive worker solidarity, and voice-oriented employer strategies. Under a 'vicious circle', these conditions are reversed. Employers' power to exploit exit options and workforce divisions grows, while labour's capacity to mobilize workers across these divisions declines.

The chapter findings show that conditions in contemporary Europe are broadly consistent with a 'vicious circle'. Labour market and collective bargaining institutions are increasingly fragmented across industries and countries. This gives employers increased scope to use precarious employment contracts and relationships to reduce labour costs and promote intensified worker-to-worker competition in labour markets and across production chains. At the same time, these developments differ in intensity and effect due to two main factors: first, persistent variation in national, sectoral, and firm-level institutions; and second, differences in worker identity and identification, at the level of individual unions or within the labour movement. Across the industry case studies, research findings show that unions are better able to fight precarity where they can access power resources from more inclusive institutions and collectivist, solidaristic forms of worker identification. These factors are complementary: inclusive institutions make it easier for unions to organize and represent diverse groups of workers, while unions rely on inclusive forms of worker solidarity to mobilize the broad forms of collective action necessary to sustain or rebuild encompassing institutions. Most crucially, labour power grounded in inclusive solidarity depends on building or sustaining coordinated bargaining within the labour movement, as well as coalition building across unions and among organizations representing workers and their communities.

Growing popular support for far-right populist parties and candidates in Europe and the US demonstrates the growing hold that exclusive forms of solidarity, based on more narrow forms of worker identity and identification, have on workers in the Global North. This trend is often attributed to expanding economic insecurity, which, in turn, encourages a backlash against the elite institutions and individuals promoting trade liberalization, as well as against groups of precarious outsiders viewed as competitors for increasingly scarce jobs. The case studies in this book show that unions can combat these divisive politics, to build inclusive forms of collective action that incorporate migrants, minorities, and other labour market outsiders most at risk of experiencing precarity and exploitation at work. However, this requires increasingly creative collective action that both looks upwards to closing gaps in welfare state, labour market, and collective bargaining institutions, and looks inwards to building inclusive solidarity across the workforce and within the labour movement.

ACKNOWLEDGEMENTS

Jens Arnholz, Chris Howell, Arne Kalleberg, Nick Krachler, Chris Tilly, and the authors of chapters in this book gave helpful comments and suggestions on earlier drafts of this introduction.

REFERENCES

Adams, Z. and Deakin, S. 2014. 'Institutional Solutions to Precariousness and Inequality in Labour Markets.' *British Journal of Industrial Relations*, 52: 779–809.
Adler, L., Tapia, M., and Turner, L. 2013. *Mobilizing against Inequality: Immigrant Workers, Unions, and Crisis of Capitalism*. Ithaca, NY: ILR Press.

Agarwala, R. 2014. 'Informal Workers' Struggles in Eight Countries'. *Brown Journal of World Affairs*, 20: 251–64.

Alberti, G. 2014. 'Mobility Strategies, "Mobility Differentials" and "Transnational Exit": The Experiences of Precarious Migrants in London's Hospitality Jobs'. *Work, Employment and Society*, 28: 865–81.

Alberti, G., Holgate, J., and Tapia, M. 2013. 'Organising Migrants as Workers or as Migrant Workers? Intersectionality, Trade Unions and Precarious Work'. *The International Journal of Human Resource Management*, 24: 4132–48.

Andersen, S. and Arnholtz, J. 2016. 'Collective Bargaining in the Shadow of Labour Migration: The Case of Danish Construction'. FAOS Working Paper.

Andrijasevic, R. and Sacchetto, D. 2016. 'From Labour Migration to Labour Mobility? The Return of the Multinational Worker in Europe'. *Transfer: European Review of Labour and Research*, 22: 219–31.

Appelbaum, E. and Batt, R. 2014. *Private Equity at Work: When Wall Street Manages Main Street*. New York, Russell Sage Foundation.

Baccaro, L. and Benassi, C. 2016. 'Throwing out the Ballast: Growth Models and the Liberalization of German Industrial Relations'. *Socio-Economic Review*, 15(1): 85–115.

Baccaro, L. and Howell, C. 2011. 'A Common Neoliberal Trajectory: The Transformation of Industrial Relations in Advanced Capitalism'. *Politics and Society*, 39: 521–63.

Baccaro, L. and Howell, C. 2017. *Trajectories of Neoliberal Transformation: European Industrial Relations since the 1970s*. Cambridge: Cambridge University Press.

Baccaro, L. and Pontusson, J. 2016. 'Rethinking Comparative Political Economy: The Growth Model Perspective'. *Politics and Society*, 44: 175–207.

Banting, K. and Kymlicka, W. eds., 2017. Introduction: The Political Sources of Solidarity in Diverse Societies. In Banting, K. and Kymlicka, W. eds., *The strains of commitment: The political sources of solidarity in diverse societies*. Oxford: Oxford University Press, pp.1–60.

Batt, R., Holman, D., and Holtgrewe, U. 2009. 'The Globalization of Service Work: Comparative International Perspectives on Call Centers'. *Industrial and Labor Relations Review*, 62: 453–88.

Bechter, B., Brandl, B., and Meardi, G. 2012. 'Sectors or Countries? Typologies and Levels of Analysis in Comparative Industrial Relations'. *European Journal of Industrial Relations*, 18: 185–202.

Benassi, C., Doellgast, V., and Sarmiento-Mirwaldt, K. 2016. 'Institutions and Inequality in Liberalizing Markets: Explaining Different Trajectories of Institutional Change in Social Europe'. *Politics and Society*, 44: 117–42.

Benassi, C. and Dorigatti, L. 2015. 'Straight to the Core—Explaining Union Responses to the Casualization of Work: The Ig Metall Campaign for Agency Workers'. *British Journal of Industrial Relations*, 53: 533–55.

Benassi, C. and Vlandas, T. 2016. 'Union Inclusiveness and Temporary Agency Workers: The Role of Power Resources and Union Ideology'. *European Journal of Industrial Relations*, 22: 5–22.

Berclaz, M., Fuglister, K., and Giugni, M. 2004. 'États-providence, opportunités politiques et mobilisation des chômeurs: Une approche néo-institutionnaliste'. *Revue suisse de sociologie*, 30(3): 421–40.

Berntsen, L. 2016. 'Reworking Labour Practices: On the Agency of Unorganized Mobile Migrant Construction Workers'. *Work, Employment and Society*, 30: 472–88.

Bohle, D. and Greskovits, B. 2012. *Capitalist Diversity on Europe's Periphery*. Ithaca, NY: Cornell University Press.

Bonacich, E. 1973. 'A Theory of Middleman Minorities'. *American Sociological Review*, 38: 583–94.

Bornschier, S. 2010. *Cleavage Politics and the Populist Right: The New Cultural Conflict in Western Europe*. Philadelphia: Temple University Press.

Bosch, G., Mayhew, K., and Gautié, J. 2010. 'Industrial Relations, Legal Regulations and Wage Setting'. In *Low Wage in the Wealthy Work*, edited by J. Gautié and J. Schmitt. New York: Russell Sage Publications.

Brinkmann, U. and Nachtwey, O. 2010. 'Krise Und Strategische Neuorientierung Der Gewerkschaften'. *Aus Politik und Zeitgeschichte*, 60: 21–9.

Çaro, E., Berntsen, L., Lillie, N., and Wagner, I. 2015. 'Posted Migration and Segregation in the European Construction Sector'. *Journal of Ethnic and Migration Studies*, 41: 1600–20.

Carr, E. and Chung, H. 2014. 'Employment Insecurity and Life Satisfaction: The Moderating Influence of Labour Market Policies across Europe'. *Journal of European Social Policy*, 24: 383–99.

Castles, S. and Kosack, G. 1973. *Immigrant Workers and Class Structure in Western Europe*. Oxford: Oxford University Press.

Chun, J. J. 2009. *Organizing at the Margins: The Symbolic Politics of Labor in South Korea and the United States*. Ithaca, NY: Cornell University Press.

CJEU 2007. Court of Justice of the European Union, Case C-341/05, Laval Un Partneri Ltd V. Svenska Byggnadsarbetareförbundet, 2007 E.C.R. I-11767.

CJEU 2008. Court of Justice of the European Union, C-346/06 Dirk Rüffert V. Land Niedersachsen [2008] Ecr I-1989.

Connolly, H., Marino, S., and Martinez Lucio, M. 2014. 'Trade Union Renewal and the Challenges of Representation: Strategies Towards Migrant and Ethnic Minority Workers in the Netherlands, Spain and the United Kingdom'. *European Journal of Industrial Relations*, 20.

Cornfield, D. 2015. *Beyond the Beat: Musicians Building Community in Nashville*. Princeton, NJ: Princeton University Press.

Doellgast, V. and Berg, P. 2018. 'Negotiating flexibility: External contracting and working time control in German and Danish telecommunications firms'. *ILR Review*, 71(1): 117–142.

Doellgast, V., Sarmiento-Mirwaldt, K., and Benassi, C. 2016. 'Contesting Firm Boundaries: Institutions, Cost Structures, and the Politics of Externalization'. *ILR Review*, 69: 551–78.

Dorigatti, L. 2017. 'Trade Unions in Segmented Labor Markets: Evidence from the German Metal and Chemical Sectors'. *ILR Review*, 70(4): 919–41.

Edwards, P. 2003. 'The Employment Relationship and the Field of Industrial Relations'. In *Industrial Relations: Theory and Practice*, edited by P. Edwards. Oxford: Blackwell.

Eichhorst, W. and Marx, P. 2011. 'Reforming German Labour Market Institutions: A Dual Path to Flexibility'. *Journal of European Social Policy*, 21: 73–87.

Emmenegger, P., Hausermann, S., Palier, B., and Seeleib-Kaiser, M. 2012. *The Age of Dualization: The Changing Face of Inequality in Deindustrialising Societies*. Oxford: Oxford University Press.

Esping-Andersen, G. 1990. *The Three Worlds of Welfare Capitalism*. Princeton, NJ: Princeton University Press.

Fairbrother, P., Lévesque, C., and Hennebert, M.-A. (eds) 2013. *Transnational Trade Unionism: Building Union Power*. New York: Routledge.

Fantasia, R. 1988. *Cultures of Solidarity*. Berkeley: University of California Press.

Frege, C. and Kelly, J. (eds) 2004. *Varieties of Unionism: Strategies for Union Revitalization in a Globalizing Economy*. Oxford: Oxford University Press.

Gordon, J. C. 2014. 'Protecting the Unemployed: Varieties of Unionism and the Evolution of Unemployment Benefits and Active Labor Market Policy in the Rich Democracies'. *Socio-Economic Review*, 13(1): 79–99.

Greer, I., Ciupijus, Z., and Lillie, N. 2013. 'The European Migrant Workers Union and the Barriers to Transnational Industrial Citizenship'. *European Journal of Industrial Relations*, 19: 5–20.

Greer, I. and Doellgast, V. 2017. 'Marketization, Inequality, and Institutional Change: Toward a New Framework for Comparative Employment Relations'. *Journal of Industrial Relations*, 59: 192–208.

Greer, I. and Hauptmeier, M. 2012. 'Identity Work: Sustaining Transnational Collective Action at General Motors Europe'. *Industrial Relations: A Journal of Economy and Society*, 51: 275–99.

Greer, I. and Hauptmeier, M. 2016. 'Management Whipsawing: The Staging of Labor Competition under Globalization'. *ILR Review*, 69: 29–52.

Grimshaw, D., Bosch, G., and Rubery, J. 2014. 'Minimum Wages and Collective Bargaining: What Types of Pay Bargaining Can Foster Positive Pay Equity Outcomes?' *British Journal of Industrial Relations*, 52: 470–98.

Grimshaw, D., Fagan, C., Hebson, G., and Tavora, I. 2017. 'Inequalities and the Dynamics of Labour Market Segmentation'. In *Making Work More Equal: Understanding the International, Societal and Systemic Effects on the Organisation of Employment*, edited by D. Grimshaw, C. Fagan, G. Hebson, and I. Tavora. Manchester: Manchester University Press.

Grimshaw, D., Johnson, M., Rubery, J., and Keizer, A. 2016. 'Reducing Precarious Work: Protective Gaps and the Role of Social Dialogue in Europe'. *Report for the European Commission (DG Employment, Social Affairs and Equal Opportunities)*.

Grimshaw, D., Rubery, J., Anxo, D., Bacache-Beauvallet, M., Neumann, L., and Weinkopf, C. 2015a. 'Outsourcing of Public Services in Europe and Segmentation Effects: The Influence of Labour Market Factors'. *European Journal of Industrial Relations*, 21: 295–313.

Grimshaw, D., Rubery, J., and Ugarte, S. M. 2015b. 'Does Better Quality Contracting Improve Pay and HR Practices? Evidence from For-Profit and Voluntary Sector Providers of Adult Care Services in England'. *Journal of Industrial Relations*, 57: 502–25.

Gumbrell-McCormick, R. 2011. 'European Trade Unions and "Atypical" Workers'. *Industrial Relations Journal*, 42: 293–310.

Gumbrell-McCormick, R. and Hyman, R. 2013. *Trade Unions in Western Europe: Hard Times, Hard Choices*. Oxford: Oxford University Press.

Haipeter, T. 2011. '"Unbound" Employers' Associations and Derogations: Erosion and Renewal of Collective Bargaining in the German Metalworking Industry'. *Industrial Relations Journal*, 42: 174–94.

Hall, P. A. and Gingerich, D. W. 2009. 'Varieties of Capitalism and Institutional Complementarities in the Political Economy: An Empirical Analysis'. *British Journal of Political Science*, 39: 449–82.

Hall, P. A. and Soskice, D. (eds) 2001. *Varieties of Capitalism: The Institutional Foundations of Comparative Advantage*. Oxford: Oxford University Press.

Hassel, A. 2014. 'The Paradox of Liberalization: Understanding Dualism and the Recovery of the German Political Economy'. *British Journal of Industrial Relations*, 52: 57–81.

Hatton, E. 2011. *The Temp Economy: From Kelly Girls to Permatemps in Postwar America*. Philadelphia: Temple University Press.

Hauptmeier, M. and Heery, E. 2014. 'Ideas at Work'. *The International Journal of Human Resource Management*, 25: 2473–88.

Heery, E. 2004. 'The Trade Union Response to Agency Labour in Britain'. *Industrial Relations Journal*, 35: 434–50.

Hermann, C. and Flecker, J. (eds) 2013. *Privatization of Public Services: Impacts for Employment, Working Conditions, and Service Quality in Europe*. London: Routledge.

Hicks, J. 1932. *The Theory of Wages*. New York: Macmillan.

Hipp, L., Bernhardt, J., and Allmendinger, J. 2015. 'Institutions and the Prevalence of Nonstandard Employment'. *Socio-Economic Review*, 13: 351–77.

Hirschman, A. O. 1970. *Exit, Voice, and Loyalty*. Cambridge, MA: Harvard University Press.

Holst, H. 2014. '"Commodifying Institutions": Vertical Disintegration and Institutional Change in German Labour Relations'. *Work, Employment and Society*, 28: 3–20.

Holtgrewe, U. 2001. 'Recognition, Intersubjectivity and Service Work: Labour Conflicts in Call Centres'. *Industrielle Beziehungen*, 8: 37–54.

Holtgrewe, U. and Doellgast, V. 2012. 'A Service Union's Innovation Dilemma: Limitations on Creative Action in German Industrial Relations'. *Work, Employment and Society*, 26: 314–30.

Höpner, M. and Schäfer, A. 2012. 'Embeddedness in Regional Integration: Waiting for Polayni in a Hayekian Setting'. *International Organisation*, 66(3): 429–55.

Hyman, R. 2001. *Understanding European Trade Unionism: Between Market, Class, and Society*. London, Sage.

Inglehart, R. and Norris, P. 2016. 'Trump, Brexit, and the Rise of Populism: Economic Have-Nots and Cultural Backlash'. *HKS Working Paper No. RWP16–026*.

Jabko, N. 2006. *Playing the Market: A Political Strategy for Uniting Europe, 1985–2005*. Ithaca, NY: Cornell University Press.

Jaehrling, K. and Méhaut, P. 2012. '"Varieties of Institutional Avoidance": Employers' Strategies in Low-Waged Service Sector Occupations in France and Germany'. *Socio-Economic Review*, 11(4): 687–710.

Kalleberg, A. L. 2009. 'Precarious Work, Insecure Workers: Employment Relations in Transition'. *American Sociological Review*, 74: 1–22.

Kalleberg, A. L. 2011. *Good Jobs, Bad Jobs: The Rise of Polarized and Precarious Employment Systems in the United States, 1970s to 2000s*. New York: Russell Sage Foundation Publications.

Kalleberg, A. L. and Hewison, K. 2013. 'Precarious Work and the Challenge for Asia'. *American Behavioral Scientist*, 57: 271–88.

Katzenstein, P. 1985. *Small States in World Markets: Industrial Policy in Europe*. Ithaca, NY: Cornell University Press.

Kinderman, D. 2005. 'Pressure from Without, Subversion from Within: The Two-Pronged German Employer Offensive'. *Comparative European Politics*, 3: 432–63.

Kinderman, D. 2016. 'Challenging Varieties of Capitalism's Account of Business Interests: Neoliberal Think-Tanks, Discourse as a Power Resource and Employers' Quest for Liberalization in Germany and Sweden'. *Socio-Economic Review*.

Korpi, W. 1983. *The Democratic Class Struggle*. London: Routledge and Kegan Paul.

Lane, C. 2011. *A Company of One: Insecurity, Independence, and the New World of White-Collar Unemployment*. Ithaca, NY: Cornell University Press.

Lembcke, J. 1988. *Capitalist Development and Class Capacities: Marxist Theory and Union Organization*. Westport, CT: Greenwood Press.

Lévesque, C. and Murray, G. 2013. 'Renewing Union Narrative Resources: How Union Capabilities Make a Difference'. *British Journal of Industrial Relations*, 51: 777–96.

Lillie, N. 2012. 'Subcontracting, Posted Migrants and Labour Market Segmentation in Finland'. *British Journal of Industrial Relations*, 50: 148–67.

Lillie, N. 2016. 'The Right Not to Have Rights: Posted Worker Acquiescence and the European Union Labor Rights Framework'. *Theoretical Inquiries in Law*, 17: 39–62.

Lillie, N. and Greer, I. 2007. 'Industrial Relations, Migration, and Neoliberal Politics: The Case of the European Construction Sector'. *Politics and Society*, 35: 551–81.

MacKenzie, R. and Forde, C. 2009. 'The Rhetoric of the "Good Worker" Versus the Realities of Employers' Use and the Experiences of Migrant Workers'. *Work, Employment & Society*, 23, 142–59.

Marchington, M., Grimshaw, D., Rubery, J. and Willmott, H. (eds) 2005. *Fragmenting Work: Blurring Organizational Boundaries and Disordering Hierarchies*. New York: Oxford University Press.

Marginson, P. 2016. 'Governing Work and Employment Relations in an Internationalized Economy the Institutional Challenge'. *Industrial and Labor Relations Review*, 69: 1033–55.

Marginson, P. and Sisson, K. 2004. *European Integration and Industrial Relations: Multi-Level Governance in the Making*. Houndsmills: Palgrave Macmillan.

Marino, S. 2012. 'Trade Union Inclusion of Migrant and Ethnic Minority Workers: Comparing Italy and the Netherlands'. *European Journal of Industrial Relations*, 18: 5–20.

Marino, S. 2015. 'Trade Unions, Special Structures and the Inclusion of Migrant Workers: On the Role of Union Democracy'. *Work, Employment and Society*, 29.

Martin, C. J. and Swank, D. 2012. *The Political Construction of Business Interests: Coordination, Growth, and Equality*. Cambridge: Cambridge University Press.

Mccollum, D. and Findlay, A. 2015. '"Flexible" Workers for "Flexible" Jobs? The Labour Market Function of A8 Migrant Labour in the UK'. *Work, Employment and Society*, 29: 427–43.

Milkman, R. 2015. 'Immigrant Workers and the Labour Movement in the USA'. In *Migration, Precarity, and Global Governance: Challenges and Opportunities for Labour*, edited by C.-U. Schierup, R. Munck, B. Likic-Brboric, and A. Neergaard. Oxford: Oxford University Press.

Mosoetsa, S., Stillerman, J., and Tilly, C. 2016. 'Precarious Labor, South and North: An Introduction'. *International Labor and Working-Class History*, 89: 5–19.

Mrozowicki, A. 2016. 'Normalisation of Precariousness? Biographical Experiences of Young Workers in the Flexible Forms of Employment in Poland'. *Przeglad Socjologii Jakosciowej*, 12(2): 94–112.

Mrozowicki, A., Karolak, M., and Krasowska, A. 2016. 'Between Commitment and Indifference: Trade Unions, Young Workers and the Expansion of Precarious Employment in Poland'. In *Labour and Social Transformation in Central and Eastern Europe: Europeanization and Beyond*, edited by V. Delteil and V. Kirov. London: Routledge.

Murgia, A. and Pulignano, V. 2016. 'The Social Construction of Precariousness: The Case of Solo Self-Employment in Italy'. Paper presented at the Work, Employment and Society Conference, Leeds University Business School, University of Leeds, 6–8 September 2016.

Oliver, R. J. 2011. 'Powerful Remnants? The Politics of Egalitarian Bargaining Institutions in Italy and Sweden'. *Socio-Economic Review*, 9: 533–66.

Palier, B. and Thelen, K. 2010. 'Institutionalizing Dualism: Complementarities and Change in France and Germany'. *Politics and Society*, 38: 119–48.

Paret, M. 2016. 'Politics of Solidarity and Agency in an Age of Precarity'. *Global Labour Journal*, 7.

Paster, T. 2013. 'Business and Welfare State Development: Why Did Employers Accept Social Reforms?' *World Politics*, 65: 416–51.

Penninx, R. and Roosblad, J. 2000b. *Trade Unions, Immigration and Immigrants in Europe, 1960–1993: A Comparative Study of the Attitudes and Actions of Trade Unions in Seven West European Countries*. New York and Oxford: Berghahn Books.

Pfau-Effinger, B. 1998. 'Gender Cultures and the Gender Arrangement: A Theoretical Framework for Cross-National Gender Research'. *Innovation: The European Journal of Social Science Research*, 11: 147–66.

Piore, M. 1979. *Birds of Passage: Migrant Labor and Industrial Societies*. Cambridge: Cambridge University Press.

Pulignano, V., Doerflinger, N., and De Franceschi, F. 2016. 'Flexibility and Security within European Labor Markets: The Role of Local Bargaining and the "Trade-Offs" within Multinationals' Subsidiaries in Belgium, Britain, and Germany'. *ILR Review*, 69.

Pulignano, V. and Keune, M. 2014. 'Understanding Varieties of Flexibility and Security in Multinationals: Product Markets, Institutions Variation and Local Bargaining'. *European Journal of Industrial Relations*, 21

Pulignano, V. and Signoretti, A. 2016. 'Union Strategies, National Institutions and the Use of Temporary Labour in Italian and US Plants'. *British Journal of Industrial Relations*, 54: 574–96.

Refslund, B. 2016. 'Sectoral Variation in Consequences of Intra-European Labour Migration: How Unions and Structural Conditions Matter'. In *Labour Mobility in the Enlarged*

Single European Market (Comparative Social Research, Volume 32), edited by J. E. Dølvik and L. Eldring. Bingley: Emerald.

Rueda, D. 2007. *Social Democracy Inside Out: Partisanship and Labor Market Policy in Advanced Industrialized Democracies*. Oxford and New York: Oxford University Press.

Rueda, D. 2014. 'Dualization, Crisis and the Welfare State'. *Socio-Economic Review*, 12: 381–407.

Samaluk, B. 2016a. 'Migrant Workers' Engagement with Labour Market Intermediaries in Europe: Symbolic Power Guiding Transnational Exchange'. *Work, Employment and Society*, 30: 455–71.

Samaluk, B. 2016b. 'Neoliberal Moral Economy: Migrant Workers' Value Struggles across Temporal and Spatial Dimensions'. In *The Commonalities of Global Crises: Markets, Communities and Nostalgia*, edited by C. Karner and B. Weicht. London: Palgrave Macmillan.

Schmitter, P. and Lehmbruch, G. (eds) 1979. *Trends Towards Corporatist Intermediation*. Beverly Hills: Sage.

Schulten, T. 2002. 'A European Solidaristic Wage Policy?' *European Journal of Industrial Relations*, 8: 173–96.

Silver, B. J. 2003. *Forces of Labor: Workers' Movements and Globalization since 1870*. Cambridge: Cambridge University Press.

Standing, G. 2011. *The Precariat: The New Dangerous Class*. London: Bloomsbury Academic.

Streeck, W. 1991. 'On the Institutional Conditions of Diversified Quality Production'. In *Beyond Keynesianism: The Socio-Economics of Production and Full Employment*, edited by E. Matzner and W. Streeck. Aldershot: Edward Elgar Publishing.

Streeck, W. 2009. *Re-Forming Capitalism: Institutional Change in the German Political Economy*. Oxford: Oxford University Press.

Streeck, W. 2016. *How Will Capitalism End? Essays on a Failing System*. London and New York: Verso Books.

Tapia, M., Ibsen, C. L., and Kochan, T. A. 2015. 'Mapping the Frontier of Theory in Industrial Relations: The Contested Role of Worker Representation'. *Socio-Economic Review*, 13: 157–84.

Taylor, P. and Bain, P. 2004. '"India Calling to the Far Away Towns": The Call Centre Labour Process and Globalisation'. *Work, Employment and Society*, 19: 261–82.

Thelen, K. 2012. 'Varieties of Capitalism: Trajectories of Liberalization and the New Politics of Social Solidarity'. *Annual Review of Political Science*, 15: 137–59.

Thelen, K. 2014. *Varieties of Liberalization and the New Politics of Social Solidarity*. Cambridge: Cambridge University Press.

Turner, L. 2009. 'Institutions and Activism: Crisis and Opportunity for a German Labor Movement in Decline'. *Industrial and Labor Relations Review*, 62: 294–312.

Umney, C. and Kretsos, L. 2015. '"That's the Experience": Passion, Work Precarity, and Life Transitions among London Jazz Musicians'. *Work and Occupations*, 42: 313–34.

Vallas, S. P. 2015. 'Accounting for Precarity: Recent Studies of Labor Market Uncertainty'. *Contemporary Sociology: A Journal of Reviews*, 44: 463–9.

Vallas, S. P. and Prener, C. 2012. 'Dualism, Job Polarization, and the Social Construction of Precarious Work'. *Work and Occupations*, 39: 331–53.

Virdee, S. 2000. 'A Marxist Critique of Black Radical Theories of Trade-Union Racism'. *Sociology*, 34: 545–65.

Vosko, L. F., Macdonald, M., and Campbell, I. (eds) 2009. *Gender and the Contours of Precarious Employment*. New York: Routledge.

Wagner, I. 2014. 'Rule Enactment in a Pan-European Labour Market: Transnational Posted Work in the German Construction Sector'. *British Journal of Industrial Relations*, 53: 692–710.

Wagner, I. 2015. 'The Political Economy of Borders in a "Borderless" European Labour Market'. *JCMS: Journal of Common Market Studies*, 53: 1370–85.

Wagner, I. and Refslund, B. 2016. 'Understanding the Diverging Trajectories of Slaughter-house Work in Denmark and Germany: A Power Resource Approach'. *European Journal of Industrial Relations*, 22: 335–51.

Wright, E. O. 2000. 'Working-Class Power, Capitalist-Class Interests, and Class Compromise'. *American Journal of Sociology*, 105: 957–1002.

Zhang, C. and Lillie, N. 2015. 'Industrial Citizenship, Cosmopolitanism and European Integration'. *European Journal of Social Theory*, 18: 93–110.

Zysman, J. 1983. *Governments, Markets, and Growth: Financial Systems and the Politics of Industrial Change*. Ithaca, NY: Cornell University Press.

2

Negotiating Better Conditions for Workers during Austerity in Europe

Unions' Local Strategies towards Low Pay and Outsourcing in Local Government

Damian Grimshaw, Stefania Marino, Dominique Anxo,
Jérôme Gautié, László Neumann, and Claudia Weinkopf

2.1. INTRODUCTION

In the wake of the 2008 economic crisis and subsequent sovereign debt crisis, governments across the EU have, to varying degrees, acted to reduce government expenditures in an attempt to restore their fiscal position (Bach and Bordogna 2013; Vaughan-Whitehead 2013). While the scale of these austerity measures has varied, there has been a convergence of reforms targeted at public sector work-forces, involving pay cuts and pay freezes, downsizing of jobs, and a renewed commitment to outsourcing and privatization (Hermann and Verhoest 2012; Keune et al. 2008; Mitchell 2009; Schulten 2012). Overall, the evidence reveals a general deterioration of pay and employment standards, especially damaging for women who are over-represented in the public sector (Rubery 2013).

The variety of austerity packages across Europe raises questions about unions' capacities to mediate and influence workers' conditions in the industrial relations heartlands of the public sector, an employment segment traditionally character-ized by relatively inclusive institutions. In many countries, governments bypassed traditional tripartite routes and enacted austerity reforms unilaterally on public sector workforces (Hyman 2015), particularly where Troika programmes were imposed (Koukiadaki et al. 2016; Marginson 2015). Furthermore, accelerated privatization and outsourcing risk stripping unions of segments of their member-ship base and weakening their bargaining power (Grimshaw et al. 2015; Hermann and Flecker 2011; Kirov and Hohnen 2015). Overall, it appears that in the once highly unionized European public sector, with its strong legacy of fair employ-ment standards, we are witnessing the emergence of *'precarious insiders'*, as pay cuts and outsourcing erode conventions of pay progress and job security. How-ever, unions are not passive actors confronted by these dynamics. A dualist thesis, associated with orthodox economics and notions of political partisanship, might anticipate that union actions would shore up employment standards enjoyed by insiders and displace cost pressures to less protected groups, such as the lowest-paid non-professional workforce and subcontracted workers (Lindbeck and Snower 1988; Rueda 2007). However, a more nuanced, non-determinist approach is needed both to account for unions' diverse interests, which tend to blur the boundaries between members' interests and those of the wider workforce (Crouch 2015: 29), and to explain empirical evidence of seemingly inclusive, solidaristic strategies. In the European public sector, these include national industrial disputes opposing austerity measures (Varga 2015; Nowak and Gallas 2014), local-level social dialogue as part of two-tier bargaining structures (Galetto et al. 2014; Grimshaw et al. 2017), local bargaining to address low pay (Johnson forthcoming), and local union opposition (also involving civil society organizations) to outsourcing (Grimshaw et al. 2015; Warner and Clifton 2013).

This chapter explores union actions affecting local government workers during a period of austerity in five European countries: France, Germany, Hungary, Sweden, and the UK. The study was designed as a 'matched comparison' of local union actions in the same sector across countries with diverse national industrial relations institutions. These five countries are characterized by different systems of public sector wage-setting and varied opportunities for local union influence (Gottschall et al. 2015; Marsden 1994). The study is also a 'contextualised comparison' (Locke and Thelen 1995), since it observes significant country differences both in the levels of macroeconomic fiscal restraint and in starting points in the drive towards austerity and pay cuts in the public sector. The central aim of the chapter is to investigate the conditions under which trade unions have been able to reduce precarious work among local government workers (in-house and subcontracted), and to promote more equitable and solidaristic outcomes. It specifically focuses on union actions against *pay precarity* (focusing on deals for the lowest paid) and against *employment precarity* (focusing on solidaristic approaches towards subcontracting). It concludes by discussing the contributory roles played by national institutions, austerity measures, and unions' power resources in shaping the prospects for pay equity and chain solidarities in Europe's public sector.

2.2. THE CONTEXT FOR COMPARISON: AUSTERITY SPENDING CUTS AND NATIONAL INSTITUTIONS

Public sector workforces across Europe seemingly faced a common challenge of having to adapt to austerity reforms in the wake of the 2008 economic crisis. The manner in which public spending cuts ripple through to the workforce at local level and affect their pay and other conditions is likely to be refracted through national industrial relations institutions (Bach and Bordogna 2013; Molina 2014), particularly the scope for joint bargaining at national and local levels and the relative influence of trade unions and government—here playing a dual role as paymaster and employer. Similarly, outsourcing decisions are shaped by a set of labour market rules and conditions, including public–private differences in industrial relations and pay conditions (Grimshaw et al. 2015). The five countries compared here have varied systems of public sector industrial relations and wage-setting arrangements. At the same time, austerity measures may affect the refractive capacities of national institutions. Following Locke and Thelen's (1995) call for 'contextualised comparisons', we therefore begin by comparing the scale and timing of austerity in each country.

2.2.1. Austerity Spending Cuts

Radically restrictive fiscal policy was a key characteristic of the resurgent neoliberal economics following the economic crisis (Crouch 2011). However, it was not pursued with the same vigour in our five countries, in response partly to differences in the degree of macroeconomic imbalances but also to differences in ideology of the ruling political elites and the capacity of surrounding institutions to shape the political response. During the period of our investigation, 2010–12, fiscal pressures were relatively moderate in Sweden and France but stringent in Germany, Hungary, and the UK.[1] In Figure 2.1, Sweden and France exhibit a cumulative positive rise in public spending throughout the 2006–14 period. For Sweden, the reason is mostly macroeconomic; it had no concerns over its public sector deficit and enjoyed very low debt levels so could continue to raise spending in line with economic growth. For France, it is a question of the timing of our fieldwork, as spending growth was cut to less than 2 per cent during 2013 and 2014 in response to spiralling government debt.

The other three countries suffered a period of fiscal retrenchment during our fieldwork. Germany and the UK experienced abrupt shocks to spending levels after 2010: while annual rises averaged around 4–5 per cent in the run-up to 2010, spending was frozen in the UK in 2011 and cut in Germany by around 1 per cent. Aggregating the three-year period, 2010–13, spending increased by just 2.6 per cent in the UK and 3 per cent in Germany, substantially less than Sweden's 9.6 per cent increase and France's 7 per cent. The UK was especially hard hit because it represented a dramatic reversal of a pre-2010 political commitment by the then Labour government to significant year-on-year rises in public spending (Grimshaw 2013). Hungary is different due to the timing of austerity. It suffered the economic crisis earlier and was one of three Central and Eastern European countries first targeted by the Troika,[2] with an injection of €20 billion in 2008. As such, Hungary experienced less than 1 per cent spending growth in 2009 and 2010 and a cut of 0.6 per cent in 2012. Moreover, from 2010 the right-wing government gradually centralized provision of public services (including public education, hospitals, and waste management) so that municipalities were deprived of key responsibilities and associated budgets. Thus, by 2010–12 spending cuts in

---

[1] Our assessment draws on OECD.Stat data for total government expenditures (see Figure 2.1) and for total government debt, 2006–15, <https://data.oecd.org/gga/general-government-debt.htm>.

[2] The label given to the representatives from the European Commission, European Central Bank, and International Monetary Fund who imposed new fiscal rules in several European countries on behalf of creditors.

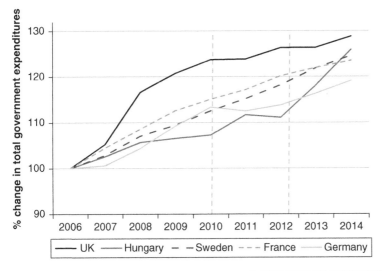

	2006	2007	2008	2009	2010	2011	2012	2013	2014
Sweden	1,591,343	1,637,064	1,705,183	1,746,133	1,801,094	1,848,385	1,903,854	1,973,692	2,027,895
UK	603,668	635,441	707,620	736,912	759,002	759,853	778,652	779,035	798,039
Hungary	12,474,690	12,796,338	13,190,523	13,308,058	13,404,821	13,996,199	13,916,287	14,890,966	16,055,295
Germany	1,069,695	1,076,099	1,116,223	1,170,508	1,219,219	1,208,565	1,224,500	1,255,570	1,290,699
France	972,839	1,016,168	1,057,610	1,100,609	1,128,022	1,151,537	1,186,020	1,207,102	1,226,746

Figure 2.1. Cumulative annual change in total government expenditures, 2006–14

Note: Data in the table are national currencies expressed at current prices.

Source: OECD.stat, <https://stats.oecd.org/Index.aspx?DataSetCode=SNA_TABLE11#>, authors' compilation.

Hungary had already accumulated significantly and were greatly felt among interviewees in the case study municipalities.

As such, local government in Germany, Hungary, and the UK experienced major financial challenges, while these were not apparent in France and Sweden. In Germany spending cuts were accompanied by reforms requiring municipalities to shoulder the additional costs of new areas of service provisions and to adapt to less generous tax relief laws. The latter led to an estimated €4.8 billion loss of municipality revenues and forced many to take out short-term loans, leading to a ballooning of debt of around €130 billion by the end of 2011. In response to severe cuts in Hungary, several municipalities issued bonds denominated in foreign currencies. However, this aggravated the situation—in some cases causing bankruptcy—and in 2013 the government had to launch a major bail-out programme. In the UK, government cuts targeted police and local government services rather than the ostensibly more politically visible areas of health and education. The highly centralized structure of UK government (Sellers and Lidström 2007) meant local municipalities had limited capacity to generate other funds, and even their limited freedoms were curtailed during 2011–13 with a centrally imposed freeze on local property tax.

2.2.2. National Institutions and Pay Reforms

Because labour costs account for a high proportion of government expenditures, austerity spending cuts are likely to translate into downwards pressures on public sector pay. However, outcomes are refracted by the country-specific character of industrial relations wage-setting institutions (Glassner 2010; Vaughan-Whitehead 2013). A key characteristic is the extent of joint regulation for public sector pay during 'normal times' (Marsden 1994; Meurs 1993). Only Sweden provides collective bargaining rights to all its public sector workforce (except very senior officials). France provides public sector collective bargaining rights, but the agreements are not legally binding (as in the private sector) and government has the final say. Germany, Hungary, and the UK only provide these rights to subgroups—to those without civil servant status (Germany), those employed in government-owned companies (Hungary), or local government workers and civil servants (UK[3]). Each country system therefore enables differential use of unilateral government intervention. There has been no unilateral employer wage-fixing in Sweden since 1965, for example, while in France unilateral government decisions have often prevailed over centralized collective bargaining. In Germany, civil servants' pay is set by government, but government must meet with union representatives twice each year and consult on all new legislation concerning working conditions. In Hungary, albeit with limited influence, tripartite consultation (including local government employers) precedes government fixing of public sector salaries. These varied systems set the scene for the use of unilateral wage-fixing and the strength of austerity-imposed pay reforms (Table 2.1).

During 2008–12, France, Hungary, and the UK applied a series of measures to cut public sector pay. Germany and especially Sweden were quite different. In

Table 2.1. Unilateral vs. joint regulation (national level) and austerity pay reforms (2008–12)

	Austerity pay reforms?		
	Weak	Medium	Strong
Unilateral	—	France: three-year freeze of *Point d'indice* (2010–13) UK: two-year freeze with small bonus for low paid (2011–13), then a 1 per cent pay cap (2013–)	Hungary: continued pay freeze (since 2006); abolished thirteenth month salary (2009); higher pay settlement for low paid (2011)
Joint regulation	Germany: reversed unilateral government decision to cut bonus (2011) Sweden: no pay cuts, new bonus for low paid	UK: one-year pay freeze in local government (2010–11)	

[3] Pay for most of the UK public sector is determined by 'pay review bodies'. The process is independent of government and includes representatives from unions and employer bodies. However, the final arbiter is government.

Germany, the government attempted in 2011 to impose increased working hours and a reduced Christmas bonus on civil servants (an estimated loss of 2.5 per cent in average earnings), but it was rejected by unions and restored in late 2011. A key point for Germany, however, is that unions acting for non-civil servants agreed to a new low rate of pay in 2005, which diminished pressures on further pay cuts. In Sweden, public sector workers faced neither a cut nor a freeze in pay during 2008–12, and in fact a small supplement was introduced for low-wage central government workers.

In the three countries where unilateral government wage-fixing is more likely, the recent trends show they experienced relatively stringent reforms during austerity. The French government unilaterally froze the value of the public sector index unit of the base wage pay scale in 2010–13, bypassing the usual process of annual centralized consultation with unions. This decision accelerated the decline of the real value of public sector base wages, which had been falling since the early 1980s. Automatic increases in the seniority premium, as well as promotions, were therefore the only remaining sources of pay increases. To compensate for the three-year index freeze, the government introduced a pay supplement but only for employees whose total nominal earnings (i.e. including bonuses and premiums) had increased less than inflation. Government interventions in Hungary far exceeded the other four countries. The government first imposed a pay freeze in 2006, and then in 2009 it cancelled the thirteenth month salary. By 2012, public sector workers had experienced a dramatic reduction in real earnings, with two in five paid at the level of the statutory national minimum wage. The UK government imposed a unilateral pay freeze (2011–13) and subsequent ongoing 1 per cent pay cap. Local government workers suffered an additional year of pay freeze during 2010–11 as the result of collective bargaining. The right-wing government at the time supplemented their strategy with a small populist pay bonus of £250 per year for two years for the lowest paid, but excluded local government workers—most likely because they had the highest incidence of low pay.

Overall, national institutions of wage-fixing play a stronger role in shaping pay reforms than the macroeconomic adjustments imposed by public spending decisions. Comparing Figure 2.1 and Table 2.1, we find that Germany and France have swapped positions: Germany imposed far more restrictive spending cuts than France, but this did not carry through into a tough unilateral reform of public sector pay, unlike France's three-year freeze of the pay index.

2.2.3. National Institutions and Outsourcing

Public spending cuts can put major pressure on public sector employers to outsource, but national institutions and labour market conditions also play a role (Grimshaw et al. 2015). Two key factors are the degree of variation in industrial relations conditions and in average earnings between public and private sectors. Public sector managers may outsource activities to evade union influence and joint regulation over pay and conditions, anticipating that private sector subcontractor employers are able to act unilaterally and quickly to adapt costs in line with (public sector) client pressures (Hermann and Flecker 2011). Also, unions are more likely to negotiate decent pay for public sector workers based on

Table 2.2. Public–private gaps[1] in collective bargaining and average pay and incentives to outsource

		Pay gap		
		Private > public	Neutral	Public > private
Collective bargaining gap	Private > public	*Zero incentives*	—	—
	Neutral	Hungary (pay penalty for non-civil servants)	Sweden, France	
	Public > private	—	—	*Strong incentives* Germany and the UK (especially female part-time workers in both)

Note: [1] This is a stylized presentation of gaps based on large numerical differences in union densities (of 20 points or more) and average earnings (10 points or more, either male or female employees).

Source: Compiled from detailed data based on a review of ICTWSS data and decomposition analyses of earnings gaps in Grimshaw et al. (2012: tables 3.1, 3.2, 3.4, figure 3.2) and Grimshaw et al. (2015: table 1).

equity across a given set of skills, job responsibilities, and experience, including gender-proofed pay differentials (Ascher 1987; Berlinski 2008; Tepe et al. 2015), which may be less likely in the private sector. To a great extent, public sector outsourcing decisions mimic private sector subcontracting arrangements, where the evidence similarly points to the role of wage cost differentials, as well as rules facilitating exit from internal employment relationships (Doellgast et al. 2016).

Overall, our five countries display considerable variation in national patterns of public–private differences, and this plays a key role shaping local outsourcing decisions (Table 2.2). Incentives to outsource public services are strongest where earnings are higher for a given occupation in the public sector than the private sector, and where unions exert greater influence through collective bargaining. Surprisingly perhaps, only Germany and the UK fit this scenario (at a national, aggregate level). In both countries, collective bargaining coverage is substantially higher in the public sector, a gap of more than forty points in both countries, and this aligns with a union density gap. Moreover, decomposition analyses[4] of public–private pay gaps suggest the German and UK public sectors pay more (for a given education and occupation) to the low paid and to women in part-time jobs, which suggests strong cost incentives to outsource low-skill, feminized services.[5] By contrast, cost-driven outsourcing would appear to be curtailed in Sweden, due to inclusive collective bargaining coverage in both sectors and convergent wage trends, and in Hungary, where the gap in bargaining coverage is narrow (despite substantially higher public sector union density). Hungarian public sector workers already experience a significant pay penalty, such that outsourcing for cost-cutting purposes would seem to be self-defeating. France is an intermediate case: bargaining coverage is very high in the private sector, and

---

[4] See, for example, Brindusa et al. (2011).

[5] It is likely that Germany's new national minimum wage (2015) and the UK's new minimum wage premium (2016) will close these pay gaps, but they were not in place at the time of our fieldwork.

the positive public–private pay gap among low-level occupations has been decreasing for years as the statutory minimum wage has increased faster than the base wage index point, overtaking the lowest pay grades in the public sector. Cost incentives to outsource are therefore generally modest or absent; in particular the large private sector utilities firms offer more attractive total compensation packages for low-skilled outsourced workers.

A further influence on outsourcing decisions in Europe concerns the EU Acquired Rights Directive (and associated European Court of Justice (ECJ) rulings), which protects a person's employment and associated conditions at the point of transfer to a subcontractor organization (for up to twelve months), albeit subject to country differences in implementation. Unions are granted strong negotiating rights over outsourcing in Sweden and Germany, including acting on behalf of a worker to refuse transfer and be redeployed with the public sector organization. By contrast, unions in the UK and Hungary have limited consultation rights, and if a worker objects to being transferred he/she will most likely be treated as having resigned rather than enjoying the rights of wrongful dismissal or redundancy compensation (Hartzén et al. 2008). There are additional peculiarities in France, Germany, and Hungary that reflect the different legal employment statuses among civil servants, other public sector workers, and private sector workers. Private sector workers providing outsourced public services used to be protected by public law in France, but this possibility was removed in 2004. Under austerity, the special legal status of civil servants may even become disadvantageous, such that unions have a perverse incentive to defend rather than oppose outsourcing as a means of improving employment conditions (Grimshaw et al. 2015).

While EU rules protect continuity of employment for transferring workers, other measures curtail union efforts to negotiate improved standards. At the time of our research, EU procurement legislation (covering all subcontracting of public services) was interpreted as prohibiting use of social clauses in public subcontracting in order to protect against the potential discrimination of bidders (Hermann et al. 2012). This view was reinforced by the 2008 ECJ Rüffert case, which ruled the German region of Lower Saxony acted unlawfully by requiring bidding firms to pay wages set in the collective agreement that was not declared legally binding. Nevertheless, empirical studies report use of social clauses in two of our five countries: Germany and the UK. Since 2010, Germany has witnessed a wave of regional governments introducing social clauses in public subcontracting, ranging from construction and public transport to security and cleaning (Schulten 2012). In the UK, unions have successfully incorporated 'living wages' into local government subcontracting. Unlike Germany, UK progress is entirely voluntary, largely uncoordinated, and patchy: among London municipalities, for example, data for May 2011 showed only five out of thirty-two municipalities required all subcontractors to pay a living wage.[6]

Other factors may also be significant in outsourcing arrangements. Local-level strategic and ideological concerns may be important drivers of actions both among employers and unions. Some employers may oppose outsourcing because they prefer to retain operational control and believe this establishes longer-term

---

[6] <http://www.bbc.co.uk/news/uk-england-london-13266095>.

protections over costs, while others outsource as part of a drive to marketize services delivery.

In summary, we anticipate that country diversity in the national institutional settings both establishes boundaries and opens up opportunities around which local actors, both unions and municipality employers, engage in social dialogue and industrial relations actions to reduce precarious work characterized by poor pay prospects and insecurities caused by outsourcing. We do not expect a set of all-encompassing, deterministic institutional effects, flowing from national to local level (Frege and Kelly 2013; Doellgast 2012). Institutional configurations may provide the necessary power resources for unions to pursue solidaristic collective actions locally, but they can also be the object of such action in situations where they no longer satisfy the self-defined interests of actors (Hall and Thelen 2005). Our research was therefore open to notions of institutional entrepreneurship (Crouch 2005), whereby local actors may be able to negotiate better outcomes for their members in ways that build on the strengths of institutional conditions and avoid their weaknesses. These concerns underpin the central question for this research, namely under what conditions can unions reduce precarious work by promoting more equitable and solidaristic outcomes for local government workers (in-house and subcontracted) during austerity in Europe? The conditions encompass national institutions (industrial relations, wage-setting, and procurement rules), employment conditions (especially public–private differences), and other local factors. Actions to reduce precarious work encompass actions against pay precarity (improved conditions for low-wage workers) and against employment precarity (solidaristic outcomes for subcontracted workers). In Section 2.3 we describe how the research was designed to investigate this central question.

2.3. RESEARCH DESIGN

Research in the local government sector in the five countries was conducted by teams based in each country and coordinated via regular project meetings. Each country team sought to identify the implications of austerity conditions for wage-setting and subcontracting practices, the mediating effects of national institutions, and the strategic responses of unions and management at organizational level. The primary data collection involved two stages: (1) the collection of national and regional data to explore the wider context of pay policies and subcontracting strategies in local government; and (2) the investigation of local responses through multiple case studies (Table 2.3). Overall we completed fifteen case studies, conducted between two and four interviews at each, and compiled documentation on staffing and procurement practices.

The rationale for the selection of municipalities in each country reflected both the general research question for the project and country specificities. In all five countries, the selection covered different-sized municipalities and/or varied population demographics (Table 2.3). In addition, the different politics of municipality governance was one of the explicit criteria in France, Hungary, and the UK; in practice this had a strong bearing on the approach to subcontracting, thereby facilitating diverse case study data. In Germany and Hungary, there was a specific

Table 2.3. A summary of case studies undertaken in the five countries

	Cases	Population	Workforce*	Factors motivating selection
France	Municipality A	100,000	3,126	• Contrasting demographics (young and
	Municipality B	60,000	1,535	high immigrant share vs. average
				demographics)
				• Contrasting politics (which shaped
				different approaches to outsourcing)
Germany	Municipality A	< 500,000	6,000	• All three in most indebted region of
	Municipality B	> 500,000	9,000	Germany (medium to large
	Municipality C	≈ 50,000	400	indebtedness in all three, ranging from
				€1.7k to €4.2k per inhabitant)
				• All Social Democrat control
Hungary	Small town	10,000	700	• Contrasting indebtedness (large town
	Large town	150,000	≈ 3,000	heavily indebted, ≈ €140m)
				• Large town is a vanguard case—strong
				right-wing public policy reforms
Sweden	Växjö	83,710	5,825**	• Contrasting approaches to
				outsourcing
	City of Goteborg	520,374	31,145**	• Contrasting political control (centre-
				right at Växjö, left-green at Goteborg)
				• Both enjoyed budget surplus
UK	North West LA1	498,800	8,907	• Contrasting local living standards
	North West LA2	308,800	1,859	• Contrasting local pay strategies and
				successes
	North West LA3	327,300	12,281	• Contrasting political control
	East LA1	125,700	1,010	
	South East LA1	1,427,400	12,652	
	South East LA2	239,700	3,888	

Notes: *Data are approximate and are not comparable since some are limited to local government administration (Germany), others include municipality-owned companies and/or schools; **permanent staff only.

concern about the consequences of high levels of indebtedness registered in some municipalities; in Germany this guided the choice of three municipalities in North Rhine Westphalia, which was the most populous and most indebted region at the time of research. In the UK one of the six cases was selected because it had opted out of the national collective agreement. Finally, in Hungary, one of the two cases was selected as a 'vanguard case' that exemplified a new style of conservative reform already established before the 2010 national elections. Overall, these contrasting case studies of municipalities provided ample scope to investigate local-level union actions and thus answer our central research question, although we make no claims here regarding the representativeness of local cases of the overall country situation.

2.4. RESEARCH FINDINGS 1: UNIONS' SUCCESS AT IMPROVING PAY AT LOCAL LEVEL

Our first set of findings covers union efforts to protect or improve pay and conditions for local government workers, especially the lowest paid. Opportunities

Table 2.4. Institutional opportunities for local-level union pay actions

	Union influence	What pay conditions?
Hungary	*Weak*: weak budget autonomy and weak union power; some influence in local government-owned companies and for 'public service employees'	n.a.
Germany	*Weak/moderate*: no wage drift in principle; very limited local autonomy	Options to use low-wage pay grade
France	*Moderate*: job rates fixed in national *grille de la Fonction Publique*	Pay premiums, bonuses (15–30 per cent of total wage) and promotions; total pay package for non-civil servants (most on fixed-term contracts)
UK	*Moderate*: pay rates fixed in national agreement but significant influence; 12 per cent of municipalities opted out of sector agreement	Fixing of job pay rates, pay bands, premiums, merit pay; weak–strong influence in opted out municipalities
Sweden	*Strong*: freedom to fix local pay rates and annual pay change subject to national minimum rise in pay bill	For all local government workers, pay rates and job grades are fixed locally

for local union pay actions ranged from weak to strong, and were shaped by the character of national agreements and the local political context (Table 2.4). Sweden and the UK provided the strongest opportunities for local engagement and negotiations in local government. In both countries, employees are covered by a national collective agreement that provides scope for further negotiations locally. In Sweden, negotiated wage increases are carried out locally but, for a majority of agreements, are subject to the constraint imposed in the national agreement of a minimum increase in the overall pay bill and/or a guaranteed individual pay rise (coordinated with the overarching framework of national agreements); 2011 data suggest around 17 per cent of workers had wages wholly determined at local level. This situation fits the country's general character of 'centralized decentralisation' (Thornqvist 1999). In the UK, local managers and union representatives have wide discretion to change conditions of employment, including pay (through job-grading decisions), sickness schemes, overtime pay, and unsocial hours premiums. Local negotiations were especially important in the 2000s in implementing a new harmonized pay scale for manual and non-manual employees which adapted an equal pay proofed, national job evaluation scheme (Perkins and White 2010). Moreover, a small group of municipalities (forty-six out of 375) operate outside the national agreement, and are relatively independent where unions have negotiating rights.

In the other three countries, there were no local negotiations on pay rates since this is entirely regulated by national collective agreement (Germany) or national legislation (France, Hungary). In Germany, local government pay is fixed by the national public service collective agreement for the federal state and municipalities, which defines classification criteria as well as pay rates. It allows very limited local freedom to adjust pay, but the 2005 agreement included two new options for local flexibility: use of a new low pay grade and (until it was abolished in the 2009–10 negotiations) a performance-related pay bonus. In France, local government pay is integrated within the unified public sector civil servants' pay scale. While relatively centralized, unions and employers nevertheless enjoyed some local discretion in the fixing and allocation of pay premiums and bonuses for civil servants, as well as on the entire pay package for employees without civil service status. The latter group accounted for almost half (45 per cent) the workforce in the two case studies, two-thirds of whom were temporary workers. Unions also exercised local influence over promotion practices. Paradoxically, the greater use of temporary contracts has brought with it an enhanced role for unions in local bargaining in France. Local union pay actions were weakest in Hungary, reflecting a significant deterioration during austerity. Local government pay is fixed by government legislation following tripartite, national 'interest reconciliation'. Decentralized collective agreements are in principle possible for public service (non-civil servant) employees and for municipal-owned company workers, following rules for the private sector. However, much depends on the degree of local budget constraints, which tend to be very restrictive, and union influence, which tends to be very weak or absent.

Describing the form of union influence as varying from weak to strong oversimplifies the inter-country variation in the form of participation, particularly where unions enjoyed high levels of *institutional power* in the form of formal consultation channels. In Germany, formal consultations also extend to works councils which, besides co-determination rights, have the right to establish a business committee in the municipality to discuss the commercial and financial situation, planned investments, partnerships with private entities, rationalization plans, and the introduction of new working and management methods. In France, unions participate in consultative bipartite committees that typically operate at the level of a grouping of municipalities and deal with employees' careers (advancement, promotions, job mobility). Through these committees, unions influence individual pay prospects, but not general wage levels. Other consultative 'technical committees' also exist to deal with work organization and health and safety issues.

Our research also revealed three types of local 'action–outcome combinations' to reduce pay precarity by protecting or improving low pay. Each combination reflected particular interactions of austerity conditions, local autonomy (for unions and employers), and evidence of coordinated union power resources and strategies (Table 2.5).

Table 2.5. Three types of local 'action–outcome combinations' on low pay

	Austerity fiscal pressures	Local employer budget autonomy	Local union influence	Actions for inclusive worker solidarity	Countries
General deterioration with patchwork of gains for low-wage workers	Strong	Weak	Weak/ moderate	Weak	Germany, UK, Hungary
Compensatory protections plus low-wage gains	Weak	Moderate	Moderate	Strong	France
Sustained improvements with varied decentralized outcomes	Weak	Moderate	Strong	Strong	Sweden

2.4.1. Deterioration (Driven Nationally) with Patchwork of Gains for Low-Wage Workers

The case studies in Germany, the UK, and Hungary are broadly characterized by stringent spending cuts combined with downward pressures on real levels of pay and relatively weak union influence at local levels. This context generated low-level industrial relations conflict and encouraged efforts by unions, where possible, to rectify matters at least for the lowest paid.

Negotiations over pay in the German municipalities we studied were shaped by both massive indebtedness and the 2005 introduction of a new low pay grade 1 in the national agreement that could be implemented locally. The new lower pay grade was justified by employers as necessary to reduce incentives to outsource. Moreover, the new pay grade provoked wide-scale conflicts across municipalities over how to value the skills required in many low-wage jobs, the range of jobs classified to the new low-pay scale, and the procedures for making local-level adjustments—all in a context of budget cuts.

The national collective agreement suggests a list of job types defined as involving 'extremely simple activities' to be included in grade 1: examples include catering and cleaning staff, toilet attendants, and cloakroom attendants. However, the case study data suggest use of the new pay grade varied, largely due to local union influence. At one municipality, managers wrongly, or unjustly, classified jobs into the new low pay grade. Works council and union representatives recounted evidence of managers describing a growing number of tasks in job descriptions as 'extremely simple', despite their requiring tangible skills, such as a foreign language or computer skills. The problem was exacerbated by municipality indebtedness, such that managers said they placed individuals on grade 1 'as a matter of principle'. A survey of the region suggests unions have enjoyed some success: only one-third of municipalities paid some employees at grade 1. In another case study, unions successfully disputed the definition of 'extremely simple activities' (e.g. with respect to the knowledge and use of kitchen-related appliances, teamwork, and physical effort) and negotiated the reclassification of ostensibly low-skill jobs to grade 2. Overall, the case studies reveal conflicting interpretations of procedural issues; while unions argued job evaluations should always be jointly negotiated, employers believed they had the right to exercise unilateral prerogative. Local actions were subject to regular audits from the regional authority to test the legality of pay grade classifications. However, these audits appeared to have the primary aim of aligning pay practices with the objective of saving public money.

In the UK, unprecedented budget cuts coupled with three years of frozen national pay set the scene for efforts by unions to improve pay locally where possible. Our case studies suggest unions were mostly effective by pressing for bottom-weighted pay settlements, a type of egalitarian pay strategy pursued by unions in low-wage segments (Heery 2000). In four of the six case studies, unions succeeded in eliminating the lowest pay points on the national pay scale and recruiting employees on to higher rates of base pay, which ranged from 7 per cent to 14 per cent above the national base rate. In each case, managers supported unions: first, because higher pay contributed towards ameliorating poverty among the local population; second, because it would reduce staff turnover and attract better job candidates (supported by detailed empirical research at one of the municipalities); and third, because it was fair compensation for increased work effort in the wake of staff downsizing (amounting to 6–30 per cent of the municipalities' workforce over the two years preceding our fieldwork). The chosen higher rate of pay in two cases was the voluntary 'living wage' (outside London), which is endorsed by the trade union movement.[7]

However, the other two UK municipalities confronted spending cuts and a national pay freeze by dismissing the entire workforce in order to re-engage everyone on to a new employment contract with changed terms and conditions. This practice provided an ostensibly effective way, from a legal perspective, of ensuring savings could be made by reducing terms and conditions of employment. In one of the cases, it involved the dismissal and re-engagement of approximately 8,500 staff on to a new contract that abolished pay premiums for weekend working, public holidays, and overtime. Local union officials told us that signing the new contract was in practice the only option available to employees:

> Well you didn't have to sign them but if you didn't you were dismissed. And if you tried to sign them under protest or say you were signing under duress they were sent back to you and told that's not acceptable—either you sign them with nothing else on the paper or if you sign under duress we'll treat you [as if] you haven't signed it.
>
> (Local union official, 2012)

In fact, all six UK case studies had downgraded premium pay for unsocial working hours and overtime hours to some extent,[8] but most had followed the 'organized practice' recommended in the national agreement of negotiating changes via local collective agreement. In response to the aggressive management tactics at North West LA3, the local union team organized a series of strikes during 2012 but only managed to restore a set of ad hoc payments to those workers most affected by the changes, including social care workers providing services to the elderly who tended to work a lot of unsocial hours (see Grimshaw et al. 2017 for details).

Hungary also fits this general type of action–outcome combination. The long-standing national pay freeze—by 2012 into its sixth year—and the abolished thirteenth month salary had generated a significant wage penalty among local government workers. Local agreements are in principle possible for employees without civil service status and workers in municipal-owned companies, but our case studies suggest meaningful collective bargaining is rare due to weak managerial budget autonomy and weak local union presence. This leaves very limited room for union influence on pay, and in practice unions were rarely able to achieve more than enforcement of mandatory minimum standards. Furthermore, labour law reforms had further limited collective bargaining in publicly owned companies by prohibiting the deviation of locally negotiated working hours, wage bonuses, and severance pay above the statutory minimum amounts. The 2012

---

[7] The UK living wage is fixed independently each year and is a voluntary initiative for decent minimum standards of pay at a level higher than the statutory minimum wage, see <http://www.livingwage.org.uk>.

[8] For example, three municipalities reduced overtime pay from time and a half (Monday through Friday) to time and a third for the first two hours of overtime in one municipality, and to basic rate payment in two municipalities. Another reduced weekend overtime to time and a half for all employees except the lowest paid, who continued to receive the nationally agreed double time payment.

Labour Code also reduced unions' local influence by granting works councils the possibility to conclude collective agreements (although not on pay) if no union is present. Despite these obstacles, in one case study negotiations did occur in publicly owned companies because unions had a strong presence. In the other municipality, where unions were weak, there was no collective bargaining over pay and no evidence of any interest representation whatsoever that could influence employment conditions. It seems only large municipalities have interest reconciliation forums that, while not legally constitutive of collective bargaining, tend to set the benchmarks for local wage agreements for public sector employees.

2.4.2. Compensatory Protections Plus Gains for Low-Wage Workers

A second scenario of action–outcome combinations consists of relatively weak fiscal spending cuts and therefore weaker pressures at national and local levels to contain pay. France is illustrative. The three-year freeze of the national index points, which applied to basic pay rates, could to some extent be compensated by union actions (agreed with local managers) to improve other parts of local government workers' pay packages, with a specific targeting of low-wage workers' pay. In both case studies, unions secured higher bonuses and premiums as compensation for the stagnation in basic pay. Unlike Germany or the UK, unions did not have the freedom to negotiate a local matching of jobs to the national pay scale, and therefore focused on adjusting a range of pay premiums and bonuses. The pay-off for managers was that more attractive pay packages would help meet difficulties in recruiting and retaining personnel.

In one case study, managers unilaterally fixed a new, simplified scale of pay supplements that consolidated the previous, more complicated structure with the aim of improving transparency, encouraging more cross-occupational mobility and establishing a more competitive position for recruiting. However, the new structure offered limited improvement for the lowest-paid (level 1) workers who were at the top of their pay grade. In response, unions organized a local strike and won a new consolidated, universal bonus of €250 for all employees in the lowest-paid category (higher than the managers' €150 offer). The deal added 12 per cent to the municipality pay bill, which was possible at the time in a context of relatively weak austerity spending constraints. The overall level of locally negotiated supplement remained high: for a newly recruited employee on the base level the monthly supplement was €269, which was around 16 per cent of total monthly pay. For higher-level jobs supplementary pay could be as much as 50 per cent of total pay (2012 data). Furthermore, in both case studies, unions were especially conscious of the standards for low-wage workers, reflective of strong inclusive solidarity actions, and negotiated annual increases to bonuses and premiums in fixed cash amounts rather than a percentage rate in order to benefit the lowest paid most.

But the wider context of changes to pay structures in France is important to consider. A major concern for unions was the flattening of age-earnings profiles in low-wage occupations ('C category' jobs), resulting from the fact that entry-level wages were de facto indexed to the national statutory minimum wage, which had increased much faster during 2008–12 than the public sector 'index point'.

To illustrate, the wage rate for someone with ten years of service in a category C job used to be 14 per cent higher than the entry-level wage in 2003, but had collapsed to just 2 per cent by 2012. Unions therefore sought to agree new local pay practices that could compensate for this flattened wage profile. Examples in our case studies included fast-track advancement for all employees, higher levels of bonuses and premiums, and new fringe benefits (such as complementary health insurance in one municipality). But differences between municipalities were important, as outcomes depended on the stringency of budget constraints and on the capacity of unions to influence local management strategy.

2.4.3. Sustained Improvements with Varied, Positive Decentralized Outcomes

Sweden's local government workforce did not suffer national pay or spending austerity, and we found unions at local level were able to continue their efforts at making egalitarian, upward pay adjustments while meeting organizational needs (especially recruitment and retention). As such, Sweden displays evidence of local-level wage-setting, like France and the UK, but in the rather different context of a nationally guaranteed pay rise and, moreover, in the absence of a nationally agreed pay scale. This is perhaps surprising to people used to thinking that Sweden operates a highly coordinated and centralized industrial relations system. However, this mostly provides a loose architecture and system for distributing resources (Thornqvist 1999). Rates of pay in Swedish local government are entirely set at local level through local collective agreements between employer and trade unions. Moreover, these agreements tend to involve *individualization* of wage-fixing through regular 'wage meetings' that increasingly seek to reflect the individual's skill and performance rather than the job's characteristics, an approach for the most part supported by unions. Nevertheless, there is variation. For example, the data revealed local use of a job evaluation system in one case study in order to combat pay discrimination (by age, sex, ethnicity) but not in the other. Also, while local union representatives in both cases were not opposed to individualized wage-setting in principle, their support was in practice relatively limited in the case of homecare workers compared to more qualified occupations (such as nurses or teachers) because it was more difficult to get a fair deal for less-qualified workers via individualized bargaining. In both cases, however, the criteria guiding the processes of individualization and differentiation of wages were negotiated jointly with unions.

As we found in France, Swedish unions exercised further local influence over wage premiums. Sweden's municipal budgets are set annually and include not only a general budget for a percentage rise in the total pay bill but also a budget for paying specific local wage premiums for occupational groups identified as hard to recruit. Examples in the two case studies included union negotiation of recruitment and retention premiums for IT specialists and nurses, reflecting national data that suggest average earnings for nurses are around 15 per cent higher in the private sector than the public sector at the top decile. However, union representatives argued that while entry pay levels were higher in the private sector, prospects for pay progression and intensity of workload (e.g. number of patients per nurse) were generally worse.

2.5. RESEARCH FINDINGS 2: UNIONS' SUCCESS AT PROMOTING SOLIDARISTIC LOCAL OUTCOMES FOR SUBCONTRACTED WORKERS

Our second set of findings concerns unions' success at negotiating better outcomes for subcontracted workers who were contracted to provide local government services. Reflecting the concerns in the literature review Section 2.2, the data confirm that two key drivers underpinned observed union actions and outcomes for subcontracted workers: (1) public–private gaps in pay and in union strength shaped outsourcing incentives and union actions; and (2) EU rights for transferring workers, along with social clauses in procurement, enabled unions in some cases to extend protections along the supply chain.

2.5.1. Gaps in Pay and Union Strength Between Local Government and Subcontractors

As anticipated, case study data for Germany and the UK revealed the strongest incentives for outsourcing owing to large perceived gaps in pay and union strength, with evidence of significantly better pay and conditions in the sampled municipalities than in the subcontractors. In both countries, unions opposed all outsourcing of municipality work because it was expected to lead to a generalized worsening of working conditions, including pay and union representation. In Germany, for example, unions were seeking more transparent cost–benefit analyses, training of union representatives in the economics of subcontracting, and clearer co-determination through provision of timely information on procurement decisions. Unions also sought to apply the rules set out in a new piece of legislation requiring subcontractors of public services to comply with current collective agreements or respect a set minimum wage. In one municipality, unions successfully negotiated with managers to limit outsourcing and even to remunicipalize some activities, despite local politicians' calls for more outsourcing. Unions won by demonstrating that in-house services were in fact cheaper. Unfortunately this was partly true thanks to the new nationally determined low pay grade 1 (see Section 2.4.1), so in fact the pay and conditions of newly recruited workers to the municipality had worsened. In another municipality, by contrast, unions made no efforts to bring cleaning services back in-house, despite the same application of the low pay grade.

A similar situation prevailed in the UK because the base rate set in the national agreement had sunk to only a little over the statutory minimum wage and therefore closed the gap with subcontractors' pay rates. But as in Germany, UK case studies varied in the application of the nationally fixed low pay rates and so the gap with subcontractors (and the associated cost incentives for outsourcing) could be quite large in some cases (e.g. where the municipality paid its workforce the UK living wage). The UK case studies, with one exception, revealed limited union actions to insource subcontracted work in order to improve pay and conditions—largely because it was seen as very difficult. Pay and conditions were universally worse in subcontractor organizations because collective bargaining was absent and employers were unwilling to align with local government terms and conditions.

The other three countries displayed a more level playing field between public and private sectors and, as such, cost and control incentives for outsourcing were weaker. In Sweden, high collective bargaining coverage combined with an increased tendency towards local wage formation had led to convergent wage formation in public and private workplaces, thereby lessening both the cost incentives for outsourcing and the wage effects. The case studies demonstrate that there were relatively limited differentials between in-house and subcontracted staff: while initial pay levels tended to be higher in the private sector, pay progression was more limited and work effort was more intensive due to tighter staffing ratios.

In Hungary, a similarly level playing field prevailed but with a shared poverty of employment conditions characterized by high use of minimum wage jobs and weak or absent union influence in local workplaces, public and private. In Hungary, therefore, outsourcing had limited impact on the wages of transferring workers and as such outsourcing decisions and union actions were generally driven by other factors, such as politics of the municipality leadership. At the same time, workers who shifted to non-union workplaces lost collective representation while unions risked losing members. Our case studies did reveal examples of effective local union actions: at one municipality unions negotiated with a subcontractor church organization to retain pay and employment conditions in its new collective agreement and also bargained for the reintroduction of benefits previously cancelled by the municipality. Unions and works councils also consulted with employers over redundancies, something that was not required by the law and contrary to the general practice.

In France, some local unions even adopted a pragmatic, surprisingly non-oppositional, approach towards outsourcing to exploit opportunities to improve employment conditions. At one municipality the employer wanted to bring outsourced services back in-house, but unions were reluctant because they had fostered collective agreements in the subcontractors that had over time delivered better pay and employment conditions. Insourcing would mean transferring workers who risked losing important fringe benefits. Furthermore, unions feared that the anticipated worsening budgetary situation of municipalities would not support future improvements in pay and conditions. These particular circumstances explain why unions in one case study supported a private company in providing school catering since pay for its employees was around 10 per cent higher than for a comparable municipal employee. The private company also committed to protect pay and employment conditions and not to redeploy transferring employees to another unit of the company.

2.5.2. Use of Employment Protection Rules and Social Clauses in Procurement

European rules dictate certain protections for transferring workers and as to whether social clauses may be incorporated into procurement contracts (see Section 2.2.3). However, our case studies reveal substantial variation between weak and medium-strong extensions of decent, negotiated terms and conditions of employment. National interpretation of EU rules certainly levelled up the minimum standards of employment protection for transferring workers: all cases except the UK confirmed rules that protected employees against dismissal at the point of transfer; Sweden went further by granting all municipality workers the right to refuse transfer; and France, Germany, and Hungary granted rights of refusal to non-civil servants or public service employees. The UK data suggest that municipality employers sought to evade employment protection rules by using a strategy known in legal cases as 'fragmentation' to reduce the possibility that the transferring staff would be covered by employment protection law (see also Adams 2012)—for example by fragmenting the services pre-transfer by geograph-ical locality or by outsourcing a series of smaller units of activity over time. While unions contested this strategy, they were unable to prevent it. European rules also recommend that subcontractors sustain the protected conditions for at least twelve months, and again this appears to have been generally respected in our case studies. However, one French case went considerably further. The local union fought to defend protections for non-civil servants when a transport service contract was won by a company with a reputation for not honouring protected conditions. The threatened workforce mounted a successful strike and won protection for the entire six-year contract period.

Given the ECJ Rüffert rulings against incorporating so-called social clauses in procurement providing for higher pay and other employment conditions, we had not anticipated finding evidence of their use. In any case, the absence of public–private pay gaps and/or collective bargaining gaps in Hungary, Sweden, and France suggested that if they were used at all it would most likely be in Germany and the UK. While there was only limited evidence of their use in the six UK cases (a living wage clause in a handful of small contracts), in Germany their use was extensive and is illustrative of a genuinely solidaristic union strategy to extend better pay and other conditions to subcontractor workforces outside unions' traditional scope for pay bargaining. The region we investigated was one of many to introduce pay clauses in various contracts for local government services, and in common with others after 2010 in fact passed legislation on their use. Accordingly, where the activity is covered by a binding sector collect-ive agreement (under the Posted Workers Act) then the subcontractor must match the minimum wage set in the collective agreement or lose entitlement to bid for the contract.[9] Because this reduces the cost incentives to outsource (combined with the new low pay grade, see Section 2.4.1), more and more municipalities were witnessing successful union actions to insource services (so-called remunicipalization).

2.6. DISCUSSION AND CONCLUSION

Our research on local government in five European countries investigated the conditions under which unions have been able to reduce precarious work among

---

[9] Legally, the contractor should fulfil all the requirements of the extended collective agreement, if these fall under the areas listed in the Posted Workers Directive, involving pay scales by skill etc., as described in the 2005 Sähköliitto decision. The remaining problem however is enforcement.

in-house and subcontracted workers and, specifically, to promote more equitable and solidaristic outcomes. The chapter has focused in particular on union actions aimed at reducing *pay precarity* among the directly employed local government workforce (by negotiating better deals for the lowest paid) and actions to reduce *employment precarity* (by extending better conditions to workers in subcontractor companies). In broad terms, the evidence suggests that the different strategies and instruments used by trade unions across the case studies were contingent on power resources deriving from both their institutional position in the regulatory framework (institutional power) and their membership base (associational power)—although the strength of these power resources differed greatly across countries as did the ability of unions to leverage their resources. The findings suggest that better regulatory outcomes in terms of defence of pay and working conditions of both directly employed and subcontracted workers have been achieved where trade unions had access to both institutional and associational power. This was most clearly the case in Sweden, with its encompassing bargaining institutions and high union density in the public and private sectors, which supported representation and regulation across the supply chain. However, our analysis for the other countries highlights some of the country idiosyncrasies— notably the legal, political, and economic factors—that also come into play.

In particular, the time and the place matter a great deal in shaping the narrative of this chapter. Where austerity spending cuts were strong, only the presence of a highly effective tripartite system of wage-fixing in the public sector could negate the adverse consequences for pay—as in Germany for example, compared to the long-term imposition of pay cuts (in real terms) in Hungary and the UK. France and Sweden offered a very interesting comparison, because spending measures either came after our period of fieldwork (France) or not at all (Sweden). This provided local employers with far greater autonomy over local budgets, which shaped union success in pay negotiations. The situations at local level in Germany and Hungary were complicated by a raft of legal reforms that devolved more and more of the financial accountabilities and generated growing problems of indebtedness among municipalities. These were important country-specific factors that framed union actions towards more equitable and solidaristic outcomes in our case studies.

The significant influence of national-level (and pan-national) institutions was further accentuated in three respects. First, national pay agreements differed in the extent to which they delegated powers to unions and employers at local level, with the clearest framework of centralized decentralization visible in Sweden's municipalities. Less coordinated systems (Hungary and the UK) generated greater potential for heterogeneity of action–outcome combinations at local level largely because they opened up a space for employer opportunism in organizations where unions had weak associational power. Second, union failure at national level to secure decent pay settlements might be said to have inspired local actions (where possible) to compensate, and even lead to unusual coalitions of local employers and unions that agreed on the need to improve pay for the lowest paid to address problems of local poverty, as we witnessed in several UK municipalities. We might even claim that local state agencies were happy to 'legitimate' raised pay for the lowest paid as compensation for the state bail-out of failing banks (after O'Conner 1973; see Grimshaw et al. 2017). Third, EU rules that protect employment conditions for workers transferring from one employer to another with recurrent subcontracting of services clearly raise the minimum standards in all European countries. In their absence, which might become a reality in the UK after Brexit, workers would have to depend on the ability of unions to mobilize members in the subcontracted companies and/or to seek to make agreements binding along the supply chain.

At the same time, the successes and forms of local union action–outcome combinations cannot be completely anticipated by national institutional configurations. Unions in France and the UK sought to further the interests of the lowest paid at local level despite no coordinating influence from national level. A key question for future research is whether or not these local-level successes in improving pay equity can feed back up to the national level so that minimum collectively negotiated standards are improved for all workers in the sector. Our evidence suggests that such gains for the low paid are highly contingent on unions' local power and resources, as well as willingness of the employer to engage. A further example concerns the gains pursued for the subcontracted workforce. The ideal national-level arrangement is typified by Sweden, where high collective bargaining coverage and convergent wage trends between public and private sectors mean that similar conditions are shared along the local government supply chain. In the UK, national rules provide for employment protection for transferring workers (as in all other EU member states). However, unlike the other countries, we found evidence of employer evasion in the UK, which quite clearly flouted the spirit of the relevant legislation. One explanation for this evasion is the structural conditions of high industrial relations gaps and high pay gaps between low-paid workers in the public and private sectors, which provides cost and control incentives to employers. The other is a growing problem that UK employers are unwilling to take on their responsibilities of ensuring wage and employment security for workers, with evidence of dysfunctional flexible employment forms such as zero hours contracts (prevalent among care workers in local authorities' supply chains for example) and false self-employment (see Rubery et al. 2016).

We conclude with an observation regarding whether or not unions adopted dualist strategies (Lindbeck and Snower 1988; Rueda 2007) by protecting standards for their core membership (mid-earners in local government) at the expense of both the non-core members (low-wage local government workers) and non-members among the subcontractor workforce. Table 2.6 locates each country in the relevant cells distinguishing between: (a) weak versus medium/strong union

Table 2.6. Comparing local action–outcome combinations: a simple test of the dualism thesis

	Weak pay equity		*Medium-strong pay equity*	
	Unprotected standards	Protected standards	Unprotected standards	Protected standards
Weak chain solidarity	Hungary	Dualist 1	UK	Dualist 2
Strong chain solidarity	—	Germany	France	Sweden

approaches towards pay equity (by targeting the interests of the low paid); (b) weak versus strong chain solidarity (by extending conditions to subcontracted workers); and (c) union effectiveness in protecting employment standards in general. If a dualist strategy were applied, we would find evidence of protected standards with weak pay equity and weak chain solidarity (Dualist 1), or possibly protected standards with medium-strong pay equity and weak chain solidarity (Dualist 2). None of the five countries fit with these action–outcome combinations. Instead, we find that Hungary has largely ineffective unions, providing limited improvements in terms of pay equity or chain solidarity and failing to protect standards. Unions in the UK did effectively raise pay for the lowest paid but in a context of falling standards and weak chain solidarity. Unions in Germany, France, and Sweden all reject the classic dualist thesis by bargaining effectively for stronger chain solidarity—in each case reflecting a specific societal approach, via social clauses (Germany), new allegiances with subcontractors (France), and inclusive collective bargaining (Sweden).

It is important to refute these simplistic dualist arguments since they get in the way of our understanding the diversity of union actions at national and local levels and figuring out the factors that assure success at improving workers' pay and employment conditions. Union actions have played a vital institutional role in managing organizational responses to austerity. While during the 1990s many European countries negotiated tripartite social pacts to respond to economic restraint and ensure sustained employment levels and economic investments (Hassel 2006), more recent examples have been scarce, only realized after the use of conflict on the side of trade unions (Rychly 2009) and often quite limited in scope (Hyman 2010). Bipartite social dialogue also faces a continuing period of difficulties, with an escalation of industrial conflicts in many European countries and a much-reduced ability of unions to protect public sector employees from job cuts and pay cuts. Our research shows that in those countries (Hungary, UK) where unions' role and position at national level has been weakened, it does not necessarily correspond to a weakening at the local level. Nevertheless, there is a risk that a patchwork of local successes, without the supporting national institutional architecture, is fragmenting employment conditions in accordance with the relative strength of the local actors involved. Lessons can be learned therefore from the ability of German and Swedish unions in particular to sustain and develop strong coordinating mechanisms to ensure better outcomes over the long term and to constrain, at least partially, the adverse fiscal consequences associated with the still-dominant neoliberal socio-economic policy approach across Europe.

ACKNOWLEDGEMENTS

This chapter draws extensively on a research project funded by the European Commission (DG Employment, Social Affairs and Inclusion, VS/2011/0141). The full research report, associated national reports and list of project team members from the five countries can be found at: <http://www.research.mbs.ac.uk/ewerc/Our-research/Current-projects/Public-sector-pay-procurement-and-inequalities>.

REFERENCES

Adams, Blair. 2012. 'Slipping through the TUPE Net'. *Procurement and Outsourcing Journal* (March/April) <http://www.dmhstallard.com/site/library/legalnews/>.

Brindusa, Anghel, De la Rica, Sara, and Dolado, Juan J. 2011. 'The Effect of Public Sector Employment on Women's Labour Market Outcomes'. CEPR Discussion Paper No. DP8468.

Ascher, Kate. 1987. *The Politics of Privatisation: Contracting out Public Services.* London: Macmillan Education.

Bach, Stephen, and Bordogna, Lorenzo. 2013. 'Reframing Public Service Employment Relations: The Impact of Economic Crisis and the New EU Economic Governance'. *European Journal of Industrial Relations*, 19(4): 279–94.

Berlinski, Samuel. 2008. 'Wages and Contracting Out: Does the Law of One Price Hold?' *British Journal of Industrial Relations*, 46(1): 59–75.

Crouch, Colin. 2005. *Capitalist Diversity and Change: Recombinant Governance and Institutional Entrepreneurs.* Oxford: Oxford University Press.

Crouch, Colin. 2011. *The Strange Non-Death of Neoliberalism.* Cambridge: Polity.

Crouch, Colin. 2015. 'Labour Market Governance and the Creation of Outsiders'. *British Journal of Industrial Relations*, 53(1): 27–48.

Doellgast, Virginia. 2012. *Disintegrating Democracy at Work: Labor Unions and the Future of Good Jobs in the Service Economy.* Ithaca, NY: Cornell University Press.

Doellgast, Virginia, Sarmiento-Mirwaldt, Katja, and Benassi, Chiara. 2016. 'Contesting Firm Boundaries: Institutions, Cost Structures, and the Politics of Externalization'. *ILR Review*, 69(3): 551–78.

Frege, Carola and Kelly, John. 2013. 'Theoretical Perspectives on Comparative Employment Relations'. In *Comparative Employment Relations in the Global Economy*, edited by Carola Frege and John Kelly. London: Palgrave.

Galetto, Manuela, Marginson, Paul, and Spieser, Catherine. 2014. 'Collective Bargaining and Reforms to Hospital Healthcare Provision: A Comparison of the UK, Italy and France'. *European Journal of Industrial Relations*, 20(2): 131–47.

Glassner, Vera. 2010. 'The Public Sector in the Crisis'. ETUI Working Paper 2010.07.

Gottschall, Karin, Kittel, Bernhard, Briken, Kendra, Heuer, Jan-Ocko, Hils, Sylvia, Streb, Sebastian, and Tepe, Markus. 2015. *Public Sector Employment Regimes: Transformations of the State as an Employer.* London: Palgrave.

Grimshaw, Damian. 2013. 'Austerity, Privatisation and Levelling Down: Public Sector Reforms in the UK'. In *Public Sector Shock: The Impact of Policy Retrenchment in Europe*, edited by Daniel Vaughan-Whitehead. Cheltenham: Edward Elgar; and Geneva: ILO.

Grimshaw, Damian, Johnson, Mathew, Marino, Stefania, and Rubery, Jill. 2017. 'Towards More Disorganized Decentralization? Collective Bargaining in the Public Sector under Pay Restraint'. *Industrial Relations Journal*, 48(1): 22–41.

Grimshaw, Damian, Rubery, Jill, Anxo, Dominique, Bacache-Beauvallet, Maya, Neumann, László, and Weinkopf, Claudia. 2015. 'Outsourcing of Public Services in Europe and Segmentation Effects: The Influence of Labour Market Factors'. *European Journal of Industrial Relations*, 21(4): 295–313.

Grimshaw, Damian, Rubery, Jill, and Marino, Stefania. 2012. 'Public Sector Pay and Procurement in Europe during the Crisis: The Challenges Facing Local Government and the Prospects for Segmentation, Inequalities and Social Dialogue'. Comparative report. Manuscript.

Hall, Peter A. and Thelen, Kathleen. 2005. 'The Politics of Change in Varieties of Capitalism'. Annual Meeting of the American Political Science Association, Washington, DC.

Hartzén, A. C., Hös, Nikolett, Lecomte, Franck, Alexandre, Marzo, Claire, Mestre, Bruno, Olbrich, H. and Fuller, S. 2008. 'The Right of the Employee to Refuse to be Transferred:

A Comparative and Theoretical Analysis'. LAW Working Paper, European University Institute.

Hassel, Anke. 2006. *Wage Setting, Social Pacts and the Euro: A New Role for the State.* Amsterdam: Amsterdam University Press.

Heery, Edmund. 2000. 'Trade Unions and the Management of Reward'. In *Reward Management: Critical Perspectives,* edited by Geoff White and Janet Drucker. London: Routledge.

Hermann, Christoph and Flecker, Jörg. 2011. 'The Liberalization of Public Services: Company Reactions and Consequences for Employment and Working Conditions'. *Economic and Industrial Democracy,* 32(3): 523–44.

Hermann, Christoph, Kubisa, Julia, and Schulten, Thorsten. 2012. 'The Struggle for Public Services'. In *Privatisation of Public Services and Impacts for Employment, Working Conditions, and Service Quality in Europe,* edited by Christoph Hermann and Jörg Flecker. London and New York: Routledge.

Hermann, Christoph and Verhoest, Koen. 2012. 'The Process of Liberalisation, Privatisation and Marketisation'. In *Privatization of Public Services: Impacts for Employment, Working Conditions and Service Quality in Europe,* edited by Christoph Hermann and Jörg Flecker. New York: Routledge.

Hyman, Richard. 2010. 'Social Dialogue and Industrial Relations during the Economic Crisis: Innovative Practices or Business As Usual?' ILO Working Paper No. 11, Geneva.

Hyman, Richard. 2015. 'Three Scenarios for Industrial Relations in Europe'. *International Labour Review,* 154(1): 5–14.

Johnson, Mathew. Forthcoming. 'Implementing the Living Wage in UK Local Government'. *Employee Relations.*

Keune, Marteen, Leschke, Janine, and Watt, Andrew (eds) 2008. *Privatisation and Liberalisation of Public Services in Europe.* Brussels: ETUI.

Kirov, Vassil and Hohnen, Pernille. 2015. 'Trade Unions Strategies to Address Inclusion of Vulnerable Employees in "Anchored" Services in Europe'. *International Journal of Manpower,* 36(6): 848–73.

Koukiadaki, Aristea, Távora, Isabel, and Martínez Lucio, Miguel (eds) 2016. 'Joint Regulation and Labour Market Policy in Europe during the Crisis'. Brussels: European Trade Union Institute (ETUI).

Lindbeck, Assar and Snower, Dennis J. 1988. 'Long-Term Unemployment and Macroeconomic Policy'. *The American Economic Review,* 78(2): 38–43.

Locke, Richard and Thelen, Kathleen. 1995. 'Apples and Oranges Revisited: Contextualised Comparisons and the Study of Comparative Labor Politics'. *Politics and Society,* 23(3): 337–67.

Marginson, Paul. 2015. 'Coordinated Bargaining in Europe: From Incremental Corrosion to Frontal Assault?' *European Journal of Industrial Relations,* 21(2): 97–114.

Marsden, David. 1994. 'Public Service Pay Determination and Pay Systems in OECD Countries'. Public Management Occasional Papers Series, No.2. Paris: OECD.

Meurs, Dominique. 1993. 'The Rationale For, and Implications Of, Centralized Pay Determination Systems in the Public Sector'. In *Pay Flexibility in the Public Sector, Public Management Studies.* Paris: OECD.

Mitchell, Daniel J. B. (ed.) 2009. *Public Jobs and Political Agendas.* Champaign, IL: Labor and Employment Relations Association.

Molina, Oscar. 2014. 'Self-Regulation and the State in Industrial Relations in Southern Europe: Back to the Future?' *European Journal of Industrial Relations,* 20(1): 21–36.

Nowak, Jörg and Gallas, Alexander. 2014. 'Mass Strikes Against Austerity in Western Europe: A Strategic Assessment'. *Global Labour Journal,* 5: 306–21.

O'Conner, James. 1973. *The Fiscal Crisis of the State.* New York: St Martin.

Perkins, Stephen J. and White, Geoff. 2010. 'Modernising Pay in the UK Public Services: Trends and Implications'. *Human Resource Management Journal,* 20(3): 244–57.

Rubery, Jill. 2013. 'Public Sector Adjustment and the Threat to Gender Equality'. In *Public Sector Shock: The Impact of Policy Retrenchment in Europe*, edited by Daniel Vaughan-Whitehead. Cheltenham: Edward Elgar; and Geneva: ILO.

Rubery, Jill, Keizer, Arjan, and Grimshaw, Damian. 2016. 'Flexibility Bites Back: The Multiple and Hidden Costs of Flexible Employment Policies'. *Human Resource Management Journal*, 26(3): 235–51.

Rueda, David. 2007. *Social Democracy Inside Out: Partisanship and Labor Market Policy in Industrialized Democracies*. Oxford: Oxford University Press.

Rychly, Ludek. 2009. 'Social Dialogue in Times of Crisis: Finding Better Solutions'. Industrial and Employment Relations Working Paper 1. Geneva: ILO.

Schulten, Thorsten. 2012. *Pay Clauses in Public Procurement*. Brussels: European Public Services Union.

Sellers, Jefferey M. and Lidström, Anders. 2007. 'Decentralization, Local Government, and the Welfare State'. *Governance*, 20(4): 609–32.

Tepe, Markus, Kittel, Bernhard, and Gottschall, Karin. 2015. 'The Competing State: Transformations of the Public/Private Sector Earnings Gap in Four Countries'. In *State Transformations in OECD Countries: Dimensions, Driving Forces, and Trajectories*, edited by Heinz Rothgang and Steffen Schneider. London: Palgrave Macmillan.

Thornqvist, Christer. 1999. 'The Decentralization of Industrial Relations: The Swedish Case in Comparative Perspective'. *European Journal of Industrial Relations*, 5(1): 71–87.

Varga, Mihai. 2015. 'Trade Unions and Austerity in Central and Eastern Europe: Did They Do Something About It?' *Transfer*, 21(3): 313–26.

Vaughan-Whitehead, Daniel (ed.) 2013. *Public Sector Shock*. Cheltenham: Edward Elgar; and Geneva: ILO.

Warner, Mildred E. and Clifton, Judith. 2013. 'Marketisation, Public Services and the City: The Potential for Polanyian Counter Movements'. *Cambridge Journal of Regions, Economy and Society*, 7(1): 45–61.

3

Cutting to the Bone

Workers' Solidarity in the Danish-German Slaughterhouse Industry

Bjarke Refslund and Ines Wagner

3.1. INTRODUCTION

The pig slaughtering and meat processing industry has historically been characterized by Tayloristic work processes and work organization. In recent years, the industry has become increasingly integrated across Europe. Germany and Denmark are among the prime producers and exporters within the European and global pig meat market. Two decades ago, wages and working conditions in the two countries were similar (Strandskov et al. 1996). However, today their labour market structures and working conditions have diverged significantly. The Danish workforce enjoys comparatively high wages and good working conditions, avoiding tendencies towards segmentation and precarious working conditions. In the German industry, on the other hand, there has been a radical growth in precarious employment, a rapid weakening of the unions, and workforce dualization, mainly based on 'posted' labour migration.

The purpose of this chapter is twofold: first, to explain the reasons behind the dualization in Germany in comparison to Denmark; and second, to examine the implications of these differences for union power as unions oppose management attempts to undermine pay and working conditions. The analysis is based on a comparison of industrial relations at slaughterhouses of the Denmark-based Danish Crown, a multinational meat producing company operating in both Denmark and Germany. Findings show how inclusive institutions support inclusive worker solidarity in the Danish case. First, at the national-sector level, Danish unions were able to mobilize traditional forms of associational and institutional power resources, such as strong worker collectivism and high union density, to bolster collective bargaining power. This allowed them to maintain or improve working conditions for the workforce and oppose pressure for labour market dualization by including labour migrants on equal terms to native workers. Weaker institutional and associational power in Germany led to growing segmentation, which in turn divided the workforce and limited union options for developing a solidaristic response. The case study reveals sporadic attempts to overcome this, but these resulted in only limited benefits for a small group of workers. The absence of traditional forms of solidarity paired with unions' inability to forge 'new' forms of more inclusive solidarity (such as organizing migrant workers) explains the associational and institutional weakness of the German meat sector union. This was associated with fragmentation of work and labour processes, both across the industry and within each production site, which led to the deterioration of working conditions. This is similar to dynamics observed in other industries experiencing vertical disintegration and competitive benchmarking across production chains (cf. Doellgast and Greer 2007; Flecker 2010; Greer and Hauptmeier 2016).

The two country cases examine how national as well as transnational dynamics are important in shaping wages, working conditions, work organization, and workers' organization and representation. At the national level, the different positions, strategies, and power resources of unions and workers presented very different options for mitigating the use of non-standard contracts and arrangements by large MNCs. In the German case, the use of posted and subcontracted labour was an important factor undermining the workers' position and lowering the companies' cost. At the transnational level, Danish and German slaughterhouses do not compete in independent markets, but are part of a global production system, which is embedded in a regional European production system. Danish production sites benefitted from the capacity of companies to segment labour markets across national borders. In the meat industry, Danish Crown and its competitors took advantage of Germany's weaker collective bargaining institutions to adopt labour practices and gain cost savings that the institutional inclusiveness and associational power of the Danish union blocked in Denmark.

The main motive for firms relocating production within the European Union has changed from being mainly about access to markets and market shares in the 1990s and 2000s to cost reductions (Brandl et al. 2010). This also occurred in the slaughterhouse industry, where Danish Crown relocated a substantial number of jobs from Denmark to lower-cost production sites in nearby countries like the UK, Poland, and, above all, Germany, affecting the balance of power between workers and management (Wagner and Refslund 2016). This suggests that capital mobility across borders is affecting outcomes in the two countries, and that there are elements of core and periphery opening up between sites, based on uneven regulation and union power in labour-intensive industries. Union strategies to counter the expansion of precarious work in this sector thus requires new strategies aimed at reinforcing encompassing sectoral institutions, strategic campaigns, and cooperation across national boundaries.

3.2. BACKGROUND AND METHODS

The case studies in this chapter are based in the slaughterhouse industry in Germany and Denmark. While both countries are considered coordinated market economies characterized by strong unions and encompassing institutions, their industrial relations systems also differ significantly (Crouch 2012). This seems to have been further reinforced by the 2008 financial crisis and the following economic crisis in Europe—at least in some industries. A key difference is that Denmark has a much higher union density (still roughly 65 per cent) and has maintained sector-based collective bargaining. The German institutional setting has shown declining union coverage and an increase in institutional regulatory voids, leading to an increase in precarious work, including for migrant workers.

The meat industry is interesting to compare in both countries because of its size and employment impact. Germany is the largest producer and Denmark the fifth largest producer of pig meat in Europe. The sector is important due to the labour-intensive work setting and history of strong unionism in both countries, and is also a significant employer of migrant workers. Wage levels in both countries were almost at the same level twenty years ago (Strandskov et al. 1996). Today, employment conditions and wages diverge significantly. This development is analysed by looking at how the big market player Danish Crown, operating in both markets, is adjusting its corporate strategy according to the different regulatory and institutional contexts, and in particular to the constraints set by the sectoral unions. This permits us to analyse differences in the organizational and institutional setting across the two countries, while holding the industry and work organization constant, since these have only minor differences.

This chapter utilizes sixty-one in-depth interviews conducted in both countries with trade unionists, workers, company management, employers' organizations, works councillors, and policymakers at the company and industry level as well as at the national and European level. The interviews were conducted between April 2011 and October 2015. The semi-structured interviews emphasized developments in industrial relations, wages, and working conditions (including worker precarity); business strategies of the firms; structural conditions, including competition; and the unions' power resources and positions. The interviews form the key data for the analysis. The chapter also draws on other sources, such as press reports and reports from unions as well as the secondary literature.

3.3. EXPLAINING PATTERNS OF PRECARIOUS WORK

Despite some differences in the size and age of slaughterhouse production sites between Denmark and Germany, industry and work processes are much alike in the two countries. Industrial slaughterhouse work is characterized by the dominance of low-skill work processes and classic Tayloristic organization. Indeed, slaughterhouse work has been described as the textbook example of Tayloristic production in the twenty-first century. However, pay, employment conditions, and the use of non-standard contracts are different in Germany and Denmark, both in the slaughterhouse sector as a whole, as well as within Danish Crown. In Denmark, wages and labour costs are very high compared with those in Germany. Wages and working conditions are still negotiated in sector-level collective bargaining between the food workers union (NFF) and the Confederation of Danish Industries (DI). The typical hourly wage level is around €25 for all workers and social security contributions make labour costs even higher. There are very strong traditions of worker representation, where union membership is the social custom and all large sites have a full-time shop steward.

In Germany a sectoral minimum wage in the slaughterhouse sector took effect in January 2014, starting at €7.75 and increasing to €8.75 by December 2016. Before its introduction, hourly wages could be as low as €3 to €5 for subcontracted 'posted' migrant workers (Wagner 2015a). 'Posted workers' are sent by their employer from one EU member state to another on fixed-term service contracts, and therefore work under partially transnationally regulated posted work contracts rather than under the normal national labour regulation of the host country. The social partners in the meat industry in principle negotiate sector-level collective bargaining coverage for all slaughterhouses. However, in recent decades the bargaining has been unstable, because the sectoral trade union NGG (Gewerkschaft Nahrung-Genuss-Gaststätten) has faced severe employer resistance to sectoral bargaining, which only ended with the signing of the 2014 collective agreement. In fact, the employers' association even dissolved at one point, depriving the union of a centralized counterpart at the bargaining table (Behrens and Pekarek 2012). The number of workers with social security coverage in slaughtering and meat processing fell from 186,717 in 1999 to 143,138 in 2014.[1] Since EU enlargement in 2004, 26,000 jobs registered via the German social security system have been downsized, while the number of posted workers who pay social security in the sending country increased to 30,000 (NGG 2013). These figures include many smaller companies and small sites, but we are mainly focusing on larger production sites and firms in this analysis.

In Germany, in-house fragmentation of production has been associated with subcontracting to firms employing posted foreign workers. Using subcontracted and posted workers for numerous parts of the work processes has become the norm in large parts of the German meat industry, where subcontractors accounted for the overall majority of sites, in some cases composing up to 90 per cent of the workforce (Wagner and Refslund 2016). This also means that the large MNCs turn over responsibilities for employment relations and practices to the subcontractors, since they do not directly manage the subcontracted workers. In contrast, the Danish meat processing industry has not seen any use of subcontractors, posted workers, or any other type of work externalization or segmentation, since the union has had the associational and institutional power (backed by the threat of strikes) to reject externalization so far.

Since in Germany works councils form the institutional base for workplace worker representation, firm fragmentation leads to segmentation of workforce representation because of the 'dual system of interest representation' characteristic of German industrial relations. Under the dual system, unions and employers are solely responsible for collective bargaining, while works councils are the main workplace employee representation bodies. In Denmark, the unions' strong collectivistic approach to wages and work organization has prevented similar attempts at labour force dualization. The sector-based collective agreement inhibits management's ability to stage competition between the production sites as a way of obtaining concessions. When there have been tendencies towards

---

[1] Statistisches Bundesamt, Genesis Online: <https://www-genesis.destatis.de/genesis/online;jsessionid= D2F7C37C6EB6828205F3102C131DB8CE.tomcat_GO_2_1?operation=previous&levelindex=3& levelid=1428400012637&step=3>.

concessions in specific sites, the national union has managed to avoid this since it would be a violation of the sector collective agreement. This is typical of Nordic industrial relations: sector-based collective bargaining remains strong in the Nordic countries, in particular in low-skill sectors like pig slaughtering, and is semi-institutionalized, e.g. through third-party mediation, following patterns from the leading sectors (Vartiainen 2011).

This general pattern, which we found based on our studies of Danish Crown, can also be observed at the German MNC Tönnies, which similarly operates in both countries. Tönnies' German sites have externalized the labour force, e.g. through subcontracting agencies, but in Denmark, Tönnies has signed the industry-wide collective agreement and abstained from any work externalization. This reinforces our claim that the power resources and institutional position of the union in the two countries are the main factors explaining differences in outcomes.

At the largest Danish Crown site in Horsens, around one-third of the workers are Eastern Europeans, mainly from Poland. However, they are employed under the exact same conditions as their Danish colleagues. All are union members as well, and the workforce is not divided into core and periphery. While the labour migrants in Germany are mainly employed via subcontractors and have precarious work contracts, in Denmark the labour migrants are fully included in the Danish industrial relations system, in terms of collective agreement coverage, employment contracts, and union representation.

The German cases shows a 'vicious circle' in which weak union power, firm segmentation strategies, and regulatory gaps facilitated by worker posting lead to greater divides in the labour movement and less success by the union in including migrant and/or posted workers (see Chapter 1). Worker posting causes regulatory gaps in Germany because free movement of services in the European Union establishes that firms can 'post' workers temporarily to another member state. This allows undercutting of pay and conditions when there is no statutory minimum wage, as was the case in Germany until 2014, and also no extended collective agreement (Wagner 2015b). However, even with a minimum wage, the cross-border nature of the worker posting and the national orientation of labour protection make enforcement of legal standards difficult (Wagner 2015c).

Danish Crown has been making headlines in Germany with regards to the poor conditions of posted workers. The subcontractors employing these posted workers should pay the statutory minimum wage. However, subcontractor workers report frequent cases of under- and non-payment of wages. They also endure highly flexible working times, employment insecurity, lack of proper work clothes for the cooling chambers, and substandard housing arrangements (Wagner 2015a).

In Denmark, the stronger organization and power of the trade union movement and the single-channel representation system unites the workforce across different employment categories and avoids labour market segmentation, for example by removing the possibility to use posted workers. In Germany, the externalization of work predominates, with many jobs taken over by foreign workers posted through staffing agencies, which are situated outside of Germany.

In Section 3.4, we use two case studies to examine how unions used different forms of associational power to prevent Danish Crown from imposing a concessionary agreement in Denmark, and to achieve representation for a group of (mostly) posted workers in Germany.

3.4. CHALLENGES IN MAINTAINING AND BUILDING INCLUSIVE INSTITUTIONS

3.4.1. Wage Bargaining in Danish Crown's Danish Production Sites: The Case of Bornholm

Danish Crown has on numerous occasions tried to lower the wages in their Danish production sites, often under the threat that the work will be relocated to production sites with lower wage levels in Germany, Poland, and the UK (Refslund 2012, 2013). While the local workers have been inclined to accept local wage concessions to avoid relocation, the outcome so far has always been rejection of any wage reductions. The main bulwark against local concessions has been the sectoral collective agreement, which makes local concessions difficult, combined with a strong collectivist tradition, which instils in the workers a solidaristic feeling obliging them to reject local concessions.

In the 2000s, the transnational threat of relocating production sites was imminent in Danish Crown's Danish operations. Relocation started with a closure of parts of production in Ringsted in 2004. This took place after workers rejected a new lower-paying wage agreement. As a result, Danish Crown moved most of this site's production to Germany. A significant number of Danish slaughterhouse jobs were moved to Germany, as well as to Poland and the UK, and Danish production sites were closed. Although this international relocation amounted to a significant job loss in Denmark (around 2,500 jobs), even more jobs were lost in recent decades to centralization and productivity improvements (Refslund 2013). The job loss is seen by the slaughterhouse union as a huge problem, but the chairman of the slaughterhouse workers union (NNF) said in 2009: 'We would rather have 6,000 good jobs than 8–9,000 insecure jobs in the Danish slaughterhouse industry.'[2] This statement continues to reflect the situation almost a decade later. Danish Crown still maintains a significant part of its production in Denmark. However, the issue of wage reductions has been a reoccurring one, both in sectoral collective bargaining and at the plant level, often backed by the threat that Danish Crown would move parts of their activities to other, cheaper production sites within the company.

One of the most recent (public) disputes was in the slaughterhouse in Bornholm in early summer 2014. Danish Crown stated publicly that it needed to cut annual costs by 3.4 million euros in its production on Bornholm in order to secure the slaughterhouse's profitability. Bornholm is an island to the east of the Danish mainland in the Baltic Sea with a population of around 40,000. Due to its isolated position, is it difficult to transport the pigs to Danish Crown's next nearest slaughterhouse in Zealand, where the pigs would have to be ferried if the Bornholm site closed. The 125-year-old slaughterhouse slaughters around 450,000 pigs a year and employs around 175 workers. During the initial wage negotiations between the company and the union (NNF), which negotiates wages via the collective agreements, Danish Crown wanted the workers to accept an 8 per cent wage reduction. The company cannot negotiate directly with the affected workers because the

---

[2] <http://www.ugebreveta4.dk/fagforbund-hellere-6000-sikre-slagtere-end-9000-us_19056.aspx>.

sectoral collective agreement makes local concessions almost impossible. Because wage reductions were rejected by the union negotiators, Danish Crown stated in a press release at the end of May 2014 that they would close the site. Following this, there was a heated public debate. Many observers, including local and national politicians, were critical of Danish Crown's decision, especially because of the large employment impact on the local community. Moreover, according to critics, the fact that Danish Crown makes a large profit made the decision to close the site problematic. The previous history of offshoring of jobs and Danish Crown's use of posted and subcontracted workers in Germany were also explicitly mentioned in the debate. Although this critique at first mainly came from centre-left politicians,[3] the site closure became a national political topic.[4] Danish Crown might have had concerns about its reputation in mind, which could also affect customer loyalty and hence sales.

Following the public announcement of the closure, the national government and the minister of business and growth stepped into the negotiations about reducing Danish Crown's costs in Bornholm. The national government promised a small tax discount and the local municipality had already offered to lower charges for wastewater treatment (of which there is a lot from a slaughterhouse) as well as electricity. Local farmers, who at the same time are owners (albeit with small shares) as well as customers at the slaughterhouse, also accepted economic compensation in order to safeguard the slaughterhouse.

Faced with public pressure, the negotiations were taken over by the DI and the national union (NNF). Ultimately Danish Crown's management accepted a five-year agreement that lowered costs for the company, but at the same time obliged the company to invest in the production site in order to secure sustained future production. The workers would still not accept any wage reductions. However, a somewhat atypical agreement was reached, where the workers invest 3.5 per cent of their wages in a fund for capital investment in the production site, e.g. for upgrading of technology. The workers can have their investment back after the five-year period, but only if the goal of reducing costs by 3.4 million euros a year is reached. A similar agreement covering all Danish Crown's Danish slaughterhouse workers had previously been rejected in a general ballot among all Danish Crown workers in Denmark. The idea at that point had been to establish a fund for employee investment in further pig production in order to secure supply to Danish Crown. In return the workers would be given a four-year guarantee that no Danish slaughterhouse jobs would be closed down. The agreement was rejected in a general ballot among the workers, despite the recommendation by the union NNF to accept the agreement.[5] A study among slaughterhouse workers showed that they did not trust the guarantee, and believed that Danish Crown would close

---

[3] For an example of this critique from leading national social-democrat MPs, see: <https://www.dr.dk/nyheder/politik/socialdemokraterne-beskylder-danish-crown-have-lav-trovaerdighed>; and from a centre-left think thank, see: <http://cevea.dk/debat/29-arbejdsmarked/736-danish-crowns-slagterilukning-er-taberstrategi>.

[4] For instance press coverage, see: <http://www.business.dk/foedevarer/sass-larsen-banker-danish-crown-og-nnf-paa-plads>.

[5] <http://politiken.dk/oekonomi/virksomheder/ECE2065867/slagteri-ansatte-kan-se-frem-til-at-miste-250-kroner-om-ugen/>.

parts of production down when the four years had passed (Kristiansen and Weber 2014). So this previous agreement was rejected by the majority of the workers because it was seen as a concession bargaining strategy. However, in Bornholm the workers were partially guaranteed their investment back and the contribution was lower, which made the agreement more acceptable for the workers.

While the transnational dimension of Danish Crown's activities were not explicitly articulated in this case, the threat of transnational mobility was still very present. After the final agreement was reached, a Danish Crown spokesperson said in an interview: '[if we do not get lower costs through taxes and/or wages] a significant reduction in the number of slaughterhouse jobs will occur in the next ten years, since they will be moved out of the country'.[6] The cost level in Denmark is constantly compared with cost levels in other Danish Crown subsidiaries abroad, and often the media coverage of the case included comparison of the wage levels for slaughterhouse workers in Denmark with their German counterparts.

The case ended with a broad agreement to reduce the cost of production; however, the slaughterhouse workers only carried a very small proportion of the cost through investing around 3.5 per cent of their wage. The workers' share can only be used to improve the production facilities at the actual site. If Danish Crown closes the site during the five years the workers are guaranteed their investment back.

3.4.2. Transnational Action in the German Meat Industry

The second case of contestation involves a group of ninety workers working for a German subcontractor at the second level down the subcontracting chain in a Danish Crown slaughterhouse. Eighty of these workers were Romanian while ten were German. These workers established a works council in order to improve their working conditions. However, the main contractor, Danish Crown, repeatedly voiced to the workers its disgruntlement over the establishment of the works council and asked them to abolish it. The works council however continued to meet, so in an attempt to get rid of it, Danish Crown gradually withdrew orders from the subcontractor, in order to phase out the whole workforce. Because of the declining orders, the subcontractor had to file for bankruptcy and had to let go of the entire workforce. None of the staff was taken over by another company or by the main contractor. However, another subcontractor tried to recruit the laid-off workers under worse employment conditions, meaning at lower pay, with no health insurance, no vacation pay, and with workers not receiving their social security payment in Germany but elsewhere.[7]

The German workers along with the Romanian workers established a works council in order to improve their working conditions. The workspace can be described as a highly flexible labour market, with low levels of jobs security and

---

[6] <http://www.business.dk/foedevarer/sass-larsen-banker-danish-crown-og-nnf-paa-plads>.

[7] The subcontractor had recruited the workers as posted workers. The absence of a statutory or sectoral binding minimum wage regulation at the time and the lack of inclusion of the meat sector in the German Posting Law meant that the workers' wages as well as social regulations referred back to the sending country context.

pay, and a fluid composition of the workforce. The segmented nature of the industry allows for the creation of ambiguous employment relations in which illegal practices, discrimination, and exploitation rarely get noticed due to the divided labour force and the isolation from the main contractor's works council. In fact, neither management nor the works councillors of the main contractor were aware of the existence of the second-level subcontractor and the working conditions of its workers.

The details of the workers' grievances related to underpayment of the promised salary, highly flexible working times, employment insecurity, lack of proper work clothes for the cooling chambers, and substandard housing arrangements. These labour practices received attention from management when the Romanian workers started talking with the German workers about establishing a works council with the subcontractor. According to one Romanian worker, it was difficult to establish solidarity because of the many nationalities at the plant. These workers were engaged in industrial work for the first time and were intimidated by management: 'there was no trade union for us, no one told us our rights and once we asked for them the employer said, if you don't like something, we will send you right back home'. However, the German workers were union members and also knew the institutional structure of the German dual system of representation, namely the in-firm possibilities for forming a works council. Due to the institutional knowledge of the German workers, they decided in unison to set up a works council, had elections, and by doing so set up a representative structure for the workers.

However, already during the election period Danish Crown management warned the workers that they should abstain from such elections and from forming the works council. One member of the works council recalls that 'we distributed flyers for the workers to inform them about our plans to form a works council and they [Danish Crown] got wind of it. Then, we put a table at the entrance in order to distribute the flyers and then management came and said, "put this away immediately" and the people who distributed the flyers were ordered to stay away from the slaughterhouse' (interview with Romanian slaughterhouse worker, 2013). The workers ignored such threats and just weeks after the works council was formed they slowly noticed that they had to work shorter shifts. The shifts and the orders for the subcontractor diminished week by week. Finally, at one point, the subcontractor filed for bankruptcy and the workforce of that subcontractor lost their jobs. However, at the same time Danish Crown hired a new subcontractor with a home base in Hungary, which posted fifty Hungarian workers to the slaughterhouse—essentially in order to take over the jobs of the subcontractor that had to file for bankruptcy. In the meantime, the workers who lost their jobs in this process were offered new contracts by a staffing agency. The conditions they were offered had lower pay and holiday allowances.

The trade union NGG organized an information event for the workers who were let go from the company in order to gain a deeper insight into the issues at hand and whether the firing occurred under lawful conditions. The workers and the union were under the impression that the workers were unlawfully laid off and aimed to file a suit against the subcontractor. The aim of the suit was to claim back pay and possibly regain the workers' jobs, even if at another firm. The NGG organized an event in order to help to organize the suit, i.e. in getting relevant documents from the workers, helping them to fill out the legal paperwork and to answer outstanding questions, explaining again what they intended to do, and managing their expectations. Also, they needed to help the workers in collecting unemployment benefits. All unemployed workers had the right to receive unemployment benefits. The German workers received these benefits because they were familiar with the system and handed in the relevant documents at the employment bureau. It was unclear how many of the Romanian workers received unemployment benefits, as many did not, or were not able to, hand in this paperwork to the bureau. Some did not have their contracts anymore, while others had left the necessary documents in their home country.

Approximately seventy Romanian workers showed up at the meeting. Most of them had little money left for outstanding bills. Some had no electricity and no running water at their houses anymore because the employer had paid for the housing, but now was no longer doing so. The NGG assisted the workers in filing the law suit in order to claim and reinstate the jobs of the subcontracted workers. Union representatives prepared all the paperwork and certificates of authority for the workers so that the union could file the suit. There was one condition, which was that the workers had to remain members for one year after they filed the suit. There were also two related law suits. The first was against the subcontractor, to determine if the laying off of the workforce was legally justified. The second was an action against another subcontractor, who tried to rehire workers under worse conditions, even though they should only be able to take over staff under the same conditions.

The NGG also clarified that suing to get the jobs at the subcontractor back was not possible in the German legal system, but rather they were trying to get another German firm to take them over. The translators assisted the workers in filling in the paperwork. There was hardly any contact between the German and the Romanian workers during the event.

NGG won the court case; and the workers were rehired by a German staffing agency to work within the same Danish Crown slaughterhouse under the same conditions. All of the Romanian workers accepted the new positions while only one of the German workers went back to work in the slaughterhouse. The other German workers decided to take work elsewhere or to receive unemployment benefits. Even though the workers were able to form a works council, Danish Crown's phaseout of the whole subcontractor prevented the works council from actually changing the status quo of employment conditions.

3.4.3. Discussing the Findings

The case studies highlight how the slaughterhouse industry has followed divergent trajectories in the integrated European market in Denmark and Germany, despite the fact that they share many characteristics and that the same MNC operates in both countries. The Danish union has successfully opposed any use of external subcontractors, and flexibility demanded by the employer is typically achieved by hiring and firing during peaks. Since the Danish union is able to maintain encompassing wages and working condition for all workers in the production site, it does not make sense for the firms to use subcontracted workers. The cases further show that the Danish workers are able to uphold solidarity across pro-duction sites at a level substantially higher than in Germany, where cross-worksite solidarity is more or less absent.

Differences in sector regulation of collective bargaining also play an important role in patterns of wages and working conditions. While hourly wages in Denmark remain well above €25, the German slaughterhouse industry implemented a minimum wage of €8.75 in December 2016. On top of that, the pension schemes are much better in Denmark and there are also large differences in, among other things, overtime pay, evening pay, and night work supplements, which are better in Denmark. Despite numerous local pressures on Danish slaughterhouse work-ers, where they were faced with concession bargaining to either reduce wages or accept job losses due to transnational relocation, the Danish slaughterhouse workers managed to maintain their collectivist consciousness and reject any wage reductions or concession bargaining. While this strategy has meant the loss of jobs in some sites, it has also meant no wage reductions, although there have been some disputes over this within the slaughterhouse workers' ranks. Concessions made in collective bargaining tend to backfire on workers in the long run, as shown in the German metal industry (cf. Benassi 2015). The collective agreements in the Danish slaughterhouse sector is settled at the sector level rather than plant level, which have provided workers with a strong bulwark against concessions despite being faced with strong transnational cost pressure (Wagner and Refslund 2016).

An interesting aspect of the Bornholm case is the workers' opposition and rejection of the proposed agreement based on employee investments or indirect wage reductions in return for job security. Here the Danish workers opposed their own union representatives in the ballot, rejecting the idea—mainly because they did not trust the job guarantees given by management, especially in the longer run (Kristiansen and Weber 2014). This confirms previous findings that Danish slaughterhouse workers are typically confident that they can find alternate employment if their job is offshored. This was highlighted in numerous interviews with slaughterhouse union representatives. It is also important to emphasize that while there has been a significant decline in overall employment at Danish Crown in Denmark, this is not only due to the transnational relocations. The majority of the job loss is explained by ongoing productivity gains from centralization and automation of production (Refslund 2013).

3.4.4. Explaining the Differences

As reported in Table 3.1, the key explanatory variables for the different trajectories are different levels of union power resources and the accompanying possibilities for forging solidarity among workers. In Denmark, the workers were able to maintain sectoral solidarity and sustain the high wage floor even on the isolated island of Bornholm, mainly through the sector-based collective agreements, which enabled the union to reject local concession bargaining. The sectoral collective agreements were backed by strong workers' collectivism at the individual sites, similar to the type of workers' collectivism Lysgaard (1961) identified in a paper mill in his classic sociological analysis of workers and their organization.

Table 3.1. Summarizing the explanatory variables

	Organizational and institutional power: bargaining coverage and structure and institutional support	Collective identity and identification
Denmark	Full coverage; single-channel representation structure; posting excluded by union strength; institutional support	Union membership as a clear norm; tradition of integration of migrants; strong tradition of collectivism
Germany	Lower coverage; dual channel representation structure; ease of posting with weaker framework; weak institutional support	Low membership density; less integration of migrants in the slaughtering sector; segmentation; divides in workforce is exploited

Union membership is a social norm at the production sites, and in practice it is often impossible not to be union member, because co-workers will not work with non-unionized workers.

In Germany, on the other hand, there were very weak foundations for any type of solidarity, due to the low associational and institutional power resources of the union and the workers. In particular, the practice of employing migrant posted workers via subcontractors has proven effective in reducing contestation from workers. The weak power base of the German slaughterhouse union in terms of membership, organizational resources, and institutional support explains the contrast with the Danish site. Even though some successes were achieved in the German case, it was fleeting and did not change the status quo of the power relations. The fragmentation of the workforce in German slaughterhouses makes it hard to sustain contestation, since there is often little or no interaction between different groups of workers, such as subcontracted and permanent staff, or even between different nationalities of migrant workers. These fragmentation tendencies are reinforced by the lack of efficient workers' representation structures at the workplace level. The Danish single representation system, where the unions and the professional shop stewards are the sole workers' representatives at workplace level, overcomes workplace fragmentation. This has a significant impact on the way the sector functions in Denmark. There was also in Bornholm a unitary approach among the local shop steward and the national union, despite somewhat clashing interests. In combination with the strong centralized collective agreements, the strong unions eliminated the firms' ability to use workforce externalization as a means to reduce wages and lower the working conditions. This shows how institutions are important in determining how flexibility is achieved in different national contexts.

Due to the fragmentation of labour processes and division between workers, often with numerous subcontractors working in the same slaughterhouse, the structural power of the slaughterhouse workers is also lower in Germany. The Danish union has prevented fragmentation of the workforce, and hence has a higher structural power, since the union can coordinate not only plant-level industrial actions but also multi-plant or national industrial actions. Furthermore, the Danish slaughterhouse workers are highly aware of the risk of concessions spreading from one site to another, so they would engage in industrial action, even when their own worksite was not involved (Refslund 2013).

The findings in the German case show how action by individual workers and lower-level union strategy can prove to be complementary to the overall institutional setting, as suggested by Hardy (2015). It also illustrates the different power bases actors can draw on. Here, the institutional power of judicial proceedings proved to be a source of power for the unions, instead of, as traditionally is the case in the German system, firm-level channels of worker representation.

We have in previous research shown how differences in unions' power resources explain much of the difference between developments in the slaughterhouse industry in the two countries (Wagner and Refslund 2016). Here we add to our previous analysis of power resource configurations by looking at how power resources interact with transnational dynamics, and how this plays out within one MNC across two national settings. Therefore, we can investigate both employers' and labour strategy to analyse the interrelationship between structural factors and the level of precarity found in the sector. Our findings suggest that the embeddedness of a union's power resources is a key explanation for diverging outcomes. Thus, it is not just the explicit differences in power resources, but also how these are embedded in the broader social system and the production system (Refslund and Sørensen 2016).

There have been some tendencies towards less inclusive forms of labour market organizations in Denmark, in particular in sectors such as agriculture and cleaning (Rasmussen et al. 2016) and the telecommunications industry (Benassi et al. 2016). However, the slaughterhouse industry is more embedded in the national institutional systems and has more powerful unions, and thus is not affected by this segmentation and the associated deterioration of wages and working conditions.

3.4.5. The Transnational Dimension

The cases discussed in this chapter illustrate the ever-closer integration of production in contemporary European capitalism, where developments in one country have significant impacts on developments in other countries. The wage dimension has been particularly influential in the European slaughterhouse industry; the very low wages of posted workers in the German industry has a significant impact on the Danish industry, contributing to strong wage pressure in Denmark (Wagner and Refslund 2016). Labour costs as well as other costs in Germany are often highlighted in wage disputes in the Danish slaughterhouse industry. Some of the most labour-intensive work processes, such as much deboning, have been moved from Danish slaughterhouses to German ones; also animals being slaughtered in Denmark are processed in Germany (Refslund 2013). But the general work processes remain largely the same across the Danish Crown group in the Danish and German production sites. The ability of the Danish workers to uphold wages and working conditions is not directly dependent on Danish Crown's use of posted and precarious workers in their German production sites, since the work processes are not segmented across national borders. While the external pressures are comparable across the two countries, what differs is their impact due to the interplay between institutions and actor strategies.

The Danish slaughterhouse workers have fought fiercely against any transfer or relocation of jobs from Denmark. Their stance against any wage reductions may have implications for the overall number of jobs in Danish Crown in Germany, but the Danish workers are not dependent on Danish Crown's application of low-wage posted workers in Germany. The decisions taken by Danish Crown on where to locate various production elements can be seen as an example of regime shopping, since the MNC is adjusting its labour market behaviour and practices to the possibilities given in each country, a phenomena discussed by, for example, Morgan and Kristensen (2006). Danish Crown is taking advantage of the subcontracted workers in Germany because it is possible for them to do that there. While the relocation from Denmark to Germany puts pressure on Danish unions, their institutional embeddedness and their ability to unify the workforce prevented this from leading to deteriorating conditions. Here, the transnational dimension of the relocation could be absorbed. The transnational dimension in the German case is the 'insourcing' of foreign labour. This leads to deteriorating employment conditions and the loss in union power in Germany because of the already weak institutional position of the trade union.

The case from Bornholm can be seen as a micro-example of some of the inherent dynamics when analysing Danish Crown's attempts to reduce the wages at Danish production sites. However, it also shows how the embeddedness of the industry in the country affects the outcome of wage bargaining, as compared to other industries that can more easily relocate production. The entanglement of local pig production with the slaughterhouses is important; a significant parameter for why Danish Crown cannot just close and move production is that the pigs produced in Bornholm (around 450,000 a year) would have to be transported off the island. While the European pig meat industry shares many characteristics with other manufacturing industries, it is more nationally embedded because of the close connection between primary production and the slaughtering and processing of the pigs. This also affects Danish Crown's general ability to offshore jobs. Furthermore, the ownership structure of Danish Crown, which is still owned by the farmers' cooperative (although Danish Crown very much acts as a traditional MNC), has an impact on the company's ability to relocate the remaining production.

While the cases have focused on national differences, it is clear that the transnational dimension is important for developments in the industry. The unions are well aware of this and the European Food Sectors Union (EFFAT) has produced material about being a posted worker in Germany in several mainly Eastern European languages. NNF is actively working for solidarity with their German colleagues, and much of the negative publicity that Danish Crown has faced in Denmark but also in Germany started with critical investigations by the NNF magazine. However, NNF does not perceive NNG as an equal partner due to its lack of power and influence, so while the union is very interested in raising the overall standards in Germany, union representatives do not perceive this as a realistic scenario in the near future. While the minimum wage in Germany has reduced some of the wage gap, there is still a significant cost reduction motive in operating in Germany rather than in Denmark. The huge differences in associational and institutional power thus confirm some previous research findings, indicating that there are substantial obstacles for cross-national union cooperation (Gennard and Newsome 2005; Greer et al. 2013).

3.5. CONCLUSION

The cases show how unions' associational and institutional power can strongly influence firms' options for externalization and fragmentation of the workforce—which in this industry occurs mainly through subcontracting to agencies employing labour migrants. While this has become the norm in the German meat processing industry, the stronger Danish unions have prevented this by using their single representation channel and strong collective norms of unionization. Nonetheless, as the case studies show, employers' attempts to fragment the workforce resulted in contestation in both countries. In Denmark, workers resent both international relocation as well as lowering wages, and in the German case we see resentment towards the widespread use of posted and agency work at very low wages and often poor working conditions. Differences in the associational power resources of the unions and the institutional support and inclusiveness of the systems explain the success of the Danish unions and the failure of the German ones in preventing the deterioration of conditions.

REFERENCES

Behrens, Martin and Pekarek, Andreas. 2012. 'To Merge or Not to Merge? The Impact of Union Merger Decisions on Workers' Representation in Germany'. *Industrial Relations Journal*, 43(6): 527–47.

Benassi, Chiara. 2015. 'From Concession Bargaining to Broad Workplace Solidarity: The IG Metall Response to Agency Work'. In *The Outsourcing Challenge*, edited by Jan Drahokoupil. Brussels: ETUI.

Benassi, Chiara, Doellgast, Virginia, and Sarmiento-Mirwaldt, Katja. 2016. 'Institutions and Inequality in Liberalizing Markets: Explaining Different Trajectories of Institutional Change in Social Europe'. *Politics and Society*, 44(1): 117–42.

Brandl, Berndt, Strohmer, Sonja, and Traxler, Franz. 2010. 'US Foreign Direct Investment, Macro Markets and Labour Relations: The Case of Enlarged Europe'. *Industrial Relations Journal*, 41(6): 622–38.

Crouch, Colin. 2012. 'National Varieties of Labour Market Exposure'. In *Capitalisms and Capitalism in the Twenty-First Century*, edited by Glenn Morgan and Richard Whitley. Oxford: Oxford University Press.

Doellgast, Virginia, and Greer, Ian. 2007. 'Vertical Disintegration and the Disorganization of German Industrial Relations'. *British Journal of Industrial Relations*, 45(1): 55–76.

Flecker, Jürgen. 2010. 'Fragmenting Labour: Organisational Restructuring, Employment Relations and the Dynamics of National Regulatory Frameworks'. *Work Organisation, Labour and Globalisation*, 4(1): 8–23.

Gennard, John and Newsome, Kirstin. 2005. 'Barriers to Cross-Border Trade Union Cooperation in Europe: The Case of the Graphical Workers'. *Industrial Relations Journal*, 36(1): 38–58.

Greer, Ian and Hauptmeier, Marco. 2016. 'Management Whipsawing: The Staging of Labor Competition under Globalization'. *ILR Review*, 69(1): 29–52.

Greer, Ian, Ciupijus, Zinovius, and Lillie, Nathan. 2013. 'The European Migrant Workers Union and the Barriers to Transnational Industrial Citizenship'. *European Journal of Industrial Relations*, 19(1): 5–20.

Hardy, Jane. 2015. 'Explaining "Varieties of Solidarity": Labour Mobility and Trade Unions in an Enlarged Europe'. *Transfer: European Review of Labour and Research*, 21(2): 187–200.

Kristiansen, Matthias Hulgaard and Weber, Søren. 2014. '*Medarbejderinvesteringer i slag-teribranchen*'. Project report. Roskilde University. Available at: <http://docplayer.dk/ 2289590-Standardforside-til-projekter-og-specialer.html#show_full_text>.

Lysgaard, Sverre. 1961. 'Arbeiderkollektivet'. Oslo: Universitetsforlaget.

Morgan, Glenn and Kristensen, Per Hull. 2006. 'The Contested Space of Multinationals: Varieties of Institutionalism, Varieties of Capitalism'. *Human Relations*, 59(11): 1467–90.

NGG 2013. 'Wenig Rechte Wenig Lohn: Wie Unternehmen Werkverträge (aus)nutzen'. Druckerei Hamburg: Sleppmann GmbH.

Rasmussen, Stine, Refslund, Bjarke, and Sørensen, Ole. 2016. 'Reducing Precarious Work in Europe through Social Dialogue: The Case of Denmark'. University of Manchester, National report Denmark, Precawo-project, European Commission.

Refslund, Bjarke. 2012. 'Offshoring Danish Jobs to Germany: Regional Effects and Challenges to Workers' Organisation in the Slaughterhouse Industry'. *Work Organisation, Labour and Globalization*, 6(2): 113–29.

Refslund, Bjarke. 2013. 'Udflytning af danske slagteriarbejdspladser? Europæisk pres på det danske arbejdsmarked'. *Tidsskrift for Arbejdsliv*, 15(1): 52–71.

Refslund, Bjarke and Sørensen, Ole. 2016. 'Islands in the Stream? Challenges and Resilience of the Danish Industrial Relations Model in a Liberalising World'. *Industrial Relations Journal*, 47(5–6): 530–46.

Strandskov, Jesper, Kristensen, Bent, and Kristensen, Anne Rohe. 1996. 'Den danske slagterisektors konkurrenceevne i europæisk belysning', Århus, Handelshøjskolen i Århus.

Vartiainen, Juhana. 2011. 'Nordic Collective Agreements: A Continuous Institution in a Changing Economic Environment'. *Comparative Social Research*, 28: 331–63.

Wagner, Ines. 2015a. 'EU Posted Work and Transnational Action in the German Meat Industry'. *Transfer: European Review of Labour and Research*, 21(2): 201–13.

Wagner, Ines. 2015b. 'The Political Economy of Borders in a "Borderless" European Labour Market'. *Journal of Common Market Studies*, 53(6): 1195–408.

Wagner. Ines. 2015c. 'Rule Enactment in a Pan-European Labour Market: Transnational Posted Work in the German Construction Sector'. *British Journal of Industrial Relations*, 53(4): 692–710.

Wagner, Ines and Refslund, Bjarke. 2016. 'Understanding the Diverging Trajectories of Slaughterhouse Work in Denmark and Germany: A Power Resource Approach'. *European Journal of Industrial Relations*, 22(4): 335–51.

4

Restructuring Labour Relations and Employment in the European Logistics Sector

Unions' Responses to a Segmented Workforce

Carlotta Benvegnú, Bettina Haidinger, and Devi Sacchetto

4.1. INTRODUCTION

This chapter compares union responses to the emergence of workers' struggles in two segments of the European logistics sector in Italy and Austria. Based on case studies of Austria's parcel delivery industry and Italy's warehousing industry, it focuses on union attempts to challenge increasingly precarious employment conditions in highly segmented labour markets, as well as their success in (re)gaining associational and positional power when faced with a changing constituency and new employment forms.

Parcel delivery and warehousing are integrative parts of a sector with systemic importance in ensuring the smooth functioning of global supply chains. At the same time, logistics has evolved into an industry in its own right, constituted by complex inter-firm networks and offering core business functions to other parts of the global economy (Coe 2014: 225–6). In both the parcel and warehousing sub-sectors, a trend towards value chain restructuring has contributed to the expansion of precarious work and to segmentation of the workforce within and across supply chains. Highly integrated logistics processes driven by just-in-time production and distribution contrast with fragmented layers of subcontracting (Gutelius 2015).

Parcel delivery and warehousing thrive on a wide range of activities and business ties among multinational logistics groups, staffing agencies, franchise companies, subcontractors, and 'self-employed' couriers. These kinds of inter-organizational contracting arrangements can lead to segmented production processes with wide-ranging consequences for industrial relations and employment conditions (Doellgast and Greer 2007; Flecker 2010). Unions find it challenging to develop effective strategies to address the demands of a new constituency of workers in non-standard and insecure employment (Meil et al. 2009; Benassi and Dorigatti 2014; Pulignano et al. 2015). Divisions among workers in fragmented layers of subcontracting are exacerbated by intersectional differences and further deepened by competition between groups of workers belonging to different establishments or firms along the value chain and network (Bonacich and Wilson 2008; Milkman 2011; Rogaly 2009; Alberti 2016). In this chapter, we ask what opportunities fragmented systems of service provision and employment still create for worker agency (Coe 2015; Drahokoupil 2015; Tapia and Turner 2013), in order to contest the expansion of precarious work in the logistics sector.

We find that unions' strategies towards precarious logistics work diverged substantially between Austria and Italy and triggered different outcomes concerning workers' solidarity and power to improve their employment situation. Austrian unions had a strong institutional standing in industrial relations and tried to prevent the emergence of precarious work by centralized collective bargaining and workers' protection systems. However, their efforts to support workers' bottom-up organizing in parcel delivery remained very limited. In Italy, grassroots organizing became stronger and more sustainable, as rank-and-file unions succeeded in gathering a 'critical mass' in warehousing and related sectors. We argue that different approaches towards worker solidarity and different institutional structures influenced unions' responses and thus worker resistance to precarious employment. Small, grassroots Italian unions were less institutionally constrained, and thus able to develop new social and informal strategies. The grassroots character of small Italian unions in warehousing allowed them to deploy workers' associational power in such a way as to make best use of their strategic position in the logistics supply chain. In Austria, unions were more constrained by strong institutions, so that grassroots organizing in parcel delivery remained transitory and local with hardly any union support. This suggests that inclusive institutions such as centralized collective agreements and encompassing labour market regulations can sometimes lag behind the development of new forms of precarious employment, such as bogus self-employment, and serve as constraints in enforcing labour standards.

This chapter is structured as follows. We first provide background on differences in union strategies and employment regulation to include and protect of precarious workers (Section 4.3). We then examine the development of employment and business practices in two segments of the logistics sector (Section 4.4). Section 4.5 identifies three crucial factors explaining successful strategies, with success defined as improving working conditions at the bottom of the supply chain. These include taking advantage of positional power to threaten to disrupt supply chains, reducing the number of links in supply chains to negotiate directly with the principle contractor, and adopting direct action with union or social movement support at the bottom of the supply chain. We argue in Section 4.6 that the reasons for unions' success or failure to adopt strategies to contest precarity are related to differences in: (1) the dominant or competing union structures in logistics, and (2) union capacity to draw on traditions of inclusive worker solidarity and direct action.

In Italy, traditional unions leave behind a growing number of precarious workers from representation and inclusion, and focus instead on better-organized industry segments to preserve the status of the 'insiders'. Here, traditional unions sustain a process of dualization of the labour market. In Austria, unions' still strong institutional power rests on their legal position, their rights in collective bargaining and wage-setting, and their position within the social partnership setting.

However, this standing is jeopardized by the blurring of clear-cut sectoral boundaries, fuelling inter-union competition and enabling employers to evade higher-wage collective agreements through outsourcing. Austria's parcel delivery sector is a case in point because unions have not developed alternative inclusive strategies to integrate different workforce groups into their representation structures. Union-supported inclusive worker solidarity across workplaces, ethnicities, and sectoral as well as firm boundaries is not seen as a priority. In Italy, we see that new and more flexible mobilizing strategies and strong solidarity bonds among workers supported by grassroots unions effectively allowed logistic workers to build associational power and to take advantage of their strategic position from the bottom of, and across, supply chains.

4.2. METHODS AND CASE SELECTION

This chapter compares two segments of the logistics industry—warehousing in Italy and parcel delivery in Austria. We examine the composition of the labour force, contract and employment relations, and legacies of unionization to explain divergences and convergences in bottom-up union responses to precarious work.

Corporate strategies in the two sub-industries shape the value chain in similar ways, and trigger associated outcomes for employment conditions. In both sub-industries, multinational logistics firms or principal contractors externalize the respective services, i.e. warehousing and parcel delivery. These supply chains consist of hierarchically segmented production, with the most vulnerable workers usually in the bottom segment (Gutelius 2015). In both sub-industries, most of these workers find themselves on non-standard contracts and in highly unstable and insecure employment (Lewis et al. 2015). In Austria's sub-industry of parcel delivery, precarious employment takes the form of (bogus) self-employment and small service providers contracted for the pick-up and delivery of parcels by logistics multinationals. Italy's warehousing subcontracting system involves cooperatives, a particular kind of business in which workers are members and formal owners. Although cooperatives originally aimed at increasing workplace democracy by involving workers in business decisions and profit sharing, in recent times the emphasis has shifted from solidarity and participation to more business-like approaches.

In both sub-industries, piece-rate payment, insecure working hours and employers' evasion of collective agreements and labour law are common. Many of the workers at the bottom of the supply chain have migrant backgrounds. This means they face precarity not only in their employment conditions but also with respect to their daily reproduction (Alberti et al. 2013). Employers use the changing composition of the labour force and pursue segmentation-focused strategies for recruitment (Peck 1996; Bonacich and Wilson 2008).

For the Austrian case, findings are based on a sectoral study on parcel delivery as part of the logistics sector.[1] Thirty-one semi-structured interviews

---

[1] 'Social Dialogue and Participation Strategies in the Global Delivery Industry: Challenging Precarious Employment Relations' (SODIPER) was a joint project between researchers and unionists in Austria, Germany, Hungary, and the Czech Republic.

with couriers—including self-employed drivers and workers employed by subcontractors—were conducted. Additionally, the Austrian team used field notes from informal conversations with more than thirty drivers during two union organizing drives. Furthermore, the project was part of a larger international collaboration in which interviews with human resource managers and other relevant experts and stakeholders were carried out, and workshops were held (Haidinger 2012).

The Italian case draws on empirical evidence from a European research project on mobile EU citizens' experiences of labour rights violations.[2] Findings are based on thirteen in-depth interviews with Italian and migrant workers employed in different warehouses inside 'Interporto', the intermodal platform of the city of Padua, and with three key informants: two trade unionists and one occupational doctor. Field notes and informal conversations were also collected during three months of participant observation at the office of the rank-and-file union Adl Cobas, as well as on the picket lines and at the meetings of shop stewards. The migrant workers interviewed come from EU (mainly Romania) and non-EU countries (especially from the Maghreb and sub-Saharan Africa). In addition, field notes from a two-week participant observation inside an express delivery warehouse and thirty interviews with workers and managers were collected.[3]

4.3. INSTITUTIONAL BACKGROUND AND UNIONS' LEGACIES

Past research has identified major institutional differences in industrial relations and employment systems between Austria and Italy. Austria and Italy are both European economies with social traditions, strong unions, and high bargaining coverage. However, union structures and approaches towards inclusive worker solidarity differ significantly (Gumbrell-McCormick and Hyman 2013).

Austria's system of industrial relations is dominated by strong social partnership and by 'centralized cartelization' (Brinkmann et al. 2008: 48–51; Firlei 2016: 394). On the sectoral level, legally binding collective agreements cover 95 per cent of employment contracts and include minimum wages negotiated by social partner organizations (unions and employers). On the company level, works councils represent workers within firms and negotiate company-based agreements. Unions' strategies build upon this dual system of representation, with unions typically pursuing consensus-oriented arrangements within firms as well as at a sectoral level. As a centralized and inclusive system, it builds upon encompassing collective agreements and labour market legislation such as equal pay rules. However, as Firlei (2016: 386) notes, in times of increasingly flexible business

---

[2] The project 'LabCit—Testing EU Citizenship as "Labour Citizenship": From Cases of Labour Rights Violations to a Strengthened Labour-Rights Regime' was co-funded by the Europe for Citizens programme of the European Union. The leading partner of the project is the Multicultural Centre Prague.

[3] Carlotta Benvegnù's PhD research project compares labour inside a multinational express delivery company in Italy (Padua) and in France (Paris), under the supervision of Devi Sacchetto and Cédric Lomba (Università degli Studi di Padova/Université Paris 8).

models, 'loopholes in the system of cartelization of labour law cut broad swaths in its provision of protection'. Hence, 'dumping opportunities of employers increased significantly'.

In parcel delivery, employer strategies in Austria include the outsourcing and subcontracting of tasks to small firms, arbitraging between collective agreements, and engaging self-employed couriers. These avoid the traditional forms of representation embedded in the highly institutionalized industrial relations system, making it impossible for unions to keep uniform wage levels and working conditions for couriers (Haidinger et al. 2014).

For parcel delivery,[4] there are three main competing sectoral collective agreements (postal service, goods transport, and light vehicle transport) with different labour regulations and minimum wages, negotiated by two unions (the postal union GPF and the transport and service union vida) and three employer organizations. There is considerable variation between the agreements and poor coordination between the unions. Self-employed couriers are neither covered by collective agreements nor by equal pay clauses.

Couriers in Austria are—if they are employed—covered by collective agreements; however, workers do not always receive the rights and remuneration due to them. In practice, withheld overtime payment or wages can be sued for after termination of the employment contract. In parcel delivery companies, workplace representation by unions or works councils is almost non-existent. The need for new organizing strategies for this new constituency of migrant workers and workers in small companies and subcontracting chains has not been a core priority for unions (Pernicka and Stern 2011; Stern 2012; Stern and Sigl 2012).

The Italian industrial relations framework has been going through deep changes in recent decades. After a long wave of strikes in the 1960s and 1970s, in the 1990s a concessionary 'neo-corporatism' emerged (Baccaro and Pulignano 2011). New forms of cooperation among social partners were developed with two levels of bargaining: national-sector and company (or sometimes district) level. For a long time the two levels provided a clear hierarchy, so the latter (local level) could only improve on working conditions provided by the national-sector agreements. During the last few years, in the wake of political and economic crises, reforms were approved (2009 and 2011) that strengthened the local level (Meardi 2014). However, today local-level agreements still concern only less than one-third (31.6 per cent) of private employees, usually in the medium-sized and large enterprises (Cnel-Istat 2015:109).

Since the mid-1990s, a series of reforms of the Italian labour market (1997 and 2003) aimed at increasing flexibility, reducing job protection and increasing segmentation. Unions' answers to the increase of non-standard jobs and employment insecurity were 'the creation of specific structures for the representation of those workers to overcome the segmentation of labour market' (Pulignano et al. 2016: 45). However, these new forms of unionizing achieved little success, particularly in big plants with a large number of atypical workers (Murgia and Selmi 2012: 185).

---

[4] For the entire logistics sector covering transport, retail, and postal workers, twelve different collective agreements negotiated by four different unions are in place.

Therefore, today the Italian labour market is characterized by high flexibility and low security, thanks to the widespread casualization of the workforce and to the erosion of the welfare state (Meardi 2014: 338). New types of labour contracts emerged, as well as other forms such as self-employment (Pulignano et al. 2015). Further, the number of people working in cooperatives surged to 1.3 million in 2011, representing 7.2 per cent of all Italian employees; of these, 58 per cent are working members, while the rest are hired by cooperatives under various types of labour contracts (Censis 2012: 7–9). In the logistics sector, the majority of the workers are employed as working members and find themselves in a peculiar and ambiguous situation. Officially, they have permanent contracts with the cooperatives, hence they are not considered as precarious workers. However, their concrete employment situation is as insecure as that of self-employed or staffing agency workers, because cooperative survival is often connected to a single contract with the client. Therefore, when this contract ends, the cooperative closes and the workers and working members lose their jobs.

As we have seen, collective bargaining in the private sector in Italy takes place both at the level of the sector and company, and the latter has become increasingly important. In logistics, only one national sectoral agreement is in force.[5] However, its application is linked to the strength of the union inside each workplace, and logistics is an unevenly unionized sector. While the three major traditional unions—CGIL (Confederazione Generale Italiana del Lavoro), CISL (Confederazione Italiana Sindacati Lavoratori), and UIL (Unione Italiana del Lavoro)— mostly focus on core, often white collar, employees, grassroots unions are more present among porters. This separation is related to traditional unions neglecting this unskilled and mostly migrant workforce. In recent years, migrant workers seeking a new form of unionism able to support their demands have joined the rank-and-file unions Adl Cobas and Si Cobas in large numbers. These unions gave legal and organizational support to their struggles. The consolidation of local-level bargaining facilitated the emerging of grassroots unions that are sometimes very strong in a single workplace.

In comparison to Italy, Austria's system of industrial relations is more highly institutionalized and more encompassing at the level of collective agreements and with respect to unions' general influence on labour law (Astleithner and Flecker forthcoming). Equal pay clauses are in place, and collective agreements cover almost all workers. However, fragmentation of collective bargaining and the recourse to self-employed couriers leave loopholes or exit options that allow employers or contractors to exploit differences in pay and working conditions. At sub-industry and company level, representation is thin in Austria and dualized in Italy. Precarious workers, for instance those in cooperatives, employed in the Italian logistics sector are joining and getting support from grassroots unions in vast numbers. However, traditional unions do not have a foothold in such workplaces. Hence, alternative inclusive union strategies incorporating different workforce groups into representation structures exist in Italy—this tendency and

---

[5] A second one, the so-called Unci-Confsal national contract, which was very convenient for employers, was rejected by the Constitutional Court in 2015. This national contract was rejected because it was not signed by representatives of employer and union organizations.

effort is not visible in Austria. Here, the representation and union support for vulnerable groups of workers in small enterprises within the parcel delivery industry is virtually non-existent. Although such workers (if they are employed and not self-employed) are formally covered by encompassing labour market legislation and collective agreements, their actual employment situation is often precarious and not in conformity with the applicable regulations. Such difficulties might also result from weak union mobilization and weak solidarity within and across workplaces.

4.4. LOGISTICS, SUPPLY CHAIN RESTRUCTURING, AND PRECARITY

As production networks became more and more globalized (Henderson et al. 2002; Dicken 2011), intermediary trade flows surged, technological innovations facilitated the cross-border movement of goods and services, and logistics advanced from an auxiliary business to a core function for accumulation (Cowen 2014; Bonacich and Wilson 2008; Coe 2014). The logistics sector is characterized by fragmented production. Storage and other warehouse operations are generally outsourced by retail and third-party logistics enterprises to a wide number of service providers, staffing agencies, or—in the case of Italy—cooperatives, while couriers in parcel delivery are often self-employed or employed by small subcontractors. The sector itself is governed by lead firms, third-party logistics providers, or multinational retailers that—as principal contractors—command a chain of subcontracted entities (Wills 2009; Gutelius 2015). In fact, we found striking similarities in the organization of the logistics production network in both our sectoral case studies. Figure 4.1 illustrates the subcontracting chains in parcel delivery and warehousing.

First, subcontracting is the main way for recruiting services within the logistics supply chain. Subcontracting firms in the form of cooperatives (Italy) or small-scale up to medium-scale businesses (Austria) compete for contracts of principal contractors. In the case of Austria, third-party logistics providers, as principal contractors, subcontract delivery services to self-employed couriers or couriers employed by small subcontracting firms via up to three chain links. Italy's warehousing industry makes intense use of cooperatives to mediate between workers and principal contractors. This 'system of cooperatives' used widely in the Italian logistics sector needs some further explanation. Italian cooperatives were founded in the middle of the nineteenth century as an instrument of workers' self-defence and to avoid mass emigration, especially in northern and central Italy. However, the expansion of the cooperative movement during the last decades brought a new business approach; in most of the new cooperatives internal democracy weakened and working conditions deteriorated (Garibaldo 2011). Those transformations are linked to increasing outsourcing practices by private companies and public administrations, to the tax breaks provided for non-profit companies, and to growing pressure on prices in the market. As a consequence, the original values and practices of cooperatives largely vanished, persisting only in certain small enterprises (Sacchetto and Semenzin 2015). Although the 'ideology of participation' is widespread, working members and in

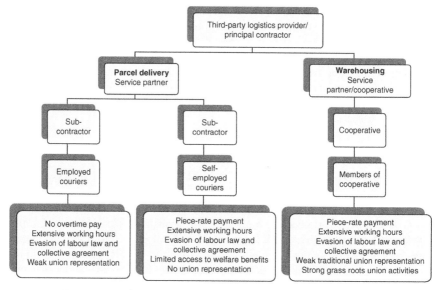

Figure 4.1. Subcontracting chains in two sub-industries of logistics

particular migrants in the logistics sector do not participate in any meetings and have very limited decisional power, if any. Some of the cooperatives in the Italian logistics sector can be rated as letter-box enterprises, as activities close down within a few years or even months without ever having paid taxes. Cooperatives often just disappear when inspected by government labour inspectors or when labour conflicts emerge. Furthermore, the relationship between the client company or principal contractor and the subcontractor can be easily dissolved when an agreement ends, effectively dismissing the workers.

The process of subcontracting to service providers and self-employed couriers, or to cooperatives and their members, lowers the cost of services for big logistics companies and makes it more difficult for workers to identify a counterpart for their claims (Wills 2009). Subcontracting allows for labour flexibility to adapt easily to fluctuations in demand, thanks to an available pool of skilled and unskilled workers. Labour processes are optimized by exploiting working conditions, long working hours, and overtime, with serious consequences for workers' health. But technology also plays a role: in courier services in Austria, workers' productivity is enhanced and controlled via electronic devices with GPS functions and radio-frequency identification systems. For warehouse workers, labour is measured by technical systems of key performance indicators with the aim to establish targets of required work effort, rendering them more accountable and monitoring them more closely (Newsome et al. 2013).

As a rule, in both sub-industries the further away from the principal contractor, the more precarious, unstable, and unprotected are the workers' employment situations. Both the (bogus) self-employed and cooperative members can expect to experience piece-rate payment and up to twelve-hour days at peak times, as well as evasive employer strategies and little union support. Diminishing regulative coverage of workplaces along the vertically structured supply chain goes hand in hand with thinning workplace representation.

Second, labour markets in the logistics sector in both countries are characterized by complex segmentation processes that intersect with labour contract forms and ethnicity. Employers use segmentation-focused recruitment strategies and exploit differences in pay and conditions across employee groups, such as migrant and native workers or workers with standard and non-standard contracts (Bauder 2006; McKenzie and Forde 2009). In Italy, the subcontracting of work in warehouses to cooperatives and the use of ethnic recruitment started in the 2000s as a way to undermine employment standards. It began as a strategy of big enterprises to adopt lean production through bypassing the 'rigidity' of core workers, who were often highly unionized. In Austria, employment contracts and hence labour standards deteriorate with the increasing length of the chain. At the bottom of the chain are self-employed couriers, often with migrant backgrounds, and small ethnic businesses with little bargaining power and in structurally disadvantaged positions in Austria's labour market. None of the third-party logistics providers employ couriers. Only the incumbent Austrian Post abstained from outsourcing the entire courier work force, after successfully bargaining for concessions on pay and conditions for new hires in the collective agreement (Haidinger 2012: 17–18).

In both countries, employers seeking to avoid compliance with collective bargaining agreements exploit the precarious labour market situation of migrant workers and their poor knowledge of labour laws. The more recently workers arrived and the less stable their living situation, the more likely they are to accept lower employment standards. At the same time, discriminatory practices inside the labour market and the link between employment contracts and work permits mean workers' only 'choice' is to take on any work available (Krenn 2013; Alberti et al. 2013). As Lewis et al. (2015: 588) underline, the difference between many migrants and other precarious workers is that the former find themselves at the nexus of both employment and migrant status, a situation of vulnerability and insecurity related to political and civil rights (see Chapter 10).

In addition, the Italian case study shows that community ties ensure the reliability of the workforce through a dual control of labour, in the workplace and community of origin. These ties also reproduce the occupational segregation of migrants in this sector. As Lusis and Bauder (2010: 38) put it: 'even though migrants can use their social capital to find work, they likely find opportunities through these channels in the secondary labour market segment'. In this context, ethnic recruitment also enforces divisions and internal hierarchies (Gilroy 2001; Roediger 1999) in the labour process, and can be used by management as an instrument for work organization and to create competition between workers.

To sum up, research on the logistics sector identifies a low-road model 'that requires the existence of groups of marginal workers' with 'low wages, preponderance of minority workers and reliance on contingent employment relationships in warehousing and distribution' (Gutelius 2015: 56). Contingent and migrant workers accept bad employment standards if the labour market is segmented, alternative jobs scarce, and social support weak, and knowledge about labour rights and workplace solidarity weak. In Section 4.5, we examine efforts by workers to build collectivist responses based on inclusive solidarity to contest this vicious circle of expanding precarious work and the decollectivization of risks, despite weak support from traditional unions.

4.5. LOGISTICS WORKERS CHALLENGING TRADITIONAL UNION STRATEGIES

Despite facing steep challenges, logistics workers at the bottom of supply chains have adopted a range of initiatives and strategies to improve their conditions and win collective representation. We compare these initiatives, focusing on the role of unions in approaching, organizing, and supporting workers and opening up union policies to a wider constituency in the two countries. Of particular interest is how unions attempted (or not) to embrace migrant workers, members of cooperatives, and self-employed couriers, and succeeded (or not) in incorporating the demands of this particular workers' segment into an overall sector policy safeguarding employment standards in logistics. We identify three crucial factors supporting successful and (under some circumstances) sustainable strategies: (1) exploiting the high vulnerability of logistics supply chains; (2) reducing the number of links in the supply chain and negotiating directly with principal contractors; and (3) adopting direct actions with union or social movement support at the bottom of the supply chain.

4.5.1. Vulnerability of Logistics Processes: High Positional, Low Associational Power

The vulnerability of logistics processes and wider production and circulation structures results in a combination of high positional and very low associational power of labour. Bonacich and Wilson (2008: 245) refer to the 'unavoidable vulnerability' of the logistics sector. On the one hand, just-in-time production principles require a smooth and steady flow of goods linking production to demand as closely as possible. On the other hand, peak seasons of delivery in the business-to-customers business (such as before Christmas), and the requirement that goods must pass through certain nodal points such as airports or distribution centres, pose a considerable potential threat for disrupting the supply chain: '[i]f it is possible to gum up the supply chain . . . a great deal of damage can be done to the company' (Bonacich and Wilson 2008: 245). Hence, workers at the bottom end of a value chain can make use of their strategically important position for improving their working conditions (Silver 2003).

On the contrary, associational power is weak in contemporary logistics, not only because of management's divide-and-rule strategies but also because the structures of interest representation are at odds with dynamic value chains and fragmented employment. Local unions have difficulty gaining access to workers in outsourced links of the logistics chain. Due to the combination of a flexible, integrated, and centrally controlled delivery process and markedly decentralized and often informal employment relations, traditional union methods of approaching workers via shop stewards are of limited use. Recruiting and/or organizing strategies focusing on direct and targeted information and action for/with the workers themselves emerged in both countries, and turned out to be more successful.

In one instance in Austria, some fifteen employees working for a third-party logistics subcontractor in Salzburg joined forces in early 2010 to set a deadline for payment of their outstanding Christmas bonus. The conflict was settled in favour of the workers after they threatened not to deliver the parcels before the deadline expired. No unions were involved in this case, though; it was a merely workers' driven action. In general, unions' direct support in Austria remained very limited. Only the transport and service union vida, as will be described, launched targeted information campaigns about workers' rights in subcontracting chains, although for a relatively short period.

In Italy, workers drew on support from social movements and rank-and-file unions to organize strikes and blockades of many warehouses in the Po Valley Region (Cuppini et al. 2015: 132), a macro-region characterized by seamless urbanization that includes most of northern and central Italy. Warehouse workers used their knowledge of the labour process to identify weak points of the supply chain (e.g. the seasonal production peaks), and were able to cause serious economic losses to their companies through blockage of the entrances of the warehouses and other actions. The companies were often forced to negotiate with rank-and-file unions as a last resort to prevent further damages. In doing so, community networks of migrant workers that connect labour inside the warehouses of the Po Valley Region were used for coordination and mutual support during the strikes. Eventually, logistics workers in Italy asked for—and often obtained—better pay and working conditions, an improvement of workplace relations, the application of the collective bargaining agreement, and the recognition of rank-and-file unions as official negotiating partners.

Both in Austria and in Italy, the combination of workplace and/or grassroots organizing and the exploitation of workers' high positional power has proven a potentially great resource for improving working conditions. However, while in Austria such direct actions can be expected to remain transitory and local, in Italy, thanks to the presence of rank-and-file organizations (Adl Cobas and Si Cobas), working conditions inside many warehouses are effectively improving in a permanent way.

4.5.2. Direct Negotiations with Principal Logistics Contractors

As already outlined, the process of subcontracting to service providers, self-employed couriers, or cooperatives via up to three chain links tends to remove principal contractors from the bargaining process. However, while subcontracting firms who compete for contracts are formally independent actors responsible for labour conditions and labour standards, in fact they remain heavily dependent on the original service provider and do not enter negotiations on an equal footing. In both case studies, workers attempted to eliminate some links of the subcontracting chain to get closer to those on whom their working conditions really depended: the principal contractors.

In Austria, self-employed couriers contracted two chain links away from a large third-party logistics provider joined forces against a subcontractor that owed them money. They decided to foreclose the subcontractor, thus 'eliminating' it from the chain. As a result, they struck a deal with the principal contractor and took over the delivery districts previously assigned to the subcontractor. Despite the structural imbalances of power among the different stakeholders within specific chain links, self-employed couriers used their positional and marketplace bargaining power combined with (temporary) associational power (Silver 2003; Brinkmann et al. 2008; Wright 2000) to contest unsatisfactory working conditions. Nevertheless, such collective action remains exceptional in a setting of high competition among workers. This is on account of the remoteness of the transnational third-party logistics companies, who set out the conditions under which people work in this sector. Again, as in the Austrian example of workers' struggles mentioned in Section 4.5.1, it was a workplace-based initiative of self-employed couriers without union support that turned out to be a successful undertaking, resulting in better contracting conditions.

In Italy, principal contractors use the threat of ending the relationship with the cooperative as a way of discouraging industrial actions. The grassroots unions countered this thanks to an agreement that introduced the so-called 'social clause', which requires principal contractors to rehire all workers in case of a subcontractor change. Nevertheless, as long as the system of subcontracting persists, the threat of putting an end to the contract and giving it to a new cooperative still exists in many workplaces.[6] Hence, workers' demands are today addressed not only to the subcontractor (the cooperative) but also directly to the principal contractors (TNT, Bartolini, UPS, DHL). With the long-term objective of cutting out the cooperatives and promoting direct employment by principal contractors, the grassroots unions' strategy is to bypass the subcontractor and negotiate directly with the client company. As the regime of union representation officially excludes rank-and-file organizations from national collective bargaining, this is an ambitious goal. However, a first important success was obtained in November 2016, when, after years of negotiating, rank-and-file unions concluded a national deal directly with three of the most important logistics companies, Bartolini, GESC, and TNT.

4.5.3. Unionizing and Fragmented Employment in Logistics

Traditional strategies of unions failed partly due to union inertia and slowness to adapt to the dynamic economic of logistics. An additional factor was the 'strategic dilemma of remaining clearly within the powerful consensus-oriented arrangement or moving more strongly towards becoming a membership organization with a stronger conflict orientation' (Astleithner and Flecker forthcoming), resulting in failing to prioritize representation of workers in precarious employment and contracts.

---

[6] This was not possible in every warehouse: in March 2017, a protest of workers employed by a porterage cooperative stopped the production of Coca Cola in Nogara (Verona), not far away from Padua. The cooperative that won the new contract refused many of the employees of the previous contractor, resulting in these workers being dismissed. Continued protest resulted in an average compensation package of about €30,000 for those who lost their jobs.

While traditional trade unions in Italy have tried to organize precarious workers, they have not been interested in organizing logistics workers because it was for a long time considered a 'marginal' sector. Storage and warehousing operations are still deemed as auxiliary activities to the factory, where the core of production takes place. Furthermore, traditional unions generally consider migrants, who represent the majority of the workers in this sector, as 'birds of passage' (Piore 1979) who are prepared to work for lower wages and worse working conditions. Recent changes in the modes of production and the development of global supply chains have put those operations at the heart of contemporary capitalism, enhancing logistics workers' positional power. Those trends have been exacerbated by the economic crisis, which left a power vacuum that opened space for self-organized protests and grassroots unions.

The Austrian logistics sector is an illuminating example of how unions' inertia in continuing to use consensus-oriented strategies undermines their ability to bargain effectively with employers in the context of a segmented workforce. The outsourcing of operational activities by big postal, transport, and logistics companies to smaller entities has laid the groundwork for employers to weaken and evade the enforcement of labour standards. The logistics sector as a whole (including postal, transport, and retail services) is regulated by twelve different collective agreements negotiated by four unions. Couriers as a particular profession working in postal, haulage, and light vehicle haulage companies are still mainly covered by three collective agreements negotiated by two unions. Minimum standards and wages differ, as does the representational structure and union strategy. In Austria, only one company, Austrian Post, still employs couriers directly. When threatened with outsourcing, concession bargaining was used to preserve this relationship (Haidinger 2012: 17–18).

The collective agreement with the weakest labour protection (light vehicle haulage) gained importance because the delivery of parcels is mainly operated by subcontracted firms. Ever fewer couriers are employed by big haulage companies and third-party logistics providers that apply a different collective agreement (haulage). Light vehicle haulage is dominated by small and medium-sized companies, which often are not inclined to admit works councils or unions into their companies (Artus et al. 2009). Hence, enforcement of even the minimum standards foreseen for light vehicle haulage is problematic. For the union vida, access to these workers is time consuming and difficult in firms where no works council is in place. Third-party logistics providers (the principal contractors) sometimes have works councils, but they have little contact with subcontractor workers.

One positive exception in this respect was an organizing campaign initiated by the union vida in 2010 to reach out to, inform, and organize couriers working in subcontracting chains. The aim of the campaign was to establish initial contact with subcontracted employees through personal conversations and two large-scale actions in front of the UPS headquarters, and to learn something about the main problems they faced at work. This direct confrontation with drivers showed that a good number of them were positive towards vida's attempts to support them. However, some voiced their fear of being observed by their employers in their contacts with unions. When asked if they would appreciate a union's or another organization's active role in supporting their struggle, most of them were interested but sceptical. This scepticism was due to the unions' previous absence from the field, and the sector's logic of exploitation, which made them feel trapped.

As we have seen, the sector is a paradigmatic example of unions' need to adopt alternatives to traditional ways of approaching, organizing, and supporting workers and to open up union policies to a wider constituency, including the self-employed. In fact, only in very sporadic cases did collective action arise from the bottom up, without institutional support from unions.

4.6. EXPLAINING SUCCESS AND FAILURE OF ORGANIZING WORKERS IN LOGISTICS SUPPLY CHAINS

In this next step, we make an attempt to explain the reasons for unions' success or failure to organize workers in logistics supply chains and ultimately to improve their working conditions. Against the background of the three factors for successful strategies discussed in Section 4.5, we identify two differences between the Italian and the Austrian cases: (1) differences in the dominant or competing union structures in logistics; and (2) differences in their capacity to draw on traditions of inclusive worker solidarity and direct action.

4.6.1. Union Structure: Membership Organization vs. Institutional Security

Traditional unions' reluctance to adapt their strategies to new economic structures and new forms of relations between workers and employers or contractors not only limits the support they can provide to logistics workers; it actually limits the spontaneous resistance of workers against their intolerable employment and working conditions (Stern 2012; Gumbrell-McCormick 2011; Brinkmann et al. 2008). This also means that institutional and organizational adaptation may greatly enhance workers' associational power and thus better position them to take advantage of the fact that the logistics processes are not only inherently vulnerable but also economically crucial for entire global production networks spanning a range of business processes and sectors.

The recognition of positional power inside the logistics supply chain led to the emergence of 'bottom-up' organizing in both case studies. On the one hand, this is the consequence of similar conditions of extreme exploitation and violation of basic laws and collective agreements in the sector. On the other hand, there is a representation gap left by traditional trade unions in both countries. While grass-roots organizing remained transitory, local, and entirely self-organized in Austria, it became stronger and more sustainable in Italy because grassroots unions gathered a 'critical mass' thanks to more flexible mobilizing strategies.

To some extent, the expansion of grassroots unions in Italy can be linked to the specific nature of the Italian trade union system showing a 'low level of institutionalization' where 'the arena of representation continued to be relatively open to newcomers' (Regalia 2012: 389). On the other hand, traditional Italian unions—CGIL, CISL, and UIL—remain very bureaucratic, and with some exceptions (i.e. the metalworkers union) their engagement is mainly constrained to high-level negotiations with the Italian government and employers' representatives. In contrast, the lean structure of rank-and-file Italian unions has been crucial to developing strong support for workers. Furthermore, as traditional unions have historical ties with some of the major cooperatives, they are considered by many workers as part of the governance of the system. Conversely, grassroots unions do not have such links and some of their leaders have common political roots with social activists supporting migrants' rights.

In Austria, an overarching umbrella organization with institutionally strong sectoral unions represents all workers, leaving little room for institutional manoeuvre for 'newcomers'. These unions sometimes even denounce alternative forms of organizing as inappropriate, radical, or too confrontational (Stern and Sigl 2012). Somehow constrained by the institutional rigidities of social partnership, and also due to a lack of ideas regarding how to mobilize workers by targeted efforts, unions have hardly reacted to critiques to better incorporate peripheral and precarious workers. In parcel delivery, most couriers—namely those who are not employed by the incumbent Austrian Post—have only the little union representation that results from legally binding collective agreements. In fact, social and working conditions in parcel delivery have been deteriorating in two ways: for self-employed couriers, collective regulations do not apply; for couriers employed by subcontractors, existing regulations are often not adhered to. The lack of workplace-based representation in subcontracted companies reflects that vida has not succeeded in developing specific strategies to address the situation of precarious workers, including migrant workers and (or in) ethnic businesses in the logistics subcontracting chain.

4.6.2. Towards Inclusive Worker Solidarity

Another explanation for the different success of grassroots strategies in the two countries is that the strong tradition of militancy in Italy is more open to encompassing solidarity with new groups compared with the more consensus-oriented direction of Austrian trade unions, where demands for better working conditions are delegated to social partnership processes. Italian grassroots unions 'build solidarity' and encourage patterns of behaviour that support mutual aid and collective action. Austrian unions do not actively prevent inclusive worker solidarity but have difficulties bridging boundaries between different sectors, different firms, core and peripheral workers, and different groups such as natives and migrant workers.

In Austria, union discourse about and attitude towards different workforce groups has only slowly and partly changed from one of 'wage dumping' to a more solidaristic framing (Stern 2012). Most unions in Austria have not yet adjusted to the new workplace realities that have followed the 'logistics revolution' and the chain logic that dominates the parcel delivery industry, and they find it difficult to access a constituency comprised of migrant workers in small enterprises without works councils or in self-employment. The cornerstone of Austrian unions' policies is to protect workers in standard employment. They rely on encompassing labour market legislation and collective agreements to protect vulnerable groups of workers in the small enterprises of the parcel delivery industry. However, unions' institutional power seems insufficient to sustain applicable labour standards and contest employers' divide-and-rule strategies. Instead of being proactively approached by unions, more often than not self-employed couriers and peripheral workers are left to their own devices.

Italian grassroots unions are often less bureaucratic and hierarchical than traditional ones, giving considerable flexibility to the agency of migrant workers, who can put in place a wide range of worker strategies according to the specific context (Alberti 2016: 98; Murgia and Selmi 2012). For example, workers were able to organize warehouse blockages for several days to force employers to rehire fired colleagues or to pay withheld wages. In other cases, they organized boycott campaigns to punish certain companies for anti-union policies and illegal working conditions. Furthermore, these labour conflicts were often supported by social movements (Cuppini et al. 2015; Tapia and Turner 2013), highlighting new ways of organizing and of raising a shared 'militant capital' (Matonti and Poupeau 2004), a set of knowledge and skills mobilized for collective actions, that can be used in very different situations. In particular, the Arab Spring of 2011 inspired migrants to overcome obstacles to improving working conditions in the warehouses and elsewhere (Perrotta and Sacchetto 2014). Indeed, while migrants strategically used their knowledge of the labour process to identify the weak points of the chain of distribution and built upon the consciousness gained in their countries of origin, local activists shared their specific skills and knowledge of the Italian context, especially regarding laws, language, and media communication.

In Italy, a combination of rank-and-file unionization and the use of ethnic networks to counter employers' divide-and-rule strategies resulted in strong and sustainable workers' resistance against employers and contractors of the logistics networks by making use of the vulnerability of the supply chain with blockades and delivery stoppages. On the one hand, rank-and-file unions approached workers directly and without reservations, providing local and labour law knowledge and militant experiences. Conversely, ethnic networks served as a stronghold for building information and solidarity networks. In the Italian logistics sector, migrant workers have been free to choose representatives from their communities, thus decreasing the distance that can exist between migrant workers and local semi-professional shop stewards. In addition, an important role in the spread of information and organization among migrant workers was played by informal channels, the Internet, and social networks as well as internal communication channels in migrant communities. These community networks that help newcomers to integrate into the host society are present in many workplaces, where they can become a resource for the union. The accumulation of power rose inside and outside the workplaces.

In this way, migrant workers were able to turn ethnic recruitment, built to ensure control over labour, into a resource for action. In this sense, 'the shared stigma and the related experience of racialization reinforce their collectivist worldview' (Milkman 2011: 365) and nourish the determination to gain 'dignity' and win what is sometimes called a 'war': 'I don't remember what year it was when we came here (to the union) together. When we started this war. . . . Because it's a war, with the cooperatives' (interview with a worker: male, 35 years old, Nigerian). The working conditions improved both because new and better collective agreements were signed and because the power relationship changed inside the warehouses. The collective agreements signed by Adl Cobas and Si Cobas compel companies (or cooperatives) in cases where the subcontractor changes to maintain staff and its labour standards and adhere to the seniority principle. Furthermore, improvements were achieved for sick payment and payments in case of injuries as well as the automatic growth of seniority with a direct impact on wages, eroding the discretion and arbitrariness of managers.

The ability shown by migrant workers in the organization of the struggles in recent years has thus obtained its record of achievements through both growth of awareness and coordination skills and also material support. In organizing these recent struggles, migrant workers proved to be successful in many ways: not only with respect to the consciousness of labour rights and an efficient coordination of skills, but ultimately to an improvement in their substantial situation.

4.7. CONCLUSIONS

In logistics, we see the pervasiveness of subcontracting, a newly composed workforce characterized by a high proportion of migrant workers, and market policies tending towards the liberalization of transport, postal, and labour markets (Holst 2015; Bonacich and Wilson 2008). Those transformations contribute to the strong segmentation and the expansion of precarious work, especially at the bottom end of the logistics supply chain. The examples of parcel delivery in Austria and warehousing in Italy not only underline striking similarities in the logic of the supply chain functioning but also in the two sub-industry's high exposure to potential disruption when workers make use of their positional power.

Struggles in warehouses can be considered as 'improbable mobilizations' if compared to 'normally accepted criteria in sociology of collective action to identify obstacles to the emergence of collective protests' (Collovald and Mathieu 2009: 120). In fact, the presence of anti-union policies, precarious status of workers, ethnic segmentation and divide-and-rule management, the supremacy of core companies or client organizations, as well as the economic crisis, are factors that should usually weaken labour struggles. Hence, it is crucial to understand to what extent workers' resistance and (non-)compliance nevertheless shape labour processes, influence value chain dynamics (Rogaly 2009), and confront a segmented labour market from the bottom of the supply chain; and what institutional and union support would best encourage the success of these struggles.

'Traditional' union strategies that target and protect core and native workers prove to be insufficient to address the concerns of vulnerable workers' situations in our cases. This finding is relevant in dualized labour markets such as in Italy's logistics sector. It is also important where encompassing labour regulations are in place, but lack efficacy and enforcement, as in Austria. Italy's case shows a successful road to improving working conditions and social protection when established channels of representation fail. Here, new forms of collective struggles succeeded thanks to rank-and-file unionization, social activist support, and the usage of ethnic networks. Ethnic networks, rank-and-file unions, and strategies which made use of the vulnerabilities of the logistics sector combined to allow strong and sustainable workers' resistance against employers and contractors. Logistics workers in Italy turned ethnic recruitment into a solidaristic weapon instead of falling into the trap of capital's divide-and-rule strategy. As Coe and Jordhus-Lier (2011: 224) underline, the boundaries between unionism and community politics can be porous, especially when connections between the inside and the outside of a workplace are strong. From this point of view, the Italian case highlights how the accumulation of power by workers unfolds 'socially' and not just within the workplace (Ricciardi 2017).

In Austria, by contrast, unions stick to their old recipes, act defensively, and leave workers to their own devices, exacerbating differences in the workforce, especially between vulnerable workers (often migrants) and standard contract workers (mostly natives). Maintaining that 'we are not in charge of the self-employed', unions focused on 'core' members, and on keeping their institutional power while neglecting atypical workers. Nevertheless, in Austria, both unions at least attempted to approach couriers in precarious employment. Also, workers self-organized to counter their structural powerlessness and to disrupt processes vital for the smooth functioning of the supply chain—even if such actions remained transitory and local.

One main lesson learned from this comparison is the need to find unconventional worker-centred and targeted ways to approach workers and to offer them legal and local support to improve their immediate work situation as well as to ensure their social reproduction. Militant action and workers' struggles have to be taken as a case in point as they can—as the Italian study greatly shows—constitute starting points for further organizing and winning members, and for reregulating the sector(s) for the better from the workers' point of view.

REFERENCES

Alberti, Gabriella. 2016. 'Mobilizing and Bargaining at the Edge of Informality: The "3 Cosas Campaign" by Outsourced Migrant Workers at the University of London'. *WorkingUsa*, 19(1): 81–103.

Alberti, Gabriella, Holgate, Jane, and Tapia, Maite. 2013. 'Organising Migrants as Workers or as Migrant Workers? Intersectionality, Trade Unions and Precarious Work'. *The International Journal of Human Resource Management*, 24(22): 4132–48.

Artus, Ingrid, Böhm, Sabine, Lücking, Stefan, and Trinczek, Rainer. 2009. 'Arbeitsbeziehungen in Betrieben ohne Betriebsrat'. *Industrielle Beziehungen*, 16(2): 180–1.

Astleithner, Franz and Flecker, Jörg. Forthcoming. 'From the Golden Age to the Gilded Cage? Austrian Trade Unions, Social Partnership and the Crisis'. In *A Rough Landscape: European Trade Unions in a Time of Crises*, edited by S. Lehndorff, H. Dribbuch, and T. Schulten. Brussels: ETUI.

Baccaro, Lucio and Pulignano, Valeria. 2011. 'Employment Relations in Italy'. In *International and Comparative Employment Relations,* edited by G. Bamber, R. Lansbury, and N. Wailes, 5th edition. New York: Sage.

Bauder, Harald. 2006. *Labor Movement: How Migration Regulates Labor Markets.* New York: Oxford University Press.

Benassi, Chiara and Dorigatti, Lisa. 2014. 'Straight to the Core—Explaining Union Responses to the Casualisation of Work: The IG Metal Campaign for Agency Workers'. *British Journal of Industrial Relations*, 53(3): 533–55.

Bonacich, Edna and Wilson, Jake. 2008. *Getting the Goods: Ports, Labor, and the Logistics Revolution*. Ithaca, NY and London: Cornell University Press.

Brinkmann, Ulrich, Choi, Hae-Lin, Detje, Richard, Dörre, Klaus, Holst, Hajo, Karakayali, Serhat, and Schmalstieg, Catharina. 2008. *Strategic Unionism: Aus der Krise zur Erneuerung?* Wiesbaden: VS Verlag für Sozialwissenschaften.

Censis. 2012. *Primo rapporto sulla cooperazione in Italia*. Roma: Censis.

Cnel-Istat. 2015. 'Progetto CNEL-ISTAT sul tema: Produttività, struttura e performance delle imprese esportatrici, mercato del lavoro e contrattazione integrativa'. Report intermedio. Roma: Cnel.

Coe, Martin Neil. 2014. 'Missing Links: Logistics, Governance and Upgrading in a Shifting Global Economy'. *Review of International Political Economy*, 21(1): 224–56.

Coe, Martin Neil. 2015. 'Labour and Global Production Networks: Mapping Variegated Landscapes of Agency'. In *Putting Labour in its Place: Labour Process Analysis and Global Value Chains*, edited by K. Newsome, P. Taylor, J. Bair, and A. Rainnie. London: Palgrave.

Coe, Martin Neil and Jordhus-Lier, David. 2011. 'Constrained Agency? Re-evaluating the Geographies of Labour'. *Progress in Human Geography*, 35(2): 211–33.

Collovald, Annie and Mathieu, Lilian. 2009. 'Mobilisations improbables et apprentissage d'un répertoire synodical'. *Politix*, 2(86): 119–43.

Cowen, Deborah. 2014. *The Deadly Life of Logistics: Mapping Violence in Global Trade*. Minneapolis: University of Minnesota Press.

Cuppini, Niccolò, Frapporti, Mattia, and Pirone, Maurilio. 2015. 'Logistics Struggles in the Po Valley Region: Territorial Transformations and Processes of Antagonistic Subjectivation'. *South Atlantic Quarterly*, 114(1): 119–34.

Dicken, Peter. 2011. *Global Shift*. Mapping the Changing Contours of the World Economy, 6th Edition. London: Sage.

Doellgast, Virginia, and Ian Greer. 2007. 'Vertical disintegration and the disorganization of German industrial relations'. *British Journal of Industrial Relations* 45 (1): 55–76.

Drahokoupil, Jan (ed.) 2015. *The Outsourcing Challenge: Organizing Workers across Fragmented Production Networks*. Brussels: ETUI.

Firlei, Klaus. 2016. 'Lohn—Und Sozialdumping—Einige Grundsätzliche Überlegungen'. *Das Recht Der Arbeit (DRdA)*, 6: 383–96.

Flecker, Jörg. 2010. 'Fragmenting Labour: Organisational Restructuring, Employment Relations and the Dynamics of National Regulatory Frameworks'. *Work Organisation, Labour and Globalisation*, 4(1): 8–23.

Garibaldo, Francesco. 2011. *Ricerca sul movimento cooperativo di Reggio Emilia*. Unpublished manuscript.

Gilroy, Paul. 2001. *Against Race: Imagining Political Culture beyond the Color Line*. Cambridge, MA: Harvard University Press.

Gumbrell-McCormick, Rebecca. 2011. 'European Trade Unions and "Atypical" Workers'. *Industrial Relations Journal*, 42(3): 293–310.

Gumbrell-McCormick, Rebecca and Hyman, Richard. 2013. *Trade Unions in Western Europe: Hard Times, Hard Choices*. Oxford: Oxford University Press.

Gutelius, Beth. 2015. 'Disarticulating Distribution: Labour Segmentation and Subcontracting in Global Logistics'. *Geoforum*, 60: 53–61.

Haidinger, Bettina. 2012. *On the Move in Global Delivery Chains: Labor Relations and Working Conditions in the Parcel Delivery Industries of Austria, Germany, the Czech Republic and Hungary*. SODIPER Synthesis Report. Vienna: FORBA.

Haidinger, Bettina, Schönauer, Annika, Flecker, Jörg, and Holtgrewe, Ursula. 2014. 'Value Chains and Networks in Services: Crossing Borders, Crossing Sectors, Crossing Regimes?' In *The Comparative Political Economy of Work and Employment Relations*, edited by M. Vidal and M. Hauptmeier. London: Palgrave.

Henderson, Jeffrey, Dicken, Peter, Hess, Martin, Coe, Neil, and Wai-Chung Yeung, Henry. 2002. 'Global Production Networks and the Analysis of Economic Development'. *Review of International Political Economy*, 9(3): 436–64.

Holst, Hajo. 2015. 'Europäisierung als Institutionelle Entbettung: Multinationale Konzerne, Finanzialisierung und die Arbeitsbeziehungen im europäischen Paketsektor'. In *Horizontale Europäisierung im Feld der Arbeitsbeziehungen*, edited by S. Pernicka. Wiesbaden: VS Verlag.

Krenn, Manfred. 2013. 'Prekäre Integration: zu den Besonderheiten eingeschränkter sozialer Teilhabe von MigrantInnen durch prekäre Arbeit'. *SWS-Rundschau*, 53(4): 382–403.

Lewis, Hanna, Dwyer, Peter, Hodkinson, Stuart, and Waite, Louise. 2015. 'Hyper-Precarious Lives: Migrants, Work and Forced Labour in the Global North'. *Progress in Human Geography*, 39(5): 580–600.

Lusis, Tom and Bauder, Harald. 2010. 'Immigrants in the Labour Market: Transnationalism and Segmentation'. *Geography Compass*, 4(1): 28–44.

Matonti, Frédérique and Poupeau, Franck. 2004. 'Le capital militant: Essai de definition'. *Actes de la recherche en sciences sociales*, 5(155): 4–11.

McKenzie, Robert and Forde, Chris. 2009. 'The Rhetoric of the Good Worker versus the Realities of Employers' Use and Experiences of Migrant Workers'. *Work, Employment and Society*, 23(1): 142–59.

Meardi, Guglielmo. 2014. 'Employment Relations under External Pressure: Italian and Spanish Reforms during the Great Recession'. In *Comparative Political Economy of Work*, edited by M. Hauptmeier and M. Vital. London: Palgrave.

Meil, Pamela, Tengblad, Per, and Docherty, Peter. 2009. *Value Chain Restructuring and Industrial Relations: The Role of Workplace Representation in Changing Conditions of Employment and Work*. Leuven: HIVA.

Milkman, Ruth. 2011. 'Immigrant Workers, Precarious Work, and the US Labor Movement'. *Globalizations*, 8(3): 361–72.

Murgia, Annalisa, and Selmi, Giulia. 2012. '"Inspire and Conspire"': Italian Precarious Workers between Self-Organization and Self-Advocacy'. *Interface*, 4(2): 181–96.

Newsome, Kirsty, Thompson, Paul, and Commander, Johanna. 2013. '"You Monitor Performance at Every Hour": Labour and the Management of Performance in the Supermarket Supply Chain'. *New Technology, Work and Employment*, 28(1): 1–15.

Peck, Jamie. 1996. *Workplace: The Social Regulation of Labour Markets*. New York and London: Guilford.

Pernicka, Susanne and Stern, Sandra. 2011. 'Von der Sozialpartnergewerkschaft zur Bewegungsorganisation? Mitgliedergewinnungsstrategien österreichischer Gewerkschaften'. *Österreichische Zeitschrift für Politikwissenschaft*, 40(4): 335–55.

Perrotta, Mimmo and Sacchetto, Devi. 2014. 'Migrant Farmworkers in Southern Italy: Ghettoes, Caporalato and Collective Action'. *Workers of the World*, 1(5): 75–98.

Piore, Michael J. 1979. *Birds of Passage: Migrant Labor and Industrial Societies*. Cambridge: Cambridge University Press.

Pulignano, Valeria, Gervasi, Luís Ortiz, and De Franceschi, Fabio. 2016. 'Union Responses to Precarious Workers: Italy and Spain Compared'. *European Journal of Industrial Relations*, 22(1): 39–55.

Pulignano, Valeria, Meardi, Guiglielmo, and Doerflinger, Nadja. 2015. 'Trade Unions and Labour Market Dualisation: A Comparison of Policies and Attitudes towards Agency and Migrant Workers in Germany and Belgizum'. *Work, Employment and Society*, 29(5): 808–25.

Regalia, Ida. 2012. 'Italian Trade Unions: Still Shifting between Consolidated Organizations and Social Movements?' *Management Revue*, 23(4): 386–407.

Ricciardi, Maurizio. 2017. 'Appunti per una teoria politica delle migrazioni: potere sociale e politicizzazione della differenza'. In *Le reti del valore: Migrazioni, produzione e governo della crisi*, edited by S. Chignola and D. Sacchetto. Roma: Derive Approdi.

Roediger, David R. 1999. *The Wages of Whiteness: Race and the Making of the American Working Class*. New York: Verso.

Rogaly, Ben. 2009. 'Spaces of Work and Everyday Life: Labour Geographies and the Agency of Unorganised Temporary Migrant Workers'. *Geography Compass*, 3(6): 1975–87.

Sacchetto, Devi and Semenzin, Marco. 2015. 'Workers' Cooperatives in Italy: Between Solidarity and Autocratic Centralism'. In *Social Economy in China and the World*, edited by P. Ngai, K. Hok Bun, Y. Hairong, and A. Koo. Abingdon and New York: Routledge.

Silver, Beverly J. 2003. *Forces of Labour: Workers' Movements and Globalization Since 1870*. Cambridge, MA: Cambridge University Press.

Stern, Sandra. 2012. 'Protektionistische Klientelpolitik oder Kampf um gleiche Rechte? Österreichische Gewerkschaften im Umgang mit un(ter)dokumentierter Arbeit'. In *Migration und Integration: Dialog zwischen Politik, Wissenschaft und Praxis*, edited by G. Biffl and L. Rössl. Bad Voslau: Verlag Omninum.

Stern, Sandra and Sigl, Lisa. 2012. 'Mülltrenners of the World, Unite! Prekär beschäftigte AbfallberaterInnen der Stadt Wien im Arbeitskampf'. *analyse and kritik*, 575: 22.

Tapia, Maite and Turner, Lowell. 2013. 'Union Campaigns as Countermovements: Mobilizing Immigrant Workers in France and the United Kingdom'. *British Journal of Industrial Relations*, 51(3): 601–22.

Wills, Jane. 2009. 'Subcontracted Employment and its Challenge to Labor'. *Labor Studies Journal*, 34(4): 441–60.

Wright, Erik Olin. 2000. 'Working-Class Power, Capitalist-Class Interests, and Class Compromise'. *American Journal of Sociology*, 105(4): 957–1002.

5

Labour Markets, Solidarity, and Precarious Work

Comparing Local Unions' Responses to Management Flexibility Strategies in the German and Belgian Metalworking and Chemical Industries

Valeria Pulignano and Nadja Doerflinger

5.1. INTRODUCTION

Nation-specific welfare and labour market institutions are often argued to moderate labour market flexibility's effects on working conditions, explaining different patterns of precarious work (Kalleberg 2009), or of segmentation and inequality in society (Emmenegger et al. 2012; Stone and Arthurs 2013; Koch and Fritz 2013). These traditional public policy instruments have declining ability to protect individuals from the social and market risks of flexible labour markets (Crouch 2015). Under these conditions, labour unions continue to play an important role in fighting segmentation (Hassel 2015) by mediating the extent to which the workforce is exposed to increasing market risks and employer demands for flexibility.

This chapter examines the processes and conditions that explain union success in fighting precarious work, based on a comparative study of multinational subsidiaries in the metal and chemical industries. In matched cases of German and Belgian plants, we examine how unions in each plant made different use of institutional and associational power resources to avoid concessions for the relatively protected standard (or permanent) workforce, while improving the conditions of the less protected non-standard (temporary and agency) workers.

In Belgium, more inclusive and encompassing collective bargaining institutions restricted the possibilities for local deviation from central agreements. Moreover, Belgian unions were able to draw on union-dominated representation structures and equal pay provisions in national legislation to resist precarious (non-standard) contracts and employment relationships. These resources were weaker in the German workplaces due to dual channel representation and weaker legislative provisions for equal treatment, allowing employers to use exit strategies to exploit differences in pay and working conditions among different groups of workers.

Findings also illustrate that power resources associated with encompassing institutions are necessary but not sufficient to explain the greater success of the Belgian unions in reducing precarious work. Associational power was indispensable for building inclusive solidarity between core, internal workers and non-standard workers, such as temporarily employed and agency workers. This was possible due to the relatively high union density among both standard and non-standard workers in Belgium,[1] as well as the unions' historically strong engagement in creating regulation that ensures similar protection in terms of social rights and entitlements for non-standard workers. Belgian unions' capacity to coordinate action between sector and workplace representation structures, as the result of the union-dominated dual representation system, further helped them to strengthen their organizational capability with the 'rank and file'.

Although the German unions also took an inclusive approach towards non-standard workers, they faced difficulty in their attempt to mobilize organizational power based on solidarity among different groups of workers. Compared to Belgium, the German unions opened up and reached out to non-standard (particularly agency) workers relatively late.[2] This lack of solidarity was exacerbated by fragmented institutions in the German chemical and metal industries and divisions between unions and works councils within the 'dual channel' system, both of which weakened the capacity of labour to mobilize among different groups of workers.

Hence, local unions in Belgium were more successful in controlling the social effects of externalization. By combining institutional with associational power resources, they reduced management's use of non-standard work, which created the basis for inclusive solidarity at the local level.

Our argument draws on Polanyi's (1944) observation that changes in employment relations generally reflect transformations in systems of power and control at the workplace. Along similar lines, we argue that to understand the extent to which and how precarious work expands, it is essential to explore the contentious politics and power mechanisms that accompany institutional change. This requires examining the resources that capital and labour deploy to impose or to defend a specific institutional order (Peck and Theodore 2007). These resources, in turn, rely on the interaction between labour market institutions and social actors' strategies at sector and local levels. Our findings contribute to developing a more dynamic and less functionalist analytical framework, which assesses the solidarity effects of labour market institutions and their change through the examination of unions' use of different power resources as responses to management strategies of segmentation across (and within) different countries and sectors (Osterman 1994; Grimshaw and Rubery 1998; Beynon et al. 2002).

As the following sections illustrate, developments in the German and Belgian metal and chemical industries show that fragmented and less encompassing institutions (especially in Germany) allow employers to exploit exit options.

---

[1] With almost 53 per cent density, Belgian trade unions are seen as much more powerful organizations than their German counterparts (ICTWSS data 2015).

[2] It is remarkable to note that in comparison with Belgium, German unions remained passive for a long time, demanding a legal prohibition of agency work. See Pulignano and Doerflinger (2013) for further analysis.

Growing use of non-standard contracts expands both segmentation in working conditions and the overall incidence of precarious work, which potentially under-mines local bargaining power. However, inclusive and strong institutions—such as in Belgium—are not an antidote per se to employers' strategic threats. Overall, to fight precarity, trade unions need to build and sustain power. This is not only a matter of inclusive institutions, but also of labour unions' capacity to overcome employer-created divides by building inclusive solidarity through mobilization across different groups of workers, in (and across) sectors covered by different collective agreements.

5.2. LABOUR MARKET TRAJECTORIES OF INSTITUTIONAL CHANGE: GERMANY AND BELGIUM COMPARED

Belgium and Germany are often classified as conservative welfare regimes, with basic welfare support for the non-employed population and an increasing division into a strongly protected group of high earners and an ever-larger marginalized group facing difficulties in finding stable employment (Esping-Andersen 1990). This 'dual' system is considered as the product of the low degree of labour market flexibility and strict dismissal protection. Yet, clustering Belgium and Germany together as 'dual' systems may pose the risk of underestimating the extent and the nature of the distinctive developments undertaken by both countries as responses to the ongoing change in the economic and political landscape. We illustrate our argument by systematically comparing Germany's and Belgium's different trajec-tories of labour market change from Fordist to post-Fordist production and employment regimes.

Since the 1980s, both Germany and Belgium have been characterized by policy reforms aimed at strengthening their economic position by increasing competi-tiveness, particularly in manufacturing, which has experienced dramatic shocks resulting from market exposure. However, these have taken different forms. In Germany, the focus moved progressively away from traditional social partner-ship and governmental regulation of economic action based on strong employ-ment protections (e.g. high dismissal protection and high costs for dismissing employees), which were typical of the 'Rhenish capitalism' of the 1960s and 1970s. From the 1980s onwards, Germany adopted policies of continuous select-ive deregulation (Buchholz et al. 2011), encouraged by international competition and structural changes towards the service economy (Carlin and Soskice 2009; Häusermann and Schwander 2012). As a result, Germany shifted progressively from modest employment levels, but relatively high equality, towards increasing occupational heterogeneity and higher labour market inequality (Eichhorst and Marx 2011; Eichhorst et al. 2015). Employment deregulation and the Hartz reforms in the 1990s and 2000s contributed to increasing labour market dualiza-tion in Germany, as restrictions on the use of atypical work (particularly fixed-term and agency work) were relaxed, and as employees who exhausted their unemployment benefits were immediately pushed to flat-rate social assistance.

The German unions could not avoid these policy reforms, although they demonstrated open resistance. One the one hand, German unions generally suffered from weakening influence on politics and business (Wiesenthal and Clasen 2003). On the other hand, inner conflicts within the DGB (Deutscher Gewerkschaftsbund) unions prevented them from joint and strong reactions (Hassel and Schiller 2010).

In contrast, labour market policy reforms in Belgium were more controlled and moderate, aimed at increasing flexibility while retaining equal treatment. Belgian trade unions traditionally relied on their strong veto power (together with the employers' associations) in social security and employment regulation. Moreover, the Belgian unions' ability to mobilize and to demonstrate their disagreement to the policy proposals through strike action contributed to helping them resist government attempts to change employment and social policy radically in the 1990s and 2000s. Belgian social policy resilience also resulted from weak government authority, because of the country's often short-lived political coalitions operating in a context of deepening federalism and growing linguistic conflicts (Emmenegger et al. 2012). Thus, the governments' attempts to reform the labour market failed. Although some reforms on social expenditures were concluded under European austerity, they did not drastically reduce the level of social protection and deregulate the labour market to the extent seen in Germany.

The specific national regulatory setting is also important to explaining differences in the extent of dualization (or segmentation) in Belgium and Germany. We refer particularly to the regulation of contractual flexibility, i.e. permanent versus temporary (agency and fixed-term) contractual arrangements. Compared to Germany, Belgian employers have relatively fewer legal incentives to use temporary (particularly agency) contracts to circumvent the strict regulation of standard (permanent) employment. The Belgian legislation foresees the use of the so-called 'temporary unemployment' schemes, which are as important as dismissal regulation and atypical work for employers to cushion the effects of potential economic shocks. Thus, the incentive to use temporary (particularly agency) work is reduced in Belgium compared to Germany (Houwing and Vandaele 2011).

In addition, Belgium has a more encompassing bargaining structure compared to Germany (Pulignano et al. 2016). In Belgium, collective bargaining at sector level is more likely to incorporate employment measures (including flexible work arrangements) than in Germany. This is explained by two factors: (1) Belgium's relatively higher organization rate (employer association and trade union density) compared to Germany; and (2) the fact that collective bargaining is more dominant at sector level than at company level in Belgium compared to in Germany. Opening clauses are increasingly common in German sector-level agreements, which has led to a variety of complementing, integrating, or derogating plant-level practices. Furthermore, sectoral social partners have weakened in Germany following the decline in union membership and the decreasing propensity of employers to organize themselves in traditional associations. Encompassing sector-level collective bargaining structures continue to be essential features of the Belgian industrial relations system. Union-dominated works councils at the local level engage in the implementation of various flexible work arrangements, which are grounded in these inclusive collective agreements.

5.3. RESEARCH DESIGN AND METHODOLOGY

We use a cross-sectoral (chemical, metal sector) and cross-national (Germany, Belgium) comparative case study design to examine how union responses in four plants run by multinationals mediate companies' flexibility strategies. Choosing workplaces of the same multinationals in two countries is important to keep the corporate company policy constant. We selected similar workplaces in terms of skill level (high), technology (high), size (more than 1,000 employees), and union presence (high). The comparison of similar workplaces allows for investigating whether outcomes across workplaces are similar or not, and if not, why this is the case and which factors are at play shaping potentially dissimilar outcomes. The empirical research focuses on workplace arrangements on wages, training, and job protection for different contractual groups of workers, because these issues were subject to local bargaining and mostly covered both core (permanent) and non-core (temporary) workers.

The German and Belgian chemical and metal sectors are of major importance for the countries' economies and labour markets, employing several million people altogether. However, especially in the past two decades, both sectors restructured due to the increased exposure to international competition. Therefore, higher levels of flexibility were an essential topic in sectoral and local bargaining. However, company strategies in both sectors differ, as patterns of externalization and outsourcing are prominent in the chemical sector, whereas the increased use of non-standard work can be observed in the metal sector. These company strategies triggered different union responses. In Belgium, collective agreements in the metal and chemical sectors set very high standards and good working conditions. In Germany, the standards tend to be good, too, but they vary across sectors. IG BCE (chemical sector) has institutionalized high levels of flexibility via opening clauses and numerous flexibility provisions to enable company- or even plant-specific agreements. In contrast, IG Metall (metal sector) has limited opening clauses in the sectoral agreement as much as possible to ensure similar standards across metal companies.

The most important characteristics of the *Chem* and *Metal* case study workplaces are illustrated in Table 5.1. *Chem* is a German multinational[3] and is one of the world's leading chemical companies, employing more than 100,000 staff globally. It offers a broad portfolio of chemical products and is active in both business-to-business and business-to-consumer markets. *Chem* invests big parts of its revenues in research and development (R&D), because innovativeness is considered a precondition for economic success. Therefore, *Chem* employs a predominantly high-skilled workforce. *Metal* (a French multinational) is one of the world leaders in transport, i.e. the production of trains and signalling techniques. Its more than 90,000 staff are highly skilled, and most of them have engineering backgrounds. *Metal*'s market leadership results from high investments in R&D and the strong technological base of its products.

---

[3] There was no country-of-origin effect regarding *Chem*'s German plant. For instance, one could have expected high equality across contractual groups due to the German tradition of co-determination, but the empirical part highlights no distinct (home country) effect in that respect.

Table 5.1. Workplace characteristics

	Chem		Metal	
	Chem-DE	Chem-BE	Metal-DE	Metal-BE
Number of staff	35,000	3,000 (about 5,000 workers on-site working in the JTU)	2,800	1,000
Workforce configuration	93% permanent workers, 2% fixed-term workers, 5% agency workers	78% permanent workers, 20% fixed-term workers, 2% agency workers	80% permanent workers, 10% fixed-term workers, 10% agency workers	80% permanent workers, 20% fixed-term and agency workers
Staff of (sub-) contractors on-site	About 10,000 (fluctuating)	About 1,500 (relatively stable)	No data available	No data available
Workplace union density	60%	85%	75%	95%
Union presence	IG BCE (minor presence: VAA, CGB)	ACV-CSC, ABVV-FTGB, ACLVB-CGSLB	IG Metall	ACV-CSC, ABVV-FTGB, ACLVB-CGSLB

Source: Archival data and interviews.

The research design allows for studying the effects of national and sectoral regulation in-depth, within matched workplaces. It thus integrates different levels when examining the processes leading to distinctive workplace arrangements. In terms of processes, we focus on local bargaining between employee representatives and management, as this defines the terms and conditions for employment in a workplace.

The main way of collecting data was via semi-structured interviews, conducted between late 2011 and early 2014. Interviews were complemented with in-depth documentary analyses of collective agreements at different levels, as well as field notes from site visits and workplace observations. Interviews were carried out at the levels of the workplace (n = 20) and the sector (n = 6). In workplaces, we talked to strategic, local, and European human resource (HR) managers to learn more about the general and local HR policy and the position of management. We also interviewed local unionists and works councillors to understand their views and role in local negotiations. At sector level, we interviewed union experts to learn more about general industry developments and collective agreements. Interviews took between 60 and 120 minutes and were conducted in the respondents' native language (i.e. Dutch, French, or German). All interviews were recorded, transcribed, and translated into English before being analysed with the help of NVivo.

5.4. UNION RESPONSES TO CORPORATE FLEXIBILITY STRATEGIES

5.4.1. The Case of *Chem*

The chemical industry has been one of the backbones of German and Belgian industry. However, global competition has changed the sector's landscape. Huge

chemical sites were transformed into chemical parks coordinated by a site oper-
ator, with chemical companies focusing on core competencies and externalizing
non-core functions. Although *Chem* has largely resisted transforming sites into
chemical parks, it has increasingly focused on core competencies and externalized
peripheral functions:

> The market forces us to focus on our core competencies. We would like to have top-
> three positions in all our markets, but of course, we strive for being the number one.
> If we do not have this position in a market, we will consider different options. We
> could invest ourselves or acquire another company or start a joint venture to reach
> the top three, or we could just sell the whole product or activity.
>
> (HR manager, Chem-BE, 2013)

Externalization decisions led to outsourcing and the creation of independent
suppliers and service companies on *Chem*'s sites. Independent suppliers are not
always covered by the favourable chemical sector agreements, and in Germany's
industry union system, they could even be represented by a different union. At the
same time, externalization strategies also fragment labour power, as *Chem*'s
decreasing size came along with smaller worker representation structures.

In Belgium (Chem-BE), outsourcing and externalization caused a workforce
reduction and a reconfiguration of the remaining staff. Of the 5,000 workers on-
site, only about 3,000 still had a contract with Chem-BE. What used to be one
large site changed to a smaller site consisting of Chem-BE—limited to its core
functions—and numerous smaller independent companies (e.g. divisions that
were sold or outsourced, amounting to about 1,200 workers) and joint ventures
(in total about 800 workers) supplying Chem-BE. The unions were not in favour
of setting up joint ventures, but they engaged in local bargaining to achieve a
'regulated' externalization to keep high levels of protection and good working
conditions for the affected workers, and to avoid inequalities across groups of
workers as well as precarious work. Specifically, they demanded the application of
the inter-sectoral collective labour agreement (CLA) no. 32[4] on transferring
employees to newly set-up firms, and specifying the possibility of creating a
'joint technical unit' (JTU). The main advantage would be that all JTU companies
would have a works council as well as trade union delegations, and that negotiated
agreements would apply to all JTU units alike. This would protect the affected
workers by setting common standards and creating high levels of equality across
units. To avoid the risk of worker resistance and industrial action by the strong
local unions (about 85 per cent density), management agreed to set up a JTU. The
unions in turn gave consent to the workers' transfer to the joint ventures. Apart
from the risk of externalization, job security was high in Chem-BE and the JTU, as
formalized by various local CLAs.

In addition to such structural changes, management increasingly used temporary workers, especially agency workers and contractor staff, to ensure numerical
flexibility. According to one unionist's estimate, there were about 1,500 contractors on average on-site daily. Chem-BE had service contracts with, for instance,

---

[4] More information on CLA no. 32 can be found here: <http://www.werk.belgie.be/defaultTab.aspx?
id=492>.

companies offering maintenance for pipes, and such companies sent a stable number of workers to the site every day. Local unions lacked a legal mandate to represent staff from contractors; however, this mandate existed for agency workers. When Chem-BE started using agency workers, they mainly replaced sick employees. This changed over time: a local unionist observed that those workers had become a 'stable population within the workforce' because of long assignments (sometimes several years). Although their numbers were relatively small, unions put this topic on the bargaining agenda to avoid long assignments and precarious conditions for the affected workers.

Generally, Belgian law requires equal treatment in pay and working conditions between agency and regular workers, but there were no clear rules on maximum assignment duration or employment trajectories. This offered space to demand workplace-specific regulation on these issues. On the other hand, management also saw problems with the existing system, as long assignments had adverse effects on agency workers' motivation and commitment. An agreement was concluded based on shared interests, as unions aimed at ensuring stability and career perspectives to agency workers, and management wanted motivated and committed workers, which was contingent upon job stability and prospects. The CLA contained two provisions. First, well-performing agency workers could participate in a screening test, and based on a positive evaluation and a suitable position, enter Chem-BE. Second, if it was known that an assignment would exceed six months, fixed-term contracts (twice renewable) were offered. Hence, the affected workers were covered by the chemical sectoral agreement and nearly all workplace agreements, increasing equality between different groups of workers. Most agency workers performed low-skill, non-chemical tasks, mainly in logistics, which had been a source of conflict in recent years. Following serious disputes and industrial action, logistics work was outsourced in the 2000s due to cost reasons; and then, after subsequent disputes, it was insourced again based on a workplace agreement setting lower wages for logistics staff. One manager observed that Belgian labour laws restricted the content of these agreements:

> If we have to take decisions like the one regarding logistics, we are constrained by the rather rigid Belgian labour laws. What we see is that employees would be willing to do much more in terms of local flexibility as long as we guarantee security, but that the labour laws are restrictive in permitting that.   (HR manager, Chem-BE, 2013)

Management preferred keeping logistics inside at a competitive price, as ensured by an earlier workplace agreement. Similarly, local unions wanted to keep as many workers within Chem-BE—even at lower wage levels—and thus within the coverage of sector and workplace agreements. They even accepted concessions to achieve this, leading to lower wages for the affected workers. However, a couple of years later, management considered the compromise not to be cost-competitive anymore because of automatic wage increases (indexation) at national and sectoral levels. According to a local unionist, the lowest logistics wage level in the Chem-BE agreement corresponded to the highest level in the logistics agreement. This caused another, imminent threat of outsourcing. By the time of data collection, local negotiations were just starting. One union representative observed the challenges associated with resisting concessions:

> At the moment, the idea persists that the established workforce does not have to give in, but that those entering the company start at a much lower level regarding the terms and conditions of employment. On the one hand, we—and also myself, personally—face a dilemma. I do not want to take anything away from anybody working here, but I also understand that the employer says 'this will be too expensive, the competition increases, so we have to outsource if nothing changes'. But on the other hand, this time, it is logistics, but then, what comes afterwards? Perhaps administrative functions, because they cost us more than in the case of outsourcing? The staff of contractors working here at our site, they already earn less compared to our internal workforce. Where is the end to this, and how does it look like?
>
> (Trade unionist and European works councillor, Chem-BE, 2013)

In sum, local unionists succeeded in reducing differences between groups of workers in local bargaining. Apart from their organizational strength in Chem-BE, they did so by using institutional resources at the national level (e.g. law setting equal treatment on agency work) and (inter-)sectoral level (e.g. CLA no. 32). Although local unions could not avoid fragmentation, they regulated it, avoided precarious work, and kept high degrees of equality across groups of workers, employed on different contracts and by different units on-site.

In contrast to the high level of externalization at the Chem-BE site and in the industry, the Chem-DE German works council attempted to keep as many (non-chemical) functions as possible in-house. The workforce on-site was reduced from more than 50,000 workers in the early 1990s to 35,000 staff in the early 2010s. While the core workforce had been shrinking, work at the margins had grown. Permanent staff enjoyed high protection, due to sectoral and numerous workplace agreements with strong standards. Furthermore, such agreements also ensured the regular provision of training and the existence of development plans. An employment guarantee—which is also linked with investments in the plant—ensures job security. Although security is provided to core staff, management demands for flexibility have increased in recent years.

> We currently find ourselves within a big process of change. I cannot look at security only; I always have to keep in mind that we still need to remain productive as well. I think that the degree of flexibility cannot be more intense than it is at present; there are basically nearly no further instruments of flexibility left. I think it's up to the employees and their representatives to find a new role for themselves. I am very happy that co-determination rights exist, and that we have a European Works Council and a supervisory board.   (Work councillor, Chem-DE, 2012)

To raise flexibility, the use of temporary contracts had increased to about 650 fixed-term and 1,500 agency workers. Chem-DE's management set up an 'internal staffing agency' (ISA) a decade ago, which directly hired workers on fixed-term contracts but treated them as internal agency workers, flexibly assigning them to departments where staff was needed. The works council agreed because the affected workers were employed by Chem-DE, implying coverage by the favourable chemical sector and most workplace CLAs. Furthermore, a workplace agreement ruled that ISA staff got two-year contracts (in exceptional cases four years, based on a sectoral opening clause if the works council agreed). ISA staff thus had a certain level of stability and remained within the chemical sector's representation domain, leading the works council to consider ISA as a better option than external agency workers employed on potentially precarious conditions. ISA workers had almost equal conditions as regular staff—according to a works councillor: 'it's basically some sort of give and take: the company opts for flexibility, we opt for security'.

Chem-DE also increasingly used external agency workers for non-chemical functions to save costs. This was possible because agency workers in Germany were covered by the sectoral agreement of the staffing agency sector, which set much lower minimum wages and standards than the chemical sectoral agreement. In addition, any agency workers supported the catering and logistics departments, which were under pressure to be outsourced due to lower wages and working conditions in sector agreements for those two industries.

> Agency work is our most important flexibility measure. Many agency workers in logistics are employed for financial reasons; they are just cheaper than permanent employees. Higher-skilled agency workers in our rather technical departments are employed for flexibility reasons. We may do some kind of spin-off or outsourcing in the logistics section based on a benchmarking with market prices. But this also largely depends on our politicians and on their plans regarding agency work.
>
> (HR manager, Chem-DE, 2012)

The works council opposed outsourcing, because the affected workers could lose their coverage by the chemical sectoral agreement and workplace CLAs—if covered by other sectors' agreements, they would experience a degradation of wages and working conditions, leading to growing inequalities in the workplace. Therefore, the works council sought to keep logistics and catering (and the numerous workers with Chem-DE contracts working in these departments) in-house and within their representation domain. It succeeded with the help of concessions it made, based on the sectoral opening clause on 'competing collective agreements' that allows for deviations from sectoral agreements for units that could be covered by (worse) agreements from other industries. This opening clause is geared towards giving works councils a resource to avoid the outsourcing of non-chemical functions, and can be seen as an example of coordination between the workplace and the sector level. The opening clause allowed management to implement an unpaid working-time extension from 37.5 hours to forty hours a week, as well as lower wages for new hires (although in practice there were no new hires for logistics and catering). The works council also agreed that numerous (cheaper) agency workers could be used in both departments. Since they were covered by the sectoral agreement for staffing agencies, they earned about a third less than logistics and catering workers with a Chem-DE contract, and were subject to worse working conditions.

> To guarantee the jobs of the logistics and catering employees we had to agree to an opening clause which states that they have to work forty hours instead of 37.5 hours per week. If new staff is recruited those employees will have a smaller salary, too. But their situation could be much worse. So far the jobs of these employees have not yet been outsourced. But many tasks are already done by agency workers who are flexibly employed according to the company's demand.
>
> (Works councillor, Chem-DE, 2012)

The agreement kept logistics and catering in-house and within the chemical sector union's representation domain; however, it had negative implications for equality across different groups of workers for three reasons. First, logistics and catering employees' deteriorating working conditions cemented inequality across groups of permanent workers within the firm. Second, the compromise led to a shrinking core workforce in the long run, as there were practically no new hires in either department. Third, the numerous cheaper agency workers had precarious working conditions, reinforcing inequality between different contractual groups. As use of agency staff was part of the agreement, the works council implicitly consented to not demanding higher standards for them. Therefore, the agreement safeguarded the shrinking core from worse conditions, but at the cost of institutionalizing the use of peripheral workers at the margins, which reinforced inequality. As mentioned before, the basis of this compromise was an opening clause in the sectoral agreement, which was positively evaluated by management: 'In my opinion it is the strength of the sectoral agreement that a lot of flexibility is provided, for example with the instrument of opening clauses. That is the precondition for good solutions and success' (HR manager, Chem-DE, 2012).

Overall, the works council succeeded in avoiding outsourcing by using a sectoral opening clause locally. However, the compromise on logistics and catering staff required accepting growing inequalities within Chem-DE's workforce. Specifically, the shrinking core was complemented by a growing number of workers at the margins, hired on temporary contracts or via external contractors and work agencies. As these workers were mostly covered by the comparably worse collective agreements of other sectors, inequality between different groups of workers on-site was cemented.

5.4.2. The Case of *Metal*

In the past decades, metal companies have reduced their in-house production depth, which came along with the increased use of suppliers, and the creation of complex supply chains. *Metal* buys about 60 per cent of its semi-finished goods, and 40 per cent are still manufactured in-house. As suppliers mostly operate in the metal sector, they are—like *Metal*—covered by metal sector collective agreements, reducing inequalities across the value chain. Furthermore, metal companies have increasingly used external staff inside their firms, especially to cut costs, increase flexibility, and circumvent collective agreements. On average, *Metal* uses about 20 per cent agency and fixed-term workers. Therefore, fragmentation strategies are pointed towards differentiating the workforce based on contracts, so processes of internal segmentation can be observed:

> We need the flexibility offered by agency work and to a lesser extent, fixed-term contracts in order to adjust our production to current needs. At the beginning of a production process, you will need more workers. But when production has stabilised and the process is running well, fewer workers are required. For these situations, we need an instrument to flexibly adjust.   (European vice president HR, Metal, 2011)

In recent years, *Metal* has shifted from a purely production-oriented industrial organization towards focusing on post-industrial services, e.g. after-market services. This shift entailed advancements in production technology, causing changes in demanded occupational profiles. It implied the need for high skill levels and a 10 per cent reduction of the global workforce in the past decade. Since *Metal's* main customers were public bodies, the budgetary pressure because of austerity measures increased the demand for cost-competitive products. Hence, *Metal* faced the challenge of manufacturing high-quality products at low cost.

Metal's Belgian plant (Metal-BE) has transformed in the last decade, reducing production to a minimum and focusing on research, product development, and engineering services instead:

> It's about giving much more to the engineering part and less to the production part. In fact, the production unit will probably become an engineering unit rather than a manufacturing unit. Gradually, the company wants to produce less and carry out more services.   (Local unionist, Metal-BE, 2012)

As a result, only 200 out of 1,000 staff were blue-collar workers, mainly involved in prototyping. Many blue-collar workers had contracts with staffing agencies because of workload fluctuation. The other agency staff (about 200 in total) worked in administration. The flexible workforce also included employees on fixed-term contracts and staff from external contractors (e.g. engineering and design companies). While the former mainly executed administrative functions, the latter worked in higher-skill product development and engineering services. Local unions had a mandate to negotiate agency workers' working conditions, but lacked this mandate for contractors. Although Belgian law stipulates equal treatment between regular and agency workers in the same (user-firm) workplace, there may be differences regarding voluntary benefits, e.g. hospital insurance, which is normally paid by the employer. Local unions wanted to extend the equal treatment principle to such benefits to reduce inequalities between regular and agency workers. Management accepted this demand under the condition that the insurance would just be paid after four months, granting the benefit only to agency workers on longer assignments. On the one hand, management wanted to avoid costly work interruptions because the strong local unions threatened industrial action. On the other hand, Metal-BE used the paid hospital insurance as a marketing instrument to attract agency workers with stronger technical and social skills. An interviewed manager observed that the insurance had positive effects on the agency workers' motivation and commitment. A CLA also stated that agency workers could participate in training if needed, formalizing a benefit that was already common practice:

> If it is necessary for the job, agency workers participate in our training programmes, then we try to find the deal with the agency that for instance we pay for the training, but we don't pay the hours for that day, so we have a kind of sharing of the costs.
> (HR manager, Metal-BE, 2012)

Hence, agency workers were treated almost equally to regular staff in Metal-BE, and regular workers enjoyed very good working conditions and high levels of job security, as specified in numerous CLAs (e.g. in terms of wages, working time, training, and development). The only difference was the contract, which implied less job security for agency workers, although long assignments prevailed. Since agency workers sometimes stayed several years in Metal-BE, local unionists considered bargaining on maximum assignment durations:

> If we put a maximum assignment duration, it would be impossible for those agency workers we have. Of course, if they immediately got a new job after leaving the plant,

we'd think differently, but with more than 20 per cent unemployment here, this is unlikely. So we ensure that someone who's unfortunately on temporary work can work here in the long term and have working experience, which is crucial, as those temporary workers will leave this plant one day, they'll be on the labour market, and they'll be able to say 'I've been working at Metal-BE for 5 years', so their experience will be acknowledged. That's why we've left the situation the way it is.

(Local unionist, Metal-BE, 2012)

Hence, the unfavourable local labour market with high unemployment made unions refrain from further workplace bargaining on agency work. What was more important than a maximum assignment duration was keeping the affected workers in Metal-BE as long as possible, to increase their work experience and their chances of finding work externally. Relatedly, local unions also abandoned demands for employment paths due to two interlinked reasons. On the one hand, unions feared that management would hire fewer agency workers due to the obligation of contractual upgrades over time, which would have created higher work pressure for the core. Furthermore, local unions viewed agency work as providing a stepping stone to other jobs under unfavourable local labour market conditions. On the other hand, because of the transformation from production to services, the number of permanent staff required in the plant for prototyping decreased. In other words, the jobs needed as a precondition to having a system of employment paths were not there anymore, and trans-formations from blue- to white-collar positions were hardly possible due to skill discrepancies.

In sum, the strong national regulation of agency work helped local unionists to negotiate high standards locally, reducing the differences between regular and agency workers. Hence, their efforts led to high levels of equality across the two groups. However, local unions refrained from further regulation of agency work because of the unfavourable local labour market situation.

Metal's German site (Metal-DE) has kept its industrial character, with a large production unit and about half of the staff executing production tasks, but the number of white-collar employees in research, product development, and other administrative functions has grown. While the core workforce enjoyed very good working conditions as specified in the sectoral agreement and in numerous workplace agreements, flexibility pressure has increased from the mid-2000s onwards, as management threatened to close the plant due to its 'unfavourable cost structure'. Therefore, the works council agreed to various flexibility measures in local bargaining to safeguard operations, although this led to deteriorating working conditions for the entire workforce:

Since 2005 we had done our very best to keep the plant competitive: we forwent wage increases, we did without the Christmas and holiday bonuses and we agreed to every flexibility measure that the management requested. All we were asking for was job security.   (Works councillor, Metal-DE, 2013)

The number of temporary workers steeply increased at the same time for cost and flexibility reasons. While fixed-term staff performed various functions, agency workers mainly executed peripheral tasks or helped with in production. They earned about one-third less compared to Metal-DE staff (permanent and fixed-term workers) for two reasons. First, the equal treatment principle set by law did not apply due to the existence of a sectoral collective agreement. Second, this sectoral agreement covering staff from agencies set lower standards regarding wages and working conditions compared to the metal sector. Management could decide to use agency workers relatively independently of the works council because of limited co-determination rights on this subject. However, according to a works councillor, 'the works council does not only feel responsible for the Metal-DE employees at this plant but for basically everybody'.

Although the works council initially remained passive, it eventually engaged in local negotiations when numbers of flexible, and thus potentially precarious, workers peaked in 2007. It demanded a quota setting an upper limit to the use of flexible contracts. Management agreed, fearing industrial action in the highly unionized site, but only under the condition that the quota was relatively high. The HR manager stated: 'We had to agree to the unions' demands regarding agency work to avoid a strike.' By formalizing the quota, however, management was guaranteed the freedom to use the negotiated amount of flexible contracts without resistance. A 20 per cent flexibility quota comprising 10 per cent agency and 10 per cent fixed-term work was implemented (extendable to 30 per cent in times of high workload). Although this limited the use of flexible contracts, their numbers were still high, and inequalities between permanent and flexible workers remained. After implementing the quota, works councillors were eager to regulate agency work further to improve the conditions of these workers. They were less concerned about fixed-term work, since these workers were covered by the same sectoral agreement and almost all workplace agreements as permanent staff. Hence, they were treated almost equally apart from the contracts' time limitation. Despite lacking co-determination rights (before the 2012 sectoral agreement), which made local bargaining regarding agency work difficult, an agreement on training was negotiated, stating that training was provided according to training needs and not contract type. If it was necessary for their function, fixed-term and agency workers also received training as 'those contracts can be extended, so we benefit if they participate in trainings' (HR manager). The works council envisaged further agreements on maximum assignment duration, pay premiums, and formalized employment trajectories. However, not only the lack of co-determination rights but also German labour law constrained these efforts, ruling that agency work can be used 'temporarily', without defining what this means in terms of (maximum) duration. This caused problems as management used the vague legal definition to justify long assignments, and works councillors could not make use of legal resources to advocate for maximum assignment durations: 'According to the proper legal definition agency workers can only be used "temporarily" to cope with a high volume of orders. But how would you define temporarily? Two weeks? Six months? Five years?' (Works councillor, Metal-DE, 2014).

The 2012 metal sector agreement could become a crucial resource in achieving further local regulation, as it grants formal co-determination rights by empowering (user-firm) works councils to conclude workplace agreements on agency work, sets pay premiums according to assignment duration (the longer, the higher the premium), and specifies contractual upgrades after having worked for two years for the same user firm. In particular, the increasing price of agency work could limit its use out of cost considerations:

> The company's leeway regarding agency work has been considerably reduced by the 2012 agreement. This development is likely to cause big problems. Agency work has

always been a very good instrument for the company, and the unions should ask themselves if they do not risk the future of our plants in Germany. Agency work has helped the German economy a lot and we need this instrument of flexibility to keep up with market pressure.   (HR manager, Metal-DE, 2014)

By the time of data collection, the works council was discussing internally how to use the sectoral agreement in local bargaining. As a next step, they agreed to demand equal pay between regular and agency workers in addition to the collectively negotiated pay premiums, increasing the annual cost of agency work for Metal-DE by another €2 million.

Overall, Metal-DE's works council engaged in regulating temporary work, but the existing gaps, especially between regular and agency workers, could not be closed, leading to sustained inequalities. The works council's actions were constrained by an unfavourable legal system that lacked a strong enforcement of the equality principle and by missing co-determination rights before 2012. This agreement, however, could become a resource in future negotiations on the workplace regulation of agency work.

5.5. DISCUSSION AND CONCLUSION

The comparison of workplaces in the Belgian and German chemical and metal sectors sheds light on how and why trade unions respond to distinctive management use of exit options when deploying flexibility strategies. These strategies were characterized by fragmentation between a core and a peripheral workforce through outsourcing in the chemical industry on the one hand, and processes of internal segmentation in the metal industry on the other hand (see Table 5.2). We examined the extent to which and how local employee representatives created more or less encompassing structures to protect workers in heterogeneous national, sectoral, and workplace contexts, as well as their effects on patterns of precarious work. Findings show that differences in unions' access to and ability to mobilize both institutional and associational power resources shaped the observed outcomes.

First, unions had different resources due to more or less encompassing institutions at national and sector level. Here, differences in the extent of encompassing country-level collective bargaining and representation structures as well as national legislation were particularly important. The delegation or derogation capacity of multi-level bargaining systems created opportunities for employers to circumvent (parts of) agreements or differentiate pay and working conditions for different groups of workers. This opportunity was greater in Germany, where the equality principle between standard (permanent) and non-standard (temporary and agency work) by law was not enforced due to the existence of a valid sector-level agreement.

Under delegation (Belgium and Germany), sector-level agreements determine a wide range of issues and allow for additional local negotiations. In Belgium, however, the delegation principle provides a set of rules to be followed by management and unions when negotiating locally, restricting the deviation possibilities

Table 5.2. Outcomes for different groups of workers

	Chem-BE	Chem-DE	Metal-BE	Metal-DE
Permanent staff	High security and good working conditions for JTU staff	High security and good working conditions	High security and good working conditions	Degradation of working conditions in previous years
Fixed-term staff	Nearly the same provisions as permanent staff	Nearly the same provisions as permanent staff, but less job security and limited prospects (internally treated like agency workers)	Nearly the same provisions as permanent staff	Nearly the same provisions as permanent staff, but less job security
Agency workers	Improved regulation, i.e. fixed-term contracts for assignments longer than six months, screening tests for permanent positions	Concessions on a relatively high use in exchange for keeping non-chemical functions in-house, by far worse working conditions compared to permanent staff due to coverage by different sectoral agreement	Job security as major difference to permanent staff, equality principle strongly enforced (also regarding training, voluntary benefits)	Attempts of better regulating agency work, slight improvement of working conditions (agreements of maximum quota, training), but still large gap compared to permanent staff due to coverage by different sectoral agreement
Staff of contractors	No negotiation mandate for local unions	No negotiation mandate for local unions	No negotiation mandate for local unions	No negotiation mandate for local unions
Others	Non-chemical functions at threat of outsourcing (logistics), concessions to keep them inside (lower wages)	Non-chemical functions at threat of outsourcing (logistics, catering), concessions to keep them inside (agency work, two-tier wage system, unpaid working-time extension)	—	—

from (inter-)sector agreements. This established strong institutional and legal mechanisms in both sectors that facilitated the extension of bargaining to new industry entrants. It reduced the employers' room for segmenting work across different groups of workers, thereby fighting unfolding precariousness. In the chemical industry, delegation mechanisms and the legally set equality principle allowed the Belgian unions to accept employers' requests for externalization while strongly regulating its social effects by using inclusive institutional resources to keep transferred workers within the union's representation domain. Similarly, local unions and union-dominated works councils easily coordinated the negotiation of high levels of equality between permanent and temporary workers in Belgium.

In Germany, conversely, the mechanisms to extend bargaining are comparably weaker because workplace agreements can derogate from sectoral agreements through opening clauses. This offered local management the opportunity to push through flexibility measures, producing segmentation effects while restricting unions' ability to resist these changes. Works councils attempted to mediate employers' segmentation threats and strategies in both industries. They tried to keep as many workers as possible within their representation domain (chemical sector), or to get them in (metal sector). They were nevertheless constrained by the non-enforced equality principle and a general context of decentralization and liberalization, which made it difficult to react strongly to management's exit strategies and avoid growing segmentation. When concluding concessions, the German works councils weakly coordinated with sectoral unions compared to their Belgian counterparts, and mainly responded based on a logic of preserving job security for the core and extending flexibility for the periphery while safeguarding the economic interests of the company. Regarding the relatively large proportion of agency workers in the metal sector, the 2012 sectoral collective agreement has become a crucial resource increasing works councils' co-determination rights on agency work by empowering them to conclude local agreements.

Second, the power of unions to organize the workforce collectively to resist employers' flexibility strategies affected patterns of union responses. In both countries, local employee representatives attempted to secure the workforces' wages and working conditions using threats of industrial action. In other words, associational power, which refers to the resources and capabilities unions develop through collective organization (Kelly 1998), was used to contest local management's ability to further fragment pay and working conditions in Germany and Belgium. Because of more inclusive national institutions in Belgium, local unions easily coordinated between sector and local-level agreements with the support of union-dominated works councils. Associational power resources deriving from workplace organizing were used to retain the encompassing bargaining structures locally, which already provided good working conditions for different groups of workers in both sectors. Conversely, the gradual weakening of sector-level bargaining and the fragmented character of national institutions in Germany led local unions in the two industries to focus mainly on recompacting the segmentation effects created by the aforementioned fragmentation.

Belgian unions were able to turn their strategies into 'real' opportunities to fight segmentation in pay and working conditions, even in workplaces characterized by corporate strategies that encouraged high flexibilization. This did not only come along with the protection of permanent workforces, but also with a variety of local agreements improving the working conditions of peripheral workers employed on temporary contracts. While security for the former remained high, local unionists bargained security and good working conditions for workers on the margins, decreasing gaps between different groups of workers, thereby successfully reducing precarious work. Conversely, in Germany the works councils were challenged by the relatively large gap in working conditions between permanent and temporary (particularly agency) workers. This gap was caused by the non-enforcement of the equality principle (due to the existence of a valid sectoral agreement) and by the different standards set by collective agreements within the metal and the chemical sectors, as well as the temporary staffing agency industry. The German works councils successfully protected the core workforces from the worsening of their working conditions and from the threat of outsourcing. In so doing, they guaranteed decent levels of solidarity within the core. The works councils at Metal-DE also succeed in limiting the use of agency work and attempted to negotiate further local agreements by leveraging strike threats. However, they struggled to improve the working conditions of the agency workers substantially due to the lack of co-determination rights for user-firm works councils until the 2012 metal sector agreement. Unlike at Metal-DE, at Chem-DE, agency work was linked to concessions with regard to avoiding externalization.

The empirical findings presented in this chapter contribute to the literature on labour market change and dualization in coordinated market economies. They add evidence to debates on the political dynamics associated with segmentation and dualization. By analysing the processes leading to workplace arrangements in the German and Belgian metal and chemical industries, we demonstrate that unions were involved in processes of capacity building by creating encompassing structures and social institutions for the protection of the working conditions of different groups of workers, thereby limiting the growth of precarious work. This is in line with recent research highlighting the distinctiveness of industry-level institutions affecting the trajectory of institutional change and workforce segmentation (Benassi et al. 2016). However, our argument and findings go further, emphasizing that the extent of solidarity outcomes are the result of the mutual relationship between change in labour market institutions shaping—and being shaped by—union strategies at both sector and workplace levels.

Our cases illustrate that unions' capacity to organize collective responses to management's exit strategies was key to achieving encompassing workplace arrangements. However, the extent to which these responses produced 'solidaristic' effects depended on the national trajectories of labour market institutional change, for instance linked to the existence of legislative principles guaranteeing equality in pay and working conditions across different groups of workers and the coordination between sector and local levels regarding bargaining and worker representation structures. These factors constituted the socio-political conditions that, in turn, affected the extent to which risks of losing protection in the different workplaces could be recollectivized as powerful actors sought to defend the institutional order (Crouch 2015), thereby contesting precarious work.

Findings illustrate that in Germany, works councils made concessions to avoid outsourcing in the chemical sector by using more agency workers and to protect 'core' workers in the metal sector. Conversely, encompassing collective bargaining and representation structures, and national legislation in Belgium, substantially reduced the unions' need to incur concessions, while producing relatively higher 'solidaristic' effects. However, our findings also illustrate that institutions alone are not enough to achieve solidarity and protection. Associational union power, based on the capacity of the unions to mobilize among different groups of workers by relying on inclusive forms of solidarity, was necessary to maintain and strengthen institutional protection. The Belgian unions gained strength based on their proactive approach to regulate flexibility right from the start, which means that their strategy was not opposing flexibility, but regulating it in all its contractual forms (including agency work). In so doing, the Belgian unions successfully organized their workers, extended inclusive solidarity, and reduced precarious work. In contrast, their German counterparts initially opposed flexible forms of work, which meant that additional regulation related to agency work was only implemented ten years after its deregulation (Pulignano and Doerflinger 2013). The chapter achieves two aims. First, it shows that the political dynamics and processes shaping workplace arrangements are important in explaining the extent to which and how trade unions are successful (or not) in avoiding segmentation and precarious work. Second, it demonstrates that local unions can play a fundamental role in fighting segmentation and precarious work by building encompassing social structures, progressively reducing the effect of workplace inequality.

The chapter also illustrates that actors build their actions through—and by acting upon—diverse institutional levels, e.g. legislation as well as bargaining and representation structures at national, sectoral, and local levels, which are mutually interdependent. Understanding how this interdependency is produced and the conditions fostering it are crucial to explaining why unions succeed or fail when responding to management flexibility strategies that challenge solidarity. This implies bridging between analyses focusing on the resilience of national institutions (Thelen 2014), and those examining the politics of institutional change at both sector and organizational levels (Benassi et al. 2016).

ACKNOWLEDGEMENTS

This chapter is drawn from the research project G.0773.11N 'Multinationals in Europe between Flexibility and Security', funded by the Flemish Research Council FWO.

REFERENCES

Benassi, Chiara, Doellgast, Virginia, and Sarmiento-Mirwaldt, Katja. 2016. 'Institutions and Inequality in Liberalizing Markets: Explaining Different Trajectories of Institutional Change in Social Europe'. *Politics and Society*, 44(1): 117–42.

Beynon, Hugh, Grimshaw, Damian, Rubery, Jill, and Ward, Kevin. 2002. *Managing Employment Change: The New Realities of Work*. Oxford: Oxford University Press.

Buchholz, Sandra, Kolb, Kathrin, Hofäcker, Dirk, and Blossfeld, Hans-Peter. 2011. 'Globalized Labour Markets and Social Inequality in Europe: Theoretical Framework'. In *Globalized Labour Markets and Social Inequality in Europe*, edited by Hans-Peter Blossfeld, Sandra Buchholz, Kathrin Kolb, and Dirk Hofäcker. Basingstoke: Palgrave Macmillan.

Carlin, Wendy and Soskice, David. 2009. 'German Economic Performance: Disentangling the Role of Supply-Side Reforms, Macroeconomic Policy and Coordinated Economy Institutions'. *Socio-Economic Review*, 7(1): 67–99.

Crouch, Colin. 2015. 'Labour Market Governance and the Creation of Outsiders'. *British Journal of Industrial Relations*, 53(1): 27–48.

Eichhorst, Werner, and Marx, Paul. 2011. 'Reforming German Labour Market Institutions: A Dual Path to Flexibility'. *Journal of European Social Policy*, 21(1): 73–87.

Eichhorst, Werner, Marx, Paul, and Tobsch, Verena. 2015. 'Non-Standard Employment across Occupations in Germany: The Role of Replaceability and Labour Market Flexibility'. In *Non-Standard Employment in Post-Industrial Labour Markets*, edited by Werner Eichhorst and Paul Marx. Cheltenham: Edward Elgar.

Emmenegger, Patrick, Häusermann, Silja, Palier, Bruno, and Seeleib-Kaiser, Martin. 2012. *The Age of Dualization: The Changing Face of Inequality in Deindustrializing Societies*. New York: Oxford University Press.

Esping-Andersen, Gösta. 1990. *The Three Worlds of Welfare Capitalism*. Cambridge: Polity Press.

Grimshaw, Damian, and Rubery, Jill. 1998. 'Integrating the Internal and External Labour Markets'. *Cambridge Journal of Economics*, 22: 199–220.

Hassel, Anke. 2015. 'Trade Unions and the Future of Democratic Capitalism'. In *The Politics of Advanced Capitalism*, edited by Pablo Beramendi, Silja Häusermann, Herbert Kitschelt, and Hanspeter Kriesi. Cambridge: Cambridge University Press.

Hassel, Anke, and Schiller, Christoph. 2010. *Der Fall Hartz IV*. Frankfurt: Campus Verlag.

Häusermann, Silja and Schwander, Hanna. 2012. 'Varieties of Dualization? Labor Market Segmentation and Insider–Outsider Divides across Regimes'. In *The Age of Dualization: The Changing Face of Inequality in Deindustrializing Societies*, edited by Patrick Emmenegger et al. Oxford: Oxford University Press.

Houwing, Hester and Vandaele, Kurt. 2011. 'Liberal Convergence, Growing Outcome Divergence? Institutional Continuity and Changing Trajectories in the "Low Countries"'. In *The Changing Political Economies of Small West European Countries*, edited by Uwe Becker. Amsterdam: Amsterdam University Press.

Kalleberg, Arne. 2009. 'Precarious Work, Insecure Workers: Employment Relations in Transition'. *American Sociological Review*, 74: 1–22.

Kelly, John. 1998. *Rethinking Industrial Relations: Mobilisation, Collectivism and Long Waves*. London: Routledge.

Koch, Max and Fritz, Martin. 2013. *Non-Standard Employment in Europe: Paradigms, Prevalence and Policy Responses*. Basingstoke: Palgrave.

Osterman, Paul. 1994. 'How Common is Workplace Transformation and Who Adopts It?' *ILR Review*, 47(2): 173–88.

Peck, Jamie, and Theodore, Nik. 2007. 'Variegated Capitalism'. *Progress in Human Geography*, 31(6): 731–72.

Polanyi, Karl. 1944. *The Great Transformation*. New York: Farrar & Rinehart.

Pulignano, Valeria and Doerflinger, Nadja. 2013. 'A Head with Two Tales? Trade Unions' Influence on Addressing Temporary Agency Workers Security while Enhancing Flexibility in Belgian and German Workplaces'. *International Journal of Human Resource Management*, 24: 4149–65.

Pulignano, Valeria, Doerflinger, Nadja, and De Franceschi, Fabio. 2016. 'Flexibility and Security within European Labour Markets: The Role of Local Bargaining and the "Trade-Offs" within Multinationals' Subsidiaries in Belgium, Britain and Germany'. *ILR Review*, 69(3): 605–30.

Stone, Katherine and Arthurs, Harry. 2013. 'The Transformation of Employment Regimes: A World-Wide Challenge'. In *Rethinking Workplace Regulation: Beyond the Standard Contract of Employment*, edited by Katherine Stone and Harry Arthurs. New York: Russell Sage.

Thelen, Kathleen. 2014. *Varieties of Liberalization and the New Politics of Social Solidarity*. Cambridge: Cambridge University Press.

Wiesenthal, Helmut, and Clasen, Ralf. 2003. 'Gewerkschaften in Politik und Gesellschaft: Von der Gestaltungsmacht zum Traditionswächter?' In *Die Gewerkschaften in Politik und Gesellschaft der Bundesrepublik Deutschland: Ein Handbuch*, edited by Wolfgang Schroeder and Bernhard Weßels. Wiesbaden: Westdeutscher Verlag.

6

The Political Economy of Agency Work in Italy and Germany

Explaining Diverging Trajectories in Collective Bargaining Outcomes

Chiara Benassi and Lisa Dorigatti

6.1. INTRODUCTION

Countries in Continental and Southern Europe were traditionally characterized by strong industrial relations institutions and encompassing sectoral collective agreements, high employment protection legislation, and, overall, well-regulated labour markets. As a result, stable employment relationships were predominant and the pay structure was relatively homogeneous and compressed (Amable 2003; Hall and Soskice 2001). In the last thirty years, however, labour market deregulation, the expansion of the private service sector, and the increase of unemployment have contributed to the growth of unstable low-paid jobs in these countries, leading to increasingly segmented and unequal labour markets (Emmenegger et al. 2012; Eichhorst and Marx 2015; Palier and Thelen 2010).

In this context, unions' responses to growing precarious work have been strongly debated. An influential stream in the political economy literature claimed that unions contribute to the 'dualization' of the labour market: they make concessions at the expense of the marginal workforce in order to maintain both the standards of wages and working conditions of their core constituencies and their (eroding) institutional bargaining power (Hassel 2014; Palier and Thelen 2010). In contrast, scholars in the field of industrial relations have analysed the conditions under which unions are likely to pursue exclusive or inclusive strategies. Findings showed a range of factors shaping unions' strategic preferences, including institutions such as employment protection legislation and the centralization of decision making (Oliver 2011; Gordon 2015); labour market competition between core and peripheral workers (Benassi and Dorigatti 2015; MacKenzie 2009); trade unions' organizational interests (Davidsson and Emmenegger 2013); and trade unions' ideologies (Benassi and Vlandas 2016; Pulignano and Doerflinger 2013; Dorigatti 2017; Marino 2012).

A second stream of literature has analysed unions' success in representing atypical workers, and therefore focused mainly on the power resources unions can use for this purpose. Studies at national, sectoral, and workplace levels showed that union effectiveness depended on their strategic ability to use a combination of institutional power derived from regulations and bargaining structures (such as union density, labour market legislation, and the structure of sectoral collective bargaining), and associational power derived from collective organization (e.g. the ability of different trade unions to cooperate and to mobilize workers) (Benassi et al. 2016; Doellgast et al. 2009; Wagner and Refslund 2016; Pulignano and Signoretti 2016; Chapter 5, this volume).

This chapter aims to contribute to this latter stream of literature by analysing the conditions supporting trade unions' success in regulating agency work in the metal sector in Germany and Italy. We focus on trade unions' effectiveness in limiting the use of agency workers, improving their pay and conditions, and increasing their rate of transition to permanent jobs. We argue that the interaction between institutional factors and internal divides within the labour movement, as well as unions' ability to overcome those divides, affect unions' capacity to represent precarious workers.

The comparative analysis shows, first, that collective bargaining's effectiveness for regulating agency work varies between the two countries and, second, that it evolved differently over time. In each country, we distinguish between two phases. In Italy, the first phase (1998–2002) is characterized by encompassing negotiated regulation constraining employers' use of agency work, while in the second phase (2003–15) collective bargaining weakened as the two more moderate unions, FIM and UILM (Federazione Italiana Metalmeccanici and Unione Italiana Lavoratori Metalmeccanici), agreed on concessions in regard to agency worker quotas and transition to permanent employment. Agency workers still benefit from legal rights to equal treatment and pay, but trade unions' ability to control the expansion of this employment form, and to improve the employment security of these workers, has progressively declined over time.

In Germany, the regulation of agency work progressively weakened during the 1990s, but the turning point were the Hartz reforms in 2003, which heavily deregulated the use of agency work; the legal regulation of the phenomenon improved only in the last few years. In the first phase (2003–6), divides between different sectoral unions and between unions and works councils prevented IG Metall from coordinating sectoral collective bargaining, with negative implications for its regulation. However, the union was later able gradually to improve the wages and employment security of these workers and to limit employers' use of this form of employment (2007–15).

Hence, we identify two different trajectories in the effectiveness of IG Metall and of the three Italian metal unions to reduce the use of agency work and to ensure better working conditions for these workers: in Italy, regulation became less encompassing; while in Germany, it set low standards and then progressively improved. These differences can be explained by looking at the interaction between national laws regulating agency work, which provide institutional power resources to labour at sectoral and workplace levels, and the divides internal to the labour movement, which undermine solidaristic action necessary to build or sustain associational power. These two factors interact over time:

labour market deregulation creates room for employer strategies to exploit the divides within labour, therefore preventing the reregulation of agency work through coordinated bargaining action. Unions can try to overcome these divides and rebuild encompassing regulation, but their success will depend on the nature and structure of the divides themselves.

The chapter unfolds as follows. The following section presents comparative data on the diffusion of agency work in Italy and Germany and illustrates the main differences in each country's legislative framework. The third section summarizes German and Italian metal unions' different strategies towards agency workers. The fourth section explains these differences based on comparative case study findings. We conclude with a discussion of the implication of our cases for studying the role of trade unions in segmented labour markets.

6.2. METHOD AND CASE SELECTION

We examine sectoral and national developments in the regulation of agency work through the analysis of collective agreements, trade unions' publications, and over sixty semi-structured interviews with trade unionists at workplace and sectoral levels. We compare broad trends at firm level through the analysis of works councils' surveys (available for the German case), trade unions' and works councils' publications, and through semi-structured interviews with plant-level employee representatives and sectoral union representatives in charge of supporting workplace bargaining in the two countries.

We focus on the Italian and German metal sector because the cases are critical for debates on the role of trade unions in labour market segmentation. The dualization literature argues that Continental and Southern European trade unions—and in particular those in core sectors such as the metal sector—exacerbate inequalities in the labour market by focusing on the protection of their members at the expense of unorganized, precarious workers (Hassel 2014; Palier and Thelen 2010). The focus on these case studies thus gives more leverage to our claim that unions are willing and, to some extent, able to extend collective agreements and negotiate employment protections for precarious workers. We look at agency work because it is the most widespread form of atypical work in the metal sector in both countries, and because its use has significantly increased over the last twenty years. In Italy, the number of agency workers with at least a one-hour assignment increased from 106,700 in 2000 to 482,100 in 2013. The majority (52 per cent) were employed in manufacturing. In Germany, there were only 42,000 agency workers in 1985, growing to over 960,000 in 2015, of which 29 per cent were employed in the metal and electronics industry. Company-level case studies in the metal sector found that agency work was concentrated in large companies and could reach 30–40 per cent of employees, constituting a stable but flexible segment of the workforce (Holst et al. 2009).

The two countries are similar in terms of their dual labour market and sectoral collective bargaining structures, but there are also some important differences. First, in Germany there is only one major trade union confederation, the DGB; while in Italy there are three main union confederations, which are distinctive in their ideological orientation. The CGIL has communist roots, CISL is catholic, and UIL used to be close to the Socialist Party. IG Metall is the only union negotiating a sectoral agreement with the German metal employers, while in Italy FIOM-CGIL, FIM-CISL, and UILM-UIL have traditionally bargained sectoral agreements together, even though FIOM (Federazione Impiegati Operai Metallurgici) represents the majority of trade union members in the sector.

Second, the German system of industrial relations is based on dual channel representation, while the Italian model is single channel. In Germany, works councillors at plant and at company level have extensive co-determination rights, and they are not necessarily union representatives—with a formal commitment to represent the interests of both the company and the company's workforce. In Italy, by contrast, workplace representatives only have consultation and information rights, and they are usually union representatives.

Third, the standards set by sectoral agreements in Germany can be amended at workplace level through opening clauses, while in Italy the favourability principle preventing workplace derogations is still widely applied. Within the context of increased employer pressure on sectoral agreements and requests for more bargaining freedom at company level, labour representatives at this level have come under pressure to reduce labour costs in order not to undermine the company's competitiveness. The wider applicability of the favourability principle thus constitutes an important power resource for Italian unions.

In Section 6.3, we explore how these similarities and differences contributed to influencing trade unions' strategies towards agency workers and their effectiveness in reducing precarity.

6.3. COLLECTIVE BARGAINING OUTCOMES FOR AGENCY WORKERS IN THE GERMAN AND ITALIAN METAL SECTOR

The success of trade union strategies in regulating agency work varied between the German and Italian metal sector in regard to three outcomes: wages and working conditions, prospects for permanent hiring, and employers' discretion in using this form of employment. In the two countries, we distinguish two phases. In Italy, the first phase (1998–2002) is characterized by positive bargaining outcomes for agency workers, while in Germany they were quite poor between 2003 and 2007. In the second phase in Italy (2003–15), the bargained regulation of agency work eroded and led to a deterioration of working standards, while in Germany (2007–15), unions managed to achieve positive bargaining outcomes, reducing the gap between permanent and temporary work.

6.3.1. First Phase

Italian law prescribes that agency workers benefit from equal treatment, and trade unions closely monitor the enforcement of this provision. Moreover, the unions responsible for negotiations in the agency sector, Nidil-CGIL, Felsa-CISL, and

UIL Temp, set additional benefits in the sectoral collective agreements immediately after the law introducing agency work was passed in 1997 (196/1997). They introduced income support in cases of sickness, accident, maternity, or unemployment, some welfare benefits (such childcare bonuses, healthcare refunds, and territorial mobility supports), and the right to further training. These benefits are provided by two bilateral funds, Forma.temp and EBITEMP, to which agencies are obliged to devolve 4 per cent of agency workers' salaries to training and income support and an additional 0.2 per cent to welfare benefits (Burroni and Pedaci 2014). While the collective agreement in the agency sector did not set any constraints on employers' use of agency work, the metal unions were able to introduce strong limitations in the 1999 sectoral collective agreement, slowing down the liberalization processes defined by the law (Altieri et al. 2005). This agreement specified the cases in which agency work could be used, and introduced a maximum quota of 8 per cent of the companies' total workforce. The sectoral agreements neither in the metal sector nor in the agency sector set transition rules from agency contracts to permanent contracts.

In Germany, sectoral collective bargaining for agency workers started with the 2003 Hartz labour market reforms, which weakened formerly strict agency worker regulations and opened a bargaining arena for unions and staffing agencies' associations. The first sectoral agreement in the agency sector, for instance, which was negotiated in 2004 by a special bargaining body comprising representatives from all sectoral unions of the German Trade Union Confederation DGB, set wages that were 30–40 per cent lower than the salaries for permanent workers in the metal sector (Benassi and Dorigatti 2015: 540). At the time, the implementation of equal pay and equal treatment rules, of limitations to the use of agency work (e.g. through the use of quotas), and of transition rules from agency to permanent contracts was left to the discretion of works councils. In some cases, such as Daimler, Audi, and Ford, works councils managed to negotiate company-level agreements regulating agency work (Benassi 2013; Dorigatti 2017). But often works councils did not regulate the phenomenon at all (Promberger et al. 2006; Wassermann and Rudolph 2007), or even used agency workers as a cheap flexibility buffer and agreed to lower wages and working conditions, such as in the case of the staffing agency at Volkswagen (Greer 2008).

6.3.2. Second Phase

In Italy, the regulation of employment conditions for agency workers has not changed in the last ten years. The collective agreement in the agency sector was renewed several times (in 2003, 2008, and 2014) and the unions were able to improve welfare provisions directed to agency workers (such as refunds for dental and medical care, income support in case of accident or disability, maternity and childcare support) (Burroni and Pedaci 2014). At the same time, the measures regarding permanent hiring and limiting the use of agency work weakened over time. In regard to the former, the sectoral agreement in the agency sector established that agency workers should be hired after forty-two months of continuous employment in 2008 but then removed the transition rule in 2014. In 2008 the metal agreement introduced the rule to hire agency workers after forty-four months of (even non-continuous) employment via an agency or temporary contract, which has been maintained so far. In contrast, the requirement to specify the reasons for hiring agency workers was relaxed over time and then eliminated from the metal agreement in 2014. Parallel to the deterioration of regulation in the metal sector, around 1,000 company-level agreements were achieved by the left-wing metal union FIOM in 2003–4, in companies such as Lamborghini (FIOM 2004). These agreements set quotas around 10–20 per cent, required employers to specify the reasons for hiring agency workers, and set a rule that agency workers should be permanently hired after about twelve months. Similar agreements were negotiated in other metal companies in the following years, often as a joint initiative of all three unions, but this regulation was never extended to the sectoral level, and therefore it only applies to a small segment of the sector's workforce.

In contrast to Italy, the regulation of agency work improved along all three dimensions in Germany. In the agency sector, the DGB bargaining body achieved an agreement in 2011, and its lowest salary level was extended by law to the whole sector until the introduction of the national minimum wage in January 2015. However, salaries remain higher in the metal sector, even though IG Metall has managed to reduce the gap between metal workers and agency workers. After a successful campaign on agency work launched in 2007, IG Metall signed a collective agreement setting equal pay for agency workers in the steel sector in 2010; furthermore, in 2012 a collective agreement between IG Metall and the staffing agencies' associations introduced a system of salary bonuses for agency workers that aims to close the gap between them and direct hires after nine months of uninterrupted assignment. The bonuses work as follows: after six weeks the agency workers get 15 per cent more, 20 per cent more after three months, 30 per cent after five months, 45 per cent after seven months, and 50 per cent after nine months. The 2012 collective agreement for metal and electronics strengthens works councils' co-determination rights in hiring companies by defining specific cases in which agency workers can be hired, and sets regulations for securing the permanent hiring of agency workers. If company agreements do not state otherwise, after eighteen months of continuous assignment, metal firms have to consider permanent hiring. After twenty-four months hiring is compulsory. In addition, the agreement strengthens co-determination rights for works councils when it comes to hire agency workers. As a consequence of the campaign and of improved co-determination, more than 1,200 agreements were signed at company level, setting better wages and working conditions for agency workers. Several workplace agreements also set maximum quotas, which, however, vary across companies.

The characteristics of agency work regulation in the two countries and in the two phases, as well as its trajectory, are reported in Table 6.1. Summing up, we can argue that the bargaining outcomes for agency workers in the metal sector diverge over time between the two countries. In Italy, agency work was initially tightly regulated through sectoral collective agreements, which progressively weakened over time. In contrast, in the German metal sector the regulation of agency work weakened after the Hartz reforms in 2003, but since 2007 it started improving thanks to collective agreements at workplace level and, most of all, at sectoral level.

Table 6.1. Regulation of agency work in Germany and Italy

Germany	Italy
2003–6	1998–2002
Employment conditions:	*Employment conditions*:
	Law: equal pay
Sectoral level (agency): lower wages than direct workers	Sectoral level (agency): additional benefits (e.g. income support and further training)
Workplace level: few company-level agreements setting equal pay	
Limits to employers' discretion:	*Limits to employers' discretion*:
Sectoral level: none (no quotas)	Sectoral level (metal): quota (8%) and definition of the cases in which agency work can be used
Workplace level: in some companies agency work used as a buffer, in some companies quotas	
Transition to permanent employment:	*Transition to permanent employment*:
Sectoral level: no rules	Sectoral level: none
Workplace level: few agreements setting transition rules	Workplace level: few workplace agreements setting transition rules
2007–15	2003–15
Employment conditions:	*Employment conditions*:
Sectoral level: sectoral bonuses (metal); minimum salary (agency)	Sectoral level (agency): strengthening of the benefits
Workplace: over 1,200 agreements setting equal pay	
Limits to employers' discretion:	*Limits to employers' discretion*:
Sectoral level: strengthening of co-determination rights for works councils	Sectoral level (metal): requirement to specify the reasons for hiring agency workers progressively relaxed (and removed in 2014)
Workplace: over 1,200 agreements setting different quotas	Workplace level: several agreements (over 1,000 *pre-contratti* in 2003–4, other later) setting quota (generally around 10–20%) and conditions for hiring agency workers
Transition to permanent employment:	*Transition to permanent employment*:
Sectoral level: obligation to hire directly after twenty-four months of assignment	Sectoral level: obligation to hire after forty-two months introduced (2008) and then lifted (2014) (agency); obligation to hire after forty-four months (2008) (metal)
Workplace level: over 1,200 agreements setting rules for transition (shorter/longer than sectoral)	Workplace level: over 1,000 *pre-contratti* in 2003–4 (plus some later) setting obligation to hire directly, usually after twelve months
Trajectory over the two phases	*Trajectory over the two phases*
Employment conditions: ↑	Employment conditions: =
Limits to employers' discretion: ↑	Limits to employers' discretion: ↓
Transitions to permanent employment: ↑	Transitions to permanent employment: ↓

6.4. EXPLAINING DIFFERENT COLLECTIVE BARGAINING STRATEGIES AND OUTCOMES

Section 6.3 illustrated the two different trajectories in the regulation of agency work at sectoral level. This cross-country variation can be explained through the interaction between two distinct power resources available to labour:

(1) institutional power resources, and in particular the evolving legislation of agency work, which granted unions and works councils different bargaining room on the issue; and (2) associational power derived from the capacity to overcome divides and promote solidaristic action within the labour movement. This section discusses how these factors interact and shows that the deregulation of the legislative framework exacerbated already existing (but at least dormant) divides within labour, which employers exploited in order to weaken restrictions on segmentation-based strategies. Labour could effectively counteract the casualization of the employment relationship when it managed to overcome such divides and coordinate bargaining activities.

6.4.1. T1-Germany: Weakening Regulation and Divided Labour (2003–6)

In Germany, agency work was first allowed in 1972 by the Temporary Employment Act, which also set strong limits on its use. The maximum duration of assignments was three months, and staffing agencies were not allowed to employ workers on contracts of the same duration as their assignment at the hiring company or to rehire the same agency worker on another agency contract right after the end of the assignment. Furthermore, fixed-term contracts were banned at the time. As the regulation was strict and agency work very limited, initially unions did not put great effort into bargaining in the agency sector. Only one collective agreement was signed in those years between the association of staffing agencies and the German white-collar union (Deutsche Angestellten-Gewerkschaft), but it applied only to white-collar workers while most of the agency workers were employed in the manufacturing sector. In the 1980s, the DGB unions refused to bargain an agreement for the whole sector with UZA, which wanted to improve the reputation of the agency sector, because the unions (including IG Metall) were radically opposed to the use of agency work and therefore did not want to show any political acceptance by bargaining on the issue (Vitols 2008). IG Metall maintained a firm opposition to agency work though the 1970s and 1980s, and in the 1989 congress it decided not to sign any collective agreement with staffing agencies because that would have weakened the union's opposition to that form of 'modern slave trade' (IG Metall 1992).

In this phase, the unions did not bargain, but they focused on lobbying political actors in order to reintroduce the ban against this form of employment instead of trying to regulate the sector (Vitols 2008: 150). However, due to the political marginalization of unions and the difficult economic conditions at the time, this strategy could not prevent the liberalization of *Modell Deutschland* initiated by the social democratic party at the end of the 1990s in order to reduce the high unemployment rate and to increase Germany's competitiveness as a production site. The reform plan 'Agenda 2010' culminated with the Hartz labour market reforms in 2003, which heavily deregulated agency work (Upchurch et al. 2009). The reforms lifted any limitation to rehiring agency workers on agency contracts and to the duration of their assignment, and eliminated the *Synchronisationsverbot* (i.e. the prohibition for agencies to hire workers for a time span corresponding to the duration of their mission in the user company). The Hartz reforms also introduced the application of the equal pay principle from the first day of assignment—since 1997 this had applied only after twelve months of assignment—but allowed its amendment via collective agreement.

Given the high unemployment rate, political and societal consensus was built around the necessity to flexibilize the labour market and to deregulate agency work. This put pressure on the DGB unions to give up their opposition strategy and to collaborate in regulating these contracts (Vitols 2008: 189–93). As illustrated by a DGB union representative in Berlin, the social democratic government pressured the DGB unions to bargain an agreement with the staffing agencies (see also Aust et al. 2007: 244; Vitols 2008: 197): 'We got the following signal (from the government): "The DGB regulates the working conditions." We then thought: "OK, if we can regulate it, then we can let ourselves in for it"' (DGB union official, 2011).

However, deregulation contributed to creating or reviving divides in the German labour movement between DGB unions (including IG Metall) and the competing Christian trade unions as well as between IG Metall and the works councils. The legislative loophole in the principle of equal pay provided more bargaining room to employers, who undermined the traditional bargaining monopoly of DGB in all other economic sectors. During the negotiations between the DGB bargaining body and two staffing agencies' associations, a third agencies' association also bargained a collective agreement with the Christian Federation of Trade Unions, setting low wages and working conditions. However, as a result of the competing agreement, the DGB signed an agreement with poor outcomes. During an interview in the headquarters in Berlin, the DGB representative indeed reported that:

> when the ink on the agreement (between the DGB and the staffing agencies) was not dry yet, the Christian unions had already signed an agreement. Then we had no influence on it anymore. We could basically only copy and paste from them and add a little something on top.   (DGB union official, 2011)

Labour market deregulation re-enforced the divide between works councils and IG Metall, which had become increasingly evident due to the decentralization of collective bargaining during the 1990s. Opening clauses started spreading as instruments of co-management at workplace level, weakening the political linkages which made works councils serve as an 'extended union arm' in the workplace (Streeck 1984). The diffusion of workplace agreements in the metal sector was also encouraged by the difficult economic conditions after reunification with East Germany and the increasing threat of outsourcing production to cheaper locations in Eastern Europe (Rehder 2003). In such negotiations, concessions on the use of agency work were made, implicitly or explicitly, in order to avoid plant closure or outsourcing or, more generally, in order to increase the cost competitiveness of production. In this context, agency workers have been used as a buffer to protect the core workforce in case of downward demand peaks (Jürgens and Krzywdzinski 2006). Most interviewees pointed out the difficult position of works councils when it comes to bargaining over agency work because they are not as politically independent from the company as the sectoral union. An IG Metall representative based in the union's headquarters explained this ambiguity:

> I think that there have always been companies which let themselves be put under pressure and, I say this all the time, were politically weak, badly organised and maybe

with a works council, which was not politicised in regard to these issues. I would also mention another category constituted by those (works councils) who were under pressure in big companies, in particular the question what happens if the company comes to me and says 'we are competing internationally, these three car models are going to be produced, and we can do it in Bochum, in Kassel or in Wolfsburg, but ultimately we can also build the car in Poland, Bulgaria or somewhere else'.

(IG Metall official, 2012)

The literature contains several examples of this type of concession bargaining. At the beginning of 2000s at Volkswagen, the works council agreed, after some resistance, to the constitution of two internal staffing agencies, WOB AG and Autovision, which were covered by collective agreements setting lower wages and working conditions (Benassi 2013; Greer 2008). However, there also are several cases in which works councils adopted more inclusive strategies and opposed agency work in order to avoid the segmentation of working conditions between different groups. This occurred at Opel (Jürgens and Krzywdzinski 2006), Daimler and Audi (Dorigatti 2017), and Ford (Benassi 2013). According to the same union official, the response of the works councils depended greatly on their political orientation and on their organizational strength.

6.4.2. TI-Italy: Strong Regulation and a United Labour Front (1997–2002)

In Italy, until 1997 agency work was banned altogether. The law introducing agency work was agreed upon by social partners during trilateral negotiations, which produced the 'Pact for Employment' in 1996. Similar to the DGB unions at the time of the Hartz reforms, unions accepted the labour market reform due to the difficult situation of the labour market after the 1993–5 recession, when the already low Italian employment rate fell to only slightly more than 50 per cent and overall unemployment rose above 10 per cent (and to as much as 26 per cent in the south and to 30 per cent among young workers) (Alacevich 2000, Molina and Rhodes 2007: 805). However, unlike in Germany, trade unions were more centrally involved in the reforms, and the new framework was stricter in constraining the use of agency work. According to the law 196/1997, agency work was prohibited for low-skill activities and permitted only under specified circumstances, e.g. for substituting workers on leave and for acquiring skills required only temporarily in production and therefore not present among the permanent workforce. Agency work thus had a strong temporary character and was limited to middle- and high-level qualifications. The law shifted the responsibility for identifying further cases in which agency work could be deployed to sectoral collective agreements, thereby encouraging its regulation within industries. Moreover, an equal treatment provision ensured that agency workers benefitted from pay and conditions equal to permanent workers. Lastly, the law introduced a compulsory contribution to a sectoral bipartite fund co-managed by employers' associations and trade unions, which primarily focused on further training. Hence, this law constituted a favourable point of departure for regulating agency work at the sectoral level and for setting sectoral standards of wages and working conditions, as described in Section 6.3. As a union representative of the CGIL union for atypical workers told us: 'the fact that the law itself, when agency work was introduced, would set certain constraints made trade unions' intervention easier to a certain extent'.

As a result, the three confederal unions for atypical workers could coordinate their bargaining strategy and negotiate with the staffing agencies' associations as a united labour front more easily than in the German case. The agreement on agency work at sectoral level set benefits in terms of training and pay between assignments that went beyond the legislative standards (Tiraboschi and Tomassetti 2015). Furthermore, the metal agreement signed by all three unions in 1999 limited the use of agency work to 8 per cent and only under certain specific circumstances. As argued by Altieri et al. (2005), the aim of the agreements was to slow down the liberalization process triggered by the law. While employers in Germany could exploit the weak legislation and competing agreements at company level and at sectoral level, the legislation and the collective agreements in Italy provided a level playing field for the whole sector in regard to the use of agency work. Therefore, the workplace agreements on agency work— only one in ten company-level agreements in Lombardy's metalworking industry during the period 1999–2001 (Ballarino 2005)—only set provisions above the sectoral standards, e.g. the amount of productivity bonus to be paid to agency workers and rules concerning the transition from agency to permanent contract.

6.4.3. T2-Germany: Overcoming Divides for Collective Bargaining and Strengthening Regulation (2007–15)

The collective agreement in Germany's agency sector was renewed in 2006 and 2010, progressively improving the standards of agency workers. In 2011, the DGB achieved a collective agreement whose lowest salary level was extended by law as a minimum wage for the whole sector in 2012, until the introduction of the national minimum wage in January 2015. Despite this agreement, the standards in the agency sector remained much lower than in the metal sector. Therefore, IG Metall still needed to raise the standards of agency workers in the metal sector in order to avoid wage dumping and to create a common bargaining floor for works councils, whose bargaining activities were very difficult to coordinate. Against this background, and given that the government was not going to agree on new strong equal pay legislation in the short term, IG Metall made bargaining at sectoral level a priority. In 2007, the 21st IG Metall Congress in Lipsia approved the launch of the national campaign 'Same Work, Same Wage', which aimed at recruiting agency workers and including them in the traditional structures of representation. The campaign was developed at two levels: IG Metall tried to engage works councillors and union officials in collective bargaining at firm and sectoral level; at national level, IG Metall focused on political lobbying, building the pressure of public opinion on employers and government through a confrontational media campaign. Agency work was represented as an unfair strategy of greedy employers, who make profits by producing negative externalities for the whole of society and by breaking the social contract characterizing the economy of postwar Germany. The initiatives included a campaign truck that was sent to different

German cities, a postcard action that made visible people's support for the initiative, and several billboards highlighting the wage differentials between agency workers and regular employees and the 'trap effect' of agency contracts. These initiatives publicly blamed employers in order to increase unions' bargaining leverage (Benassi and Dorigatti 2015).

Thanks to the above-mentioned campaign, IG Metall could regain control over the standard-setting process at workplace level by encouraging works councils to pursue the same bargaining goals. Even though existing research suggests that there still is variation across plants (e.g. Benassi 2013; Pulignano and Doerflinger 2013), the campaign has clearly influenced workplace bargaining in the intended direction. A few years after the beginning of the campaign, more than 1,200 firms had signed agreements setting quotas for the utilization of agency work, better working conditions for agency workers (such as equal pay with direct workers), and stronger co-determination rights for works councils (IG Metall 2017). Most of all, however, IG Metall took advantage of its monopolistic bargaining position and negotiated sectoral agreements that improved the wages and working conditions of agency workers. In 2010 an equal pay agreement was achieved in the steel sector, while the 2012 metal collective agreement broadened co-determination rights and set transition rules. Parallel to the annual sectoral bargaining round, IG Metall conducted a separate and successful bargaining round on salary bonuses directly with the staffing agencies, because the hiring companies cannot negotiate higher wages for agency workers given that they are not those workers' direct employers. In order to put pressure on the staffing agencies and the employers on the issue of agency work, IG Metall refused to negtiate wages for the metal sector and threatened strikes until the salary bonuses were agreed.

These sectoral agreements helped to limit cross-company competition, as an IG Metall representative who was in charge of the campaign suggested:

> It makes sense to say: 'Collective agreements are there in order to switch off salary competition among workers.' There should be competition about the product, the services, but not about the salaries. The agency workers brought this competition in the companies and a company alone cannot really regulate it without putting itself at risk and therefore it was necessary and right to regulate it at national level and through the hiring companies (rather than the agencies) and through politics.
>
> (IG Metall official, 2011)

The legislation partly supported this reregulation process of agency work, even though it introduced neither the equal pay principle nor the equal treatment principle. In regard to wages, in 2010 the Federal Labour Court declared the Christian union 'not able to conduct collective bargaining' because it was too weak to ensure good standards of wages and working conditions for its members. As a result, even the past collective agreements were declared as non-valid, and many agency workers were able to claim additional salaries from their (former) employers and social security (Hensche 2016). Furthermore, in 2012 a legal minimum wage for the agency sector was introduced. The legislation also tried to prevent companies from substituting the permanent workforce with cheap, flexible agency workers by specifying in 2011 that companies should hire agency workers only on a 'temporary basis', even though the legislation does not clearly define the term 'temporary' (Bundesagentur für Arbeit 2016), and since 2012 by prohibiting companies from rehiring dismissed workers on agency contracts. Furthermore, co-determination rights have been expanded. Different decisions of the Federal Labour Court have specified that: employers need works councils' approval for hiring agency workers; that they need to provide information on the characteristics of agency workers, their job position, and the length of the assignment; and that works councils can refuse the hiring of agency workers who are not only 'temporarily' employed and have the right to contest the dismissal of permanent workers if agency workers are employed in the company as their job positions are considered as 'free' (DGB 2013). Finally, since 2013 the number of agency workers also counts towrads determining the size of works councils (IG Metall Zoom 2016).

The reregulation of agency work offered additional support to the initiatives of works councils and unions. For instance, the law specifying that agency workers can be employed only temporarily was used by the BMW works council in Leipzig to bring the management to the local labour court because agency workers were employed for years in the same job positions without any prospects of securing a permanent contract (Benassi 2013). The same legislative change provided a good basis for the collective agreement achieved by IG Metall in 2012, which allows works councils to prevent the hiring of agency workers if they do represent a threat to the standards of permanent workers, e.g. substitution of permanent contracts through agency contracts (IG Metall Bezirk Mitte 2012).

6.4.4. T2-Italy: Expanding Divides and Weakening Regulation (2003–15)

In Italy, during the period 2003–15, we observe a progressive liberalization of agency work, both enabled by and conducive to deepening ideological divides among the three unions at national and sectoral level. Labour market flexibility figured at the centre of growing disagreement both between state and employers, on the one side, and unions, on the other, but also among unions themselves (Molina and Rhodes 2007). Social concertation on labour market reforms was abandoned at the beginning of 2000s due both to the opposition of the new government against this decision-making mechanism, but also to the increasing scepticism of the employers' association Confindustria. Furthermore, in 2001, the centre-right Berlusconi government presented the 'White Paper' containing provisions for labour market flexibilization, including a modification of the rule on dismissal protection (art.18). These measures led to extensive social protests and were initially opposed by all three unions. Still, union solidarity proved shaky, as unions differed in their willingness to cooperate with the government. In March 2002, CGIL called a demonstration in Rome against the government's proposal of reforming art.18, attended by approximately three million people. In April, the three unions together called a very successful general strike. However, in July, CISL and UIL (with the support of the autonomous unions CISAL and UGL) signed the social 'Pact for Italy' with the government, which they considered the best possible outcome in that difficult situation and still better than the government's unilateral intervention. In contrast, CGIL continued its opposition, calling another general strike in November (Negrelli and Pulignano 2008). The 'Pact for Italy' was translated into the labour market reform in 2003, which, among other measures, also liberalized agency work. The law 30/2003 introduced the open-ended agency work (or staff-leasing), weakened the linkage between agency work and the temporary needs of employers, and relaxed companies' obligation to provide specific reasons for their use of agency work. This provision limited the room for bargaining quotas for agency work at workplace level, which could be set only through sectoral collective bargaining.

Deregulation affected the power balance in the bargaining round between the metal trade unions and the employers' association Federmeccanica in 2003. Federmeccanica wanted to adjust the standards of the sectoral collective agreement to the new legal framework, by removing the constraints on the use of fixed-term and agency work. The left-wing union FIOM is a member of the trade union confederation CGIL, which had heavily mobilized Italian workers against the labour market reform. FIOM sought to maintain constraints on the use of agency work and fixed-term work in the sectoral agreement and to introduce stricter rules requiring agency workers to be hired on permanent contracts after eight months of assignment. The other two unions, FIM and UILM, while also aiming to reduce the impact of the law, were willing to accept a compromise with employers and to adapt the collective agreement to the new normative framework. During the tough bargaining round, the union front split and a separate collective agreement was signed between Federmeccanica and the two moderate unions, FIM and UILM. Similar to the German case, employers took advantage of the divides in the labour movement. The regulation of agency work was deferred to a specific commission that was charged with defining what to delegate to collective bargaining. However, the commission was never actually called to life and therefore the law applied.

FIOM later tried to re-enter negotiations by focusing on the workplace level. At stake was not only the regulation of precarious work in workplaces, but also the ability to bargain at sectoral level in the future. This is clearly explained in the following quote by a FIOM trade union official:

> We have started bargaining on these issues (agency work) especially after the separate agreement of FIM and UILM. We needed those issues in order to show that we were rooted in the workplace, that we bargained and that the present contract was not OK and then we managed to achieve the sectoral agreement again in 2008. I mean, the workplace agreements (*pre-contratti*) did not start because there was a problem with precarious work. That was also the reason, obviously. The separate contract went a step backwards due to the legislation, but for us there was a fight about the sectoral agreement to be achieved again.   (FIOM official, 2016)

In the following years, unity of action was shortly resumed both at workplace and at sectoral level. The workplace campaign launched by FIOM showed employers that a collective agreement without the largest union could lead to conflicts in workplaces. Hence, the majority of the employers' association's members pushed for reopening negotiations with FIOM, and a unitary agreement was signed in 2006. The agreement foresaw the set-up of a specific bargaining commission, which, among other things, should achieve an agreement regulating fixed-term and agency contracts, and setting maximum quotas. However, in the following agreement in 2008 the parties did not introduce any specific limitations, but defined mechanisms for the direct and permanent hiring of non-standard workers after forty-four months of assignment through fixed-term or agency contracts. The longer time frame reflected the new legislation: The centre-left government elected in 2006 signed a social pact with the social partners, which was subsequently translated into law. The new law abolished staff-leasing (reintroduced in 2009 by the newly elected Berlusconi government) and introduced a maximum duration for fixed-term work (thirty-six months). As argued by the former FIOM's general secretary, this last provision strongly constrained the bargaining positions of the social partners:

> In 2008 we had already agreed on the total length of assignment considering both agency and fixed-term contracts, but the employers did not want to sign because at the same time there was a discussion in regard to the legislation. And when the legislation came into force, saying that there were thirty-six months[1] only for fixed-term contracts, etc., we were screwed. Even at FIAT we had agreed a shorter total length of assignment than the one which was imposed by the new legislation.
>
> (Former FIOM official, 2016)

The unity of action both at the sectoral and national level was short-lived. In 2009, a separate confederal agreement on the collective bargaining system was signed by the employers' association Confindustria, CISL, and UIL. In the same year, Federmeccanica pushed for introducing the possibility to derogate at plant level the norms of the sectoral collective agreement, leading to a new split in the union front: FIOM refused to sign, but FIM and UILM did.

In the following years, labour market reforms and separate collective agreements in the metal sector continued. Both in 2012 and 2014, labour market reforms have excluded trade unions and have been pursued unilaterally by the governments. Trade unions' exclusion has been explained through their declining attractiveness as bargaining partners for the government, as they seemed to be incapable of promoting innovative solutions, and were losing their power as veto players (Culpepper and Regan 2014). The two labour market reforms lifted the remaining limits on employers' use of agency work. In 2012, the obligation to justify the use of agency work was lifted for the first contract and it was removed altogether in 2014, so agency work can now be used at will. This trend was reflected in the collective agreements at sectoral level, where the collectively bargained regulation of agency work was progressively relaxed according to the liberalization pursued by the governments. In particular, while the temporal limitation of forty-four months is still in place, the collective agreements have been progressively weakened to the point where the obligation for employers to justify the use of agency work has been removed.

---

[1] The interviewee refers to the law passed by the Prodi government in 2007, which set the maximum time for fixed-term contracts at thirty-six months. As a consequence of the change in the normative framework, the employer association Federmeccanica first refused to negotiate with the unions on the maximum length of non-standard contracts, and then signed for a maximum amount of forty-four months for the sum of periods with fixed-term or agency contracts.

6.5. DISCUSSION AND CONCLUSIONS

This chapter has compared collective bargaining outcomes for agency work between the German and the Italian metal sector, across two time periods. We identify two main differences: the trajectory of collective bargaining and the effectiveness of negotiated regulation. Regulation was initially strong but progressively weakened in Italy, while it weakened and then improved in Germany. As for the first dimension, in Germany collective bargaining took place primarily at national level in the agency sector and at workplace level in the metal sector during the first phase (2003–6). The law, which originally restricted the use of agency work, was most heavily deregulated in 2003. This opened up divides respectively between the DGB unions and the Christian unions and between unions and works councils, which prevented collective bargaining from setting good standards for agency workers. The bargaining strategies shifted to the sectoral level in the second phase (2007/215), as IG Metall coordinated workplace bargaining and, most of all, achieved a sector-wide collective agreement setting wage bonuses for agency workers in 2012.

Collective bargaining on agency work evolved differently in Italy. In the first phase (1998–2002), unions used sectoral collective agreements in order to introduce more favourable conditions for agency workers in the agency sector. Furthermore, metal collective agreements set additional constraints to employers' use of agency work, slowing down the liberalization process. However, in the second phase (2003–15) unions' ability to resist deregulation progressively eroded, as the union front split over the labour market and collective bargaining reforms, and the most militant sectoral trade union was excluded from the national negotiations. With the aim of regaining a seat at the negotiation table, FIOM pushed its workplace representatives to achieve workplace agreements setting better conditions for agency workers and constraints on employers. However, such gains could never be extended to the whole sector, since, with the exception of a short parenthesis between 2006 and 2009, collective bargaining was led by the two moderate unions.

The second difference consists in the effectiveness of regulation for agency workers between the two countries. In Italy, agency workers still enjoy equal pay and treatment thanks to the legislation, while in Germany the sectoral agreement just reduces the gap between agency workers and permanent workers without eliminating it. For this reason, the agreement was also criticized by the service unions, especially ver.di, which found the provision of sectoral salary bonuses insufficient as this does not really achieve equal pay. However, the transition period from an agency to a permanent contract is shorter in Germany than in Italy, and strengthened co-determination constrains employers' use of agency work.

The differences in the capacity of trade unions to regulate agency work effectively in the two countries and in the two time periods can be explained through the interaction of two main factors: the evolution of legislation on agency work and the divides characterizing the two labour movements. First, the progressive deregulation of legislation on agency work affected the institutional power resources available to labour at national, sectoral, and workplace levels: In Germany, the Hartz reforms in 2003 allowed the amendment of equal pay by collective agreement and lifted most limitations to hiring (and firing) agency workers. The reregulation of agency work by law has been slowly taking place since 2011. In Italy, the legislation on agency work was strict until the major liberalization reform of 2003, and then the deregulation continued. As a result, the first collective agreements for the agency sector (in 2004 in Germany and 1998 in Italy) set lower wages and working conditions in Germany than in Italy, reflecting the different power resources granted to trade unions by the legislation. While Italian law established a rigid framework setting equal pay for agency workers, the legislation in Germany allowed derogation through collective agreements. This loophole was then exploited by employers and a first divide opened up between DGB unions and Christian unions. Furthermore, the deregulation of agency work exacerbated the differences in terms of bargaining strategies between IG Metall and works councils. Without a common wage floor for the whole workforce in the metal sector, works councils agreed on concessions concerning agency work under the pressure of reducing labour costs and preventing outsourcing. Furthermore, works councils had limited co-determination rights on agency work by law, which made the regulation at company level even more difficult.

Similarly, in the second phase in Italy the labour front split along ideological lines in conjunction with deregulation. The different strategic orientations of the sectoral unions made it possible for employers to obtain concessions in sectoral collective agreements signed with the other two unions, FIM and UILM. Hence, even if FIOM workplace representatives were able to negotiate more favourable agreements in some workplaces, it was impossible to extend them to all agency workers through sectoral agreements. In contrast, the bargaining monopoly of IG Metall enabled the union to regain control over agency work through a campaign initiative targeting works councils and union officials, which resulted in a sectoral agreement applying to all agency workers in the sector. The campaign also contributed to putting pressure on the legislator, leading to better regulation of agency work.

Our case studies thus point to the crucial role of the interaction between two factors: national legislation and the structure of divides within the labour movement. These two factors reinforce each other, building virtuous or vicious circles (see Benassi et al. 2016 for a similar argument). In particular, the virtuous circle between encompassing national legislation and coordinated bargaining on agency work in Italy was reversed by employers and the government, which weakened regulation and the institutions of collective bargaining, exploiting the ideological divides between the unions. However, our empirical evidence also suggests that a vicious circle can be reversed and turned into a virtuous one if labour can overcome divides and build associational power based on solidarity. This power, in turn, can be mobilized to establish more encompassing institutions. Similar to Italy, employers in Germany also exploited the divides in the labour movement in order to obtain concessions. However, thanks to its bargaining monopoly at the sectoral level, IG Metall was able to overcome those divides to organize a successful campaign to coordinate workplace bargaining and achieve better standards for agency workers at the sectoral level. In contrast, FIOM could not lead collective bargaining initiatives at the sectoral level because FIM and UILM were negotiating separate agreements with the employers' associations; therefore, its bargaining activity was confined to the workplace, where the balance of power is more favourable to employers.

Our study has broader implications for those interested in how labour can successfully regulate precarious work. In particular, divides within the labour movement undermine the ability of labour to respond effectively to labour market deregulation and the casualization of the employment relationship. They derive from a mix of ideological and institutional factors. The divide between different unions, present mainly in Italy, is rooted in differences in their ideological orientations and willingness to compromise with governments and employers. The divide between unions and works councils, typical of the German system, is rooted in the institutional design of labour representation, as works councils are formally independent representation bodies committed to the company's work-force and to the company itself. This difference is important for understanding at which level such divides are more likely to be exploited, as well as the strategies for overcoming them. In Germany, IG Metall could still 'enforce' its monopolistic bargaining position and lead sectoral bargaining initiatives, while the divisions among Italian unions, which have the same institutionalized bargaining rights, allowed employers to pursue a divide-and-rule strategy and prevented the development of sectoral bargaining on agency work. More intra-union negotiations and initiatives to promote shared understanding would probably be necessary in order to overcome ideological divides and constitute a united labour front against precarization.

ACKNOWLEDGEMENTS

Field research for this chapter was supported by the Hans-Boeckler Foundation (research project 'Bargaining along the Value Chain: Italy and Germany Compared').

REFERENCES

Alacevich, Franca (ed.) 2000. *Emergenza occupazione: ruolo delle parti sociali, concertazione e contrattazione collettiva in Italia*. Firenze: Cisl.

Altieri, Giovanna, Oteri, Cristina, and Pedaci, Marcello. 2005. 'Dal lavoro interinale alla somministrazione di manodopera: primo monitoraggio su cosa cambia per le Agenzie per il lavoro e per le imprese utilizzatrici'. Rapporto IRES. Rome: IRES.

Amable, Bruno. 2003. *The Diversity of Modern Capitalism*. Oxford: Oxford University Press.

Aust, Andreas, Pernicka, Susanne, and Feigl-Heihs, Monika. 2007. 'Moderner Sklavenhandel? Gewerkschaftliche Strategien im Umgang mit Leiharbeit'. In *Die Unorganisierten Gewinnen*, edited by Susanne Pernicka and Andreas Aust. Berlin: Sigma.

Ballarino, Gabriele. 2005. 'Strumenti nuovi per un lavoro vecchio: Il sindacato italiano e la rappresentanza dei lavoratori atipici'. *Sociologia del Lavoro*, 97: 174–90.

Benassi, Chiara. 2013. 'Political Economy of Labour Market Segmentation: Agency Work in the Automotive Industry'. ETUI Working Paper 2013.06. Brussels: European Trade Union Institute.

Benassi, Chiara, Doellgast, Virginia, and Sarmiento-Mirwaldt, Katja. 2016. 'Institutions and Inequality in Liberalizing Markets: Explaining Different Trajectories of Institutional Change in Social Europe'. *Politics and Society*, 44(1): 117–42.

Benassi, Chiara and Dorigatti, Lisa. 2015. 'Straight to the Core: The IG Metall Campaign towards Agency Workers'. *British Journal of Industrial Relations*, 53(3): 533–55.

Benassi, Chiara and Vlandas, Tim. 2016. 'Union Inclusiveness and Temporary Agency Workers: The Role of Power Resources and Union Ideology'. *European Journal of Industrial Relations*, 22(1): 5–22.

Bundesagentur für Arbeit. 2016. *Der Arbeitsmarkt in Deutschland: Zeitarbeit in Deutschland—Aktuelle Entwicklungen: Nürnberg, Bundesagentur für Arbeit*. Nürnberg: Bundesagentur für Arbeit.

Burroni, Luigi and Pedaci, Marcello. 2014. 'Collective Bargaining, Atypical Employment and Welfare Provisions: The Case of Temporary Agency Work in Italy'. *Stato e Mercato*, 101: 169–93.

Culpepper, Pepper and Regan, Aidan. 2014. 'Why Don't Governments Need Trade Unions Anymore? The Death of Social Pacts in Ireland and Italy'. *Socio-Economic Review*, 12(4): 723–45.

Davidsson, Johan Bo and Emmenegger, Patrik. 2013. 'Defending the Organisation, Not the Members: Unions and the Reform of Job Security Legislation in Western Europe'. *European Journal of Political Research*, 52(3): 339–63.

DGB. 2013. 'Betriebsrat und Leiharbeit'. Available at: <http://www.dgb.de/themen/++co++023ac7d8-34d2-11e3-9a92-00188b4dc422/@@dossier.html>.

Doellgast, Virginia, Batt, Rosemary, and Sørensen, Ole H. 2009. 'Introduction: Institutional Change and Labour Market Segmentation in European Call Centres'. *European Journal of Industrial Relations*, 15(4): 349–71.

Dorigatti, Lisa. 2017. 'Trade Unions in Segmented Labor Markets: Evidence from the German Metal and Chemical Sectors'. *ILR Review*, 70(4): 919–41.

Eichhorst, Werner and Marx, Paul. 2015. *Non-Standard Employment in Post-Industrial Labour Markets: An Occupational Perspective*. Cheltenham: Edward Elgar Publishing.

Emmenegger, Patrik, Häusermann, Siljia, Palier, Bruno, and Seeleib-Kaiser, Martin. 2012. *The Age of Dualization: The Changing Face of Inequality in Deindustrialising Societies*. Oxford: Oxford University Press.

FIOM. 2004. 'Quadro riassuntivo provvisorio dell'iniziativa precontrattuale'. Available at: <http://archivio.fiom.cgil.it/contrattazione/pre-ccnl/quadro.htm>.

Gordon, Joshua C. 2015. 'Protecting the Unemployed: Varieties of Unionism and the Evolution of Unemployment Benefits and Active Labour Market Policy in the Rich Democracies'. *Socio-Economic Review*, 13(1): 79–99.

Greer, Ian. 2008. 'Organized Industrial Relations in the Information Economy: The German Automotive Sector as a Test Case'. *New Technology, Work and Employment*, 23(3): 181–96.

Hall, Peter A. and Soskice, David. 2001. *Varieties of Capitalism: The Institutional Foundations of Comparative Advantage*. Oxford and New York: Oxford University Press.

Hassel, Anke. 2014. 'The Paradox of Liberalization: Understanding Dualism and the Recovery of the German Political Economy'. *British Journal of Industrial Relations*, 52(1): 57–81.

Hensche, Martin. 2016. *Handbuch Arbeitsrecht: Arbeitnehmerüberlassung (Leiharbeit, Zeitarbeit)*. Available at: <http://www.hensche.de/Rechtsanwalt_Arbeitsrecht_Handbuch_Leiharbeit.html>.

Holst, Hajo, Nachtway, Oliver, and Doerre, Klaus. 2009. *Funktionswandel von Leiharbeit. Neue Nutzungsstrategien und ihre arbeits- und mitbestimmungspolitischen Folgen: Eine Studie im Auftrag der Otto Brenner Stiftung*. Frankfurt am Main: OBS-Arbeitsheft 61.

IG Metall. 1992 *'Moderner Sklavenhandel': Fremdfirmeneinsatz durch Leiharbeit und Werkverträge. Eine Handlungsanleitung für betroffene Betriebsräte und Arbeitnehmer-Innen*. Frankfurt am Main: IG Metall.

IG Metall. 2017. Gleiche Arbeit—Gleiches Geld. Available at: <https://www.gleichearbeit-gleichesgeld.de/initiative/ueber-die-kampagne/>.

IG Metall Bezirk Mitte. 2012. 'Mehr Fairness bei Leiharbeit'. Available at: <http://www.igmetall-bezirk-mitte.de/gruppen/leiharbeit/>.

IG Metall Zoom. 2016. 'Urteile'. Available at: <http://www.igmetall-zoom.de/urteile>.

Jürgens, Ulrich and Krzywdzinski, Martin. 2006. 'Globalisierungsdruck und Beschäftigungssicherung: Standortsicherungsvereinbarungen in der deutschen Automobilindustrie zwischen 1993 und 2006'. WZB Discussion Papers SP III, 2006, Social Science Research Centre, Berlin.

MacKenzie, Robert. 2009. 'Union Responses to Restructuring and the Growth of Atypical Labour in the Irish Telecommunication Sector'. *Economic and Industrial Democracy*, 30(4): 539–63.

Marino, Stefania. 2012. 'Trade Union Inclusion of Migrant and Ethnic Minority Workers: Comparing Italy and the Netherlands'. *European Journal of Industrial Relations*, 18(1): 5–20.

Molina, Oscar and Rhodes, Martin. 2007. 'Industrial Relations and the Welfare State in Italy: Assessing the Potential of Negotiated Change'. *West European Politics*, 30(4): 803–29.

Negrelli, Serafino and Pulignano, Valeria. 2008. 'Change in Contemporary Italy's Social Concertation'. *Industrial Relations Journal*, 39(1): 63–77.

Oliver, Rebecca. 2011. 'Powerful Remnants? The Politics of Egalitarian Bargaining Institutions in Italy and Sweden'. *Socio-Economic Review*, 9(3): 533–66.

Palier, Bruno and Thelen, Kathleen. 2010. 'Institutionalizing Dualism: Complementarities and Change in France and Germany'. *Politics and Society*, 38(1): 119–48.

Promberger, M., Bellmann, Lutz, Dreher, Christoph, Sowa, Frank, Schramm, Simon, and Theuer, Stefan. 2006. *Leiharbeit im Betrieb: Strukturen, Kontexte und Handhabung einer atypischen Beschäftigungsform. Abschlussbericht*. Nürnberg: Hans-Böckler-Stiftung.

Pulignano, Valeria and Doerflinger, Nadja. 2013. 'A Head with Two Tales: Trade Unions' Influence on Temporary Agency Work in Belgian and German Workplaces'. *International Journal of Human Resource Management*, 22(24): 4149–65.

Pulignano, Valeria and Signoretti, Andrea. 2016. 'Union Strategies, National Institutions and the Use of Temporary Labour in Italian and US Plants'. *British Journal of Industrial Relations*, 54(3): 574–96.

Rehder, Britta. 2003. *Betriebliche Bündnisse für Arbeit in Deutschland: Mitbestimmung und Flächentarif im Wandel*. Frankfurt am Main: Campus Verlag.

Streeck, Wolfgang. 1984. *Industrial Relations in West Germany: A Case Study of the Car Industry*. London: Heinemann Educational Publishers.

Tiraboschi, Michele and Tomassetti, Paolo. 2015. 'La riforma del lavoro a termine alla prova della contrattazione'. Working Paper ADAPT, 101.

Upchurch, Martin, Taylor, Graham, and Mathers, Andy. 2009. 'The Crisis of "Social Democratic" Unionism: The "Opening Up" of Civil Society and the Prospects for Union Renewal in the United Kingdom, France, and Germany'. *Capital and Class*, 34 (4): 519–42.

Vitols, Katrin. 2008. *Zwischen Stabilitaet und Wandel: Die Sozialpartnerschaft in Deutschland und die atypische Beschaeftigungsform Zeitarbeit*. Hamburg: Verlag Dr Kova.

Wagner, Ines and Refslund, Bjarke. 2016. 'Understanding the Diverging Trajectories of Slaughterhouse Work in Denmark and Germany: A Power Resource Approach'. *European Journal of Industrial Relations*, 22(4): 335–51.

Wassermann, Wolfram and Rudolph, Wolfgang. 2007. 'Leiharbeit als Gegenstand betrieblicher Mitbestimmung: Anforderungen und Arbeitsressourcen von Betriebsräten in Betrieben mit hohem Leiharbeitnehmeranteil. Ergebnisse einer Befragung von Betriebsräten in Betrieben des Organisationsbereichs der IG Metall im Frühjahr 2007'. Working Paper 148. Hans-Böckler-Stiftung.

7

Union Campaigns against Precarious Work in the Retail Sector of Estonia, Poland, and Slovenia

Adam Mrozowicki, Branko Bembič, Kairit Kall, Małgorzata Maciejewska, and Miroslav Stanojević

7.1. INTRODUCTION

This chapter addresses the problem of trade union responses to the precarization of work in the retail sector in Estonia, Poland, and Slovenia. The retail sector is an example of a low-paid sector, in which trade unions face similar challenges associated with high levels of non-standard employment (Carré et al. 2010). The global economic crisis of 2007–8 and the subsequent downturn led to increased competitive pressure on wages and working conditions (Mrozowicki et al. 2013). As a result, unions in all three countries have become increasingly active in organizing and representing precarious workers (Trif et al. 2016). At the same time, their strategies and success have been shaped by each country's distinctive industrial relations system (Bohle and Greskovits 2012; Kohl 2009).

In this chapter we ask two questions. First, what impact have sectoral characteristics, institutional factors, and trade union strategies had on patterns of precarious work in retail workplaces across Estonia, Poland, and Slovenia? Second, are new patterns of solidarity emerging in the retail sectors of these three countries following the economic downturn? We consider precarious employment as a relational category defined, on the one hand, by the expansion of non-standard employment contracts and, on the other hand, by the expansion of low-paid jobs and growing insecurity in pay, job security, social status, and career progression (Arnold and Bongiovi 2012; Heery and Salmon 2000; Vosko 2010). It is often assumed that precarization increased in Western capitalist countries 'with the erosion of the "Fordist bargain" and the "standard employment relationship" roughly since the 1970s' (Mosoetsa et al. 2016; Standing 2011), in addition to the crisis of collectivist and solidaristic trade unionism. However, even if precarity can be seen as a norm for all capitalist societies, it takes different forms and varies in intensity across time periods and regions. Precarious employment patterns that developed in Central and Eastern Europe (CEE) following the return of capitalism can be seen as partially driven by similar factors as in the Western capitalist countries (Heery and Salmon 2000; Standing 2011). Yet its forms also reflect a specific institutional context marked by the legacies of variegated state socialist regimes and their pathways of capitalist transformation. This chapter is centrally concerned with the impact of different types of CEE political-economic regimes, including the 'neoliberal' regime in Estonia, the 'neocorporatist' regime in Slovenia, and the 'embedded neoliberal' regime in Poland (Bohle and Greskovits 2012; Crowley and Stanojević 2011), on the forms of the precarization of work and union attempts to counteract it.

We can distinguish between several theses in the literature regarding the effects of institutional and sectoral factors and trade union power resources on trade union strategies towards precarious employment (Benassi and Dorigatti 2015; Benassi and Vlandas 2016; Pulignano and Signoretti 2016; Mrozowicki 2014; Trif et al. 2016). One argument holds that encompassing institutions increase unions' institutional power, understood as the ability of unions to regulate employment conditions through collective bargaining and political/legal leverage (Doerre et al. 2009; Doellgast et al. 2016: 575). However, unions' institutional power is not reducible to favourable institutions, but is dependent on unions' structural and especially associational power resources as well.[1] Our earlier studies on the retail and automotive sectors demonstrated that Slovenian trade unions' higher institutional power tended to support collective bargaining solutions to the problems of precarization that followed the 2007 global economic crisis. By contrast, unilateral responses predominated in Estonia and Poland, where the institutional power of unions was weaker (Mrozowicki 2014; Mrozowicki et al. 2013).

Second, sectoral characteristics are often argued to influence the types and levels of workers' organization in trade union responses towards precarious work (Carré et al. 2010; Geppert et al. 2014; Jany-Catrice and Lehndorff 2002). Following Wright (2000) and Silver (2003), we distinguish between structural power that results from workers' location and role within the economic system, particular sector, or workplace, and associational power, reflecting the formation of workers' collective organization and its internal features. In sectors such as retail, in which the structural power of workers is limited, trade unions have to rely more on various forms of associational power (Silver 2003). Research on precarious worker organizing provides evidence that the types of associational power that are crucial to success are those linked to union capacities to build links with workers' communities beyond workplaces, utilize their discursive power to address new targets of claims (states, customers, MNCs), and build new, solidaristic identities among the workers themselves (Chun and Agarwala 2016; Sarmiento et al. 2016). Framed in the language of power resources theory, unions both need new kinds of network embeddedness (solidarities manifested into horizontal and vertical links with other unions and civil society organizations) and narrative resources (i.e. 'the existing stock of stories that frame understandings and union actions and inform a sense of efficacy and legitimacy') (Lévesque and Murray 2010: 339).

---

[1] In this chapter we distinguish between 'formal institutions' and 'unions' institutional power'. Although the two often overlap, we follow here Doerre et al. (2009) in that institutional power is past 'structural and organisational power . . . incorporated into societal institutions'. Also, we posit that this power that is built into institutional structure needs to be constantly supported and defended if it is to function as a power resource.

In this chapter, we examine how institutional differences in industrial relations, sectoral characteristics, and union resources interact to influence the paths available to unions, as well as their degree of success in limiting precarious employment and establishing ties of solidarity across workforce segments. Our main argument is twofold. On the one hand, labour's responses to precarization have differed due to the variegated industrial relations systems, which influence both sectoral forms of precarity and union resources. These differences reflected opportunities and constraints embedded in distinct institutional contexts. Because of their institutional resources, Slovenian unions can be seen as most successful in counteracting precarization out of three cases studied. On the other hand, we observe innovative approaches emerging in all three countries, some of which transcend institutional opportunities and constraints. These innovations reflect the strategic choices of sectoral- and company-level trade union leaders (Turner 2009) as well as the dynamics of workers' collective mobilization as union members and citizens capable of building up new ties of solidarity within and across the sector. Thus, rather than seeing union responses as determined by institutional context, we interpret them in terms of strategic utilization of various context-bound options in the course of ongoing social struggles in the countries studied.

The chapter is divided into three main parts. First, we discuss our research methods and rationale for selecting the empirical cases of companies and countries. Next, we present background to the analysis of precarious work in retail. This includes a discussion of the meanings and mechanisms of precarization and the role played by employment characteristics and industrial relations. In the body of the chapter, we present our empirical analysis in a country-by-country fashion, which enables us to explain differences in patterns of solidarity (and the lack of thereof) by referring to interactions among institutions, sectoral characteristics, and actors' strategies at three levels (national level, sectoral level, and company level). Finally, we engage in a comparative discussion aimed at a more systematic analysis of conditions, forms, and limits of new solidarities emerging in the retail sector in Estonia, Poland, and Slovenia.

7.2. METHODS AND CASE SELECTION

This chapter examines the responses to the precarization of work by organized labour in a sector (retail) with an overall high incidence of precarious work and differentiated power resources of unions to counteract precarity. Empirical data are drawn from interviews with unionists from six multinational food retailers and expert interviews with sectoral and national-level union officials and employer representatives conducted between 2011 and 2016. We also analysed secondary data, including press reports and sectoral employment statistics taken from corporate reports. In total, we conducted nine interviews in Estonia, sixteen interviews in Poland (plus twenty-one background interviews carried out in 2002–11), and ten interviews in Slovenia.

The three countries selected for this study represent three different types of capitalist regimes that evolved in Central and Eastern Europe after the end of state socialism. Bohle and Greskovits (2012: 3) distinguish between the neoliberal type

(Estonia) marked by the 'combination of market radicalism with meagre compensation for transformation costs', the embedded neoliberal type (Poland) characterized by a 'permanent search for compromises between market transformation and social cohesion', and the neocorporatist type (Slovenia) manifested by 'negotiated multilevel relationships among business, labour, and the state'. Regional varieties of industrial relations systems developed in parallel to changes in political economies. Slovenia, with its legacy of strong working-class mobilization, stood out as an exception in which encompassing institutions of tripartite economic coordination and multi-employer collective bargaining emerged (Crowley and Stanojević 2011). In Estonia and Poland, neocorporatism never really developed or took a more 'illusory' form (Ost 2000) and single-employer collective bargaining is dominant. Nevertheless, due to the legacy of independent unionism (NSZZ Solidarność) in the 1980s, overall Polish unions possess stronger power resources than their counterparts in Estonia, which was marked by a general weakness of bottom-up workers' movements both before and after the system change.

Research has also shown that the characteristics of employment at the sectoral and company levels mediate institutional effects on the incidence and forms of precarious work in CEE countries (Trif et al. 2016; Mrozowicki et al. 2013). The retail sector is characterized by sharp, cost-based competition and strong downward pressure on wages and other employment conditions throughout the Western world, with non-standard forms of employment becoming more common (e.g. Carré et al. 2010; Jany-Catrice and Lehndorff 2002). Our earlier work indicates that the economic crisis following 2007 offered retail employers further leeway to justify and accelerate the expansion of low-paid and unstable employment (Mrozowicki et al. 2013). Therefore, the main time frame for our analysis is the years 2008–15, although we also acknowledge that earlier developments are relevant for the precarization of retail work.

The multinational companies analysed in the case studies have different countries of origin but share some common characteristics. They all are among the five largest food retailers in each country, making them influential for the overall picture of employment conditions in the sector as a whole (Table 7.1). They have adopted similar business models and strategies, which, in all but one (EE1) case, were based on the diversification of shop formats as well as the spread of low-wage, insecure, and precarious jobs. In all of the companies, wages were rather low (compared to the nationwide average), companies made use of functional flexibility and multi-skilling, and employees experienced work intensification (particularly after the crisis).

7.3. PRECARIOUS WORK AND INDUSTRIAL RELATIONS IN THE RETAIL SECTOR

The case study companies have broadly similar working conditions, typically with low pay and high insecurity. However, we found differences in patterns of precarious work at both company and national level, and we show that these differences can be explained by two sets of factors. First, institutions at national and sectoral level affected overall patterns of precarity as well as unions'

Table 7.1. Overview of companies

	Estonia		Poland		Slovenia	
	EE1	EE2	PL1	PL2	SI1	SI2
1. Market share in food retail (country level)	9% (5th largest, 2013)	17% (2nd largest, 2013)	3.3% (5th largest, 2014)	4.8% (4th largest, 2014)	33% (largest, 2016)	23% (2nd largest, 2016)
2. Home country	Finland	Sweden	France	UK	Croatia	Austria
3. Number and structure of shops	8 HM (2016)	14 HM, 24 SM, and 46 hard discount shops (2016)	96 HM, 138 SM, and 468 convenience stores (2014)	70 HM, 88 compact HM, and 296 SM (2014)	22 HM, 390 convenience stores, 62 SM and smaller formats (2014)	47 HM, 34 SM, 13 mega-markets, two city stores
4. Number of employees in the country	1,000 (2016)	2,700 (2016)	16,000 (2014)	29,934 (2014)	11,000 (2014)	4,300 (2014)
5. Trade union presence	Estonian Trade Union of Commercial and Servicing Employees (ETKA)	Estonian Trade Union of Commercial and Servicing Employees (ETKA)	NSZZ Solidarność	NSZZ Solidarność; August '80, NSZZ Solidarność '80, the Confederation of Labour OPZZ, and Trade Union of Retail Employees	Trade Union of Worker's in Trade Sector in Slovenia (SDTS affiliated to ZSSS); Trade Union of Commerce of Slovenia (STS affiliated to KS-90)	KNSS (Confederation of New Trade Unions of Slovenia); SDTS (affiliated to ZSSS); STS (affiliated to KS-90)
6. Collective agreement	Company level	No	No	No	Sectoral and company level	Sectoral level

Notes: HM = hypermarkets; SM = supermarkets. The names of companies were made anonymous.

Sources: (1) Eesti Konjunktuuriinstituut (2015) for Estonia, Dlahandlu.pl for Poland, Delo (2014) for Slovenia; (2–4) company home pages for Estonia, annual reports and CSR reports for Poland, annual reports (AJPES) for Slovenia.

institutional resources to combat precarization through collective bargaining. These include industrial relations structures, collective bargaining coverage, and the role of the state in regulating employment conditions. Second, unions relied on associational power derived from union membership structure, density, and solidarity links with other unions and civil society organizations to supplement these institutional resources or overcome their relative weakness.

In Estonia, industrial relations institutions are the least encompassing of the three countries, despite formal institutional support for national tripartite dialogue and sectoral- and company-level collective bargaining. This makes the situation of retail workers particularly vulnerable, regardless of their employment status and forms. There are two sectoral-level unions that retail workers can join: the Estonian Trade Union of Commercial and Servicing Employees (ETKA) is active in several retail chains (including in the companies studied here), while the Estonian Communication and Service Workers' Trade Union (ESTAL) is only present in one. Most big retail employers are joined under the employers' federation Kaupmeeste Liit, but they are not interested in sectoral collective agreements. While the situation of overall precariousness and limited segmentation could potentially help to organize workers, trade unions lack both institutional as well as associational power, industrial relations are fragmented, and collective bargaining takes place mainly at the company level. There is no sectoral-level collective agreement, and union density has remained at around 1 per cent in the sector and 6.5 per cent nationwide, while collective bargaining coverage is 23 per cent (Visser 2016). The tripartite institutions at the national level are weak and virtually ignored by government, while the sectoral level constitutes 'the absent middle' between the two levels (Glassner 2013; Kallaste and Woolfson 2013).

Non-standard contracts are usually not considered as a necessary cost-saving alternative for Estonian employers, because employment protections associated with standard employment contracts are rather weak (Turk and Nurmela 2012), the national minimum wage is fairly low (employers usually have to pay above minimum wage to attract and keep employees), and inspection of working conditions is limited. A representative of the sectoral-level retail union observed that the new Employment Contracts Act of 2009 increased labour market flexibility and made the employment conditions even less secure and more employer-dominated than before:

> Well ... let's say the new Employment Contracts Act [of 2009] is like ... you can interpret it very differently. Secondly, it gives a lot of freedom to negotiate. They say we have a FLEXIBLE law. But what does it mean for service workers? For service workers it means that they work until 10.00 pm, until 11.00 pm. Well, actually until 11:30 [pm], because the work does not end when you close the shop. There is no more extra pay for evening work ... In a lot of cases extra pay for night work is written into the employment contract that means that basic salary already contains night extras.
>
> (Interview, ETKA official, 2014)

Company-level data from the Estonian companies EE1 and EE2 confirm the prevalence of standard contracts. In both MNCs, open-ended full-time contracts were the dominant form of employment, although part-time work was also used and services like cleaning and security were outsourced. EE1 used temporary agency workers (TAWs) and temporary contracts during periods of increased workload, like holidays, but the share was low.

Poland's formal institutions are more or less comparable to those in Estonia; however, its industrial relations structure is somewhat more favourable for unions. The most important trade unions in the sector include the National Section of Commerce of NSZZ Solidarność, the Federation of Trade Unions of Employees in Co-operatives, Production, Commerce and Services in Poland (affiliated to the All-Poland Alliance of Trade Unions (OPZZ)), the radical Free Trade Union August '80, and the Confederation of Labour OPZZ. The only relevant employer organization is the Polish Organisation of Trade and Distribution (POHiD), representing thirteen large (mostly transnational) retail chains. However, it refuses to join sectoral-level collective bargaining. As a result, similar to their Estonian counterparts, Polish unions operating in the retail sector find themselves in an environment of decentralized, company-level bargaining, with no sectoral-level collective agreement. Union density is very low (some 2 per cent in the sector, 12 per cent nationwide in 2015) and nationwide collective bargaining coverage is limited (35 per cent in 2012, cf. Visser 2016). Yet, different from Estonia, NSZZ Solidarność benefitted from early international contacts, resource transfer from foreign trade unions, including the Service Employees International Union, and strategic leadership decisions to pool union resources from various sectors. The union used these resources to start organizing campaigns in the late 1990s, enabling it to unionize a proportion of workers in large, multinational retail chains.

As compared to Estonia, the precarization of employment in Polish retail was more closely linked to segmentation in the sector, which reduced unions associational power. First, trade unions are not present in small family-owned shops, convenience stores and franchise systems, as well as temporary work agencies. The majority of their members have open-ended contracts in the largest, multinational stores. Second, employers easily make use of strong inter-union rivalry, which is much more present in Poland than in Estonia and Slovenia, to counteract workers' associational power. In addition, in the mid-2000s, non-standard employment began to expand, creating additional lines of division among the workforce. This was due in part to the flexibilization of the Labour Code in the wake of Poland's accession to the European Union (2002–4) and cost-cutting employer strategies. Polish employers began to employ workers on temporary, civil law contracts and encouraged self-employment, in which case the minimum wage does not apply. Precarization took different forms in two segments of the sector. In the largest retail chains, stores increased their use of temporary work agencies and part-time jobs. In the small and medium-sized enterprises, precarity was related to the use of franchises and the spread of self-employment. As observed by an employer representative:

> If you create a system which has more than 4,000 shops, with 70–80 m² of sale area on average per shop, in which 3–4 people work, usually a family, you influence it by a certain standard. From the perspective of HR management in a corporation, it is precariat. And from a perspective that they are entrepreneurs bounded by a contract, it is self-employment, a provision of service called 'management and running a shop'.
> (Interview, representative of POHiD, 2015)

Accordingly, both Polish companies studied made extensive use of non-standard employment contracts. In addition, cleaning and security services were outsourced, similar to the Estonian cases. In PL1 the share of TAWs and workers with temporary employment contracts was very high (fluctuating between 30 and 70 per cent), but the share of part-timers was limited. By contrast, PL2 employed workers directly with employment contracts, and the share of temporary workers was lower. Yet (forced) part-time employment was more common than in PL1.

Compared to Estonia and Poland, in Slovenia industrial relations structures can be seen as the most encompassing. During the first decade of transition, Slovenia developed into a sort of coordinated market economy (Hall and Soskice 2001) with relatively good macroeconomic performance, a centralized collective bargaining system with an almost 100 per cent coverage, and a relatively generous welfare state. This system proved quite resilient in the face of shocks that started to occur in the mid-2000s, when Slovenia joined the European Union and basically fulfilled all required conditions to adopt the euro. Social and political conflicts escalated after 2008. Successive attempts by various governments to enforce unilateral decisions were opposed and quite frequently brought down by the massive demonstrations and referendums organized by unions. Union density that was relatively high (around 40 per cent nationwide) until 2003 (Stanojević 2015) dropped thereafter (20–25 per cent nationwide and some 15 per cent the retail sector in 2014), but the trade union movement, nonetheless, retained its mobilizing strength, at least at the national level.

In the retail sector, the most important social partners in the sector are the Trade Union of Workers in the Trade Sector (SDTS), which is a member of the Slovenian Association of Free Trade Unions (ZSSS), and KS 90—the Trade Union of Commerce of Slovenia. SDTS is the only union representative at the sector level and thus the only signatory to the sectoral collective agreement on the part of organized labour. At the company level in SI1, where both unions are representative, they cooperate and negotiate collective agreements with the employer together. On the employer side, the crucial actors are the Slovenian Chamber of Commerce, the Association of Employers of Slovenia, and the Chamber of Commerce and Industry of Slovenia. There is a collective agreement in the sector and there are also some collective agreements at the company level. As the extension mechanism is applied, the sectoral collective agreement covers all companies in the trade sector and employees (excluding student workers, but including temporary agency workers).

Despite the presence of strong and encompassing institutions, precarious employment in Slovenia began to expand in the 1990s and further increased in the mid-2000s. Firms were under growing pressure to improve their international competitiveness during the process of EU accession. As a result, wage levels in many companies could be maintained only by resorting to labour intensification and flexibilization of work, which increased the penetration of atypical forms of employment (Stanojević 2010). However, following the 2007 crisis the labour market situation worsened and some traditional retailers sought to replace the regular workers that left the sector with atypical, mostly precarious jobs. Discounters significantly expanded their operations, and mostly relied on part-time (Labour Code-regulated) jobs. Developments in Slovenia thus started to resemble Poland; however, the stronger institutional and associational power of trade unions made it more difficult for employers to adopt fully 'the' segmentation strategies.

In both Slovenian case study stores, SI1 and SI2, non-standard forms of employment were quite widespread. Most of the unionists we interviewed reported that traditional retailers, as well as SI1 and SI2, offered almost exclusively fixed-term contracts to new employees. Both retailers also used student work, which is an extremely flexible labour arrangement performed mostly on a part-time basis. Also, although TAWs did not represent a high share of total number of employees on the company level, they represented a very large share of warehouse workers.

It can be argued that crisis solidified the differences across the three countries that had emerged in the pre-crisis period. The outcomes in terms of the diversified employment precarization patterns are demonstrated in Table 7.2.

The share of part-time employees oscillates between 10 and 12 per cent in all three countries (see Table 7.2), and in Estonia and Slovenia the share has increased since 2008 by three percentage points, indicating a common cost-cutting strategy of retailers (cf. Carré et al. 2010; Grugulis and Bozkurt 2011). Still, part-time work is less common than in many European countries due to the generally low wages associated with it. In Poland, self-employment plays a greater role than in Estonia and Slovenia, due to the large number of small family shops and franchises. In Slovenia and Poland, the share of employees with temporary contracts is quite high—respectively 17.8 per cent and 36.7 per cent—with the higher Polish figure reflecting strong employer-driven segmentation. In both countries, in an attempt to bypass the costs related to standard employment, employers also use service

Table 7.2. Basic employment dimensions in the sector (2014)

	Estonia	Poland	Slovenia
1. Employment share (section G47) in total employment	8.0%	9.1%	7.9%
2. Employment change (2008–14)	−5.3%	−3.8%	−9.9%
3. Temporary employment share in total employees (section G) (change 2008–14)	3.0% (1.0%)	36.7% (2.7%)	17.8% (−2.4%)
4. Part-time employment share in total employees (section G) (change 2008–14)	11.4% (3.0%)	10.2% (−0.1%)	12.7% (3.1%)
5. Self-employment share in total employment (section G) (change 2008–14)	9.8% (−1.5%)	21.3% (1.3%)	8.0% (4.0%)
6. Number of employed persons per enterprise (average) (G47.110) (2013)	39.3	6.7	38.6
7. National-level minimum wage (2014)	€355	€394	€789.15
8. Gross monthly wage (section G47) (% of the average wage) (% of the national minimum wage)	€735 (69.5%) (207%)	€603.23 (153%)	€1,184.77 (151%)
9. Estimated union density	1.2%	2%	15%
10. Sectoral-level collective agreement	No	No	Yes

Notes: Temporary employment category (3) is ambiguous as it includes both Labour Code employment and non-Labour Code employment forms. G: wholesale and retail trade; repair of motor vehicles and motorcycles. G47: retail trade, except of motor vehicles and motorcycles. G47.110: retail sale in non-specialized stores with food, beverages, or tobacco predominating.

Source: (1–5) Eurostat LFS; (6) Structural Business Statistics Eurostat; (7–8) national statistical offices; (9–10) Mrozowicki et al. 2013.

contracts extensively, excluding workers from some rights guaranteed in the Labour Code. These include civil law contracts in Poland and, in Slovenia, extensive utilization of country-specific student work, which is used mainly due to its flexibility and not lower wages.[2] In Estonia, on the other hand, a rather low level of employment flexibilization in terms of contractual arrangements can be observed. Seen from a different angle, in Estonia even *regular employment is almost completely flexibilized*. The sector can be seen as low wage in all three countries, based on the proportion of sectoral gross monthly wages relative to national averages. However, there are also significant differences between wage levels. Gross monthly wages in 2014 were €603.23 in Poland (i.e. 66.8 per cent of the national average, 153 per cent of minimum wage), €735 in Estonia (69.5 per cent of the national average, 207 per cent of minimum wage) and €1,184.77 in Slovenia (76.9 per cent of the national average, 151 per cent of minimum wage). Although the 2007 global financial crisis depressed economic activity in retail, average wages increased relatively fast in the Slovenian retail sector due to a sharp increase in the minimum wage, indicating the important role of articulation of union struggles above the sectoral level.

7.4. UNION STRATEGIES TOWARDS PRECARIOUS WORK

Different patterns of precarization and sectoral characteristics pose specific challenges for unions in the retail sector. At the same time, union approaches to regulating precarity are influenced by confrontations between capital and labour at the national and sectoral level. Institutional factors and power resources delimit the range of approaches at unions' disposal, but are also, at least to some extent, a condensed result of their past struggles. In this section, we first summarize the unions' approaches and their successes (or failures) in a country-by-country fashion. We then explain these outcomes in terms of the factors listed in Section 7.1: in particular, union power resources and institutional embeddedness. We conclude with a very brief discussion of some common limitations and challenges of the approaches observed.

7.4.1. Strategies and Outcomes

The strategies that Estonian retail unions apply at different levels are interrelated and mostly initiated by the sectoral union ETKA, to which most company-level retail unions are also affiliated. First, Estonian unions, including those in the retail sector, are trying to secure better labour legislation by lobbying the government and striving for increases in the minimum wage through negotiations at the national level. This has a direct influence on the remuneration of retail workers, as retail is a low-wage sector. Although the institutional framework for tripartism

---

[2] It has to be noted that Eurostat figures on temporary employment (Table 7.2) also partially include non-Labour Code employment (such as civil law contracts).

at the national level exists, the unions lack the power to back it up and social dialogue usually brings them meagre results. Unions have succeeded in gaining slow minimum wage increases and stopping further flexibilization of the Labour Code (initiated by employers and the government). Unions were not able to stop government's unilateral changes to the new Employment Contracts Act in 2008, which increased flexibility in the labour market for all workers. They did manage to stop, but not improve, planned changes in the collective labour law in 2012, including more restrictive rights to strike, by lobbying the government, organizing small-scale protest action, and also getting help from the International Labour Organization (Kall 2017). Importantly, unlike in Poland and Slovenia, Estonian trade unions did not build any significant coalitions with other civil society organizations or political parties in their efforts to counteract precarious work.

Social dialogue in Estonian retail has been further impeded by the fact that the employers' federation in retail is not willing to engage with sectoral-level collective bargaining. In order to overcome this critical weakness and strengthen associational power, the Baltic Organising Academy co-sponsored by Nordic trade unions was established in 2010. Thanks to strategic decisions of its leadership, the main retail sector federation ETKA joined the academy and has undertaken US-inspired, centrally planned organizing campaigns financed with the support of the Finnish private service sector union PAM since 2012.[3] The Estonian members of BOA are committed to investing 'at least 35 per cent of the campaign-generated membership fees into organising work' (Häkkinen 2013: 7). Some resource redistribution is needed to organize and represent precarious workers in retail, due to low membership in this sector. The important problem was overcome by international solidarity, followed by internal redistribution. The organizing campaign produced some tangible results, most notably a company-level collective agreement in EE1 that improved wages and other employment conditions (see Table 7.3).

In both Estonian case study companies, organizing has raised union density and enhanced the monitoring and fulfilment of labour standards. Unionized employees who have the support of ETKA have become more aware of their rights and less afraid of demanding better conditions. Further, in both companies trade union campaigns contributed to raising wage levels and employment standards—as employers sought to demonstrate that they could improve conditions without a collective agreement—hence helping to counteract wage-based precarization. Notwithstanding these results, the unions' approach suffers from certain limitations. The scale of organizing campaigns is relatively small and they targeted only two retailers, thus most of the sector stays uncovered. Also, temporary workers are generally not union members in both EE1 and EE2 (although their share is very small). In addition to organizing, ETKA also employs media-oriented instruments and engages with the dissemination of benchmarks on employment standards (informing workers about safety and health issues) as well as limited mobilization, such as gathering signatures against wage cuts in some shops during the crisis. Servicing in the retail sector is not very extensive, as

---

[3] PAM is Palvelualojen ammattiliitto PAM (in Finnish) or Service Union United PAM (in English).

Table 7.3. Trade union instruments addressing the problems of precarious work and outcomes

	Estonia	Poland	Slovenia
Instruments			
Organizing	US-styled organizing in large MNCs (since 2012 in EE1, 2014 in EE2)— BOA, sector level	The legacy of US-styled organizing in MNCs— sector and national level, no TAWs, routine and protest-based recruitment in PL1 and PL2	Recruiting with elements of organizing—company level (some TAWs in SI1, no TAWs in SI2)
Servicing	Rather limited, mostly sectoral level	Rather limited, company and sector	Extensive, at the sector and national level
Collective bargaining	Company level, limited, no sectoral-level CB	Company level, limited, no sectoral-level CB	Extensive, collective agreement at the sector level
Mobilization	Limited protests, company and national level, union-dominated	Cyclic protests, all levels, social campaigns involving political parties and NGOs	National level, broad coalitions and social campaigns
Outcomes			
General outcomes	*Extensive precarization* across the sector and islands of good practices in EE1 and EE2 (*limited segmentation*)	The early stage of nationwide legal changes aimed at reducing precarious work (*moderate precarization*) and *extensive segmentation*	Sectoral-level and national-level regulation—*reduced precarization* via collective bargaining and legal changes and *moderate segmentation*
Detailed outcomes	Increasing union density in some MNCs, monitoring/ benchmarking labour standards, some wage increases at the company level, CA in EE1	Increasing union density in some MNCs and legal changes thanks to social campaigns at national and sectoral level aimed at reducing wage-based precarity and insecurity	Increases of wages at the sectoral level, counteracting precarization at the sectoral and national level, greater inclusion/coverage of non-standard employees
Shortcomings	Wage increases still small, no sectoral-level CAs, limited density, limited coverage of non-standard employment, limited coverage of employees beyond certain stores	No sectoral-level CAs and company-level CAs in MNCs, limited inclusion and coverage of non-standard employees, and limited access to workers in micro-companies	No provisions in sectoral-level CAs for precarious (equal treatment of TAWs and Labour Code-regulated fixed-term and part-time workers enshrined in the law)/non-standard employees, limited union organizing at the company level

Notes: Grey-shaded areas are dominant instruments. CA = collective agreement, CB = collective bargaining, TAW = temporary agency workers, MNC = multinational company, BOA = Baltic Organising Academy.
Source: Authors' research.

resources are limited, but ETKA's members are given legal support, counselling, and different courses. As non-standard workers rarely become union members, their access to these services is restricted. The most general result is continuous precarization across the sector, which is countered neither by the emergence of the islands of good practices in two unionized retail chains nor by significant legal changes triggered by union actions.

Similar to the Estonian case, in Poland a national tripartite institutional structure exists, but has not been used for vigorous social dialogue. For some observers, far from constituting the mainstay of unions' institutional power, the national-level tripartite institutions seem to be an empty institutional shell in Poland (Ost 2000). Being short on institutional power, Polish trade unions began to address the problems of non-standard and low-paid employment at the national level in the late 2000s through some novel, mostly mobilization-based instruments. They managed to frame precarious work as a social problem through mass media campaigns, cyclic street protests, as well as national and international pressure for legislative reform. Union demands included strengthening the Trade Union Act to improve union representation of precarious workers, raising the minimum wage, and creating a minimum hourly wage for civil law contracts, as well as measures counteracting the expansion of civil law and fixed-term employment contracts (cf. Maciejewska and Mrozowicki 2016). The retail sector unions were at the forefront of these activities, including the National Section of Commerce of NSZZ Solidarność, which was involved in nationwide campaigns to raise the minimum wage to 50 per cent of the national average wage and in the 'Sisyphus' campaign against the expansion of 'junk contracts', involving spots on the Internet and in national media. In some campaigns, non-union actors were also involved. These included political parties, such as the right-wing Law and Justice Party and the small left-wing party Together; and social movements, such as the coalition of the anarchist movement and trade union Workers' Initiative that organized Amazon distribution centres. The legal reforms aimed at reducing temporary and civil law employment were implemented in the course of electoral campaigns of the Civic Platform (in 2014–15), as well as following the victory of the Law and Justice Party in the 2015 parliamentary and presidential elections.[4]

Trade union density in the retail sector is as low in Poland as in Estonia. However, Solidarność was able to overcome this obstacle by combining international support and the advantages of being a general union, which allowed it to tap union resources from other sectors for organizing campaigns. The efforts of trade unions did not result in a sectoral collective agreement, nor did they bring collective agreements to a successful conclusion in any of the major retail chains. But the outcomes of retail unions' actions are not negligible and some even reach non-standard workers. The accomplishments in PL1 include, *inter alia*, the transformation of 5,000 fixed-term contracts to open-ended contracts in 2011 and a new policy guaranteeing open-ended contracts for the employees with seniority longer than fifteen months, as well as salary increases secured by a company–union agreement.[5] In PL2, in the course of company-level consultations

---

[4] Even though the reforms could indicate the increase in union institutional power, it has to be noted that the most of them were unilaterally implemented by the government rather than negotiated with the trade unions who initially inspired them.

[5] The company agreements (in Polish, *porozumienie*) in PL1 and PL2 have no status of collective agreements—they are not registered as collective agreements and concern only specific problems at work. Yet, they were seen as binding as they resulted from the company–union consultations of company policies.

and company–union agreements, the unions achieved a reduction in the scope of collective redundancies and an increase in redundancy payments. They also began to represent the interests of merchandizers (employed by external companies), and successfully opposed the project to monitor cashiers' scanning time. Finally, they managed to remove a temporary work agency infamous for bypassing some of the Labour Code and health and safety regulations. Still, in none of the companies were TAWs and self-employed (in the PL1 convenience stores) recruited, as union leaders consider them either non-eligible due to legal regulations or too unstable to invest in their organization. As explained by one of the trade union leaders, 'We have nothing to offer them' (interview, sectoral representative of NSZZ Solidarność, April 2015). Another unionist (from PL2) observed: 'We don't accept people without open-ended contracts as we know they would be fired by the employer' (interview, representative of NSZZ Solidarność in PL2, October 2015).

Following trade union organizing campaigns at the turn of the 1990s and 2000s, working conditions began to improve in large supermarkets and hypermarkets, as well as discounters belonging to MNCs in Poland—in particular as compared to the disorganized segment of small shops. However, trade unions still lack the strength to bring the sectoral employers' organization to the bargaining table, negotiate a sectoral-level agreement, and reduce workforce segmentation. As a result, unions have focused on increasing their associational and institutional power through social and political campaigns combined with company, sector, and nationwide protests aimed at building solidarity within the sector and across other sectors. Initial tangible results can already be observed.

Similar to Estonia and Poland, Slovenia has established national tripartite institutions. The Slovenian government also tried to bypass tripartite institutions and unilaterally pass neoliberal reforms (including the introduction of mini-jobs in 2011) in more or less the same manner as the Estonian government did. This is, however, where the similarities end—the unions in Slovenia effectively deflected reforms and brought down the government in a series of referendums. Furthermore, only 'neocorporatist' Slovenia has a sectoral collective agreement covering the whole trade sector, with both social partners claiming that social dialogue in the sector is good. Greater institutional and associational power, with approximately 15 per cent union density in retail, makes the need for organizing less acutely felt in comparison with the other two countries. The general outcome of these encompassing institutions is less precarious conditions for workers in both standard and non-standard employment. The situation is changing, however, due to increasing difficulties with recruiting and organizing workers in the hostile environment of discounters and smaller employers.

At the national level, the dominant union strategy is to influence labour and social legislation through tripartite negotiations. For example, the labour market reform in 2013 lowered the level of employment protection for regular workers (with rather negative outcomes for retail employees) while at the same time introducing a host of measures aiming at halting the expansion of precarious work. While a similar outcome was present in Poland, it was unilaterally introduced by the government rather than collectively bargained with employers and unions. In addition, similar to Poland but with more substantial results in terms of legislative outcomes, Slovene trade union confederations were involved in broad, nationwide, class-based campaigns. These involved coalitions with other civil society organizations (e.g. the 2011 ZSSS campaign against mini-jobs, together with a student organization) or with a political party (e.g. the 2015 parallel campaigns for the redefinition of the minimum wage, including trade union confederations and a political party positioned to the left of the social democrats). Both campaigns disproportionally affected the situation of retail workers.

At the sector level, the dominant tactics differ according to the workforce segment that is targeted. As regards the part-time, fixed term, TAW,[6] and regular workers (all within Labour Code employment), the main instrument of regulation is the sectoral collective agreement. Equal treatment of TAWs and Labour Code-regulated fixed-term and part-time workers, are enshrined in the law, which means that the provisions in collective agreements apply to them, too. However due to the perceived trade-off between interests of regular and atypical workers, there are no provisions specifically regulating the latter's working conditions. In fact, when asked about the reasons for not including issues concerning atypical workers in the collective agreement, union representatives often referred to a trade-off between the interests of regular and atypical workers:

> UNION REPRESENTATIVE: We could do it, certainly, we could do it. Now, the question is how much we could actually achieve, what would we have to forgo in order to get it.
> INTERVIEWER: Would you have to give up certain rights of regular workers?
> UNION REPRESENTATIVE: Yes, yes, probably so.
> (Interview, union representative, March 2016)

Hence, unions apply a separate strategy towards atypical precarious workers and try to attract them with servicing (legal support, tourist capacities, and loan guarantees). This is, however, not to say that non-standard workers are ignored at the company level. For instance, one of the unions in SI1 managed to organize some agency workers that were treated unequally in respect to regular workers performing the same job. Also, the SI1 company-level union systematically engages in inter-firm solidarity practice as it regulates the working conditions of employees in convenience stores operating as franchises via its relations with the management of the franchisor. This practice was also found in another large state-owned petrol retailer in Slovenia, where the union was strong enough to demand the cancellation of the franchise agreement in cases where the franchisee commits serious breaches of labour laws or if the wages paid are lower than in franchisor-operated petrol stations covered by a company-level collective agreement.

7.4.2. Explanations

Comparatively, the retail sector in all three countries can be considered as precarious, but the concrete forms and extent of precarization differ between

---

[6] In Slovenia the law stipulates that TAWs have to be treated equally as workers employed directly by the company. Hence, the provisions of collective agreements apply to them as well. A similar law is also present in Poland. However, it only applies to hired employees, while the majority of the retail sector TAWs are civil-law workers.

the countries and companies studied. In this respect, the main dividing line seems to run between Estonia, where the share of non-standard work is relatively low, and Poland and Slovenia, which both feature a more segmented workforce. In Estonia, precariousness is virtually a universal feature of retail sector work, and so unions pursue a relatively undifferentiated approach, seeking to build *internal solidarity* and through this to increase *associational power*. In Poland, one segmentation line runs between workers in large retail MNCs, on the one hand, and small and medium-sized enterprises with self-employed workers and franchises, on the other. A second segmentation line cuts into the workforce of the MNCs themselves, dividing those in regular jobs from temporary employees, including those on fixed-term contracts of employment (Labour Code), TAWs, and civil-contract workers (non-Labour Code). In this context, considerable resources would be needed to unionize the segment of temporary workers marked by high turnover, promising only short-term results at best. The segment of small enterprises and the self-employed appears almost totally impenetrable for traditional organizing instruments. Under these conditions, the most promising venue for building solidarity across segmentation divides seems to be radicalization and mobilization by *framing the discourse*. This is the first step to increasing associational power through protest actions that go beyond the workplace level. In Slovenia segmentation is also a problem, but the difficulties with unionization of temporary workers seem less severe. Much larger financial resources allow sectoral unions to apply a somewhat differentiated approach, with certain services attracting many non-standard and low-paid workers.

Turning to institutional variables, tripartite institutions are established in all three countries, but only in Slovenia are unions in a position to pose a credible threat in case the tripartite dialogue is bypassed. This indicates that unions' associational power may be crucial for them to access institutional power through formal institutional structures—or for these structures to even function. Features of institutional regulation at the sectoral level are in place in all the countries studied, such as extension mechanisms, the favourability principle, or the presence of representative employer organizations. However, union density rates of 1–2 per cent in Estonia and Poland (as compared to 15 per cent in Slovenia) are hardly conductive to sectoral multi-employer collective bargaining. This higher density underpins Slovenia's firmly established collective bargaining institutions in retail, which also regulate many aspects of the working conditions of atypical workers. Hence, the major difference between Slovenia and the other two countries does not concern institutional structure but rather union power. The weak enforcement of formal protective labour market institutions that do exist in Estonia provides further support for the argument that union power is more critical than formal institutions.

Indeed, unions' most important power resources enabling them to build ties of solidarity in Poland and Estonia derive from union *network embeddedness*. This involves the articulation between unions operating in the sector and union structures at different levels: at the national (confederation) level in Poland; and at the international level in both countries, through Estonian unions' cooperation in the Baltic Organising Academy (currently) and through the cooperation between the SEIU and Solidarność in Poland. Slovenian unions have also relied on network embeddedness to support their campaigns. For example, the surge in the national minimum wage in 2010, which benefitted retail workers, was to a large extent a generalized outcome stemming from the wage increase in a major exporter of home appliances. Mini-jobs legislation that was successfully resisted at the national level threatened workers in retail (and some other parts of the low-paid and precarized service sector) more than workers in other industries. In addition, the fact that in Slovenia the collective agreement in the retail sector covers TAWs (with no derogations allowed), though clearly an institutional feature, is owed to national-level negotiations in which unions exchanged statutory guarantees of equality of treatment against concessions to capital in other areas. In sum, institutions may well constitute tools at unions' disposal when it comes to constructing inclusive union strategies. Nonetheless, they are but a solidified outcome of past organized labour's struggles and, if they are to be preserved, they have to be constantly backed up by unions' power resources and capacities of making use of them by union leaders (and members) at various levels within trade union structures.

The importance of union power resources is further underscored if we look at patterns of mobilization and relations with the government. The stronger the unions are, the more prominent is the role of mobilization. In Estonia, where unions' associational power is very low and where they lack narrative resources legitimizing social protests,[7] the unions are merely *lobbying* the government. Though unions in Poland are considerable stronger at the national level than in Estonia, those in the retail sector lack the resources necessary to unionize non-standard workers and those employed in the small and medium-sized enterprises segment. They thus find it difficult to apply traditional instruments. However, in the post-2007 crisis period, Polish unions changed tack and began organizing large-scale mobilization actions, which are more demanding in terms of resources than mere lobbying and where the *addressee* of actions are both 'the people' and the government. The legacy of social movement unionism, present in Poland (as the legacy of Solidarność) and missing in post-Soviet Estonia, seems to be crucial in explaining this difference. Finally, Slovene unions' power may be institutionalized, but when these institutions are under threat, the unions are still able to bring 'the people' to the streets and voting polls. At the same time, they are much less able to persuade workers to strike today than in the early 1990s when the industrial relations structure was formed—which makes mobilization a *fall-back option* even when unions are engaged in 'peaceful' negotiations. The militancy of Slovene unions can also be explained by their much stronger power at the national level than at company level. They thus rely on national mobilization and coalitions to sustain institutional power, and to try to compensate for their virtual invisibility and cooperativeness in a growing share of companies (Stanojević and Kanjuo-Mrčela 2016).

---

[7] In Estonia, discourse on class and inequality issues has been generally marginalized and instead national/ethnic and 'transition culture' discourses have dominated that have legitimized the existing inequalities and created ethnic divisions (Helemäe and Saar 2015). This has made it difficult for the representatives of labour to legitimately counteract market-oriented policies (and the expansion of precarious employment) by bringing 'the people' to the streets.

7.4.3. Common Limitations and Challenges

Looking at the explanations in this section, it appears as if the past actions of organized labour in the three countries could be almost *in toto* explained in terms of structural forces and resources inherited from past struggles. This is, however, an illusion of perspective—we have to bear in mind the fact that if structural forces in a capitalist society are constantly exerting pressures for reshaping the society according to the needs of capital, not least by segmenting and atomizing the workforce, virtually every collective act of defiance on the part of working-class organizations palpably points to the importance of *agency*. The various forms of strategic union responses to the problems of precarious work would be difficult to uphold without the innovativeness of trade union leaders and members at various levels of trade union structures. What then are the challenges that lie ahead for organized labour with respect to rebuilding the unity of the working class in the face of pressures for further segmentation and atomization?

Our conclusion at this stage is that the challenge all three labour movements face if they are to rebuild their power resources and counter precarization is to relink political and economic struggles, although each from a different angle. In other words, the political aspects of workers' solidarity, which are often lost in the technical aspects of organizing and collective bargaining (Simms et al. 2012), are the *sine qua non* condition to counteract precarization. Notably, the efforts to build links with workers' communities beyond workplaces, which was said to be crucial in precarious workers' organizing in other contexts (Chun and Agarwala 2016; Sarmiento et al. 2016), are still relatively weak in all three countries studied. In Estonia, where organizing campaigns of precarious retail workers have already borne some fruit, the challenge seems to be linking these clear, though limited, economic achievements at the company level to a more politically oriented approach that could reach beyond the workplace level. The need for such a reorientation towards a more political, class-based movement appears even more pressing among Poland's highly segmented workforce and internally conflicted unionism. This change of course might just be starting to get under way if the recent turn towards protest actions is complemented with some innovative form of organizing atypical workers. In Slovenia, the political momentum of the unions at the national level proved crucial in warding off even more intensive precarization and segmentation. If these institutional protections are not to recede, they need to be reinforced with a stronger union presence in economic struggles at the company level. The way to address these challenges is not defined by initial conditions in any of the three cases—it is only the collective agency comprising both organizational as well as political efforts that can provide a solution.

7.5. CONCLUSIONS

This chapter examined how sectoral characteristics, institutional factors, and trade union strategies towards precarious work have shaped patterns of new solidarities in the retail sector following an economic downturn, based on a comparison of three CEE countries with variegated political-economic and industrial relations systems. Our analysis suggests that institutional differences influenced the forms and extent of precarious work. In Estonia, precariousness is nearly a universal feature of retail sector work and standard employment dominates, while in Poland and (to a lesser extent) Slovenia, the retail workforce is more differentiated between and within shops, and atypical employment is rather widespread. While Estonia represents a case of the most extensive precarization of all workers in the sector regardless of the types of their contracts, the situation in Poland is marked by greater precarization of those in non-standard contracts as compared to those with standard contracts, which reflects very limited organization and representation of the latter. The attempts to advance workforce precarization in Slovenia have been most seriously constrained thanks to union power resources and mobilization capacities at the national level.

More generally, the chapter has demonstrated how opportunities and constraints embedded in the institutional context have influenced union resources and responses to precarization. Our analysis supports the role of encompassing institutions, including high coverage of collective agreements, as a tool to combat precarious work (Doellgast et al. 2016; Mrozowicki 2014). However, we conclude that unions' associational power (Lévesque and Murray 2010; Silver 2003) and institutional power (Doerre et al. 2009: 37) are crucial for the institutions to function and bring gains for labour. Only Slovenian retail unions—with their higher union density rate and occasional support from other unions, political parties, and social movements—are in a position to guarantee the continuation of bipartite and tripartite social dialogue and to regulate the conditions of atypical workers. Poland and Estonia both have favourable regulatory frameworks, which could potentially be used to improve the situation of precarious workers through tripartite social dialogue and multi-employer collective bargaining. However, as suggested by Ost (2000, 2009), these institutions remain illusory as long as they are not backed by strong unions who are able to bring employers—by their mobilizing capacities—to the bargaining table. In such a context, in order to combat precarious work more effectively, both Polish and Estonian unions have also tried to increase their associational power by making use of their network embeddedness, cooperating with national and international unions. The Polish unions have also made use of narrative resources and conducted different mobilization actions directed to a wider audience, including social campaigns in mass media and the Internet. In order to succeed in reducing precarious work, the successful construction and use of narrative resources to mobilize the people and to conduct more politically oriented actions might be crucial.

ACKNOWLEDGEMENTS

The data used for this report have been partially gathered within the research project PRECARIR, 'The Rise of the Dual Labour Market: Fighting Precarious Employment in the New Member States through Industrial Relations', financially supported by a grant from the European Commission, DG Employment, Social Affairs and Inclusion [project no. VS/ 2014/0534], within the project 'Industrial Citizenship and Labour Mobility in the EU: A Migrant Centered Study of Estonia-Finland and Albania-Italy Labour Mobility', funded by the Academy of Finland and the Estonian Ministry of Education and Research funded project 'Alternatives at Work and Work Organisation: Flexible Postsocialist Societies'.

The work on the conceptual part of the chapter was also supported by the project PREWORK ('Young Precarious Workers in Poland and Germany: A Comparative Sociological Study on Working and Living Conditions, Social Consciousness and Civic Engagement') funded by the National Science Centre in Poland and the German Research Foundation (DFG), the NCN project number UMO-2014/15/G/HS4/04476, the DFG project number TR1378/1-1.

REFERENCES

Arnold, Dennis and Bongiovi, Joseph. 2012. 'Precarious, Informalizing, and Flexible Work: Transforming Concepts and Understandings'. *American Behavioral Scientist*, 57(3): 289–308.

Benassi, Chiara and Dorigatti, Lisa. 2015. 'Straight to the Core—Explaining Union Responses to the Casualization of Work: The IG Metall Campaign for Agency Workers'. *British Journal of Industrial Relations*, 53(3): 533–55.

Benassi, Chiara and Vlandas, Tim. 2016. 'Union Inclusiveness and Temporary Agency Workers: The Role of Power Resources and Union Ideology'. *European Journal of Industrial Relations*, 22(1): 5–22.

Bohle, Dorothea and Greskovits, Bela. 2012. *Capitalist Diversity on Europe's Periphery*. Ithaca, NY and London: Cornell University Press.

Carré, Francoise, Tilly, Chris, Van Klaveren, Marteen, and Voss-Dahm, Dorothea. 2010. 'Retail Jobs in Comparative Perspective'. In *Low-Wage Work in the Wealthy World*, edited by Jérôme Gautié and John Schmitt. New York: Russell Sage Foundation and Harvard University Press.

Chun, Jennifer J. and Agarwala, Rina. 2016. 'Global Labour Politics in Informal and Precarious Jobs'. In *The Sage Handbook of the Sociology of Work and Employment*, edited by Stephen Edgell, Heidi Gottfried, and Edward Granter. Los Angeles: Sage Reference.

Crowley, Stephen and Miroslav, Stanojević. 2011. 'Varieties of Capitalism, Power Resources, and Historical Legacies: Explaining the Slovenian Exception'. *Politics and Society*, 39(2): 268–95.

Delo. 2014. 'Diskontne trgovine v Sloveniji rastejo, tudi domače'. Available at: <http://www.delo.si/gospodarstvo/podjetja/diskontne-trgovine-v-sloveniji-rastejo-tudi-domace.html>.

Doellgast, Virginia, Sarmiento-Mirwaldt, Katja, and Benassi, Chiara. 2016. 'Contesting Firm Boundaries: Institutions, Cost Structures, and the Politics of Externalization'. *ILR Review*, 69(3): 551–78.

Doerre, Klaus, Holst, Hajo, and Nachtwey, Oliver. 2009. 'Organizing: A Strategic Option for Trade Union Renewal?' *International Journal of Action Research*, 5(1): 33–67.

Eesti Konjunktuuriinstituut. 2015. *Muutuv konkurentsiolukord toidukaupade tarneahelas ja ebaausad kauplemistavad*. Tallinn: Eesti Konjunktuuriinstituut.

Geppert, Mike, Williams, Karen, Wortmann, Michael, Czarzasty, Jan, Kağnicioğlu, Deniz, Köhler, Holm-Detlev, Royle, Tony, Rückert, Yvonne, and Uçkan, Banu. 2014. 'Industrial Relations in European Hypermarkets: Home and Host Country Influences'. *European Journal of Industrial Relations*, 20(3): 255–71.

Glassner, Vera. 2013. 'Central and Eastern European Industrial Relations in the Crisis: National Divergence and Path-Dependent Change'. *Transfer: European Review of Labour and Research*, 19(2): 155–69.

Grugulis, Irena and Bozkurt, Ödül. 2011. 'Why Retail Work Demands a Closer Look'. In *Retail Work*, edited by Irena Grugulis and Ödül Bozkurt. Houndmills: Palgrave Macmillan.

Häkkinen, Mika. 2013. *The Baltic Organising Academy: How to Build a Multinational and Multisectoral Organising Program?* Available at: <http://library.fes.de/pdf-files/bueros/warschau/10342-20131128.pdf>.

Hall, Peter. A. and Soskice, David. 2001. 'An Introduction to Varieties of Capitalism'. In *Varieties of Capitalism: The Institutional Foundations of Comparative Advantage*, edited by Peter A. Hall and David Soskice. Oxford: Oxford University Press.

Heery, Edmund and Salmon, John. 2000. 'The Insecurity Thesis'. In *The Insecure Workforce*, edited by Edmund Heery and John Salmon. London and New York: Routledge.

Helemäe, Jelena and Saar, Ellu. 2015. 'Estonia: Visible Inequalities, Silenced Class Relations'. *East European Politics and Societies*, 29(3): 565–76.

Jany-Catrice, Florene and Lehndorff, Steffen. 2002. 'Who Bears the Burden of Flexibility? Working Conditions and Labour Markets in the European Retail Trade'. *Transfer: European Review of Labour and Research*, 8(3): 504–20.

Kall, Kairit. 2017. 'Post-Crisis Innovation within Estonian Private Sector Unions'. In *Innovative Union Practices in Central-Eastern Europe*, edited by Magdalena Bernaciak and Marta Kahancová. Brussels: ETUI.

Kallaste, Epp and Woolfson, Charles. 2013. 'Negotiated Responses to the Crisis in the Baltic Countries'. *Transfer: European Review of Labour and Research*, 19(2): 253–66.

Kohl, Heribert. 2009. *Freedom of Association, Employees' Rights and Social Dialogue in Central and Eastern Europe and the Western Balkans*. Berlin: Friedrich Ebert Stiftung.

Lévesque, Charles and Murray, Gregor. 2010. 'Understanding Union Power: Resources and Capabilities for Renewing Union Capacity'. *Transfer: European Review of Labour and Research*, 16(3): 333–50.

Maciejewska, Małgorzata and Mrozowicki, Adam. 2016. 'The Rise of the Dual Labour Market: Fighting Precarious Employment in the New Member States through Industrial Relations (PRECARIR). Country Report: Poland'. CELSI Report No. 13. Bratislava: Central European Labour Studies Institute (CELSI). Available at: <http://www.celsi.sk/en/publications/research-reports/detail/13/the-rise-of-the-dual-labour-market-fighting-precarious-employment-in-the-new-member-states-through-industrial-relations-precarir-country-report-poland/>.

Mosoetsa, Sarah, Stillerman, Joel, and Tilly, Chris. 2016. 'Precarious Labor, South and North: An Introduction'. *International Labor and Working-Class History*, 89: 5–19.

Mrozowicki, Adam. 2014. 'Varieties of Trade Union Organizing in Central and Eastern Europe: A Comparison of the Retail and Automotive Sectors'. *European Journal of Industrial Relations*, 20(4): 297–315.

Mrozowicki, Adam, Roosalu, Triin, and Bajuk-Senčar, Tatiana. 2013. 'Precarious Work in the Retail Sector in Estonia, Poland and Slovenia: Trade Union Responses in a Time of Economic Crisis'. *Transfer: European Review of Labour and Research*, 19(2): 267–78.

Ost, David. 2000. 'Illusory Corporatism in Eastern Europe: Neoliberal Tripartism and Postcommunist Class Identities'. *Politics and Society*, 28(4): 503–30.

Ost, David. 2009. 'The Consequences of Postcommunism: Trade Unions in Eastern Europe's Future', *East European Politics and Societies*, 23(1): 13–33.

Pulignano, Valeria and Signoretti, Andrea. 2016. 'Union Strategies, National Institutions and the Use of Temporary Labour in Italian and US Plants'. *British Journal of Industrial Relations*, 54(3): 574–96.

Sarmiento, Hugo, Tilly, Chris, Garza Toledo, Enrique de la, and Gayosso Ramírez, Jose Luis. 2016. 'The Unexpected Power of Informal Workers in the Public Square: A Comparison of Mexican and US Organizing Models'. *International Labor and Working-Class History*, 89: 131–52.

Silver, Beverly. 2003. *Forces of Labor: Workers' Movements and Globalisation Since 1870*. Cambridge: Cambridge University Press.

Simms, Melanie, Holgate, Jane, and Heery, Edmund. 2012. *Union Voices: Tactics and Tensions in UK Organizing*. Ithaca, NY: Cornell University Press.

Standing, Guy. 2011. *Precariat: A New Dangerous Class*. London: Bloomsbury Academic.

Stanojević, Miroslav. 2010. 'Vzpon in dezorganizacija neokorporativizma v Republiki Sloveniji'. In *Neosocialna Slovenija: Smo lahko socialna, obenem pa gospodarsko uspešna družba?*, edited by Urban Vehovar. Koper: Annales.

Stanojević, Miroslav. 2015. 'Sindikalne strategije v obdobju krize'. *Teorija in praksa*, 52(3): 394–416.

Stanojević, Miroslav and Kanjuo Mrčela, Aleksandra. 2016. 'Social Dialogue during the Economic Crisis: The Impact of Industrial Relations Reforms on Collective Bargaining in the Manufacturing Sector in Slovenia'. In *Joint Regulation and Labour Market Policy in Europe during the Crisis*, edited by Aristea Koukiadaki, Isabel Távora, and Miguel Martínez Lucio. Brussels: ETUI.

Trif, Aurora, Kahancová, Marta, and Koukiadaki, Aristea. 2016. *PRECARIR. The Rise of the Dual Labour Market: Fighting Precarious Employment in the New Member States through Industrial Relations (2014–2016). Comparative Report.* Dublin: DCU. Available at: <http://www.dcu.ie/sites/default/files/dcubs/comparative_report_precarir_2016_final.pdf>.

Turk, Pirjo and Nurmela, Kirsti. 2012. 'Estonia: EWCO CAR on Working Conditions in the Retail Sector'. Available at: <http://www.eurofound.europa.eu/observatories/ eurwork/comparative-information/national-contributions/estonia/estonia-ewco-car-on-working-conditions-in-the-retail-sector>.

Turner, Lowell. 2009. 'Institutions and Activism: Crisis and Opportunity for a German Labor Movement in Decline'. *ILR Review*, 62(3): 294–312.

Visser, Jelle. 2016. 'ICTWSS Database. Version 5.1. Amsterdam: Amsterdam Institute for Advanced Labour Studies (AIAS)'. University of Amsterdam. September 2016.

Vosko, Leah. 2010. *Managing the Margins: Gender, Citizenship and the International Regulation of Precarious Employment.* New York: Oxford University Press.

Wright, Erik Olin. 2000. 'Working-Class Power, Capitalist-Class Interests, and Class Compromise'. *American Journal of Sociology*, 105(4): pp. 957–1002.

8

Better Strategies for Herding Cats?

Forms of Solidarity among Freelance Musicians in London, Paris, and Ljubljana

Ian Greer, Barbara Samaluk, and Charles Umney

8.1. INTRODUCTION

A Vancouver restaurateur posts a Craigslist ad asking for solo musicians to 'play [for free] in our restaurant, promote their work and sell their CD . . . only for special events which will eventually turn into nightly event . . . Are you interested to promote your work?' A reply: 'I am a musician with a big house looking for a restaurateur to promote their restaurant and come to my house to make dinner for my friends and I. This . . . will eventually turn into nightly event if we get positive response . . . are you interested to promote your restaurant?'

This reply highlights the absurdity of expecting musicians to work for free at a profit-making restaurant. But this arrangement would be common in most European or North American cities. Indeed, when the British Musicians' Union (MU) publicly criticized the 2012 London Olympics committee for expecting musicians to work for free, the *London Evening Standard* dismissed their concerns: 'The Musicians Union is indignant that performers at the Olympics and Jubilee celebrations are being asked to perform for free. But frankly, many would pay to be invited to showcase their talents: at momentous national events, surely they should be glad to play their part?'

In our three cities—London, Paris, and Ljubljana—venues, promoters, and intermediaries routinely exploit musicians' unpaid labour. Ongoing salaried jobs exist at many orchestras or theatre companies, but these represent only one part of the market. Our focus is on freelance musicians, most of whom are self-employed and engaged in multiple relations with various actors that offer their services, hire them to perform, or act as channels for dissemination and distribution of their music. These mostly one-off engagements are precarious in both the senses identified in this book—they lack an ongoing employment contract and involve employment insecurity—and are the norm for most working musicians. In the freelance segment a large reserve army of recent graduates and amateurs pushes down pay and other standards. Unpaid jobs are attractive to many musicians in this market because they are presented as career-development opportunities to access new audiences.

MU officials compare organizing musicians with 'herding cats'. We argue that this reflects the aspirations of musicians as creative workers in the context of anarchic and competitive markets. Musicians' desire to work can inspire a fatalism about material conditions that is common to all three cases and which severely limits the organizing potential of unions and institutions. Nonetheless, different forms of solidarity do exist, including ones organized by trade unions and collectives. In France and Slovenia action is directed at protecting highly encompassing welfare institutions that mitigate the consequences of precarity for freelance musicians. Unions help individual members navigate the market through legal advice and events, as well as advocacy for various kinds of state support. Collectives help their members increase their creative autonomy through better access to performance opportunities, while sharing publicity and cutting out profit-extracting intermediaries such as booking agents. Because the advocacy work of unions and collectives is mainly aimed at the state, institutional differences explain some variation in their strategies, but in all cases their effect on precarity is limited by musicians' aspirations and the features of the market.

In this chapter we examine the collective action of freelance musicians in these cities. First, we introduce the basic problem of organizing musicians in this market. Then we compare the state institutions that shape the lives of musicians, and two forms of musicians' collective action: trade unions and collectives. Collectives are an example of communitarian activity which, through creating shared projects and opportunities, assist artists in becoming more 'entrepreneurial'; a kind of solidarity termed 'artistic social entrepreneurship' by Cornfield (2015) and as 'associational' by Umney and Kretsos (2014). Cornfield's (2015) 'artistic advocates', who seek to advocate for greater union consciousness among musicians, did exist among our participants, but struggled to gain traction. We conclude with broader implications for studying collective action of creative workers in highly anarchic and competitive market situations.

8.2. METHODS

This research is based on around seventy qualitative interviews with musicians including numerous trade unionists and members of collectives. Our sample was primarily freelancers working in jazz, world, and popular music domains. Participants were recruited through snowball sampling, beginning with initial contacts who acted as gatekeepers to the wider 'scene'.

The cities are chosen because they are all the centres of large-scale music production and consumption in their respective countries. The countries represent diversity in the institutions that govern the workplace: unlike Britain, both France and Slovenia have welfare institutions specifically aimed at supporting self-employed performing musicians. They also represent diversity in terms of the artistic division of labour: while Paris and London are both unchallenged as global centres of cultural production, Ljubljana's musicians struggle with the replacement of their work by imported recorded music, which they see as part of a broader fight against the global homogenization of cultural and music production.

8.3. THE MUSIC INDUSTRY: ANARCHIC AND HIGHLY COMPETITIVE MARKETS

Freelance musicians operate in an industry where market conditions frustrate the enforcement of labour standards and reinforce their precarity. Musicians transact their business through one-off, often informal agreements with bar owners, restaurant managers, festival promoters, individuals, or organizations looking for entertainment at private functions. This work is attained through word of mouth, personal contact networks, individual musicians prospecting potential clients, or intermediaries such as booking agencies that link clients with bands or musicians. A musician can become a link in the chain by recruiting band members for an engagement, often at the behest of an agent or directly through clients; in Britain this is called a 'fixer'. The fixer–agent relationship usually involves a significant power imbalance owing to the number of options available to most agents and can be characterized by problems such as late payments. The ability of agents to divert work around a large pool of musicians means participants are often afraid to raise these issues (Umney and Kretsos 2014). However, lower links in the chain—those between fixers and their band members—tend to be more egalitarian and embedded in social norms, particularly around pricing.

Markets for music and musicians are fragmented. Symphony orchestras, for example, frequently offer salaried positions, sometimes quasi-permanent, in Europe and North America, usually covered by collective agreements. In our three countries the classical sector depends heavily on state subsidies. Musical theatres also offer large numbers of ongoing positions that can last weeks or months; while these may be freelance positions, the terms agreed for freelancers may be regulated by collectively agreed guidelines. The recording industry generates lucrative streams of funding for record companies, top-selling singers and bands, and other intermediaries, and derives large surpluses from providing content to be used by technology companies to sell hardware or advertising. However, most of the musicians we interviewed were earning money by performing at festivals and clubs, providing background music in restaurants or at corporate functions, and, in some cases, working in theatres or on cruise ships or teaching.

These markets are highly competitive, with a large industrial reserve army whose size is unquantifiable. Freelancers include a spectrum, from well-established professional musicians to 'wannabes' attempting to enter the market while topping up their wages through other means (often teaching, or sometimes jobs entirely outside of music), and hobbyists who do not envision a career in music at all but pursue it as an occasional interest. For freelance musicians, who work solely in areas of writing, recording, and performing, self-employment is generally the only option, and others might combine self-employment with elements of employment in teaching or other, more regular types of work (Coulson 2012). This turns musicians into entrepreneurs, who are tasked with finding work, securing their own income, and insuring themselves against contingencies, such as illness, periods of leave, old age or accidents. This not only represents an enormous financial risk, but also makes musicians responsible for marketing themselves and for other administrative tasks associated with self-employment, as one accordionist in Ljubljana told us: 'every freelancer is like a little enterprise and apart from one's core activity one needs to master various other skills'.

Musicians have to operate like a small enterprise and have to act as producers, promoters, and distributors of their work. This entrepreneurship work is, however, not something musicians have chosen to do. Since most musicians did not initiate their careers with an entrepreneurial drive or think of themselves as businesses, they can be called 'accidental entrepreneurs' (Coulson 2012: 251). The individual negotiation of the market is, as we will show, for many musicians augmented by collective self-organization. Moreover, state institutions can play a role in easing the financial burdens of self-employment, as is the case in Slovenia.

The freelance segment of the music business is anarchic. The lack of an employment relationship makes it difficult to apply collective bargaining and employment law. Requests for unpaid work are very common even for established professionals (Musicians Union 2012), leading the MU to issue guidance such as that shown in Figure 8.1. Furthermore, several of our interviewees valued informality, partly as a response to the onerous administrative tasks associated with being an entrepreneur. As a Parisian musician told us:

> In fact, for jazz musicians, it's very difficult to unionize because we work on our instrument, we are passionate about jazz, about musicians, etc., and in jazz there aren't many people that are going to say 'right, I'm going to do the paperwork' . . . That's the reverse of what we do.   (Saxophonist, 2014)

While there are norms and agreements, they are usually informal and enforced in an uneven way. Employers are adept at giving musicians reasons why they should not be paid. Particularly in rock and pop, they may advertise events as a 'battle of the bands', a name that tempts up-and-coming groups to work for free, or even pay to play, in exchange for the dubious promise of publicity for the winner. Organizers may extract unpaid labour by advertising events as charity shows (so musicians waive their fee) or demanding that musicians do publicity themselves ('you can play here, but only if you bring an audience'). In the case of unwritten arrangements, employers may renege on agreements. One interviewee reported being told by a bar manager that his gig had never actually taken place. Another musician recounted being taken up to an attic after the performance and told the fee was being reduced.

In our interviews, a significant minority of artists were quick to justify their poor conditions, saying things like 'if you want money, get an office job'. If they pursue their passion as a career, in other words, they should be willing to forfeit their right to material security. This applied far more to situations where musicians had more control over their performance (such as bar or club gigs under their own name) than it did to weddings or corporate functions in which musicians had no influence on the content of the work, indicating a trade-off between worker autonomy and reliable fee expectations (Umney and Kretsos 2014).

Other musicians rationalized taking low-paid work by repeating their employers' arguments summarized above. Such gigs could build networks and a reputation, finesse a work in progress, or constitute performance purely for enjoyment. Moreover, because these motivations were widely accepted as legitimate, criticizing other musicians for tolerating poor conditions was viewed as taboo.

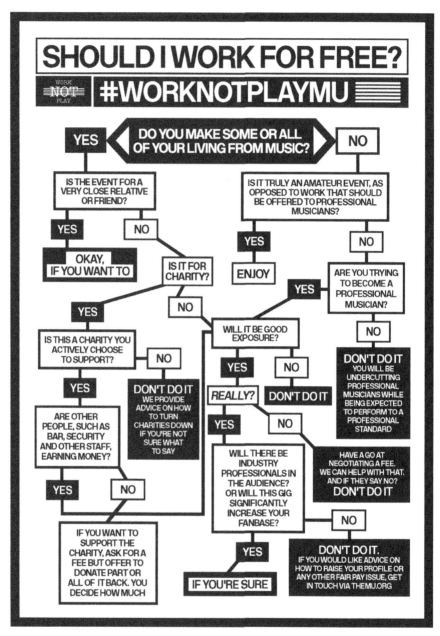

Figure 8.1. Poster from the Musicians Union's 'Work not Play' campaign
Source: Grassrootsy (2015).

Resistance was typically sporadic and isolated: simply walking away, exchanging angry emails, or getting into arguments with buyers of their services. At times, confrontations could be violent: for example, one Paris jazz musician described how a bar manager had refused to pay her band after it had played, so she snatched his iPhone and threatened to smash it on the floor unless cash was forthcoming. The tactic was successful, but it was a response born of a power imbalance and isolation.

From the interviews it was evident that there were some shared ideas about what constitutes acceptable working conditions. In Britain, for example, there was a rule of thumb for minimum payment—£150 per person per engagement—which was applied to private function work and which had not changed in two decades. But musicians do not always hold others to these standards. In a few cases, respondents talked about musicians who egregiously breached these informal social expectations—repeatedly acting in bad faith to undercut others—and were ostracized as a result. But this outcome was rare, suggesting the need for stronger attempts to foster solidarity. We also came across occasions where musicians used word of mouth and social media to publicly attack employers who treated other musicians badly.

In these basic market features there is not much variation between the three countries. There are, however, differences in the way local markets have been affected by external forces and the economic downturn. In Ljubljana—which, compared to London or Paris, is a small city on a peripheral location—local music production has become increasingly crowded out by forces of the globalized market, and since the economic downturn it has been faced with lack of demand and austerity-driven shrinkage of public funds. France has historically been stronger in its attempts to promote domestic musicians through public funding. However, in the experience of participants, this was being undermined by austerity pressures and intermediaries' preferences for importing internationally renowned stars to headline festivals.

The statutes and collective bargaining rules that govern workplaces do not function with musicians outside of theatrical and orchestral settings because there is no employment relationship; what rules and agreements are made tend to be informal and easily violated. This happens in the context of intense competition between musicians for gigs. Musicians themselves find it difficult to enforce norms, whether formal or informal, due to their own conflicting career aspirations. Nevertheless, we have described some everyday forms of conflict and resistance.

8.4. STATE INSTITUTIONS

Despite the evident weakness of industrial relations institutions, music is not a self-regulating market: state institutions shape behaviour in various ways. For example, Slovenia and France both offer state support for individual musicians, with eligibility requirements and financial support having significant implications for freelancers' working lives. They provide a kind of support that is encompassing enough to support, up to a point, precariously employed 'labour market outsiders'. In addition, governments fund festivals and concerts, which provides support for particular kinds of musicians. A third aspect of governance—which was particularly important in Slovenia—has to do with copyright, which determines how royalties are collected and paid to musicians when their music is broadcast, performed live, streamed online, or downloaded.

In London there is very little institutional support for musicians. Musicians seeking welfare support go through the same channel as everyone else, Jobcentre Plus, which tightly controls the activities of job seekers (Greer 2015). One participant who had experience working in both Britain and France, compared his experience in London to his experiences as a job seeker in Paris dealing with advisors at Pôle emploi. While in Britain he had been subject to numerous unhelpful requirements, he described the French experience as more supportive:

> As long as they can see that you're genuine, and you're genuinely looking for work, and not just scamming the system . . . They can tell: I've seen them get arsey with dole-hounds . . . I went to them and they said 'What do you do?' Musician. 'Oh, ok, fine, good. You should go to this dole office which is a specialized office for people working in the field of the arts.' So I went there and all I had to do to keep getting RMI [*Revenu Minimum d'Insertion*, a flat-rate social-assistance benefit] was that every three months I had to go to an interview with this woman who was so excited to hear about everything I was doing musically—because she was into jazz as well—she was like 'oh, great! Let me know when you're playing'. And then she was like, 'Oh, I know someone who works for a jazz magazine, you should try and get a review there' . . . She was trying so hard to help me and get me leads . . . They try and direct you to gigs but often it's stuff like 'Disneyworld needs some musicians'. The best gigs won't be advertised at the dole office. (Guitarist, 2014)

Not only is the general benefits system less punitive for French musicians, there is in addition a specific benefit aimed at them. The *intermittents du spectacle* (IdS) status provides a monthly minimum income for arts sector workers, intended to compensate for the fluctuations in their employment and the forms of work they would do that would otherwise remain unpaid (such as rehearsing, composing, and administration). When a job is undertaken, employers and employees are required to pay social insurance contributions and fill in paperwork declaring that the engagement took place. The criteria for accessing these payments are purely quantitative: musicians must undertake 507 hours of such 'declared' work in a 10.5 month period.

Intermittence contributes to the stability of musicians' working lives by giving them a predictable source of monthly income. It does not, however, eliminate precarity. While *intermittent* musicians may not need to worry as much as counterparts outside the system about their monthly earnings, whether they will be able to renew the status at the end of the 10.5 month period can be a source of profound worry. *Intermittent* status also affects the labour process of its beneficiaries. As one bassist puts it:

> The advantage of *intermittence* is that once we have unlocked our rights to the status . . . we will have an unemployment which will allow us to live and be able to present new repertoire, listen to new concerts . . . The rehearsals we do are never paid. When we do *residences du travail* we are rarely paid. For some concerts, sometimes we aren't paid because it's to develop repertoire. And *intermittence* allows us to live at those times when we have less concerts and where we're really working on future projects. (Bassist, 2014)

Intermittence thus facilitates activities like recording; one saxophonist had been able to stand the costs of recording an album because of the status and described it as 'a kind of subsidy for creativity'.

IdS contributes to the structure of the Parisian labour market. Those who receive it may feel less under pressure to do 'bill-paying' music jobs, such as private function work, which do not advance their artistic project. This was the experience of some interviewees. One saxophonist, who had worked in both Paris and London, compared the higher level of artistic specialization he attained in the latter case, compared to the need for a musician to be a 'jack of all trades' in the former. But this depends on the level of ease with which a musician is hitting their declarations. For musicians facing potential loss of this status, it could impose the exact opposite pressure, to do more function work, since this was more likely to be 'declared'.

IdS has been under pressure in recent years. In 2003, eligibility criteria were tightened (the 10.5 month timeframe had previously been an entire year). This precipitated a strike wave, called initially by the main musicians' union, Confédération Générale du Travail (CGT)-SNAM, but sustained by various insurgent groups who saw the dispute as a key battle in the development of a 'precariat' movement in France (Bodnar 2006). More recently, the French employers' federation, MEDEF (Mouvement des entreprises de France), called for complete suppression of IdS, and then for its retrenchment (Chastand 2014). While such changes would be negotiated with national unions (notably the CGT and the Confédération française démocratique du travail), other groupings such as Coordination des intermittents et precaires are excluded from negotiations but play an important role in mobilizing to defend the statute.

There are other criticisms of IdS that do not stem from employer hostility. There is the argument that, by subsidizing interruptions to employment, *intermittence* permits employers to maintain workers in perpetual underemployment (Menger 2012). Among our participants there were also political and ideological objections. Many saw the system as more favourable to technical staff who could be attached to particular productions for extended periods. By contrast, musicians who earned a living performing in highly casualized one-off engagements were likely to find it harder to meet eligibility requirements, as one bassist told us: 'we represent the perfect *intermittents*. Those that have a different employer all the time. And we are defended by those that have a single employer all the year round!' Questions of legitimacy may arise, given that many musicians may contribute towards it without getting enough declarations to get anything back. Many interviewees argued that the system favoured musicians in genres prioritized by French cultural policy and therefore had better access to publicly funded venues. As a result, they perceived IdS as a form of 'institutionalization' recasting the musician as a *fonctionnaire*.

IdS is undermined by the prevalence of 'black' employment, informal engagements where social contributions are not paid, and which do not contribute towards musicians' eligibility. This kind of work is more common in smaller venues such as bars, restaurants, and clubs than in function work or venues that receive state subsidies. Those interviewees that had been working in Paris since the 1990s had perceived a marked decline in publicly funded venues. Where the bar and club scene had once been a more casualized supplement to publicly subsidized performances, it was now the main source of work for most participants.

While a small minority of Parisian participants had participated in strikes and mobilizations in defence of IdS, most preferred low-level informal manifestations of solidarity. In these, IdS was a complicating factor. By imposing heavy burdens on individuals to meet eligibility criteria, *intermittence* can be a source of individualization—two interviewees who had worked in both France and the UK tended to think that musicians in the former case guarded their positions in bands more jealously, because the stakes of retaining 'good' (i.e. declared) work were higher. One of these summarized the English attitude as 'everything's shit anyway so let's be friends'. But it is also an object of solidarity: where bands are only partly declared (as is common with *contrats de cession*) it was usually the case that musicians would share the declarations out on a 'to each according to his/her need' basis. Given the dynamics of supply and demand, participants perceived little scope to pressure employers to declare more reliably.

The problem of conflicting motivations is exemplified by the experience of one participant, who had sought to use his *association* as a forum for 'collective reflection' on pricing. We might liken this to what Cornfield (2015) terms 'artistic advocacy'. *Associations* may provide rehearsal space or legal advice to musicians or act as channels for receiving public subsidy, but they rarely have a political role. The interviewee in question described meeting opposition when talking about the goals of his association, eventually becoming reluctant to publicize it for this reason. The conflicting motivations acting on musicians can thus be exacerbated by the individualized and quantitative criteria for *intermittent* status, and this, in turn, can be a barrier to solidarity among Parisian musicians.

Unlike in France, the Slovenian welfare state does not offer a guaranteed income to eligible musicians. But it does offer assistance to self-employed persons in culture, including musicians, in the form of state-covered social protection contribution costs. To register with the Ministry of Culture as a self-employed person in the field of culture, annual income has to be below a certain threshold (€19,839.86 gross in 2016) and outstanding cultural achievements must be demonstrated. Outstanding achievements are measured through state, professional, or international awards, published critiques, reach of national and international publics, and through artists' contributions towards the development of an area of work that falls under shortage occupations.[1] Unlike France, the criteria are thus qualitative rather than quantitative.

For these musicians the state covers their compulsory pensions, disability and health insurance, and contributions for parental security and for employment from the state budget. This status lasts for three years and can be renewed according to the above eligibility criteria. However, those above fifty years of age and with a twenty-year lasting right to state contributions gain a permanent status until they reach retirement age. While these subsidies do not bring any direct net income to the musicians, they cover social protection contributions which would normally fall under the gross income, thus unburdening musicians from risks that have otherwise been offloaded to other types of self-employed persons and brings some social and financial security during parental leave, health leave, and retirement.

---

[1] Ministry of Culture, criteria to gain access to state funded social protection contributions: <http://www.mk.gov.si/si/storitve/postopki/statusi_in_pravice/pogoji_za_pridobitev_pravice_do_placila_pri spevkov_za_socialno_varnost_iz_drzavnega_proracuna/>.

There is one exception, however. Although all interviewed freelance musicians who did not earn their core income through teaching or other means had the status of self-employed person in culture that included state-covered social contribution costs, some of them struggled to demonstrate their eligibility because of improper measurements and criteria and lack of recognition of their music work or particular genres. For instance, in some music genres no awards existed, non-commercialized authors had limited access to the media and consequently fewer opportunities to receive critiques or increase their public outreach, and some music genres were not recognized as professions. The state also offers other one-off subsidies for cultural activities for which artists compete on public tenders. These funds have, however, been shrinking due to austerity measures starting in 2009. Public funding and access to public assets has been politically important because it fostered local music and cultural production and distribution that cannot equally compete on the globalized market, and has thus enabled local non-commercial musicians to participate on the market.

The British welfare state does not make allowances for artists; there is little public policy to address the problems of precariously employed musicians. France and Slovenia, by contrast, both have a social insurance fund for musicians and state funding that reaches the freelance musicians we interviewed. This has implications for what unions do: in Slovenia and France, unions focus more on advocacy and the defence of and access to state subsidies, while the British MU focuses more on individual services. These institutions do mitigate precarity but in ambiguous ways. While having a guaranteed income reduces some of the pressure to work paying gigs and creates more scope for family life, Parisian interviewees also discussed at length the extra incentive for getting 'declared' gigs created by the eligibility criteria for IdS, which can further normalize low prices. In Slovenia the efforts of musicians were also geared towards promoting local music in the face of Western imports, using broadcasting, public spending, copyright, and other changes for leverage; it is impossible, however, to say how effective that has been.

8.5. TRADE UNIONS

Despite the widespread view among trade unionists that freelance musicians are difficult to organize, in reality some musicians do join unions in all three cities. These unions have three main functions. First, they set a framework of rules through collective bargaining and unilateral lists of prices, although these are for most freelancers a dead letter. Second, they provide services to help musicians navigate the market, including legal advice and courses on negotiation and marketing. Third, they do advocacy and campaigning. What we do not see are effective strategies to bring the market under control, for example, by increasing and enforcing overall minimum standards.

The MU's role is multifaceted and varies across the UK musicians' labour market. It has a collective bargaining function in sectors where established institutions, such as orchestras or musical theatre companies, employ musicians regularly. For instance, an important employer of musicians in London is the West End, where the MU negotiates a collective agreement with the Society of

London Theatres. It also bargains with individual orchestras and ballet or operatic ensembles to set terms for regularly employed musicians. In these cases it also negotiates to set baseline contracts for musicians who are taken on more casually, through Orchestral Freelance Agreements. On the MU's website, musicians can find the agreed guidelines for pay rates and working hours for their employer. These engagements are often accessed via 'fixers' who recruit bands for production companies who are required to respect these guidelines. There is wide variation above them depending on the profile of individual performers, and they may look to cut out potential 'troublemakers' who are seen to be too rigid in following MU rules.

In more casual contexts such as function, club, or bar work, the MU plays a different role. The level of casualization, the transient nature of buyer–seller relationships, and the sheer size of London's reserve army of musical labour, appear highly unconducive to collective bargaining. Correspondingly, the union recruits and retains members through servicing. For instance, its provision of discounted insurance tends to be highly valued by interviewees, as does its legal advice services, and it organizes events for members such as networking sessions.

The MU does not limit itself to service provision. It has tried to influence the terms of the labour market, but what it can achieve in this respect is limited by various factors we will describe later in this section. It sets and publicizes guideline rates and working hours for one-off engagements, which it tries to promote among musicians. Generally, it seeks to raise the profile of working conditions as a question among musicians, whether they are members or not. It released the 'Fair Play Guide', which makes recommendations regarding the kinds of behaviour musicians should or shouldn't be prepared to accept, and which cautions against strategies to extract free labour such as 'Battles of the Bands' or dubious invocations of charitable status. The highest-profile current initiative is the 'Work not Play' campaign, launched after an MU-commissioned study found that more than half of respondents reported having been asked to work for free in the preceding year (MU 2012). 'Work not Play' encourages musicians to report requests for unpaid work, so the campaign can then name and shame offenders on its website.

These measures depend on a particular form of organization, in which individuals need to embed social expectations in their own decision making when engaging with multiple potential employers and clients. It implies that musicians should negotiate harder with buyers, and in extreme cases reject work for the long-term good of the profession as a whole. For musicians without a well-established career as an in-demand performer this is very difficult. MU guidelines had a low profile among our London participants, for several reasons.

First, the structure of the musicians' labour market in these contexts is highly porous, with a very large constituency that is only partially integrated into it. This reserve army comprises many people for whom paid music work is more accurately characterized as a hobby, undertaken sporadically alongside other sources of income. Such people may well even be union members, if they perceive this to be a sign of prestige as a 'proper musician', or else value the services. This kind of musician would face prohibitively high entry barriers to working in an orchestral or theatrical production (and would have little incentive given the time commitments), but has less difficulty in one-off performances where the job brief may simply be to provide background music for an audience with little specialist knowledge. In this porous and open market, a significant proportion of the music labour force is unconcerned about MU rates.

Second, even among the more dedicated professional musicians in our sample, there is scepticism about setting collective fee guidelines. Musicians may see a financial benefit in working for less, if it contributes to building their name recognition or developing a particular project. Our interviews also detected a recurrent sense of fatalism: poor conditions are the price to be paid for having your passion as your job. Furthermore, even where musicians were individually conscious of the problem of poor pay, decisions were seen as individual, and that it was illegitimate to impose collective expectations on the kinds of work others should not accept.

A final reason for the weakness of MU guideline rates may be the low visibility of the union in musicians' workplaces. Employment relationships are transient, and even ostensibly stable units—such as function bands that get very regular work—are characterized by rapidly shifting personnel. A musicians' chair in a function band does not necessarily entail that individual turning up for every engagement. Instead, they control a position which may regularly be 'depped out' to other contacts when diary clashes emerge. This is also a means of cementing reciprocal relationships between others playing the same instrument. This economy of replacements means that even ostensibly stable function bands have fluctuating line-ups. Hence, while musicians often profess strong communitarian sentiment and form powerful social bonds with other musicians, these bonds tend to spread across a diffuse network of bands and projects, rather than being located in particular workplaces. Consequently, the absence of a stable bargaining unit is not just due to disparate buyers, but disparate co-workers.

Parisian trade unionists tend to be primarily concerned with mobilizing to defend IdS, and some of our interviewees had been involved. One, for instance, had recently performed live in front of the Ministry of Culture as part of a protest against mooted reforms. But this was a very rare case, for reasons similar to those preventing union mobilization in the UK. As Proust (2010) has argued, it tends to be difficult for French unions to mobilize at grassroots level, given the conflicting motivations of arts workers. As in Slovenia, unions may play a role in supporting individual workers' access to social security *contributions*. One participant, for instance, had had administrative problems in getting his declarations processed, and the union was able to advise him in making progress with the Pôle emploi bureaucracy. But the clear quantitative eligibility criteria for IdS may diminish the demand for these kinds of services, compared to Slovenia.

Like the MU, CGT-SNAM does set minimum condition guidelines, but among our interviewees these had barely any recognition. Indeed, in some respects, *intermittence* may make solidarity among musicians harder to realize since it imposes a heavy but clearly defined burden on individuals. To one respondent drummer this meant an overriding concern first and foremost with hitting individual declaration targets. As we have shown in more depth elsewhere, this could further weaken social price norms (Umney 2016). For some participants, the question of whether a gig would be declared or not was more important than the question of price. One guitarist reported being asked the following question on various occasions: 'Do you want to be paid or do you want to be declared? It's one or the other.' Consequently, musicians find quite personalized balancing acts between declared and undeclared work. In the words of another guitarist: 'I have my own arrangement with the social system.' Many participants were very well informed about the pressures on IdS and could be forthright in articulating the need for a political defence of it, but this tended to be in quite an informal way, prioritizing discussion with others as a means of countering media misrepresentations, rather than through union membership per se.

The comments on trade unionism in this section reflect the situation across France more generally, where union membership is low but support for 'union causes' comparably high. Another participant, a jazz drummer, talked about support for the system, but in a manner that reflects the 'underground' preference of jazz musicians: they might sign petitions or attend demonstrations, but would never go to a union meeting.

In Ljubljana unions are also weakened by the transient and informal nature of the work. In addition, the Slovenian music scene is heavily burdened by several competing and divided collective organizations that have emerged due to unresolved issues concerning copyright and other related rights. The largest union for freelance musicians is Glosa (Trade Union of Culture and Nature in Slovenia) that represents cultural workers in general. It organizes various cultural workers under different Trade Union Conferences, among which is also the Conference for Musicians (Glosa-SKG), an umbrella body for musicians' unions. Much smaller is the musicians-only union, the Union of Slovenian Musicians (SGS), established in 1994 and more recently revived.

One goal of Slovenian trade unionists has been the re-establishment of a national award for music that would benchmark standards for music work and provide a much-needed reference for musicians when applying for state subsidies. In 2015 they succeeded, and the ceremony was accompanied by relevant discussions around the contemporary issues in the music industry. As one Glosa-SKG activist told us: 'Musicians' trade unions, we wanted to re-establish a national music award... in order to do that we started talks with the public RTV Slovenia... to film and broadcast the event... but certain people blocked it... and this would be a professional award... it would act as a reference for musicians, and also as an eligibility to apply for tenders and the status (of self-employed person in culture with state-covered social contributions). This was a non-invasive way to start attracting new members: 'We decided... to approach musicians through positive things and establish our name through that' (Glosa-SKG activist, 2014). Glosa-SKG was attempting to build itself up by gaining musicians' trust by empowering local musicians and increasing their access to public subsidies, which was also something that interviewed musicians were looking for when they turned to unions.

Another way of increasing access to subsidies came from SGS, which was assisting singer-songwriters with their petitions to the Ministry of Culture for their specific genre to get officially recognized as a profession. This recognition enables proper assessment of their work that increases their access to state subsidies and grants them appropriate classification for copyright and also acts to better preserve the linguistic and cultural heritage of Slovenia. Both unions have also been advocating changes of the Media Act, including an increase of quotas of

Slovenian music in media broadcasting. These demands are a result of external pressures visible in an increasingly privatized media landscape characterized by the rapid rise of commercial radio stations that import Western models (Golčar 2004; Bašić-Hrvatin et al. 2004) and crowd out local non-commercialized music production and the demand for it.

A longstanding goal of Glosa has been an encompassing collective agreement that includes a diverse range of self-employed persons in culture. These endeavours initially departed from precarious conditions of bogusly self-employed (yet economically dependent) journalists on the public RTV Slovenia and have been run by Glosa's Conference for freelancers in the area of culture and information (Glosa-SUKI). They proposed two important legal changes, writes a Glosa-SUKI representative on their website: 'the acknowledgment that self-employed persons in culture do not employ others... and that as such a self-employed person [in legal terms] counts as a worker with workers' rights... the second change introduces a horizontal income comparison between self-employed and employed public worker, and this would need to be achieved every time an employer would be co-financed by the state budget'.[2] This proposal recognizes self-employed as workers and thus grants them the right to social dialogue and collective agreements. The proposal is under consideration by the government, but according to the President of Glosa-SUKI has stalled because 'it is being heavily disputed by private non-governmental organizations that use freelancers for projects and programs co-financed by the Ministry of Culture'.[3]

Furthermore, the musicians' representative supports this initiative and sees this collective agreement as a solution to improving the condition of freelance musicians and increase their employment protection:

> [The collective agreement] could define how many gigs per year in what sum... we discussed setting tariffs... how much would a gig cost in relation towards certain amount of people, by such a bend in such a place... minimum fee per gig... This would be a 'one stop shop', this would be a collective agreement for self-employed, that would include overall tariffs, their rights and protective mechanisms, etc.
>
> (Glosa-SKG activist, 2014)

The collective agreement would be a 'one stop shop' governing fees, rights, and protection mechanisms. Such a collective agreement could also set criteria of a certain amount of music work required per year which would then disqualify all hobby musicians. Thus far, setting up common employment conditions have only been achieved by unions when they were negotiated within a common workplace, such as a music festival: 'we only achieved that once, we successfully bargained that food, lodging and daily allowance is provided to all musicians, who were performing at that festival' (former SGS activist, 2014).

Slovenian music industry unions are more actively involved in advocating for musicians in the management of copyright and the pursuit of royalties than their London or Paris counterparts. While the MU provides advice services on

---

[2] Samozaposleni v kulturi in samostojni novinarji v Sloveniji—Quo vadis?: <http://www.sindikat-glosa.si/assets/suki/samozaposleniquovadis26012016.pdf>.

[3] SUKI-Glosa boj z mlini na veter: <http://www.sindikat-glosa.si/assets/suki/boj-z-mlini-na-veter2612016.pdf>.

copyright and lobbies the government in support of policies that are more favourable to copyright holders, there is currently much controversy in Slovenia over copyright, and unions were more active in debates regarding the collection and distribution of performance and mechanical royalties to authors. This management is currently divided between various competing organizations, among them SAZAS (Association of composers and authors for protection of copyright in Slovenia), Zavod AIPA (Slovene collecting society for asserting rights of authors, performers, and producers of audiovisual works), and its sister organization Zavod IPF (Slovene collecting society for asserting rights of performers and producers of phonograms). Glosa-SKG is advocating for the so-called 'one invoice' for collecting royalties, which, according to a study conducted by the Faculty of Economics at the University of Ljubljana, would significantly reduce the administrative costs and allow the beneficiaries of copyright and related rights to obtain more resources.[4] Currently, however, previously mentioned managing organizations seem to have little interest in establishing this policy. While these managing organizations are caught in power struggles, non-commercialized freelance musicians receive few royalties or other support from them. Glosa-SKG and all interviewed musicians held grudges, particularly against SAZAS, which has according to them worked in a very non-transparent and non-cooperative manner and favoured commercialized over non-commercialized authors.

Union functions for freelance musicians vary, often in response to the institutional context, but one commonality is a lack of enforcement power in most musical workplaces. This stems from market structures and worker aspirations that are common to all cases. The MU is mainly focused on individual services, and its largest campaign is aimed at public education rather than state policy. CGT-SNAM is mainly present in preserving IdS. The Slovenian musicians unions that operate under wider union efforts to better the conditions of all cultural workers have a much wider range of activities, including an innovative collective agreement that would cover all self-employed cultural workers operating under state funding.

8.6. COLLECTIVES

An alternative form of solidarity among musicians is the collective. Many musicians we met in London and Ljubljana had been part of networks of like-minded musicians that created and operated new performance spaces and opportunities for production. Some collectives resembled small businesses, with a closed-off core of members that see successful collectives as commodifiable 'brands'. Others, especially in Ljubljana, where musicians faced being crowded out of the market, pursued a more radical vision of music making—one interviewee spoke of 'cultural self-supply'. This distinction is thus comparable to the one Cornfield (2015) makes between 'artistic social entrepreneurs', who use community resources to

---

[4] *Delo*, 'One Invoice for Collecting Royalties': <http://www.delo.si/kultura/dediscina/enotna-poloznica-za-pobiranje-nadomestil.html>.

support entrepreneurialism, and 'artistic advocates', who seek to push a more trade union-centred mentality. The more politicized 'artist advocacy' in the Slovenian case, however, is shaped by austerity and the threat to localized music production from an influx of mass Anglophone culture.

In Paris, the word 'collective' was used far less frequently, and methods of self-organization among musicians tended to take the form of the quasi-formal 'associations' described above. Some had a fledgling political purpose, as described previously, while others, such as the Union des Musiciens de Jazz in Paris (with which some interviewees had worked) were more established and channelled funding into rehearsal spaces and organizing concerts. The majority existed as a legal vehicle to establish *contrats de cession* or to apply for and receive grants. Because of this more technical and instrumental character, associations are distinct from the kinds of self-organization we describe in this section. Self-organized collectives were more frequently brought up by interviewees in London and Ljubljana.

A collective, in London jazz music, tends to refer to a loose network of musicians with more or less defined membership boundaries. Members may cooperate to secure access to venues where they share out performance opportunities, support each other in publicizing and administrating concerts, and to some degree even constitute the nucleus of a ready-made audience for their members' gigs. Each collective tends to comprise various different bands with overlapping personnel. They are united by an artistic agenda and/or a neighbourhood.

This can constitute a form of mutual aid. Collectives can give musicians space for collective self-expression that is somewhat sheltered from market pressures. Sometimes, collectives may have explicitly communitarian goals; one participant, for instance, described hers as being a means of making music participation more accessible in her relatively deprived part of London.

On the other hand, collectives are not generally incubators of professional solidarity: they tend to focus on building local scenes and expanding networks of contacts. Indeed, most collective work we came across revolved around 'door-money' engagements, where there was no fee for the band but where bar takings or entry fees would be divided up at the end of the night. They thus advance the material interests of their participants, not by challenging poor pay, but by building name recognition and securing access to work. They can become relatively closed-off, perhaps even cliquish, once established. In the ones we came across, entry was generally closed to non-founding members. The 'branding' value of a successful collective implies an implicitly entrepreneurial logic, an ambiguity expressed by one member:

> This is the very internal debate that's going on at the moment within the collective. What are we trying to do? None of us actually want to be promoters, but in reality that's kind of what we're doing. We're running this promotions company for other bands, and our bands when we want to play there. And that doesn't really sit comfortably with any of us. Because we're all kind of artistically minded, slightly anti-business, you know? There was this meeting the other week . . . [in the email follow-up discussion] people were starting to use terms like 'band liaison officer'. Sort of corporate terminology. So I sent an email asking what that meant! I don't really know the answer to that—it's an ongoing debate. I think we all just see each other as

musicians who are doing something mutually beneficial, giving us a platform for our original music, trying stuff out in front of an audience. As for the future, I'm not sure.

(Bassist, 2014)

In Slovenia, collectives were more likely to have an overtly political agenda. In Ljubljana the local labour market for musicians and the welfare arrangements that once supported them have shrunk due to external market pressures, privatization of public services and assets, and the economic downturn and austerity. While local musicians are being increasingly crowded out, we witness musicians' collectives, in some cases, attempting to create an alternative market segment. There we spoke to members of collectives founded on egalitarian principles that had created alternative venues and production and distribution channels. They also built new relationships with venues, asking them to commit to pre-agreed pay rates in return for booking them for well-attended cultural events. While these collectives fight to improve material conditions for musicians, they have also projected a radical political message against the privatization and commercialization of venues and distribution channels.

For example, one self-managed collective built a strategic relationship with one venue. There the general agreement was that the self-managed collective has complete autonomy over the cultural programme and the venue allocates fixed funds to finance events they organize, as one musician told us:

The owner is paying [from the bar], so that every musician gets €50 or the band €200, every band gets €200 . . . We played on Friday . . . we were three and there was €60 and on top the tips, so each got €85 . . . This is the first bar in Ljubljana, unique, musicians badly needed it, that also elsewhere similar things will emerge now upon its example so that [the] music scene becomes alive, because it's practically dead.

(Bassist, 2014)

Although the performance fees are lower than before the crisis, the tariffs are agreed in advance, and the collective has been applying for public funds to raise them to an acceptable fixed minimum level of €100 per person per gig. This semi-autonomous space has contributed to the revival of the performing scene, which suffered due to the economic crisis and lack of demand. Members of the collective are already established within the scene and use their networks to cut out intermediaries.

This includes previously mentioned organizations responsible for collecting copyright royalties, especially SAZAS, which is, according to one musician, described as a destructor of local culture: 'And why is SAZAS responsible for destruction of local culture? Simply because many clubs couldn't afford to have concerts anymore, because they wanted too much money. The clubs abolished live performance . . . We have a rule. A condition to play [within their semi-autonomous place] is to give up your copyright, because this is the only way we can fight them' (Bassist, 2014). The demand to give up rights is not coercively exercised but is the musicians' strategy against representational injustice that in effect lowers their fees and decreases their possibilities to perform in smaller, less commercialized, and self-managed venues. Rather than actively engaging with divisive politics and management of copyright, non-commercial freelance musicians tend to rebel by giving up their copyright in order to avoid payments to SAZAS, which is seen as favouring commercialized authors.

Moreover, one accordionist established a self-managed record company to connect freelance musicians and to unburden them from the self-entrepreneurial labour needed for production, promotion, and distribution of their artistic work: 'This is now nine, ten years ago, when I wanted to use my multi-layered knowledge in order to connect the freelance music scene, maybe not that much connect as to create a sort of service, which then developed into [a record company], which would offer a platform to freelancers in order to publish and promote music' (Accordionist, 2015).

This record company acts as a creditor that does not charge interest, for those musicians who would otherwise self-publish. It unburdens freelancers from self-managerial work, offers them a platform to publish and promote their music, and opens up possibilities for cooperation. It employs 'radical transparency', giving everyone involved an overview of finances and prices. Contracts usually give authors two years to return the credit, and unlike other record companies they do not dispossess authors of copyright. To further promote the authors they established a non-profit institute, which enables them to organize events and apply for public funding, as the organizer told us:

> This is the first year that we received some funds for the festival, I hope it will also be available for the next three years. If the conditions will not drastically worsen in our country, which means that now we have certain funds available that enable us to do 5–6 concerts. Normally that also means that we publish 5–6 albums, these two things are very connected . . . I think we will also put more focus on this in the future. Because only publishing music, without creating a certain pulse beside, it's a drop in the ocean. There is no effect.　(Accordionist, 2015)

Since 2009 the institute has organized yearly music festivals, where musicians who publish with their record company are presented and can distribute their work. The quote shows that they aim to put more focus on distribution and hope that they will have continued state support. They also air the published music on their online radio station. Overall the enterprise is presented on the webpages of both entities as 'a creative field that opens up possibilities and supports capabilities for creation, performance and access to music'. The growing self-managed enterprise is thus aiming to increase local musicians' capabilities within the production, performance, and consumption process of the global market. Through years of work the enterprise built a trustworthy reputation among musicians and the expert public. Especially for younger musicians, involvement in this enterprise provided access to networks and work. It involves around 120 musicians, and through their mailing list they also try to engage musicians in wider issues regarding their rights and representation. However, despite attempts the organizer reports little willingness for collective action among musicians:

> The awareness that we have to come together is still not anchored within most of these people . . . There is a possibility to authorize and then we suggested one [from One Music Society], who has a good knowledge of this . . . at the end we collected 20–30 authorizations, which is something but still too little for concrete bargaining power. While on the other hand you have pop-folk music, which has a pretty well-organized union and they collect 200 signatures. Then they can decide how the IPF [Society for asserting rights of performers and producers of phonograms] will function, etc.
>
> (Accordionist, 2015)

Through their mailing list they also try to address issues around representation. They cooperate closely with the collective One Music Society that has the most politicized agenda of all collectives. As one of their members explains, they engage in a variety of activities in order to address musicians' rights and challenge the basic epistemic issues regarding how the public interest should be defined: 'One activity is education, [the] second activity is acoustic ecology, the third is copyright law in connection to collectives . . . Then, it is the overall cultural politics and status of self-employed or free culture and overall national programme for culture. Basically the common denominator is how to distribute public funds, how to define public interest' (Sound designer, 2014).

To this end they petition against sound pollution in the Old Town of Ljubljana that comes from various privatized places that play commercialized radio stations and take away the space for local musicians. Through petitioning and public engagement they try to achieve the protective status of local music which would equal the protective status of architectural cultural heritage. Overall they challenge the epistemic issues of public reasoning (Sen 2005) that define public interest in the recognition and funding of local culture and cultural heritage.

Since their success in changing the workings of structural institutions is limited, they also create autonomous space for musicians to perform, record, and distribute their music. One member calls this self-organizing model a 'cultural self-supply' that compensates for failed welfare institutions and provides a space for local musicians to perform and produce by circumventing any intermediary extractors of profits and creating a direct 'sharing economy' with the audience. The main aim is to provide top recording facilities completely free of charge for musicians, while gigs for the wider public are only organized each Saturday. These are always recorded and published on their YouTube channel, yet financed exclusively by tips. Several of our interviewees had played there and, though appreciative of the work of the collective, one musician pointed to problems regarding poor material rewards that only come from tips: 'When people came to our concert there was €120 in the hat . . . Their work is great, everything is great, but I'm talking about people, about the audience' (Guitarist, 2014).

In all of the above-mentioned collectives, the problems of the market—especially that of poor remuneration and no artistic control—were recognized and acted on collectively. In some cases, this took a more market-facing, 'entrepreneurial' form, whereas in others it was more market-contesting. This difference was attributable to the institutional context in the cities concerned. In addition to improving conditions for performance, Ljubljana's collectives also offer an alternative space for production and distribution and an alternative platform for political engagement and representation. In no case did we see evidence of collaboration between unions and collectives, although in Ljubljana there was some mutual recognition and criticism.

8.7. CONCLUSION

In all cases of collective action, we observe freelance musicians struggling in this market. Competition is intensified by a large reserve army, exacerbating problems of income insecurity that are part of being a freelancer, and generating administrative tasks and a need to self-promote. Many of the better-paid gigs (such as private functions) involve little or no creative autonomy, which is what many musicians have told us they value most of all. Differing welfare institutions do not mitigate the existence of short-term contracts, but they do temper income insecurity in the short run. Moreover, they influence the forms of solidarity that exist, since collectives and unions adapt to engage with the institutional context. The qualitative criteria employed in the Slovenian system creates greater scope for unions to assist workers in accessing welfare support compared to France. However, market structure and worker aspirations limited unions' mobilizing capacity in workplaces in all three cases.

The most obvious contrast between the countries is the lack of institutional support for freelance musicians in London compared to Paris and Ljubljana, in terms of both funding and welfare provision. This does not mean lower status distinctions in London, however: in place of state support for musicians, financial support from families becomes all-important (Umney and Kretsos 2015). It also does not eliminate precarity in Paris and Ljubljana, even among those musicians who are covered. It does mean that in Paris and Ljubljana collective action is more politicized and aimed at the state: in Paris this included a strike, and in Ljubljana an attempted collective agreement. In both cases these hinged on government institutions not tasked with regulating the workplace, and in Ljubljana there was another difference, namely a lively politics of cultural self-protection as the capital of a small peripheral country. Table 8.1 summarizes the examples of regulation in the three cities.

Throughout this book, union strategy is highlighted as a way to avoid a downward cycle of narrow self-interest, institutional dualization, and employment precarity, and move towards a virtuous cycle of broadly solidarity, encompassing institutions, and greater security. That we observe neither of these paths can be explained in a way that echoes the criticisms found in other chapters of the 'dualization' discussion in comparative political economy.

Table 8.1. Examples of regulation for freelance musicians

	State	Union	Collective
London	Very little; generalized welfare regime	Servicing role; attempts to establish widespread norms and practices	Communal support for artistic entrepreneurs
Paris	Welfare system based on quantitative criteria	Advocacy and mobilizations to protect welfare system	[Associations]: means of acquiring funding; administrative functions connected with welfare system
Ljubljana	Welfare system based on qualitative criteria	Advocacy and mobilizations to protect welfare system and establish better management of copyright; services to help musicians access welfare eligibility; attempts at collective agreement	Communal support for artistic entrepreneurs; 'cultural self-supply' and political advocacy

Unions and collectives do not have the tools at their disposal to reduce their members' precarity, because their efforts to regulate the terms of exchange on the market are limited by their members' aspirations. This, however, does not mean that they are narrowly self-interested representatives of labour market 'insiders'. To the contrary, they are helping their members to include themselves in the market by getting paid for what they do and show solidarity via an advocacy role aimed at expanding the size of the market (through protecting state funding), increasing musicians' revenue streams (through intervening in copyright policy, as in Slovenia), and mitigating income insecurity (through protecting social insurance schemes, as in the Parisian strike). Collectives tend to be more specialized, but they similarly work to include musicians in the market through advocacy. In addition they create spaces for musicians to do their work, whether motivated by a radical vision of 'cultural self-supply' or a small-business mentality focused on market access. These forms of solidarity can be quite inclusive and aimed up at shoring up encompassing institutions, but they do not reduce precarity for working musicians.

The notion of a 'union strategy' seems to have weak traction in the context of music, in part because of the incongruity of managerial and military language where so much collective action is outside of trade union administrative structures, in collectives or the everyday struggles of individual working musicians. The 'herding cats' metaphor used by union officials themselves suggests another reason, namely, that planned and systematic attempts to control the market are easily frustrated by the aspirations and actions of working musicians themselves.

ACKNOWLEDGEMENTS

The study presented in this chapter arose from a wider research project entitled 'The Effects of Marketization on Societies' and supported by the European Research Council (#313613).

REFERENCES

Bašić-Hrvatin, Sandra, Kučić, Lenart, and Petković, Brankica. 2004. *Media Ownership: Impact on Media Independence and Pluralism in Slovenia and Other Post-Socialist European Countries*. Ljubljana: Mirovni Inštitut.

Bodnar, Christopher. 2006. 'Taking It to the Streets: French Cultural Worker Resistance and the Creation of a Precariat Movement'. *Canadian Journal of Communication*, 31(3): 675–94.

Chastand, Jean-Baptiste. 2014. 'Le MEDEF veut supprimer le regime des intermettents'. *Le Monde* Blogs. Available at: <http://emploi.blog.lemonde.fr/2014/02/12/le-medef-veut-supprimer-le-regime-des-intermittents/>.

Cornfield, Daniel. 2015. *Beyond the Beat: Musicians Building Community in Nashville*. Princeton, NJ: Princeton University Press.

Coulson, Susan. 2012. 'Collaborating in a Competitive World: Musicians' Working Lives and Understandings of Entrepreneurship'. *Work, Employment and Society*, 26(2): 246–61.

Golčar, Bojan. 2004. 'Mrtvorojeni otrok' države s prevelikim številom rtv-organizacij?' *Media Watch*, 20/21: 22–7.

Grassrootsy. 2015. 'Should You Play that Free Gig?' Blog, 15 April 2015. Available at: <http://www.grassrootsy.com/2015/04/15/should-you-play-that-free-gig/>.

Greer, Ian. 2015. 'Welfare Reform, Precarity and the Re-commodification of Labour'. *Work, Employment and Society*, 30(1): 162–73.

Menger, Pierre-Michel. 2012. 'Job Growth and Unemployment Increase: French Flexible Labour Markets and their Insurance Shelter in the Performing Arts'. *Economia della Cultura*, 22(1): 17–34.

Musicians Union. 2012. *The Working Musician*. London: Musicians Union.

Proust, Serge. 2010. 'Syndicalisme et délitement du salariat artistique: la CGT et les groupes mobilisés autour du régime de l'intermittence'. *Sociologie du travail*, 52(3): 374–88.

Sen, Amartya. 2005. 'Human Rights and Capabilities'. *Journal of Human Development*, 6(2): 151–66.

Umney, Charles. 2016. 'The Labour Market for Jazz Musicians in Paris and London: Formal Regulation and Informal Norms'. *Human Relations*, 69(3): 711–29.

Umney, Charles and Kretsos, Lefteris. 2014. 'Creative Labour and Collective Interaction: The Working Lives of Young Jazz Musicians in London'. *Work, Employment and Society*, 28(4): 571–88.

Umney, Charles and Kretsos, Lefteris. 2015. '"That's the Experience" Passion, Work Precarity, and Life Transitions among London Jazz Musicians'. *Work and Occupations*, 42(3): 313–34.

9

Fighting Precariousness

Union Strategies towards Migrant Workers in the UK, France, and Germany

Maite Tapia and Jane Holgate

9.1. INTRODUCTION

The rise of a precarious migrant workforce presents challenges as well as opportunities for trade unions across and within countries. Organizing precarious workers[1] creates particular problems for labour unions as they struggle to organize sectors and jobs where these workers are to be found. That said, organizing precarious *migrant* workers presents an even greater challenge for unions who struggle without appropriate resources and staff to organize and recruit this particular group of workers. Migrants, regardless of their skill level, are disproportionally employed in informal or low-wage jobs, creating patterns of occupational segregation where discrimination and insufficient union protection leave workers in a vulnerable and precarious state (Cornfield 2014). Yet, at the same time, unions and groups of migrant workers in these growing, precarious, and low-wage sectors are engaging in campaigns to reduce the economic and social inequalities many of them encounter in the labour market. Our chapter focuses on union strategies towards migrant workers and the extent to which unions are trying to build inclusive solidarity to counter the segmentation strategies of employers—in other words, union strategies that could overcome the 'vicious circle' associated with expanding precarity described in the introduction to this book (see Chapter 1).

This chapter builds on our previous book, *Mobilizing Against Inequality: Unions, Immigrant Workers, and the Crisis of Capitalism* (Adler et al. 2014), and examines union strategies towards precarious migrant workers in the UK, France, and Germany. Specifically, we compare migration policies at national and peak levels and specific union/migrant worker campaigns at more local levels across these countries as well as within each country. We focus on dimensions of scale and agency to examine the extent to which national trade union policies (positive

---

[1] We draw on Kalleberg 2009 and Kalleberg and Hewison 2013 and define precarious workers broadly as individuals on non-standard contracts, lacking employment security, and without, or with minimal, employment protection.

as they might be towards organizing migrant workers) are actually acted upon at a localized, workplace level in terms of concrete organizing strategies.

We show that at a national level the umbrella labour organizations or confederations—the British Trades Union Congress (TUC), the German Deutscher Gewerkschaftsbund (DGB), and the French Confédération Générale du Travail (CGT)—have changed their policies over time, becoming more open and welcoming towards migrant workers. However, specific union strategies towards migrant workers differ substantively. Thus, even though the policy framework at a *macro level* is quite similar across the UK, Germany, and France, we detect significant differences in union approaches at the *micro level* when examining the organizing or advocacy work that is happening on the ground in the workplace or locality. It is here that union strategies diverge as local actors deal with the practicalities of putting national union policies on integration of precarious migrant workers into practice. Our findings show that institutional and associational power resources (i.e. the power held by unions through their participation in labour market or government institutions and the strength of the membership) and union ideology (i.e. particular union orientation influenced by the national, socio-political, and cultural context) really matter for the specific approaches taken by unions at the micro level.

Furthermore, we also find differences at the micro level in union strategies *within* each country. We argue, however, that union responses are still the outcome of ideology and the power resources held by individual unions. In other words, even though scholars have critiqued national models of immigrant integration, we still believe that the responses within each country—while not completely similar—tend to be the result of the broader national and institutional context. In the UK, where multiculturalism has been the dominant narrative and practice, approaches to the inclusion of migrant workers have tended to target specific groups for organizing, often using government funding. We categorize union responses in the UK as broadly a 'recognition of difference' approach towards migrant workers. In France, the labour movement largely follows the French tradition of republican assimilation, where workers are workers, not specifically precarious *migrant* workers. Here, unions often target their demands towards the state, and migrant struggles have regularly been framed around civil rather than labour rights. We show that union strategies in France therefore often, but not exclusively, take on a 'civil rights approach'. In comparison, unions in Germany have tended to take an 'institutional approach' towards precarious migrant workers by focusing on collective representation through works councils or leadership positions within unions in order to counter labour market segmentation. As unions have weakened and many migrants in Germany find themselves outside these traditional institutional structures, we argue that taking on an institutional approach towards migrant workers has resulted in shortcomings at the local level.

9.2. CONSISTENCY AND VARIATION IN UNION POLICY AND STRATEGY TOWARDS MIGRANT WORKERS

Over the past few decades, processes of liberalization have led to the erosion of socially protective and redistributive organizations like labour unions (Greer and Doellgast 2013; Baccaro and Howell 2011). At the same time, we have seen growing hostility towards migrants as national media and politicians use migration as a political weapon in this period of austerity and social unrest. As a consequence, there is urgency for unions to counteract these tendencies as they result in growing inequality and precarity across society—not just for migrant workers. Examining union strategies towards precarious migrant workers is an area that highlights the challenge of institutional disorganization, as many immigrants find themselves at the periphery of the labour market and subject to racism and xenophobia at work as well as in wider society. It is also where unions—as institutions whose raison d'être is to curb labour exploitation—have found organizing these groups difficult, as the migrant division of labour has sectioned off these workers from core jobs where traditional union membership was previously located.

Our research shows how unions are attempting to break out of past strategies where migrants were excluded from representative structures, and examines why unions are adopting different approaches to organizing precarious migrant workers. Penninx and Roosblad (2000) have been useful in thinking through the factors that influence outcomes. These authors describe three dilemmas that unions have faced over time: cooperating versus resisting the recruitment of foreign workers; including or excluding foreign workers from their structures; and granting migrant union members equal or special treatment. To explain differences across countries, Penninx and Roosblad (2000) point towards four possible explanatory variables: the power and structure of the trade unions; the conditions of the economy and labour market; the broader societal and historical context; and characteristics of migrant workers themselves. According to the authors, to explain the variance in trade union responses we need to take into consideration the intersection of all four factors. Recently, their paper has been revisited to take into account the contextual changes in Europe since the early 1990s. Marino et al. (2015) illustrate that while all three dilemmas are still valid, unions should not just behave as labour actors, but need to act more broadly by fostering civic alliances, which often means promoting internal organizational and cultural change to make this happen.

Other writers have examined union policies towards migrant workers and linked these to specific company outcomes. Pulignano et al. (2015), for example, examine why the actual protection of agency migrant workers is weaker in Germany than in Belgium, even though in both countries the unions appear, on paper, to commit to similar policies. They emphasize the importance of institutional embeddedness and show how the institutional power resources of Belgian unions, including their role in policymaking, the existence of the Ghent system, and union-dominated works councils, are critical in facilitating their political action by regulating employment for agency workers through agreements with the government and employer associations. In Germany, the sectoral agreements are not as strong because the institutional power resources of unions are much weakened. During the latter part of the last century, there was increasing decentralization of collective bargaining at local level resulting in deviation from collectively agreed wages and conditions. This resulted in migrant agency workers not receiving the same protection as permanent workers and the establishment of dual labour markets with separate and worse collective agreements for agency workers (most of whom were migrants). In other words, according to Pulignano et al. (2015), while individual union strategies are important, they cannot be fully understood without taking into consideration the institutional context or power resources available to the actors.

The contribution of our chapter lies in linking union policy to specific strategies on the ground, taking into consideration how institutional and associational power resources *as well as* specific union ideology influence unions' strategic capacity. First, by institutional and associational power resources we are referring to the power held by unions as a result of their participation in institutions to affect change (for example, through collective bargaining with employers, or with governments to influence labour market policy), and the strength of collective organization (the willingness of members to take action). Second, unions are not purely rational actors, but have distinctive logics of action or ideological orientations that are derived from their embeddedness in a national context. As scholars have shown, this ideology will most likely affect the union strategies adopted towards organizing (migrant) workers (e.g. Connolly et al. 2014; Marino 2012; Benassi and Vlandas 2016). We draw upon Hyman's (2001) work on union identity, which explains how a union's ideology creates its very being or character, and which argues that most unions' identities can be located at some point within a triangular module between market, class, and society, depending on the emphasis they place on each of these elements. While heuristic in nature, the model is helpful in approximating where the *dominant* ideology of a union lies, and this then provides a useful way in which to understand the different organizing approaches adopted. For example, the 'class' corner represents an ideology of class division and class struggle, whereas the dominant ideology for unions in the 'market' corner is primarily to regulate wage labour relations, and the 'society' corner represents unions whose primary concern is to coexist with other organizations in the wider framework of civil society campaigns for social justice. Of course, most unions tend to incorporate elements of all three, but because of their history, culture, and politics, would orientate themselves towards a certain point within the triangle, which gives them a particular identity and organizing approach. This model is therefore useful in understanding how a union's identity might affect its strategy towards involving or incorporating migrant workers into the union. For example, a union operating in a sector of low-paid precarious workers with a strong commitment to civil society campaigns for social justice is perhaps more likely to seek to bring migrant workers into membership and activism than a union whose primary focus is regulating wage labour relations. In the latter case, the union's focus may be much narrower (pay and conditions) and only concerned with improving the living standards of its current members. As we will show in our research, if we apply this model to the unions we studied, we can see that it is dynamic and not fixed. Thus we find that each of these unions have, to some extent, shifted their ideological orientation towards the more societal dimension and have taken action outside their own union structure as they seek to engage with migrant workers. But overall, union identity (and thus practice) is still reflective of each union's particular orientation between market, class and, society, as influenced by the wider national, socio-political, and cultural context in which the unions are operating. As Hyman asks, though, an important question in understanding union orientation is: Whose interests count for most, and which interests are most relevant for union representation and bargaining policy? We argue that the policy, practice, and priorities of a union that forms its identity will affect the behaviour or strategy it adopts towards migrant workers.

9.3. METHODOLOGY: DATA COLLECTION AND ANALYSIS

This research had its origins in the United States, where scholars were studying innovations in the organization of migrant workers. They expanded via a research grant to Europe, in order that we might better understand the factors that encourage unions to integrate these workers into their structures. While the choice of countries was to some extent influenced by our funding, there were some important points of useful comparison. Each country has a long history of migration and union policy towards migration; in each country union views on the recruitment and organization of precarious migrants have changed over time; and in each country we can observe case studies where unions are actively organizing in specific places or sectors. Further, a common factor across countries was the level and extent of precarity: migrant workers in the UK, France, and Germany had a common experience of precarious employment, lack of access to welfare provision, and, in many cases, were operating in the grey economy often due to their irregular citizenship status.

Our data gathering starting point was at the grassroots level and was based on inductive research. First, though, we began with in-depth literature reviews on trade unions and migrant workers in each of the three countries to provide context. We shared this information among the country research teams in a day-long seminar in November 2011, where we discussed the similarities and differences in attitudes (both historical and current) to the integration of migrant workers in unions. Once we had synthesized this material, we began our data collection by interviewing key figures in unions in each of the countries, and from these initial interviews we identified union campaigns that we might study in greater depth. The research thus resulted in over 200 interviews with practitioners and twenty in-depth case studies. This was followed by a two-day workshop involving the research team and union participants from each country, where we analysed the core themes arising from the case studies.

Our analytical approach was to start from the macro level and burrow down to the micro level to get a clear understanding of what was taking place and why, and how the macro-level policies towards migrant workers were translated into specific micro-level strategies by the trade unions in each country. This is what we will look at next.

9.4. THE MACRO-LEVEL CONTEXT: UNION MIGRATION POLICIES IN THE UK, FRANCE, AND GERMANY

Since the postwar period, we find a similar story regarding migration policy within the UK, French, and German unions. After World War II, an economic boom paired with labour shortages encouraged a growing number of immigrants to live and work in those countries. While each government encouraged foreign workers to come and take jobs to rebuild the economy, the TUC, CGT, and DGB strongly opposed immigration, claiming that these migrant workers refused to integrate with indigenous workers, or considered migrant workers as competitors to native workers that undercut wages and living standards. Between 1945 and the early 1970s, unions in all three countries were often described as racist and exclusive, as the practice was either to prevent migrant workers from entering the labour market, keep them out of unions, and if that did not work, exclude them from union benefits. And thus, up until the 1970s, unions adopted a classic restrictionist position towards migrant workers (for more details see, for example, Fine and Tichenor 2012; Adler et al. 2014; Wrench 2000; Blévis and Pezet 2012; Chin 2007; Kühne 2000).

From the early 1970s onwards, as governments tried to push through more restrictive and discriminatory legislation, unions in each country shifted their migration policy from a more restrictive to a more inclusive and solidaristic approach. These policy shifts within the unions were prompted by a number of events. In the UK, increasing pressure from black and white rank-and-file union members, high-profile industrial disputes involving migrant workers, and the rise of the far-right National Front all played a role in the reversal of the TUC's stark anti-immigration policies (Holgate 2009). In France, important strikes by migrants at the workplace, as well in society, pushed some unions to advance the rights and participation of immigrants within their structures. Migrant workers, for example, took an active and prominent role during the May 1968 strike waves, the 1970s housing strikes, as well as the 1970s and 1980s strikes in the auto industry (Turner 2014). In Germany, the DGB recognized that migrant workers were no longer just *Gastarbeiter* or a temporary workforce, but were there to stay and were even increasing in numbers. At the same time, German trade union density was in decline, so there seemed to be instrumental reasons for the unions to stop resisting the inflow of migrant workers (Budzinski 1979).

Finally, over the past decade, many employers have intensified their segmentation-focused strategies to exploit differences in pay and conditions based on race or ethnicity. Unions are responding by trying to include migrant workers into their representation structures and build solidarity among different groups of workers, often in communities beyond the workplace. Some common root causes can be detected: unions in each country suffer from a decline in power resources and therefore recognize that migrants are important to rebuild labour. But at the same time, they also put emphasis on collectivist forms of worker identity and share concerns about an expanding precarious workforce across the labour market. Most recently, for example, the TUC put out a briefing to strongly condemn the 2015 Immigration Bill that was being pushed through Parliament, as it 'scapegoats migrants for social and economic problems caused by austerity and bad employers' (TUC 2015). This legislation, now law, criminalizes undocumented migrants, introduces English-language requirements for public sector workers in a customer-facing role, and requires document checks by landlords and banks, among other issues. The TUC therefore emphasizes the importance of collective bargaining and union representation to prevent further labour market segmentation, and accentuates the role unions can play in offering English-language classes, for example, through UnionLearn. In its framing, the TUC shifts the blame away from migrants and focuses instead on 'bad bosses'.

Given this context, we examine to what extent and how these revised macro-level union policies are currently translated into micro-level union strategies in the workplace. In other words, we emphasize particular union strategies—some successful, others unsuccessful—towards integrating migrant workers into their structures and the broader society.

9.5. MICRO-LEVEL UNION STRATEGIES TOWARDS MIGRANT WORKERS IN THE WORKPLACE

While it is not possible to classify each approach to recruiting and organizing precarious migrant workers precisely into one neat and tidy box, we do believe that in each country we can identify an overall characterization. For example, in the UK, organizing initiatives tend to be based on a 'recognition of difference approach' and the importance of self-organization, reflecting the country's historical adoption of multiculturalism. French unions have implemented what could be categorized as a 'citizens'-rights approach' where the focus has been on campaigns around the regularization of undocumented workers directed at the state. In Germany, an 'institutional approach' has been adopted; an example of this would be the creation of spaces for individual migrant workers to integrate into union or works council structures through leadership development.

9.5.1. Organizing Initiatives towards Precarious Migrants in the UK

While there is no one-model-fits-all approach of the UK trade unions towards organizing migrant workers, three main strategies can be highlighted: involving migrant workers through training and learning initiatives, through organizing campaigns, and by setting up separate structures. Most of these tend to be implemented through a 'recognition of difference approach'.

First, scholars in the UK have examined the potential of union education to revitalize the labour movement (Findlay and Warhurst 2011; Rainbird and Stuart 2011; for a more critical analysis, see McIlroy 2008). When focusing more specifically on migrant workers, studies have shown with caution how union learning can be a means to stimulate membership as well as to organize migrant workers (Mustchin 2012). While learning initiatives are important, 'more established organizing and bargaining processes and the identification of griev-ances among vulnerable workers appear more fundamental to improving levels of union representation and organization among migrant workers' (Mustchin 2012: 22). In the UK, government funding has facilitated the role of the unions in providing workers access to training and learning initiatives. The Labour govern-ment, for example, established the Union Learning Fund in 1998 to develop the capacity of trade unions and to create union learning representatives (ULRs). ULRs were a new type of union activist and were more likely to be black, women, young, or recent hires (Stuart et al. 2010).[2] While these learning initiatives have been small-scale and highly volatile, as they depend on government funding (Perrett and Martínez Lucio 2008),[3] they have been one of the main channels for UK trade unions to include migrant workers into their structures.[4]

A second strategy taken up mostly by the union Unite (formerly the Transport and General Workers' Union) has been to engage in comprehensive organizing campaigns to gain new members. While most of these campaigns are not targeted specifically towards migrant workers, they have often taken place in low-wage sectors where these workers are located. Based on a US model of organizing, their 'Justice for Cleaners' campaign engaged in organizing mostly migrant workers in the cleaning sector in London. This campaign was, however, quite exceptional as early on it relied heavily on the involvement of a community organization (now called Citizens UK). While this model of community and social movement unionism might be on the rise in the US or Australia, it is not yet part of the strategic vision of UK unions.[5]

Finally, compared to other countries, the UK labour movement has also focused on structural solutions to enhance the integration of migrant (especially black and minority ethnic or BME) workers. Unions like the large public sector union Unison have created self-organized structures to encourage the participa-tion of BME workers. These structures, while not without controversy, can be considered 'special opportunity' structures trying to go beyond just equal treat-ment of workers as workers. According to Wrench (2004), the weak institutional power of British unions and low levels of political legitimacy have pushed the unions to become even more open and inclusive towards migrant workers. In addition, these special structures can be understood in light of the British model of multiculturalism, or trying to give enough space to self-organize and protect the distinctiveness of migrant workers.

---

[2] Currently in the UK there are about 24,000 ULRs, and they are given paid time off by the employer in order to undertake their role in a similar way to health and safety reps and shop stewards.

[3] Between 2005 and 2009 the government set up a Union Modernization Fund. This fund supported unions such as the TGWU, Unison, and the GMB towards integrating migrant workers into their unions, but was abolished in 2010 when the Conservative government came to power.

[4] The general union, GMB, for example, used ESOL (English for speakers of other languages) training to reach out to migrant workers and set up a Migrant Workers Branch. Unfortunately, the branch became unsustainable and once workers received their free skill and language training, the branch dissolved and the GMB leadership wasn't able to transfer the mostly Polish migrant workers into other local branches (Heyes 2009; James and Karmowska 2012).

[5] Some changes are underway though: for example, with Unite creating Unite Community Membership, or membership not restricted to a particular workplace but opening it up to community members.

In sum, to a certain extent the union strategies reflect policy shifts towards a solidaristic model and a greater ideological orientation of the union towards 'society' (based on Hyman's typology of union identity). In terms of specific union strategies, we detect a focus on 'recognition of differences'. The emphasis is put on learning and training initiatives (drawing on institutional power resources via government funding for training) as well as on setting up separate structures specifically for migrant workers, reflecting the multicultural, historical context in the UK—even though these are not always set up without controversy. Finally, while migrant workers have joined UK unions through organizing campaigns, these campaigns often did not strategically target migrants but happened to take place in sectors, such as the cleaning sector, in which migrant workers dominate.

9.5.2. Organizing Initiatives towards Precarious Migrants in France

Similar to the UK, there is not one single strategy that French unions have taken to integrate migrant workers. Instead, when examining organizing initiatives towards migrant workers we found at least three distinct approaches, often couched within each of the three main French confederations.

First, since the mid-2000s, the CGT has been the most visibly active in providing support to undocumented workers. Even though they supported migrant workers during the 1970s and 1980s, the struggles of migrant workers took place outside the workplace and the CGT did not lead these efforts. During the mid-2000s, however, partly because of critical 'bridge building' by CGT union activists, the union focused its efforts on mobilizing thousands of undocumented migrant workers, or *sans papiers*, to demand better living and working conditions (see also Kahmann 2015; Tapia and Turner 2013). Their demands arose from the migrant workers themselves, were picked up by the union, and were directed at the state and employers, focusing specifically on the issue of regularization. In doing so, the struggle of the migrant workers broke with the past and created a shift from a humanitarian issue to a labour fight. As a next step, the union, together with other civil society organizations and some other union confeder-ations, joined in a coalition effort—the Collective des Onze (C11)—to create wider civil society pressure on the national government to ease regularization criteria, among other issues. This emphasis on mobilizing migrant workers can also be found in the confederation Solidaires Unitaires Démocratiques, often described as a combative union with anarcho-syndicalist roots (Turner 2014; Connolly 2010).

Since the official start of the 'Sans Papiers' campaign in April 2008, and despite low union density in France, the union has been able to mobilize thousands of undocumented migrant workers demanding regularization. This campaign has been extremely significant not just for the many undocumented migrant workers who are seeking regularization, but also for the French labour movement. Even though the unions in France have strong institutional power resources through their involvement in collective bargaining agreements, their union density—while always low compared to other countries and because of its industrial relations system—has now dropped to below 10 per cent. In addition, a 2008 law now requires unions to demonstrate a certain percentage of support from employees in workplace elections as a necessary condition of getting 'representative' status.

To a certain extent, therefore, building this coalition between labour, NGOs, and migrant workers, signals the union's attempt to re-establish itself as a membership organization within the broader society.

A more modest approach towards migrant workers can be found in the French Democratic Labour Confederation (CFDT) with Christian-Democratic roots (but more secular since the 1960s). Historically, the CFDT and CGT have been competing with each other to recruit members. While the CGT is often characterized as focusing on aggressive, public mobilization campaigns, the CFDT takes a more moderate organizing approach. During the housing strikes of the 1970s, for example, the CFDT was able to reframe the discourse around immigration and portray immigrants living in slum housing as victims of injustice rather than as workers trying to undercut the wages of the French (Blévis and Pezet 2012). Nonetheless, the union was not very successful in encouraging foreign workers to be active within its structures. The union translated publications, set up an immigration secretariat, and formed language groups to promote migrant integration into wider society. So here, rather than creating active, public movements, the CFDT tends to focus inwards, emphasizing internal union policies towards migrant workers. During the more recent 'Sans Papiers' movement, the union signalled its support in 2009, but has been worried about retaliation against undocumented workers due to the public face of the campaign.

Finally, the FO (Force Ouvrières) decided not to join the coalition of eleven organizations to fight publicly for the regularization of undocumented workers. This union focuses on individual empowerment and worker training rather than highly public demonstrations, similar to some UK unions. A local FO branch in Paris in the cleaning industry, for example, conducted a more low-profile campaign focusing on the rank-and-file education of undocumented migrant workers, because the FO leadership considered it too risky to carry out public demonstrations by undocumented workers (see, for example, Quintin 2009).

In sum, French unions have, overall, taken different approaches towards migrant workers where the framing of precarious immigrant worker rights has been much more focused as a civil rights or societal issue. This was particularly the case in the CGT, where campaigns were targeted at the state more so than employers, although less so with other unions/federations who additionally focused on education and training at the workplace level. And even though the French unions have strong institutional power resources, their declining membership is disconcerting and could lead to weakening of associational power. Building alliances with civil society actors could re-establish them as a membership-based actor within society.

9.5.3. Organizing Initiatives towards Precarious Migrants in Germany

In contrast to the British 'Justice for Cleaners' and French 'Sans Papiers' campaigns, we did not find evidence of any large-scale mobilization efforts by German trade unions and migrant workers. This does not mean that German unions do not have concerns about the precarity of migrant workers, but rather it shows how union identity and ideological orientation towards historic industrial relations practice influences the different strategic approaches adopted by the unions. In Germany, we found the primary response towards migrant workers was to attempt to deal with the legacy of dualization at an institutional level, where past approaches to dealing with the increase of agency labour (often migrants) tended to focus on maintaining wages and working conditions of core constituencies at the expense of marginal workers (see Chapter 6, this volume). This was done by mentoring in an attempt to get migrant workers to take on leadership roles within unions or works councils to integrate and educate them in the workings of the union. The limitation of this 'institutional approach' is that it does, of course, require migrants to be already employed in union-organized sectors and workplaces. While many are, for example in the metal, construction, and meatpacking sectors, unions have tended to neglect the issue of lower wages and worse conditions for agency workers leading to significant differentials with little incentive for agency workers to join the unions (Benassi and Dorigatti 2015). Only in the last ten years have German unions become more proactive in bargaining national sectoral agreements to improve the working conditions of agency workers (e.g. Chapter 6, this volume), but Germany's dual bargaining arrangements (via works councils and the trade unions) have resulted in division and obstacles to this being achieved at the workplace level. The externalization of work is largely being taken up by foreign workers employed by agencies, and unions have few strategies or ability to interact with or to organize these workers at the workplace level (see Wagner 2015 and Chapter 3, this volume). For example, without the means (as a result of language barriers, high turnover, and workers' fear), and ideological commitment to organize at the grassroots level, regulation and collective agreements are easily bypassed, thus creating greater isolation between 'core' and 'peripheral' workers.

Further, adopting an institutional approach does not address the issue that much of the precarious migrant workforce is predominantly to be found in unregulated and precarious work—outside of the influence or benefits of any collective agreement. German unions that are more used to formal collective bargaining through social dialogue are finding that these traditional national and sectoral institutional approaches are much weakened. This perhaps suggests the need to break out of this familiar territory, if they wish to engage with migrant workers who are currently far removed from union coverage and protection.

Some of the organizing initiatives we studied involve the formation of migration committees or migration centres. For example, in about 20 per cent of its 164 administration offices, IG Metall has set up migration committees (Adler and Fichter 2014; Trede 2010). These committees are mainly service-driven and are trying to promote members with migration backgrounds into union leadership positions. Their activities include services such as language seminars, legal advice, assisting seniors with retirement issues, and training. In 2008, ver.di started a migrant worker 'drop in centre' (MigAr) to give low-wage migrant workers legal advice and assist with wage abuses among other issues. This centre was set up after the ver.di regional office in Hamburg fought against the mistreatment of an undocumented au pair worker in Hamburg (Adler and Fichter 2014). The difference between these initiatives and those from the UK are that these are institutional responses and mainly 'service based', and are thus not about the self-organization of migrant workers around the most pressing issues of concern in their workplace or union.

An important initiative trying to transcend existing institutions has been the creation of the European Migrant Workers Union (EMWU) by the German construction union IG BAU (Industriegewerkschaft Bauen-Agrar-Umwelt) in 2004. This case of transnational migrant worker organizing represented a radical shift from the way German workers are organized. Instead of being organized nationally by sector, this union for migrant workers was intended to cut across national and to some extent industrial boundaries. The EMWU, however, failed to attract substantial membership and develop into an independent viable organization. It was too service-driven, making it financially unsustainable, and did not develop a vibrant organized grassroots membership base. The EMWU focused mainly on legal support and advice, such as trying to regain lost wages for individual migrant workers. In addition, IG BAU had some contradictions in its own strategy: for example, it was encouraging the organizing of precarious migrant workers, while at the same time it favoured legislation to restrict the access of migrant workers to the labour market and worked with the labour inspectorate to enforce these rules. Finally, other unions were unwilling to support this transnational approach, did not recognize their union membership, and instead protected their own institutional structures (for more, see Lillie and Greer 2007; Greer et al. 2013).

Our findings in sum were that, in Germany, some unions have begun attempts to include migrant workers into their structures, but this is largely where there are still strongholds of co-determination and representation through works councils and unions. Where there is an absence of strong German institutions in some of the lower-paid, less-regulated sectors (e.g. care, food processing, hospitality, retail), however, there has not been a great deal of migrant worker organizing. Yet it is in the peripheral labour market outside of collective agreements where the most precarious migrant workers are in need of union representation and support. The gradual weakening of union power, the tendency to shift collective bargaining from the national to local level, the growth in segments of the labour markets no longer regulated by collective agreements, the import of posted workers from other European countries, and the creation of 'mini-jobs' (casual low-paid part-time work), thus present huge challenges for unions in Germany trying to adapt their industrial relations strategies to fit this new industrial/economic reality (Bosch and Weinkopf 2008).

9.6. EXPLAINING THE DIFFERENCES AND SIMILARITIES BETWEEN AND WITHIN COUNTRIES

So how do we explain the similarities and differences we have observed in our cross-country study? First, it is clear that at the macro-level attitudes towards the recruitment, organization, and inclusion of precarious migrant workers appear to be converging. Historically, the policies of the TUC, CGT, and DGB were largely protectionist and in some cases xenophobic. At the end of the 1960s and early 1970s, a gradual shift took place and unions adopted more inclusive policies. While unions in earlier periods responded to employer segmentation and growing competition with strategies that sought to exclude migrants, later on unions became more inclusive and adopted anti-discrimination policies, or pushed for a stronger participation of migrant workers.

While union policies at a national level are quite similar across the countries, at the micro level, however, we find that the individual case studies highlight different strategic responses in local union practice, reflecting historical institutional developments. This divergence in approach, which is observed both within and between countries, requires some explanation as to why it differs from the convergence that is taking place at national level. In the UK, there has been some migrant worker organizing in the workplace, albeit limited; the focus has been on training and learning initiatives to integrate migrant workers into union structures or on setting up separate structures—the 'recognition of difference approach' mentioned earlier. Here we would argue that there is a lack of industrial/class-based organizing of precarious migrant workers (i.e. around terms and conditions or collective bargaining). Given the UK's historical emphasis on multiculturalism, these separate structures and training initiatives are one way to integrate migrant workers, *as migrant workers*, into the unions. In France, the republican ethos has overall tended towards the view of *workers as workers*, despite their differing backgrounds. As such, the key campaign around the organizing of precarious migrant workers—the 'Sans Papiers' campaign—has been at community level and was not constructed in a workplace setting around employment issues (or even the labour market). Instead, the campaign was around the undocumented status of workers or around their poor housing conditions. Although it should be acknowledged that at least for the *sans papiers*, the debate and campaign did begin to shift from civil society to a more labour-centred issue, with the unions taking on a greater role while the campaign lasted. In terms of the other French case studies, the main approach from unions has been in terms of servicing and supporting precarious migrant workers through training and rights awareness rather than specific workplace/industrial organizing strategies to achieve recognition or collective bargaining.

In Germany, the gradual erosion of the trade unions and works councils as well as the expanding immigrant-rich sectors without any co-determination rights or collective bargaining coverage has made any meaningful locally based union action towards migrant workers very challenging (Bosch and Weinkopf 2008). The institutional approach to attempt to integrate migrant workers into unions and works councils through leadership development is, of course, important. However, focusing only on institutions as the way forward at a time of institutional disorganization is perhaps flawed, especially as many precarious migrant workers are to be found outside traditional workplaces covered by collective bargaining. Thus, while in the past German unions could reach institutional inclusiveness through legally extending the collective bargaining agreements to cover entire sectors, this practice is not straightforward (see, for example, Pulignano et al. 2015). As a consequence, German unions would need to go beyond their institutional comfort zone (e.g. engaging in mobilizing migrant workers in the community by building alliances with other groups), to reach out and improve the working conditions of the migrant workers. Their institutional power resource is still important and essential to providing opportunities for some migrant workers, but might fail to address the precarious situation of most migrants who are working in non-union-organized sectors.

Earlier in the chapter we mentioned Hyman's (2001) framing of unions according to where they lie in term of their ideological orientation between market, class, and society. Clearly, this is a broad categorization, as individual unions could well be found at a different point within the framework, but at a national level we believe this is a useful way of understanding how our countries differ in their approach to precarious migrant workers. In the UK the key problem unions face is a weak institutional framework and lack of power resources at the level of the state, as well as across sectors and workplaces. Their ideology towards migrants was about advocating for social and labour rights and thus, we argue, fits (in Hyman's terminology) most closely between market and society in its orientation. Here the focus was very much on campaigns and education that clearly expressed and recognized multiculturalism and a recognition of difference between migrants and other workers.

On the other hand, the institutional power resources utilized by unions in France were largely directed towards getting the state to accept the citizenship rights of migrants. Unions worked in coalition with civil rights organizations by mobilizing their members to push for legislation to force employers to provide greater security for migrant workers as well as more welfare rights for those falling below the floor of rights. This civil rights approach fits more closely between the class and society axes of Hyman's framework of union identity.

Of the three countries, Germany has the strongest institutional structures at firm, industry, sector, and state levels to regulate collective bargaining, but has felt the decline of these in the recent period. Nevertheless, for unions in Germany (where they exist), the workplace remains the source of institutional power and it is here where attention has been focused on attempting to get migrant workers to play a role in union structures through leadership development. Unions' ideological orientation has been primarily between class and market through institutions with less focus on organizing at societal level, as is the case in France and the UK.

9.7. CONCLUSION

This comparison and multi-scalar analysis assists in our understanding of the role unions, as key actors in the employment relationship and wider society, are able to play in combatting inequality and discrimination towards precarious immigrant workers. It shows as well the specific strategies unions take to prevent further labour market segmentation. Unions in all three countries have struggled to draw on traditional bargaining approaches, given their decreased institutionalized bargaining power, especially in those segments of the economy where migrant workers are located.

Scholars have critiqued national models of immigrant integration and have emphasized variation within countries (Bertossi and Duyvendak 2012). Our analysis also shows differences in union strategies within each country. Yet, to a certain extent, these responses are still outcomes of the broader, national traditional spheres in which unions build solidarity as well as the institutional and associational power of unions within the national context.

Based on these findings, we argue that union strategies towards migrant workers are important not just for the migrant workers, but as a way to defend the rights of all workers. As a result, the strategies towards the migrant workers should not just be about delivering a service, but should involve broader organizing strategies to build greater associational power; for example, through building coalitions. The 'Sans Papiers' campaign was able to move the issue of undocumented workers from the margins to the centre and gain public legitimation. While this might not result in any immediate membership increase for the unions, building inclusive solidarity is part of the original goal of unions, which is to strive towards equality or social justice for all. We argue therefore that in the French case, notwithstanding its limitations, the strategy of coalition building with other actors in society might be the most effective strategy to reduce the precariousness of all workers. Given the weak institutional and/or associational power resources that unions in all three countries face, the importance of building coalitions comes to the forefront.

To conclude, we want to draw out some important implications given these different union strategies. The processes of dualization (or more critically described as processes of liberalization)[6] affect unions as well as migrant workers themselves. Labour unions, as redistributive and protective institutions, have been weakened through the dualization processes and have started to look for ways to revitalize and counter growing labour market segmentation by building solidarity across different groups of workers. Migrant workers often find themselves on the periphery or as outsiders who do not enjoy the same benefits as insiders. In addition, they have been faced with growing hostility, especially during periods of austerity. Migrant workers have therefore become important to unions, not just as a constituency—to grow in membership numbers—but also as a way to go back to the roots of unionism and fight for better working and living conditions for the working class as a whole. We detect, however, immediate shortcomings when unions do not break out of their traditional institutional channels in order to reach migrant workers. Given that migrant workers often find themselves at the periphery of the labour market, already outside the established institutional channels, many remain out of reach. We have seen this play out especially in the German case. Indeed, research has already shown that unions that are less institutionally embedded within the political system are more likely to strengthen their commitment towards migrant workers than unions that are highly involved in collective agreements or social partnerships (see also Wrench 2004). In France, unions will focus more on mobilization as a

---

[6] Dualization assumes there is a group of 'insiders' or core workers that enjoy good pay, benefits, job security, unionization, and so on, while at the same time there is a growing group of 'outsiders' or workers at the periphery that are not unionized, and don't enjoy the same level of pay, benefits, and job security. When we talk about processes of liberalization more broadly, scholars argue that due to government deregulation and the expansion of employers' discretion, even the so-called 'core' is getting smaller and don't enjoy these good working conditions anymore. As a result, a more general shift towards liberalization is taking place that affects the insiders as well as outsiders (e.g. Baccaro and Howell 2011).

way of improving the lives of migrant workers and integrating them into their structures and society. At the same time, their focus is primarily on civil rights directed at the state, which might not be sufficient to counter the liberalization processes felt at the workplace. In the UK, the unions often feel restricted in their action repertoires due to the lack of funding and set up special structures within the unions to give migrant workers a voice. These structures, however, have been heavily critiqued and it is unclear to what extent they have contributed to membership increase or, more importantly, to a change within the culture and organization of the union.

Based on our findings, we argue that in each country unions would perhaps benefit from focusing on the initiatives at a local level led by the migrant workers themselves at the workplace as well as in the broader community. In line with Marino et al. (2015), unions might need to promote internal and cultural changes within their own structures and act more as a social and political actor, fostering civic alliances, as a means to break out of their own traditional structures. Union power and structures, changes in the labour market, as well as the institutional context are important in understanding union strategies. However, unions could benefit from gaining a deeper understanding of the migrant workers themselves, their organizing capacities, background, and characteristics, when engaging in strategies to counter the tendency towards processes of dualization.

ACKNOWLEDGEMENTS

The research for this chapter was funded by the Hans Böckler Foundation, for which we are very grateful. We also want to thank the editors for their extensive comments on our draft.

REFERENCES

Adler, Lee and Fichter, Michael. 2014. 'Germany: Success at the Core, Unresolved Challenges at the Periphery'. In *Mobilizing against Inequality: Unions, Immigrant Workers, and the Crisis of Capitalism*, edited by Lee Adler, Maite Tapia, and Lowell Turner. Ithaca, NY: Cornell University Press.

Adler, Lee, Tapia, Maite, and Turner, Lowell (eds). 2014. *Mobilizing against Inequality: Unions, Immigrant Workers, and the Crisis of Capitalism*. Ithaca, NY: Cornell University Press.

Baccaro, Lucio and Howell, Chris. 2011. 'A Common Neoliberal Trajectory: The Transformation of Industrial Relations in Advanced Capitalism'. *Politics and Society*, 39(4): 521–63.

Benassi, Chiara and Dorigatti, Lisa. 2015. 'Straight to the Core—Explaining Union Responses to the Casualization of Work: The IG Metall Campaign for Agency Workers'. *British Journal of Industrial Relations*, 53(3): 533–55.

Benassi, Chiara and Vlandas, Tim. 2016. 'Union Inclusiveness and Temporary Agency Workers: The Role of Power Resources and Union Ideology'. *European Journal of Industrial Relations*, 22(1): 5–22.

Bertossi, Christophe and Duyvendak, Jan Willem. 2012. 'National Models of Immigrant Integration: The Costs for Comparative Research'. *Comparative European Politics*, 10(3): 237–47.

Blévis, Laure and Pezet, Eric. 2012. 'CFTC/CFDT Attitudes towards Immigration in the Parisian Region: Making Immigrant Workers' Condition a Cause'. *Urban Studies*, 49(3): 685–701.

Bosch, Gerhard and Weinkopf, Claudia. 2008. *Low-Wage Work in Germany*. New York: Russell Sage.

Budzinski, Manfred. 1979. *Gewerkschaftliche und betriebliche Erfahrungen auslaendischer Arbeiter. Untersuchung in einem Chemie- und einem Metallbetrieb in Baden Wuerttemberg.* Frankfurt: Campus Verlag.

Chin, Rita. 2007. *The Guest Worker Question in Postwar Germany*. Cambridge: Cambridge University Press.

Connolly, Heather. 2010. 'Organizing and Mobilizing Precarious Workers in France: The Case of Cleaners in the Railways'. In *Globalization and Precarious Forms of Production and Employment: Challenges for Workers and Unions*, edited by Carole Thornley, Steve Jefferys, and Beatrice Appay. Northampton, MA: Edward Elgar Publishing.

Connolly, Heather, Marino, Stefania, and Martínez Lucio, Miguel. 2014. 'Trade Union Renewal and the Challenges of Representation: Strategies towards Migrant and Ethnic Minority Workers in the Netherlands, Spain and the United Kingdom'. *European Journal of Industrial Relations*, 20(1): 5–20.

Cornfield, Daniel. 2014. 'Integrative Organizing in Polarized Times: Toward Dynamic Trade Unionism in the Global North'. In *Mobilizing against Inequality: Unions, Immigrant Workers, and the Crisis of Capitalism*, edited by Lee Adler, Maite Tapia, and Lowell Turner. Ithaca, NY: Cornell University Press.

Findlay, Patricia and Warhurst, Chris. 2011. 'Union Learning Funds and Trade Union Revitalization: A New Tool in the Toolkit?' *British Journal of Industrial Relations*, 49(1): 115–34.

Fine, Janice and Tichenor, Daniel J. 2012. 'An Enduring Dilemma: Immigration and Organized Labor in Western Europe and the United States'. In *Oxford Handbook of the Politics of International Migration*, edited by Marc. R. Rosenblum and Daniel J. Tichenor. Oxford: Oxford University Press.

Greer, Ian, Ciupijus, Zinovijus, and Lillie, Nathan. 2013. 'The European Migrant Workers Union and the Barriers to Transnational Industrial Citizenship'. *European Journal of Industrial Relations*, 19(1): 5–20.

Greer, Ian and Doellgast, Virginia. 2017. 'Marketization, Inequality, and Institutional Change: Toward a New Framework for Comparative Employment Relations'. *Journal of Industrial Relations*, 59(2): 192–208.

Heyes, Jason. 2009. 'Recruiting and Organising Migrant Workers Through Education and Training: A Comparison of Community and the GMB'. *Industrial Relations Journal*, 40(3): 182–97.

Holgate, Jane. 2009. 'The Role of UK Unions in the Civic Integration of Immigrant Workers'. Available at: <https://www.ilr.cornell.edu/mobilizing-against-inequality>.

Hyman, Richard. 2001. *Understanding European Trade Unionism: Between Market, Class and Society*. London: Sage.

James, Phil and Karmowska, Joanna. 2012. 'Unions and Migrant Workers: Strategic Challenges in Britain'. *Transfer: European Review of Labour and Research*, 18(2): 201–12.

Kahmann, Marcus. 2015. 'When the Strike Encounters the Sans Papiers Movement: The Discovery of a Workers' Repertoire of Actions for Irregular Migrant Protest in France'. *Transfer: European Review of Labour and Research*, 21(4): 413–28.

Kalleberg, Arne. 2009. 'Precarious Work, Insecure Workers: Employment Relations in Transition'. *American Sociological Review*, 74(1): 1–22.

Kalleberg, Arne and Hewison, Kevin. 2013. 'Precarious Work and the Challenge for Asia'. *American Behavioral Scientist*, 57(3): 271–88.

Kühne, Peter. 2000. 'The Federal Republic of Germany: Ambivalent Promotion of Immigrants' interests'. In *Trade Unions, Immigration and Immigrants in Europe 1960–1993: A Comparative Study of the Actions of Trade Unions in Seven West European Countries*, edited by Rinus Penninx and Judith Roosblad. New York: Berghahn Books.

Lillie, Nathan and Greer, Ian. 2007. 'Industrial Relations, Migration, and Neoliberal Politics: The Case of the European Construction Sector'. *Politics and Society*, 35(4): 551–81.

Marino, Stefania. 2012. 'Trade Union Inclusion of Migrant and Ethnic Minority Workers: Comparing Italy and the Netherlands'. *European Journal of Industrial Relations*, 18(1): 5–20.

Marino, Stefania, Penninx, Rinus, and Roosblad, Judith. 2015. 'Trade Unions, Immigration and Immigrants in Europe Revisited: Unions' Attitudes and Actions under New Conditions'. *Comparative Migration Studies*, 3(1): 1–16.

McIlroy, John. 2008. 'Ten Years of New Labour: Workplace Learning, Social Partnerships and Union Revitalization in Britain'. *British Journal of Industrial Relations*, 46(2): 283–313.

Mustchin, Stephen. 2012. 'Unions, Learning, Migrant Workers and Union Revitalisation in Britain'. *Work, Employment and Society*, 26(6): 951–67.

Penninx, Rinus and Roosblad, Judith. 2000. 'Introduction'. In *Trade Unions, Immigration and Immigrants in Europe 1960–1993*, edited by Rinus Penninx and Judith Roosblad. Amsterdam: Amsterdam University Press.

Perrett, Robert and Martínez Lucio, Miguel. 2008. 'The Challenge of Connecting and Coordinating the Learning Agenda: A Case Study of a Trade Union Learning Centre in the UK'. *Employee Relations*, 30(6): 623–39.

Pulignano, Valeria, Meardi, Guglielmo, and Doerflinger, Nadja. 2015. 'Trade Unions and Labour Market Dualisation: A Comparison of Policies and Attitudes towards Agency and Migrant Workers in Germany and Belgium'. *Work, Employment and Society*, 29(5): 808–25.

Quintin, Marion. 2009. 'The CGT Campaign Supporting the "Sans-Papiers"'. Available at: <https://www.ilr.cornell.edu/mobilizing-against-inequality>.

Rainbird, Helen and Stuart, Mark. 2011. 'The State and the Union Learning Agenda in Britain'. *Work, Employment and Society*, 25(2): 202–17.

Stuart, Mark, Cook, Hugh, Cutter, Jo, and Winterton, Jonathan. 2010. 'Evaluation of the Union Learning Fund and UnionLearn'. Center for Employment Relations, Innovation, and Change, Leeds University Business School.

Tapia, Maite and Turner, Lowell. 2013. 'Union Campaigns as Countermovements: Mobilizing Immigrant Workers in France and the United Kingdom'. *British Journal of Industrial Relations*, 51(3): 601–22.

Trede, Olivier. 2010. 'The IG Metall and the Integration of Immigrant Workers in Kiel'. Case study prepared for Labor Unions and Civic Integration of Immigrant Workers Research Project, Cornell University.

Turner, Lowell. 2014. 'France: Battles for Inclusion, 1968–2010'. In *Mobilizing against Inequality: Unions, Immigrant Workers, and the Crisis of Capitalism*, edited by Lee Adler, Maite Tapia, and Lowell Turner. Ithaca, NY: Cornell University Press.

TUC. 2015. 'Briefing Immigration Bill'. Available at: <https://www.tuc.org.uk/international-issues/migration/tuc-briefing-immigration-bill>.

Wagner, Ines. 2015. 'Rule Enactment in a Pan-European Labour Market: Transnational Posted Work in the German Construction Sector'. *British Journal of Industrial Relations*, 53(4): 692–710.

Wrench, John. 2000. 'British Unions and Racism: Organisational Dilemmas in an Unsympathetic Climate'. In *Trade Unions, Immigration and Immigrants in Europe 1960–1993*, edited by R. Penninx and J. Roosblad. New York: Berghahn Books.

Wrench, John. 2004. 'Trade Union Responses to Immigrants and Ethnic Inequality in Denmark and the UK: The Context of Consensus and Conflict'. *European Journal of Industrial Relations*, 10: 7–30.

10

Unions and Migrant Workers

The Perspective of Estonians in Finland and Albanians in Italy and Greece

*Sonila Danaj, Erka Çaro, Laura Mankki,
Markku Sippola, and Nathan Lillie*

10.1. INTRODUCTION

Labour migrants, particularly those from poorer countries, have long been re-garded as vulnerable to labour market segmentation, discrimination, and exploit-ation. This is in part due to their status as 'outsiders' within a society. This results in limited legal and social rights (Lillie and Simola 2016; Anderson 2010), and is linked to their labour market position, migration motives, and expectations (Piore 1979). Their precariousness makes them a problem for unions, who must decide whether to try to represent them or exclude them (Penninx and Roosblad 2000). Representing migrants presents practical challenges. There is now a large body of literature that shows it can be done—mostly based on case studies of unions either adapting their strategies to better organize and represent migrants (cf. Berntsen 2016; Milkman 2000; Holgate 2005) or of migrants self-organizing and successfully representing themselves (Anderson 2000; Chapter 4, this volume). Although inspiring, these cases remain exceptional—migrants, while not 'unorga-nizable', remain a difficult group for unions to organize and represent.

Based on a series of biographic interviews with Estonian migrant workers in Finland and Albanian workers in Italy and Greece, we make the case that when migrants join unions, it is usually a result of an individual movement out of precarious and sometimes informal work into secure, formal work relations. Such secure jobs for migrants are more available where there are inclusive national institutions of labour market regulation and a strong trade union workplace presence. Although in all three countries, the migrants were quite passive and instrumentalist in their relations to unions, they nonetheless generally joined when working in unionized contexts, as a way of conforming to workplace norms. For the migrant workers we interviewed, work precarity and a (lack of) union involvement went hand in hand. Both were largely a function of the migration experience and of entering the job market from the low end. Our interviewees usually began their migrant careers working in precarious jobs, with many progressing over time into better and more secure positions. Finland had the most encompassing labour market regulation and the strongest shop floor union presence, and consequently also the shortest path out of precarity. The highly segmented nature of the Greek labour market inhibited integration, ensuring that many migrants remained in the informal sector and also detached from unions. Italy stood somewhere in-between, with both a large informal sector as well as opportunities to move into less precarious work in union-regulated workplaces.

10.2. UNION IDENTITY AND SOLIDARITY

In order to evaluate the degree to which migrants assume a union identity and normative framework, we first need to define the framework. The ideal type can be derived from classic works of labour history and sociology, which generally tell a story of workers in the same workplace and geographic space relying on one another at work, sharing social networks in community and leisure activities, and finding common cultural reference points (cf. Brody 1993; Gilbert 1992; Koo 2001; Thompson 1968). These workers form solidaristic bonds and working-class cultures, which enable them to build class-based associational power (Wright 2000). This does not mean the workforce becomes a homogenous mass as pre-existing social formations are wiped away, but rather that ethnic and other divisions can be bridged through a process of class-based framing (Fantasia 1989).

Worker collectivism is simultaneously ideological and rational, being based not on disinterested altruism, but rather on enlightened self-interest. If workers have strong solidaristic norms, their organizations are powerful. If their organizations are powerful, their material interests are well represented. Collectivism serves the economic interests of workers, which in turn shores up the organizational stability of unions (Chapter 1, this volume). Kimeldorf (1988: 166) observes, in his study of dock unions in the United States, that: 'It is with the promise of delivering these [economic] goods that unions are born. Whether they endure, however, depends not only on how well they deliver on their economic promise, but also on the socially constructed meanings that in the course of history come to be attached to the union, its mission, and its leadership.' Although collectivism serves economic purposes, it fits logically into a non-economic normative system, the power of which lies in its moral integrity as much as in its utility. If its integrity is violated, the utility disappears as well. This working-class identity is in part strategically socially constructed, but it also reflects and incorporates other identities: the community the workers live in or come from, the occupational community of the crafts and/or professions, or in the case of ethicized labour markets, the ethnic group from which the workforce is drawn.

This is similar to 'instrumental collectivism' (Bradley 1999; Lockwood 1996: 57–8), which resolves the tension between individualism and collectivism inherent in collective action. Instrumental collectivism differs from individualism in that individuals recognize their own weakness in relation to their employer, which is why they turn to unions to gain power (Healy at el. 2004: 452). Layered over the instrumental collectivist rationality, however, are normative structures built up and reproduced through collectivist narratives. These are not necessarily easily transmitted outside their social milieu, but serve to ensure the sustainability of union organizations by attaching normative values to union membership, goals, and participation in collective actions.

For this reason, identities that create strong solidarity are also ones with strong potential to be exclusive. Bonacich's (1972) theory of ethnic antagonism, for example, presents ethnic and other exclusive identities as a double-edged sword: they are a ready-made source of organization, community, and solidarity, but their exclusivity also provides employers with ready-made fissures to exploit. From the side of the unions, building solidaristic norms that appeal to migrant workers can be challenging. National cultures of solidarity are very specific; we think of an 'international working class' only in the abstract, but concretely workers' actual associations, narratives, and norms refer, almost entirely, to national collective experiences. These national narratives are likely to be exclusive of migrants. For example, as Mulinari and Neergaard (2005) observe from interviews of immigrant union activists in Sweden, many native Swedes see immigrants as outsiders, whom they assume cannot be full participants in the collective historical experience of Swedish working-class struggle.

Constructing multicultural and inclusive unions is challenging, as it goes to the heart of union organizational identity, but it can be done (Virdee 2000; Chapter 9, this volume). As Marino (2015) argues, organizational inclusion depends on union legitimacy and recognition that is reflected and supported by the active participation of migrant workers on the shop floor and in the union structures. The many examples of grassroots self-organization by precarious workers, in contexts where unions might have been available in theory at least (Mattoni and Vogiatzoglou 2014; Della Porta et al. 2015; Chapter 4, this volume) suggest a degree of dissatisfaction, or insufficiency of trade union action, and perhaps a perception of a distinctive worker identity with specific interests that separate them from core workers. When special structures for migrant workers and/or precarious workers are created, there is a need for balance between autonomy and integration to make their work meaningful for migrant representation and participation within the union.

It is worth noting that the survival mentality of the migration experience as well as the migrants' historical and cultural background might contradict union norms, and inhibit the development of a union consciousness. It has often been observed that migrant workers are more likely to accept precarious working conditions, and reject or at least be reluctant to claim labour rights (Piore 1979; Çaro and Danaj 2015; Lillie 2016). This is particularly the case for short-term mobile workers and recent immigrants. Workers whose mobility prevents integration may never have an opportunity to be effectively represented by unions (Berntsen and Lillie 2016). In the early phase of the migration experience, workers often find themselves operating in the informal or semi-informal economy, which, combined with an irregular residence status, deepens their dependence on the employer and increases their willingness to accept substandard working conditions (Çaro and Danaj 2015; Mankki and Sippola 2015). Temporary regular migrant workers might also sometimes strategically accept precarious working conditions, while employing pragmatic responses to cope with them until they can find better jobs (Berntsen 2016). The intersection of the migrant and precarious statuses puts migrant workers in a more vulnerable and marginalized position

(Alberti and Danaj forthcoming) often in less unionized sectors or in the informal economy working in workplaces with no union presence (Holgate 2011). In the case of workers from Eastern Europe, home country experiences of trade unionism are also believed to have an impact on their values and response to organized labour. Referred to in the literature as post-socialist 'quiescence' (Crowley 2002), imposed solidarity during socialist regimes has pushed workers towards individualism, which has been reinforced by a void of collective understanding and expectation during the transition period (Stenning and Hörschelmann 2008).

The literature suggests that as migrants abandon their migrant mentality, and become more embedded in the host society, they also become more likely to absorb union perspectives (Gorodzeisky and Richards 2013; Kranendonk and de Beer 2016). They move from ignorance and indifference towards appreciation of the role unions play during their integration process, with the shift often coinciding with their transferral from the underground economy to formal employment, usually in unionized sectors and workplaces (Gorodzeisky and Richards 2013). In other words, their membership is determined not only by their own inclinations, individually or collectively, but also by the presence of appropriate structures to facilitate their organization in that segment of the labour market where they operate.

10.3. CASE SELECTION AND DATA

This chapter draws on 148 biographical interviews of labour migrants conducted between 2013 and 2016 in Finland, Italy, and Greece. In Finland, Estonians were interviewed, while in Italy and Greece the interviewees were Albanian. We draw on individuals as cases with life trajectories of their own, and then nest these in comparative national cases, where we can see how different national job market/labour union/migration regulation nexuses result in different patterns of precarity and union engagement among migrant groups.

The Estonian migrants we interviewed had been living and working in Finland for between one to over ten years, whereas Albanian migrants had been living in Greece and Italy for between ten and twenty-five years. The difference between the groups can be traced to the different migration statuses and regimes. Nevertheless, in all three host countries, most of the migrants described work histories of mostly or entirely poorly paid labour-intensive jobs. Table 10.1 provides a more detailed account of the interviewee backgrounds.

The biographic interviews followed Mrozowicki's (2011) three-phase interview structure. Interviewees were first asked to tell the story of their migration experience. After their initial narration, questions were asked for clarification. Then, migrants were asked more specific questions on their working lives and relationship with unions. Where possible, follow-up interviews were conducted (fifty), allowing us to chart their integration progress (or return migration) and their changes in jobs and union membership status, as well as opinions about unions. This interview technique, combined with the follow-up interviews, allows us to analyse change over time backwards to the period of initial entry, to the present, and then in some cases forward to the follow-up. Across these periods, we track

Table 10.1. Migration and employment profile of the respondents

		Finland	Italy	Greece	Total
Gender	Women	28	24	26	78
	Men	23	30	22	75
Type of migration	Informal entry	0	32	31	63
	Currently resident	45	54	35	134
	Commuters	6	0	5	11
	Circular/seasonal	0	0	8	8
Type of employment	Formal	50	49	24	123
	Informal	0	10	12	22
	2+ jobs	0	12	8	20
	Unemployed	1	1	11	13
	Retired	2	0	1	3
Sector	Services	4	10	15	29
	Cleaning	20	8	7	35
	Domestic	0	9	14	23
	Construction	17	12	5	34
	Manufacturing	3	9	3	15
	Highly skilled	3	11	1	15
	Other	2	6	5	11

the relationship of precarity and migrant integration to union status—both in fact and based on each worker's perception. We also conducted twenty-one thematic interviews with trade unionists in the three host countries. To protect the participants' identity, we use codenames throughout the chapter.

10.4. FINNISH, ITALIAN, AND GREEK NATIONAL CONTEXTS

The migration narratives and union attitudes of our respondents clearly fell into patterns consistent with the industrial relations backdrop of the host country, with more effective union regulation leading to shorter periods of precarity and greater possibilities to move into secure union-protected employment.

All three countries show clear signs of segmentation, with migrants located mainly in industries like care, cleaning, construction, hospitality, and other services characterized by substantial levels of precarity. However, there are also substantial differences in terms of union structures, status of the labour migrant workforce, and union strategies for migrants' representation and inclusion. Finland has a highly regulated industrial relations system with 70 per cent union density, 90 per cent collective bargaining coverage, and union workplace representation at 60 per cent (Eurofound 2015a). The informal sector plays a relatively small role. Since Estonia is an EU country, Estonians are legally allowed to work in Finland, and, in principle, are protected by Finnish labour laws and collective agreements. Estonians often begin to work in Finland in the informal or semi-formal sector, but there are sometimes opportunities in the formal sector as well. Some Finnish unions have made special efforts to represent migrant workers and to include them in union activities.

Italy also has strong and encompassing trade unions. Collective bargaining coverage in the Italian private sector is 97 per cent, trade union density 36.9 per cent, and workplace representation 28 per cent (Eurofound 2015b). Italy, however, has a large informal sector, which is an important provider of (precarious) employment, but which is also very difficult for the unions to regulate. Many migrants are employed in this sector (Bonifazi and Marini 2014). Albania is not in the EU, and Albanians do not have an automatic legal right to work in Italy. Informal migrants to Italy have frequently used paths to formalization. It is therefore common for Albanians to begin in precarious informal sector work, but enter into the formal sector, and then become union members as they integrate. Italian unions have instituted special structures and services for migrants.

Greece has a weaker and less encompassing labour movement than either of the other two countries. Until 2013, collective bargaining coverage in Greece for the private sector was 89 per cent, but workplace representation only at 14 per cent (Eurofound 2015c). Greek unions have been deeply affected by the economic crisis and austerity reforms through budget cuts and unilateral governmental decisions, which have led to a continuous decline in union density (Vogiatzoglou 2015). There is also a large informal sector, in which migrant workers are typically employed (Dendrinos 2014). Albanian migrants in Greece are often stuck in precarious employment in the informal sector, with few opportunities to move into formal employment. We did not find evidence of effective union programmes promoting the inclusion of Albanian migrants in Greece.

Twenty-five per cent of migrants in Finland are from Estonia and another 30,000 Estonian workers are commuting (Statistics Finland 2013). Although there are no exact figures, estimates on the unionization rates among migrant construction workers were at 12–14 per cent in 2012 (Alho 2013), and in the private service sector, the Service Union United (SUU) declared that only 4.4 per cent of their members were non-Finnish (SUU union official, 2014). Albanians are the second largest immigrant group in Italy at around half a million (ISTAT 2016). The unionization rate of immigrants of all ethnicities in the unions is rather low but progressively increasing since the establishment of special structures for migrant services (Marino 2012). Albanians are by far the largest migrant group in Greece at around half a million. Albanian migration to Italy and Greece was largely irregular, therefore most of the workforce was located in the informal labour market, to which some have returned during the economic crisis (Çaro and Danaj 2015; Triandafyllidou and Maroukis 2012). Despite a large migrant workforce, there are no reliable data on the unionization rates of migrants in Greece.

10.5. COMPARING MIGRANT PRECARITY AND UNIONIZATION

In all three host countries, migrants tended to enter mostly into precarious jobs. In the Italian and Greek cases, this usually meant entering into the informal economy. Extended residence usually had a positive impact on migrants' labour market integration. In Finland and Italy, this often also meant union membership. In Greece, most of our respondents only joined out of an immediate and pressing

Table 10.2. Union membership among the respondents

	Finland	Italy	Greece
Union members at some point	27	19	4
Union members who subsequently left the unions	3	3	3
Never been union members in host country	18	30	38
Unknown	6	4	3
Total	51	54	48

need for representation, which did not seem to arise directly from the integration process. Informal sector employment discouraged unionization in Italy and particularly in Greece (See Table 10.2).

Most of the literature about migrant unionization is really about migrant mobilization, because the reality of precarious work is often such that unionization and mobilization are one and the same. The weak union presence and employer anti-unionism, endemic to the labour market segments where migrants are most present, tends to make unionizing a drastic, high-risk decision and a radicalizing process (see, e.g., the contributions by different authors to Milkman 2000; Berntsen 2016; Chapter 4, this volume). Very few of our interviewees related such experiences. Instead, the response among those with favourable attitudes towards unions was, more or less, one of cost–benefit analysis, fitting into the workplace/host society, and a relatively weak and non-ideological union attachment.

10.5.1. Integration and Union Consciousness

In our Finnish and Italian cases, it is clear that taking up union membership was a step in the integration process, and reflected an adherence to local workplace norms rather than a mobilization experience to gain rights as migrant workers. It tended to be associated with a movement from more precarious to less precarious work situations. In the Greek case, this dynamic was less visible, primarily because of the severe labour market segmentation, accentuated by the economic crisis. Those who operated in the informal job market were generally detached from unions and afraid of associating with them, while those in formal employment usually perceived membership either as a choice they could make, or as something they *should* do as a part of belonging in the host country workplace. *Inclusive and comprehensive institutions* of the Finnish union movement, and to a lesser extent of the Italian one, allowed many migrants to take a shorter and more accessible integration path out of precarity. This was the case because unions ensured some secure jobs were available for the migrants to move into as part of their integration paths: the stronger unions in the Finnish case meant that some jobs (in cleaning, for example) that might have been precarious in Italy or Greece were relatively secure in Finland. The weaker unions in the Greek case meant that secure jobs for migrants were exceedingly rare.

During the initial period of mobility into the host country job market, all of our participants experienced a period of precarity, during which union membership was not perceived as a realistic option. For Albanians in Italy and Greece, most of the migrants we interviewed entered either as irregular migrants or as labour migrants whose right to remain was dependant on their employment. This immigration status made them highly compliant with employer demands, increasing their willingness to work under flexible and precarious conditions. The Estonian migrants also tended to enter the Finnish job market in low-paid precarious jobs in the semi-formal sector. They often began as 'posted workers' or worked for firms under somewhat dubious arrangements. For example, Aleksandr, currently working a permanent position in construction, first came as a posted worker in a firm of which he states: 'They hire a lot of Estonians, give them work for a couple of weeks and then send them back home. And take on the next set of workers' (2014). In another example, Valdo, a construction worker who is nowadays in permanent employment in a Finnish firm, first came to work for a firm with Estonian ownership (2014). He did not get his salary paid from that firm, and decided to appeal to the construction workers' union for help to get the employer to pay his salary; at this point he also changed his job.

The typical integration pattern was that the migrants eventually moved out of informal/semi-informal employment into more formal and often unionized jobs. In Finland, this could be in the same sector—as cleaning and construction are more or less properly regulated industries—but might mean a switch from an Estonian-owned to Finnish-owned, or from a smaller to a larger employer. Out of the seventeen construction workers interviewed, only eight were union members, much less than the 80 per cent density claimed by the Finnish construction workers' union. Most of those who were non-union worked for Estonian-owned small subcontractors, which are typically not unionized, even when they operate in Finland (see Sippola and Kall 2016). Also, Finnish small firms do not normally have an active union presence. Three of our informants gave this as the reason why they were not union members. As Jaan, a construction worker, put it, union recruiters are not that active 'in the smaller enterprises, but in bigger ones they start asking immediately. It is more or less obligatory there' (2014). Because Finnish collective bargaining in construction occurs at the industry level, and agreements are legally extended across the sector, small employers operating in Finland are legally obliged to follow the collective agreement, even when there are no union members present. In general, our interviewees believed that Finnish employers and large establishments usually abide by collective bargaining agreements. Smaller companies did not always do so (although they must legally).

In Finland, our informants often related their decision to join to the unions' positive reputation in the Finnish society, both as normal, mainstream institutions, and as successful representatives of workers' interests. As Vello, a construction worker, put it: 'one is supposed to be there [i.e. in the union]' (2014). Helena, for example, who has been working in cleaning for five years, argued that SUU's (the service union's) negotiations with the employers' associations had increased her salary over the years (2014). The reason why she joined, however, was a combination of the fact that her fellow workers were members, and an informed decision about the benefits of union membership. She became a member after having repeatedly discussed it with a Finnish colleague. Indeed, several respondents spoke of how they learned about unions through colleagues, both Finnish and Estonian. As Aleksandr, a construction worker, pointed out: 'the guys at work were always saying that it is good to belong to the union' (2014).

It was also common in Italy for migrant workers to become union members when moving into more secure positions. Albanian workers in the highly unionized construction industry related that union membership was required in the workplace. For example, Altin, a construction worker, was uncertain to which union he belonged, but he still joined because it was expected in his workplace (2015). And those working in manufacturing considered union membership fees as a part of normal workplace practice. For these workers, membership did not usually go further than paying dues; although they had greater knowledge and awareness of unions' role, this did not translate into engagement. As with the Estonians in Finland, being employed by small firms or by firms owned by co-nationals discouraged union membership. Several interviewees employed in small-scale carpentry firms managed by an Albanian owner, for example, were not unionized. We did not find any union members working formally in hospitality, but all of the workers in manufacturing and in construction were members.

The first and most common reaction towards questions about Greek trade unions among Albanian workers was disregard, short and simple 'no' answers, and even lack of knowledge of what trade unions are, confusing them with different associations or organizations such as the labour inspectorate. This was especially pronounced among women who had worked only in the informal economy. Most seemed nervous or even afraid that being involved with unions would put them on the wrong side of an unwritten social contract between themselves and their Greek employers. Some of the migrants, especially those with particularly long work hours, assumed union membership would be excessively time consuming. In the few cases where they had been associated with unions, it was as a result of turning to them for help in extreme situations, such as work-related injury or dismissals.

The Greek unions also confirmed the difficulty in reaching Albanian workers. Informal employment excludes the regulatory role of trade unions:

> It is almost impossible to get access in the informal market. Workers involved in the black market are very difficult to find let alone mobilise, the grey market is easier.... we try to spread the word, e.g. distribute brochures with information in different languages, also in Albanian, but we do not reach much of the informal market and precarious work nowadays.   (PAME, Migrants Secretariat, 2016)

10.5.2. 'A trade union is an office you go to when you have a problem'

In all three host countries, with a few exceptions, migrants described their interactions with unions in instrumental terms. Aside from becoming union members to show colleagues that they adhere to workplace norms, respondents emphasized the role of union management in unemployment schemes in Finland, support for handling migrant-related issues in Italy, and contesting wrongful termination in Greece. The instrumentalist view might also explain the low level of engagement in union activity among migrants in all three case studies. Furthermore, during the current economic crisis, several of our respondents experienced increased precariousness and therefore distanced themselves from the unions, in particular in Greece.

Many Estonian workers interviewed rationalized their decision to join unions on individualistic lines, in particular because Finnish unions provide unemployment benefits. This instrumental motivation is visible in the way workers readily quit the union when they felt it was no longer useful to them or when their circumstances changed. In some cases, this was because they considered the membership fees to be too high. For example, Peeter, a lorry driver, stopped paying union fees because they were too expensive (2015). Similarly, Terje, a female personal assistant and accountant for an Estonian-owned construction firm, left the union and joined the private Assured Unemployment Fund (YTK), because its fee was cheaper (2016). Although Finnish unions are the usual point of access to unemployment benefits in Finland, it is also possible to join a private fund. Marju, a female factory worker, neglected membership payments and eventually left the union (2016). She seemingly regarded union membership as pointless even though her fellow workers (all Finns) belong to the union. The only situation under which she might consider rejoining was if her employment situation were to become more insecure. These explanations for leaving the union confirm the instrumental aspect of migrants' initial unionization: rather than identifying with the union, they related to it as a service, which they decided was not worth the money.

Most of the Albanian migrants we interviewed regarded Italian unions as useful service providers. They mentioned the unions' help with problems related to working life, such as wrongful or unpaid salaries, injuries at work, retirement pensions, health leaves and benefits, wrongful termination, and liquidations. Luan, for example, who worked in construction and had once been an informal worker, praised the union officials for their support and mediation when his informal employer refused to pay him the agreed wages (2015). However, most of our informants praised the competence of the special structures for migrants, which provide services in helping migrants regularize their residence status and renew their work permits: 'It is a huge structure with various offices for the different problems you might have. If you are a foreigner, if you have documents, don't have documents, if you have . . . everything' (Edlira, hairdresser, 2015). However, as the special structures provide assistance to all migrant workers, regardless of membership, it reinforced the perception of unions as problem-solving and service-providing institutions rather than as solidarity organizations. As Edlira says, a trade union is an office you go to when you have a problem.

The association of the unions with the services they offer is also detectable in the explanation we were given for not engaging with unions as 'not having any problems'. This instrumental understanding of the unions and access to their services positively influenced the perception about unions in general, but did not necessarily increase Albanian migrant workers' likelihood to become union members. Unlike the Finnish unions' unemployment benefits, membership is not a precondition for access to Italian unions' migrant services. We also found three cases of migrant workers who had left the unions. For one of them the shift in status from employed to self-employed led to the adoption of an employer's viewpoint, whereas the other two workers left because they were not satisfied with union performance in the workplace and more broadly.

In the Greek case, the ineffectiveness of unions in representing precarious workers in the context of austerity had damaged their image among Albanian migrants. Among our interviewees, there were only four Albanians who had ever been union members, and three out of these left the unions because they were disappointed with them or when they lost their jobs. All of these individuals asked for union support after they were fired, but the union was unable to help them recover their job:

> When I got fired, I went to the trade unions . . . They used to be strong and the employers were scared of them but not anymore. When I lost my job, they should have provided assistance to me because I was fired without any reason but instead they told me 'It is the crisis don't you see, what can we do to him [employer].' I have paid for ten years my membership to them and for what? For nothing!
>
> (Alban, construction worker, 2015)

10.5.3. Union Activism

Few of the workers we interviewed were union activists. Despite being disinclined towards activism, in Finland some of the Estonian workers ended up as lay activists because of the proactive policy of the SUU to recruit shop stewards. As one Estonian shop steward told us, 'They [SUU officials] told me that every company has to have a shop steward. [I was asked because] I'm old, reliable, and maybe because I can speak some Finnish' (2014). While the union's policy of pushing to recruit activists managed to persuade some Estonians to become shop stewards, these were not always the right sort of people, or were discouraged by internal union politics. The same respondent felt that although she was a shop steward she did not get enough support from the union and was sidelined by the union officials during dispute settlement procedures. Another worker, who served for only a short time, said she had never wanted to be a shop steward in the first place but had been pressured into it by the union (2016). The Estonian union activists all reported that they faced hostility from their Finnish employers because of their union engagement.

Some passive members of the Finnish unions reported having previously been more active. The case of Kadri, a barmaid, is illustrative (2014). She had been an active shop steward in Estonia, where she was an initiator of industrial action against a proposal by the employer to introduce tests for workers to keep their jobs, and the union she represented ran a successful campaign. However, despite being a union member for the whole three-year period she had worked in Finland, she did not express enthusiasm for Finnish union activities. Kadri implied that her passivity was related to the more humane attitude of the management in Finland towards workers.

Among the Albanians in Italy, we found only one migrant worker with a high level of commitment, and who had become a union officer responsible for two sectors in her region. A university graduate who could not find employment in her field, she had worked in a factory. When the workplace representative was about to retire, she was encouraged to run. This eventually set her on the path to becoming a paid union official.

10.5.4. Sending-Country Effects or Post-Socialist Quintessence?

Both Estonia and Albania are post-socialist countries, which opened their economies to capitalism in the early 1990s. Some scholars have hypothesized that the
historical experience of state socialist 'transition belt' unionism, followed by
emancipation through a rapid transition to market capitalism, caused a post-
socialist 'quiescence' (Crowley 2002), guiding workers to reject unions and to be
less assertive about workers' rights. The post-socialist 'getting-rid-of-Communist-
institutions' atmosphere has definitely left its imprint on Estonian and Albanian
workers, and there is a notable absence of knowledge of unions, or of the solidarity
and assertiveness about rights one occasionally encounters from Western European
workers. However, individualist and utilitarian attitudes towards unions are common also in Western Europe (Schnabel 2002), and the acceptance of poor wages
and working conditions is long recognized as a characteristic of labour migrants
generally (Piore 1979).

Both Albanian and Estonian workers made reference to the post-communist
experience, but its effect on union membership was ambiguous. Some workers did
associate unions with the communist past. As one of them put it:

I. Are you a member of a trade union?

Q. What? We are not in communism anymore. In capitalism, we solve our
own problems. I go to the employer and I say 'listen here, I will work hard,
I will come when you ask for, I want my salary to be X and I want Sunday
off.' If she does not agree I will go to the next one.   (Albana, cleaner and
babysitter, 2015)

The reasoning of Albana, who works in Greece, is illustrative of younger Albanians,
reflecting a pro-market attitude consistent with an experience of very flexible work
in the informal economy. In her case, it also reflected a survival strategy for the
crisis and the austerity measures, and a reality of not having access to effective
union representation.

However, being in the union during communist times also normalized union
membership for some older Albanians. Estonian workers more often associated
unions with the Soviet regime institutions they wanted to discard. The individual
biographies in our case study do not directly exhibit strong associations between
unionism and workers' past experiences with communism, but rather show
indifference towards unions, which, as a post-soviet 'social custom', is indirectly
linked to the eradication-of-everything-associated-with-communism ideology
(Sippola 2014). On the other hand, being part of the union is something 'normal'
for older Albanian workers, as indicated by the case of Skifter, who has been a
union member in Albania, in Greece, and in Italy (2015). He first joined the union
when he was working as a miner in communist Albania. When he moved to
Greece at the beginning of the transition period in the early 1990s, he started work
as a construction worker, and soon joined the union there and remained a union
member until he left Greece permanently. Later, when he moved to Italy, he again
joined one of the unions, considering it to be normal practice. However, during
the interview he expressed his dissatisfaction with union politics; therefore, he had
decided to withdraw his membership. The influence of the communist experience

has seemingly faded away after a long migration experience, although it has not necessarily brought him closer to the unions. His detachment also reflects his lack of regular employment in the last two years as a result of the crisis.

10.5.5. Economic Crisis and Survival

Although the economic crisis and austerity has affected all three host countries, the impact has been much more substantial in Greece, somewhat less in Italy, and much less in Finland. Finland has seen public spending cuts, rising un-employment rates, and increased precarization (Ministry of Economic Affairs and Employment of Finland 2016), but unions managed to forestall a proposed wholesale reform of the industrial relations system. In Italy, labour market deregulation, the introduction of non-standard forms of employment, and recent austerity measures have led to further labour market segmentation (Dell'Arringa 2012). Greece, of course, is in a class of its own, with the crisis producing almost 1.5 million jobless workers and a general unemployment rate of 27.5 per cent (Monastiriotis 2011; Matsaganis 2013), while migrants' unemployment reached 35 per cent (OECD 2015). Differences in the impact of the crisis and austerity are very clear in the biographies of the migrants.

Most of our informants had migrated to Finland when the economic crisis hit Estonia. Although they were aware of the economic crisis' impact on Finland, they argued it had not affected them personally. Nonetheless, in our follow-up inter-views we found that at least one had returned to Estonia, one had become unemployed, and one's employment situation had not improved as she hoped as a result of graduating from a Finnish vocational school. She explained that this was because now the crisis had hit Finland too.

For Albanians in Italy, the recent crisis made employment in sectors like construction and hospitality more precarious, causing some to fall back into semi-formal or informal work arrangements. Fear of losing their jobs led to a renewed acceptance of poorer terms and conditions, and caused them to regard unions as a threat to their ability personally to make exploitive deals with employers. At the same time, the crisis negatively influenced migrant workers' perceptions of union power and position. Prior to the economic crisis, unions were considered strong and powerful. Several of our interviewees mentioned that they thought Italian trade unions had been weakened by the crisis. The Italian unions' policy of sometimes settling back pay cases for less than the sum owed is one example. Landi (lorry driver, 2015) told us that instead of fighting to collect all the unpaid salaries, the union-hired lawyer negotiated partial payments. Landi felt it was wrong for the union to accept less than what the employer had originally agreed to pay him.

The case of Albanian migrants in Greece showcases the effect of austerity measures on precarious migrant workers even more starkly. The construction industry was particularly hard hit. Among our interviewees, eleven workers were laid off and only three still work in construction. Migrant women in the female-dominated domestic care industry had been more successful in keeping their jobs, but this was due to a willingness to present themselves as flexible, cheap, and undeclared (Çaro and Lillie 2016). Deregulation of labour markets and increased precarity and vulnerability were hindering unions in representing migrant workers, especially in the private sector where union membership has declined steadily.

Prior to the economic crisis, unions had been active in collective bargaining for minimum wages and collective agreements that had relatively widespread coverage over the formal sector. Due to the economic crisis, the rise of informality brought a further decline in union membership. 'Now it is the state that decides about the minimum wage, the pension schemes, and re-compensation for redundancies' (GSEE, International Affair and Legal Counselor, 2016). The confidence crisis is very pronounced among Albanian migrants who in hard times trust only their hard work and social networks (Çaro and Danaj 2015). There is a general belief among our informants that if they show 'loyalty' by not turning to the trade unions or other structures in case of exploitation, termination, or even injuries, the employer will rehire them when an opportunity arises:

> Even if union offices exist I know nobody that goes there nowadays . . . We all are afraid that we will be fired, there is the crisis, and everywhere applies the law of the jungle, workers and employers just get what they can from each other. My husband was fired and did not receive any compensation. He did not ask for it. It was the right decision because the same employer when the firm expanded rehired him. Had he complained the employer would not have taken him back. It was like an unwritten and unspoken agreement between them.   (Lena, domestic worker, 2015)

As this quote suggests, Albanian migrants in Greece for the most part pursue individualistic strategies of flexibility and compliance with the demands of the employer. As a result of the crisis, many of those who had at some point moved into secure jobs moved partially or completely back into the informal economy in order to survive. Instead of using the social capital of integration to contest precarization (as can be seen, for example, in the cases described in Chapter 4, this volume), many Albanian migrants in Greece have fallen back on utilizing their subordinate ethnic and gendered position in the segmented labour market to secure employment, if necessary on less desirable terms than before.

10.6. CONCLUSION

Weak union attachment and a superficial or non-existent commitment to union norms, even among migrant union members, means that union membership among migrants is largely a reflection of personal circumstances. Transition to formal employment in Finland and Italy has usually been accompanied by union membership, in particular in the highly unionized industries, where membership is normalized. This confirms previous research findings (e.g. Gorodzeisky and Richards 2013; Marino et al. 2015). At the point of entry into the host country job market, the migrants had little contact with unions, and were deeply suspicious of unions and union motivation, finding themselves at the intersection of social isolation, poor labour market position, and uncertain legal status. This precarious situation usually changed with extended residence in Finland and Italy— particularly for those who found formal permanent employment in highly unionized industries and who gained familiarity with their labour rights. Inclusion in the core workforce, combined with extended residence in Finland and Italy, resulted in the adoption of workplace norms similar to the country of residence. This did not occur in Greece, mainly because most Albanian workers remained excluded from 'core' jobs throughout their migration experience. Furthermore, the harsh individual consequences of the economic crisis increased the distance between Albanian workers and the Greek unions.

Among migrant union members, migrant workers' understanding of the unions was predominantly instrumentalist. The structures and the competences unions have in each country dictated the form of instrumentalism. Access to union unemployment benefits served as an incentive for union membership among Estonian workers. In the case of Albanians in Italy, the union special structures for migrants provide services regardless of membership. As a result, although Albanian workers in Italy contacted unions with their grievances, they unionized predominantly only when their workplace was unionized. In Greece, Albanians were quite disconnected from Greek unions, which was related to the fact that most had only held informal jobs, or returned to informality as a result of crisis, and therefore were not part of the core workforce.

The literature on migrant unionization based on case studies of union campaigns suggests that the union organizing process can be a consciousness-raising event, empowering workers by encouraging them to take a direct role in improving their conditions. Our data suggest that these sorts of experiences are exceptional. It would be wrong (in almost all cases) to say that the unionized migrant workers in our interviewee group became converted or radicalized as a result of their union membership; rather, union membership was a step to join the labour market 'insider' group, and reflected a normalization of unionism in the migrants' workplaces. Those migrants who remained in the informal sector continued to lack knowledge about unions, and remained suspicious of them. Even those who evidenced in their interviews that they understood and appreciated the role of unions tended towards instrumentalist interactions with them, rarely sharing union norms.

Furthermore, one might expect migrants with established positions in the host society to act collectively when austerity threatens their jobs. In contrast, among the Albanians, a more common reaction to the economic crisis was for workers to embrace precarity—including forgoing union protections and labour rights—as a survivalist repertoire to fall back on in hard times. This attitude was prevalent in the Greek context, and also occasionally in Italy. This strategy was not visible among the Estonians in Finland, but neither were the effects of the economic crisis so severe. Finally, a number of the Albanian respondents had pursued social advancement through entrepreneurship, instead of shifting into secure jobs, and these voiced anti-union inclinations even when they were well integrated.

Our analysis suggests that despite the efforts unions have made to include migrant workers in all three countries, they still largely operate within their comfort zone, i.e. representing workers in secure jobs. However, the number of secure jobs an economy has to offer makes a substantial difference for outcomes, and here union strength and encompassing institutions matter. Union services, special structures for migrant workers, and efforts to recruit migrant activists were all visible among interviewees. The first two at least were appreciated by migrants, but these efforts failed to imprint on them the solidarity logic of the unions—i.e. the connection between the unions' normative logic and the unions' collective instrumentality. Instead, most of the migrants interviewed in all three countries continued to perceive unions in individual-instrumentalist terms. Migrant unionization seems linked to their labour market integration and employment stability more than to specific union efforts. Unions are successful in unionizing migrant workers predominantly when they come out of their precarious (informal) employment, and lose them again when their precariousness deepens. This means that unions need to recognize the interconnectedness of migrant and precarious worker statuses and address them accordingly in order for their inclusive strategies to be more successful.

ACKNOWLEDGEMENTS

The research in Finland and Italy was funded by the Academy of Finland's Project Grant #265572, and the one in Greece by the Regional Research Promotion Program Project Grant #AL_225.

REFERENCES

Alberti, Gabriella and Danaj, Sonila. Forthcoming. 'Posting and Agency Work in British Construction and Hospitality: The Role of Regulation in Differentiating the Experiences of Migrants'. *The International Journal of Human Resource Management*. DOI 10.1080/09585192.2017.1365746.

Alho, Rolle. 2013. 'Trade Union Responses to Transnational Labour Mobility in the Finnish-Estonian Context'. *Nordic Journal of Working Life Studies*, 3(3): 133–53.

Anderson, Bridget. 2000. *Doing the Dirty Work? The Global Politics of Domestic Labour*. London: Palgrave Macmillan.

Anderson, Bridget. 2010. 'Migration, Immigration Controls and the Fashioning of Precarious Workers'. *Work, Employment and Society*, 24(2): 300–17.

Berntsen, Lisa. 2016. 'Reworking Labour Practices: On the Agency of Unorganized Mobile Migrant Construction Workers'. *Work, Employment and Society*, 30(3): 472–88.

Berntsen, Lisa and Lillie, Nathan. 2016. 'Hyper-Mobile Migrant Workers and Dutch Trade Union Representation Strategies at the Eemshaven Construction Sites'. *Economic and Industrial Democracy*, 37(1): 171–87.

Bonacich, Edna. 1972. 'A Theory of Ethnic Antagonism: The Split Labor Market'. *American Sociological Review*, 37(5): 547–59.

Bonifazi, Corrado and Marini, Cristiano. 2014. 'The Impact of the Economic Crisis on Foreigners in the Italian Labour Market'. *Journal of Ethnic and Migration Studies*, 40(3): 493–511.

Bradley, Harriet. 1999. *Gender and Power in the Workplace*. London: Macmillan.

Brody, David. 1993. *Workers in Industrial America: Essays on the Twentieth Century Struggle*. Oxford: Oxford University Press.

Çaro, Erka and Danaj, Sonila. 2015. 'Being the Good Worker: What it Means for Albanian Labour Migrants to be Successful in the Italian Host Society'. *SASE 27th Annual Conference. Inequality in the 21st Century*. 2–4 July, London, UK.

Çaro, Erka and Lillie, Nathan. 2016. 'Feminized Migrant Labor in Austere Times: The Case of Albanian Migrants to Greece and Italy'. Marketization and Neoliberal Restructuring in Europe, ILR School, Cornell University, USA, 2016.

Crowley, Stephen. 2002. 'Explaining Labor Quiescence in Post-Communist Europe: Historical Legacies and Comparative Perspective'. *Working Paper* No. 55. Center for European Studies in Central and Eastern Europe.

Dell'Arringa, Carlo. 2012. 'Il ruolo degli immigrati nel mercato del lavoro italiano'. Predisposto dall'ONC-CNEL in collaborazione con il Ministero del Lavoro e delle Politiche Sociali.

Della Porta, Donatella, Silvasti, Tiina, Hänninen, Sakari, and Siisiäinen Martti (eds) 2015. *The New Social Division: Making and Unmaking Precariousness.* London: Palgrave Macmillan.

Dendrinos, Ioannis. 2014. 'Youth Employment Before and During the Crisis: Rethinking Labour Market Institutions and Work Attitudes in Greece'. *Social Cohesion and Development,* 9(2): 117–32.

Eurofound. 2015a. 'Finland: Working Life Country Profile'. Available at: <http://www.eurofound.europa.eu/sites/default/files/ef_national_contribution/field_ef_documents/finland_0.pdf>.

Eurofound. 2015b. 'Italy: Working Life Country Profile'. Available at: <http://www.eurofound.europa.eu/sites/default/files/ef_national_contribution/field_ef_documents/italy.pdf>.

Eurofound. 2015c. 'Greece: Working Life Country Profile'. Available at: <http://www.eurofound.europa.eu/sites/default/files/ef_national_contribution/field_ef_documents/greece.pdf>.

Fantasia, Rick. 1989. *Cultures of Solidarity: Consciousness, Action, and Contemporary American Workers.* Los Angeles: University of California Press.

Gilbert, David. 1992. *Class, Community and Collective Action: Social Change in Two British Coalfields, 1850–1926.* Oxford: Clarendon Press.

Gorodzeisky, Anastasia and Richards, Andrew. 2013. 'Trade Unions and Migrant Workers in Western Europe'. *European Journal of Industrial Relations,* 19(3): 239–54.

Healy, Geraldine, Bradley, Harriet, and Mukherjee, Nupur. 2004. 'Individualism and Collectivism Revisited: A Study of Black and Minority Ethnic Women', *Industrial Relations Journal,* 35(5): 451–66.

Holgate, Jane. 2005. 'Organising Migrant Workers: A Case Study of Working Conditions and Unionization at a Sandwich Factory in London'. *Work, Employment and Society,* 19(3): 463–80.

Holgate, Jane. 2011. 'Temporary Migrant Workers and Labor Organization'. *workingUSA,* 14(2): 191–9.

ISTAT. 2016. 'Bilancio Demografico Nazionale: Anno 2015'. ISTAT. Available at: <https://www.istat.it/it/files/2016/06/Bilancio-demografico-2015-1.pdf?title=Bilancio+demografico+nazionale+-+10%2Fgiu%2F2016+-+Testo+integrale.pdf>.

Kimeldorf, Howard. 1988. *Reds or Rackets? The Making of Radical and Conservative Unions on the Waterfront.* Los Angeles: University of California Press.

Koo, Hagen. 2001. *Korean Workers: The Culture and Politics of Class Formation.* Ithaca, NY: Cornell University Press.

Kranendonk, Maria and de Beer, Paul. 2016. 'What Explains the Union Membership Gap between Migrants and Natives?' *British Journal of Industrial Relations,* 54(4): 846–69.

Lillie, Nathan. 2016. 'The Right Not to Have Rights: Posted Worker Acquiescence and the European Union Labor Rights Framework'. *Theoretical Inquiries in Law,* 17: 40.

Lillie, Nathan and Simola, Anna. 2016. 'The Crisis of Free Movement in the European Union'. *Mondi Migranti,* 3: 7–19.

Lockwood, David. 1996. 'Sources of Variation in Working Class Images of Society'. In *Class: Critical Concepts,* volume 4, edited by John Scott. London and New York: Routledge.

Mankki, Laura and Sippola, Markku. 2015. 'Maahanmuuttajat suomalaisilla työmarkkinoilla: intersektionaalisuus ja "hyvä kansalainen" työmarkkina-aseman määrittäjänä'. *Työelämän tutkimus,* 13(3): 193–208.

Marino, Stefania. 2012. 'Trade Union Inclusion of Migrant and Ethnic Minority Workers: Comparing Italy and the Netherlands'. *European Journal of Industrial Relations*, 18(1): 5–20.

Marino, Stefania. 2015. 'Trade Unions, Special Structures and the Inclusion of Migrant Workers: On the Role of Union Democracy'. *Work, Employment and Society*, 29(5): 826–42.

Marino, Stefania, Penninx, Rinus, and Roosblad, Judith. 2015. 'Trade Unions, Immigration and Immigrants in Europe Revisited: Unions' Attitudes and Actions under New Conditions'. *Comparative Migration Studies*, 3(1).

Matsaganis, Manos. 2013. *The Greek Crisis: Social Impact and Policy Responses*. Berlin: Friedrich Ebert Stiftung.

Mattoni, Alice and Vogiatzoglou, Markos. 2014. 'Today, We Are Precarious. Tomorrow, We Will Be Unbeatable: Early Struggles of Precarious Workers in Italy and Greece'. In *From Silence to Protest: International Perspectives on Weakly Resourced Groups*, edited by D. Chabanet and F. Royall. Burlington: Ashgate Publishing.

Milkman, Ruth (ed.) 2000. *Organizing Immigrants: The Challenges for Unions in Contemporary California*. Ithaca, NY: Cornell University Press.

Ministry of Economic Affairs and Employment of Finland. 2016. 'Employment Bulletin'. Available at: <http://julkaisut.valtioneuvosto.fi/bitstream/handle/10024/75584/TKAT_September_en_2016.pdf?sequence=1>.

Monastiriotis, Vassilis (ed.) 2011. 'The Greek Crisis in Focus: Austerity, Recession and Paths to Recovery'. *Hellenic Observatory Papers on Greece and Southeast Europe*. London: Hellenic Observatory.

Mrozowicki, Adam. 2011. *Coping with Social Change: Life Strategies of Workers in Poland's New Capitalism*. Leuven: Leuven University Press.

Mulinari, Diana and Neergaard, Anders. 2005. '"Black Skull" Consciousness: The New Swedish Working Class. *Race and Class*, 46(3): 55–72.

OECD. 2015. 'Trade Union Density'. Available at: <https://stats.oecd.org/Index.aspx?DataSetCode=UN_DEN>.

Penninx, Rinus and Roosblad, Judith. 2000. *Trade Unions, Immigration, and Immigrants in Europe, 1960–1993: A Comparative Study of the Attitudes and Actions of Trade Unions in Seven West European Countries*, volume 1. New York and Oxford: Berghahn books.

Piore, Michael. 1979. *Birds of Passage: Migration and Industrial Societies*. Cambridge: Cambridge University Press.

Schnabel, Claus. 2002. 'Determinants of Trade Union Membership'. Diskussionspapiere No. 15. Friedrich-Alexander-Universität Erlangen-Nürnberg, Lehrstuhl für Arbeitsmarkt- und Regionalpolitik.

Sippola, Markku. 2014. 'Balancing Between Exit, Voice and Loyalty: Labour Market Policy Choices in Estonia'. In *The Contradictions of Austerity: The Socio-Economic Costs of the Neoliberal Baltic Model*, edited by Jeffrey Sommers and Charles Woolfson. Oxford: routledge.

Sippola, Markku and Kall, Kairit. 2016. 'Locked in Inferiority? The Positions of Estonian Construction Workers in the Finnish Migrant Labour Regime'. *Comparative Social Research*, 32: 197–222.

Statistics Finland. 2013. *Rajahaastattelututkimus 2012*. Helsinki: Tilastokeskus.

Stenning, Alison and Hörschelmann, Kathrin. 2008. 'History, Geography and Difference in the Post-Socialist World: Or, Do We Still Need Post-Socialism?'. *Antipode*, 40(2): 312–35.

Thompson, Edward Palmer. 1968. *The Making of the English Working Class*. Harmondsworth: Penguin Books.

Triandafyllidou, Anna and Maroukis, Thanos. 2012. *Migrant Smuggling: Irregular Migration from Asia and Africa to Europe*. Basingstoke: Palgrave Macmillan.

Virdee, Satnam. 2000. 'A Marxist Critique of Black Radical Theories of Trade-Union Racism'. *Sociology*, 34(3): 545–65.

Vogiatzoglou, Markos. 2015. 'Precarious Workers' Unions in Greece and Italy: A Comparative Study of their Organizational Characteristics and their Movement Repertoire'. PhD thesis, European University Institute. Available at: <http://cadmus. eui.eu/bitstream/handle/1814/37908/2015_Vogiatzoglou.pdf?sequence=1&isAllowed=y>.

Wright, Erik Olin. 2000. 'Workers Power, Capitalist Interests and Class Compromise'. *American Journal of Sociology*, 105(4): 957–1002.

11

The Puzzle of Precarity

Structure, Strategies, and Worker Solidarity

Steven P. Vallas

11.1. INTRODUCTION

More than a generation has passed since the work regime known as Fordism first began to unravel. For a time, theorists hoped that post-Fordist regimes might succeed in aligning the interests of labour and capital to a fuller extent than had previously been the case. Such hopeful views were especially evident in the discourse of the 1980s and 1990s as in the literature on flexible specialization (Piore and Sabel 1984), the high-performance work organization (Appelbaum et al. 2000), and the post-hierarchical workplace (Zuboff 1988; Saxenian 1994), among many other outlooks. Since that time, however, economic realities have adopted a different and far starker form. Paradoxically, economic crises have seemed to increase the power of neoliberal doctrines, engulfing a growing proportion of the labour force in ever-rising levels of economic uncertainty and job insecurity (Hacker 2006; Kalleberg 2011; Standing 2011).

How can we make sense of this trend? What are the structural and cultural forces that account for the rise of precarity? And how are the institutional characteristics of different societies likely to modify the neoliberalization process? Answers to these questions have remained elusive, despite the burgeoning debates that have unfolded across much of the advanced capitalist world. Although the theme of precarity lies at the centre of much social and political theorizing (Giddens 1991; Bourdieu 1998; Bauman 2000), our theoretical models of precarious work have lagged behind economic reality. This absence has taken its toll in many ways, contributing to a broader sense of paralysis in the face of wrenching economic and political change.

This is the context in which *Reconstructing Solidarity* appears. Its goals are ambitious and its mode of presentation all too rare. The arguments it contains represent the culmination of a collective effort on the part of scholars concerned with major theoretical questions that hold equally great practical import. Key to the volume's value is the original conceptual model it proposes in an effort to address the puzzle of precarity—that is, how to explain the varied forms that employment assumes in an era of liberalization and generalized risk. My task in this concluding chapter is to assess the volume's contributions, to subject them to critical scrutiny, and to highlight some of the major issues that future researchers will need to address as they build on the theoretical and empirical basis which this volume provides.

This chapter begins by developing a critical exegesis of the Doellgast–Lillie–Pulignano model. It then selectively extracts certain themes from the volume's case studies, which have sought to apply the model to a host of sectors throughout the European continent. Next, the chapter develops a friendly critique of the model, drawing largely on literature from economic and organizational sociology, the better to foster the kind of interdisciplinary dialogue contributors have worked to sustain. The chapter closes with some necessarily speculative remarks on the tasks that confront workers, labour organizations, and policymakers in an era of rapid structural change.

11.2. STRUCTURE, STRATEGY, AND SOLIDARITY: AN INTEGRATED VIEW

The point of departure for this volume lies in the fractured state of scholarship that exists among scholars studying the work regimes that have unfolded in the wake of neoliberalism. In the view of the editors, one schism warrants especially close attention: that which separates the European tradition of comparative political economy from critical sociological studies of work. As the editors make clear, both scholarly traditions have generated invaluable insights, but both have remained plagued by important analytical limitations as well. To address these limitations, the authors invoke a conceptual toolkit drawn from their own field—the study of employment relations—using it to generate a conceptual synthesis that holds greater promise than either approach could achieve. This is not an instance of a jurisdictional competition, but quite the opposite: an effort to conjoin complementary perspectives, each with its own strengths, producing a theoretical model that is stronger and more analytically powerful as a result.

The rationale for their approach rests on a trenchant critique of existing models. To be sure, scholars working in comparative political economy have identified important institutional differences that distinguish capitalist societies from one another. They have also led an important debate over just how enduring cross-national differences are likely to be in the contemporary era. Although some theorists envision an overarching liberalization process likely to overwhelm the traditional protections workers have enjoyed in the past, others envision a heightening of the dualizing tendencies that labour markets have exhibited in the past (Rueda 2007; Palier and Thelen 2010; Thelen 2012). The problem with much of this literature, the editors contend, is its implicit reliance on what Beck (2007) has called methodological nationalism—an analytical habit that tends to reify the characteristics of the nation state and to fashion generalizations couched at the macro-social level of analysis. This view too easily overlooks important variations in labour market dynamics that exist *within* given nations, and which have less to do with nationally distinctive institutional patterns than with the combination of conditions that exist irrespective of national context.

For their part, critical sociologists of work have exhibited an oddly mirrored set of analytical limitations. Critical sociologists have generated a rich literature on the precarization of work at the level of the firm, industry, or occupation (Smith 2001; Padavic 2005; Hatton 2011). But since it typically lacks any comparative focus, such research can only rarely account for structural and cultural variations in the neoliberal trend.[1] Given the barriers that exist between these two perspectives, scholars have found it difficult to solve the puzzle of precarity—the variability that accompanies the neoliberalization that has unfolded across the advanced capitalist landscape.

Doellgast, Lillie, and Pulignano wish to change this state of affairs. Borrowing from the field of political economy, the editors assign a central place to the provisions and protections afforded by the state—specifically, welfare state policy, labour regulations, and state-sanctioned collective agreements—mindful that these institutional conditions impinge on the degree of economic dependence that workers experience in their relation to capital. The key issue is whether state provisions and protections are broadly inclusive of all workers, or instead encompass only a subset of the labour force. They reason that inclusive institutional conditions are likely to prevent capital from exploiting loopholes, or inequalities, among different groups of workers; exclusive patterns have the opposite, divisive effect, fostering fissures in the labour market that redound to capital's advantage.

The editors are keenly aware that more is involved than political and economic factors. They recognize the importance of processes involving collective identities and symbolic boundaries, as has been shown in literature on split labour markets (Bonacich 1976; cf. Tilly 1998). In such instances, racial, ethnic, and religious categories can become deeply embedded within the workings of the labour market, differentially situating workers in relation to one another and thus to capital as well. Where such conditions foster particularistic identities on the part of workers, the organizational strategies that labour unions adopt are especially likely to favour labour market 'insiders', thus fostering the dualization trend that scholars often expect. The opposite is the case, however, where workers embrace a more inclusive identity. Here, a broader, class-based orientation on the part of labour organizations is likely to arise, in turn supporting strategic orientations on the part of unions that resist economic divisions and inequalities among workers' ranks. The latter strategy is presumed to work in defence of *all* workers, not least because it avoids the trap of perpetuating a reserve army of labour that employers would use to erode the labour market power of incumbent groups.

Thus the model that Doellgast, Lillie, and Pulignano propose envisions a causal matrix at the macro-social level whose elements include structural, cultural, and strategic determinants. Crucially, these elements can combine in two ideal-typical ways. Where institutional conditions are inclusive, including the great bulk of the labour force, a level playing field emerges that empowers workers and reduces their dependence on capital. Cultural divisions are less salient, and workers become more likely to present a united front in relation to both employers and the state. The associational power of trade unions is likely to expand, in turn

---

[1] Some sociologists do conduct comparative analysis of work; see in particular Sharone 2014 and Sallaz 2009, who build on earlier work by Bendix 1956 and Gallie 1978.

helping protect or enhance labour's bargaining position and its capacity to shape the role of the state. Under these conditions, a 'virtuous circle' results, and employers have little choice but to adopt strategies towards labour that allow workers to exercise 'voice' (Hirschman 1970). By contrast, where institutional conditions adopt an exclusive form, and where workers are divided by fragmented or particularistic identities, the opposite dynamic is likely to obtain. Here, capital is likely to rely on a more coercive strategy towards labour—'exit'—that exploits social and economic divisions among the workforce. Here, a downward spiral emerges whose feedback loops set in motion an ongoing deterioration in wages and job security. Here one expects a 'vicious circle' that intensifies the precarization trend.

The editors present their framework as a heuristic device, mindful that no actually existing societies will perfectly exhibit either the 'virtuous' or the 'vicious' dynamic. Yet they do see a broad trend gripping many European societies, moving work regimes from the 'virtuous' towards the 'vicious' end of the continuum. But they insist that such a trend is likely to be complex, uneven, and marked by important variations which their causal model can explain. The implication is twofold. First, dualization ceases to be a structural necessity; rather, it represents one possible outcome whose emergence occurs only under the specific conditions identified in the model. Second, the effects of liberalization are also viewed in contingent terms. Where inclusive identities arise, and union strategy acts on the mission of labour solidarity, workers will enjoy far stronger ability to challenge the deterioration of their position in the labour market, with more favourable work regimes emerging as a result. Motivating their analysis, then, is the hope that social scientific analysis can explicate the social and institutional forces that the workers' movement confronts, thus placing labour's strategic outlook on a more reflexive footing.

11.3. THE MODEL APPLIED

The chapters in this volume richly substantiate the Doellgast–Lillie–Pulignano framework. With some variation, the contributors reject the tenets of methodological nationalism in favour of a research strategy that uses the sector as the unit of analysis and compares the employment relations that arise within different institutional and cultural contexts. The chapter address a wide array of blue- and white-collar settings, whether in manufacturing contexts (e.g. meat processing, metalworking, and chemical sectors), services (logistics, retail, the arts), or local government. The chapters also address the complexities that arise when migrant workers are recruited into host communities, the better to understand the challenges that socio-demographic divisions portend for worker solidarity. Since the contributors describe a broad and varying set of outcomes, with evidence of workers' relative success at resisting precarization under specific circumstances, the results provide an empirical basis for guarded optimism, suggesting that the problems workers experience under neoliberalism are by no means insoluble.

These features are apparent in three chapters that address the sharp divisions that can emerge between 'regular' and agency workers, as when firms utilize outsourcing strategies that erode the security and wages that workers previously enjoyed. In their study of warehouse and delivery workers in the Italian and Austrian logistics sector (Chapter 4), for example, Benvegnú et al. develop a rich analysis of the shifts that have reconfigured the work situations of warehouse and package delivery workers. These workers are employed in a complex web of supply chains and subcontracting arrangements that place native and migrant workers within different segments of the labour market. In the Austrian logistics sector, rigidly institutionalized patterns of collective bargaining left little room for activism at the local level, thereby tending to reproduce the labour market segmentation that plagued regular and agency workers alike. But their Italian counterparts faced a different set of circumstances. Since collective agreements were less firmly established in the Italian sector, and since political divisions confronted employers with elements of uncertainty, grassroots mobilization became more feasible, enabling activists to devise imaginative tactics that succeeded in making egalitarian gains. The Pulignano and Doerflinger study (Chapter 5) found a similar pattern of variation in the work situations of 'regular' and agency workers. Studying chemical and metalworking plants situated in Germany and Belgium, these authors report that collective agreements in the German plants limited the agency of local works councils, fostering dualist union strategies that favoured the interests of 'regular' employees. In the Belgian plants, however, a different outcome emerged. Because the Belgian unions enjoyed greater power resources and were more centrally embedded within Belgium's collective bargaining system, they were far better able to act in unison in relation to capital, limiting employers' ability to utilize agency employees. Finally, Benassi and Dorigatti (Chapter 6) studied metal workers in Germany and Italy, and again explored how unions addressed the division between 'regular' and agency workers over time. In this study, workers in the German metal sector established important limits on the employer's use of agency employees, limiting any dualization trend. In Italy, precisely the reverse occurred: here, labour's initial advantages decayed over time, with agency workers growing more vulnerable as employers gained the upper hand.

Two important lessons can be gleaned from these studies. First, these results suggest that worker solidarity and union strategy are indeed consequential. Different work regimes seem to emerge as these factors vary, in other words, indicating that labour struggle and organization do have effects of their own. The dualization trend is by no means a necessary outcome, then, but is instead a malleable trend. Second, these studies begin to provide a nuanced portrait of the dynamics that unfold beneath the surface of the nation state. German work regimes are sometimes prone to dualization but at other times not, depending on the characteristics that impinge at the sectoral level. These chapters thus trouble established analytical habits, showing the value of an approach that remains alive to intranational variations.

Evidence of varying labour market outcomes is apparent elsewhere as well. For example, the study by Grimshaw et al. (Chapter 2) explores how public sector unions in five European nations (the UK, Hungary, Sweden, France, and Germany) have responded to a politics of austerity that threatens government workers with pay cuts, outsourcing, and eroded job security. Again, this study finds little evidence of a particularistic orientation of the sort that dualization theorists expect. Especially in Germany, France, and Sweden, the trend was one in which unions 'reject[ed] the classic dualist thesis by bargaining effectively for stronger chain solidarity', thereby establishing greater unity among workers holding distinct positions in the labour market. The implication is that a 'nuanced, non-determinist approach is needed' that sees dualization as but one contingent outcome. Likewise, Refslund and Wagner's study of Danish Crown's meatpacking plants in Denmark and Germany (Chapter 3) again shows how unions can adopt an inclusive, egalitarian posture even in the face of powerful outsourcing threats. Since workers at the German plant were unable to form such solidary ties, however, their union's power suffered as a result. This opened the door to the fragmentation of their work and the deterioration of their working conditions. In the Danish plant, by contrast, workers enjoyed a strong sectoral tradition of collective bargaining and union membership both at the local and national level, even when faced with the threat of capital flight. The result was that the Danish workers were able to limit the company's ability to exploit posted employees.

Yet if workers and their unions have clearly achieved important successes, these chapters also provide evidence of the profound challenges that workers face in addressing the precarization trend. A particularly thorny issue stems from the native/immigrant division, which emerges in several of these chapters. For example, the study by Danaj et al. (Chapter 10) explores the difficulties that unionization encountered among Estonian migrants to Finland and Albanian migrants to Italy and Greece. Here one begins to appreciate the enduring barriers that separate native and migrant workers and that undercut efforts to incorporate migrants within labour organizations. Such barriers are equally pronounced in the study by Tapia and Holgate (Chapter 9), who are concerned with the unionization of migrants in the UK, France, and Germany. Common findings emerge in both these studies: while union responsiveness, efficacy, and reputation favour migrant incorporation, inclusive forms of solidarity are simply difficult to achieve, especially where (as is often the case) the life circumstances of migrant workers require them to adopt a narrowly instrumental view of union membership. One can speculate that such ethnic divisions have only grown more pronounced in the wake of the xenophobic movements that have gained energy in the wake of the refugee crisis that has emerged in the aftermath of civil wars plaguing the Middle East.

11.4. THEORETICAL CHALLENGES

The studies collected in this volume provide compelling substantiation of the Doellgast–Lillie–Pulignano approach and begin to demonstrate its analytic power. Evaluating its success as an explanatory model, however, requires that we subject it to critical scrutiny, probing its assumptions and exploring any possible omissions. This section adopts such a critical inquiry, beginning at the micro-social level of the workplace and firm and then moving upward through meso- and macro-levels of analysis.

1. Doellgast–Lillie–Pulignano have implicitly (and insightfully) used Hirschman's classic *Exit, Voice and Loyalty* (1970) as an important resource for their model.

As they show, when employers have no alternative, they will allow workers to exercise 'voice' at the point of production, acceding to workers' demands. Yet when employers can behave otherwise—that is, when loopholes exist that employers can exploit—capital will resort to economic coercion as a lever with which to enhance its power over labour. This reasoning holds obvious pertinence in an era marked by widespread offshoring and regional inequalities in economic conditions.

Yet there is reason to believe that the exit/voice binary may not suffice to capture the mechanisms that employers use in their effort to gain control over labour. Studies in both the organization studies and labour process traditions, for example, have consistently shown that capital is often able to adopt organizational and cultural mechanisms with which to limit labour struggle and organization at the level of the firm or establishment. For example, Kunda's influential study (1992) revealed that firms in the high-tech sector are able to devise powerful forms of 'normative control' that erect salient boundaries around employee orientations towards work and management. In his analyses of the retail and other sectors, du Gay found evidence that 'enterprise culture' had redefined worker consciousness, encouraging workers to adopt a market-friendly outlook that impeded the formation of a counter-discourse (du Gay 1996; du Gay and Salaman 1992). Alvesson and Willmott (2002) go further, and suggest that the tools at capital's command now extend into the regulation of employee identity, which becomes an important site of organizational control. In their study of a call centre, Fleming and Sturdy (2011) suggest that recently, more 'natural', neo-normative forms of labour control have evolved which allow workers to 'just be themselves'—a pattern that elicits high levels of commitment to the firm to a degree that wages and benefits would not predict.

Interestingly, virtually all of this research has been conducted in liberal market economies, where works councils are notably absent. This point underscores the need for a fuller understanding of managerial control strategies established under different circumstances. Key are the tensions and contradictions such structures betray, and the possibilities they may provide for worker intervention. Even potent forms of cultural control have been found to be fragile under certain conditions, and even to provide workers with the social and cultural resources they need to oppose unilateral management actions (Vallas 2003, 2016). Arguably, such micro-level dynamics warrant especially careful consideration in an era when centralized bargaining systems are delegating more and more issues downward to the level of the firm. The point here is that the question is not merely whether worker solidarity develops in a narrowly exclusive or broadly inclusive form. Pertinent too—and perhaps increasingly so—is the question of whether employers can entice workers to feel a sense of loyalty towards the firm (Burawoy 1985).

2. Many of the studies in this volume use the *sector* as the basic unit of analysis. The research strategy they use has held the sector constant while allowing institutional conditions, solidarity, and union strategy to vary, thus isolating the impact these variables have on employment relations. This is a fertile research strategy, as these studies attest. But implied in this approach is a tendency to use the sector concept in a relatively unexamined way, as if it entailed a technical or economic category with which to classify firms producing the same or similar goods or services. Though organizational sociologists have used such an approach

in the past (cf. Scott and Meyer 1983), they have increasingly found reason to embrace a different view, premised on the organizational *field*. In so doing, they have opened up a different set of assumptions and findings than are envisioned by the contributors to this volume (DiMaggio and Powell 1983; Emirbeyer and Johnson 2008; Fligstein and McAdam 2011, 2012). Their reasoning may hold potential value for future researchers to note.

Especially in the hands of scholars such as Fligstein and McAdam, organizational fields are viewed as meso-level social orders that harbour their own structural and cultural dynamics, and these hold great relevance for the strategic orientations that firms are likely to adopt. In this view, fields are socially constructed domains that are internally stratified, yet their participants nonetheless come to share a common set of rules, operational norms, and interpretive frames. Although fields can exhibit elements of stability, they are inherently dynamic, owing to both exogenous and endogenous factors. Endogenous sources of change stem from the ongoing struggle between incumbents and challengers, and from shifting coalitions that can arise among firms, investors, and suppliers. Change often has exogenous sources, too, as when shocks occur due to shifts in state policy or to product or process innovations that can disrupt the field's boundaries. Fligstein has shown, for example, that shifts in a field's regulatory environment can alter the position that different groups of executives hold within the firm, thus altering the strategic actions the firm is likely to adopt (Fligstein 1987, 1990). The point is that the fields in which firms are embedded are more than technical or economic categories—they are also interaction orders that generate strategic dispositions, collective identities, and norms in ways that are not driven by considerations of profit and loss alone. Patterns of solidarity may not only shape the strategic orientations of *workers* (which the model acknowledges) but also the orientations of *employers* (a point which the model omits).

The potential value of the field concept lies in its ability to generate lines of inquiry that might fruitfully extend the Doellgast–Lillie–Pulignano model. It suggests, for example, that decisions to expand the use of agency employees, or to divert capital to lower-cost sites, may reflect underlying shifts in the firm's environment, instability in the coalitions to which it belongs, or an infusion of 'conceptions of control' (Fligstein 1990) previously found in adjoining fields. A good example is provided by Ho's (2009) study of the shareholder conception of the firm, which migrated from elite Wall Street investment firms outward into adjoining fields, recasting the strategic orientations that firms embraced and redefining their relations to employees (Hatton 2011). The point is that by tracing the actions of firms to the fields in which they are embedded, we are in a better position to anticipate and understand the dynamics that drive employers' strategic orientations, and to show instances where state policy has hidden yet significant effects on workers (Palier and Thelen 2010). We may also be in a better position to propose counter-strategies as a result (Reich 2016).

3. A further consideration raised by the Doellgast–Lillie–Pulignano model involves its emphasis on the importance of state policy—i.e. institutional conditions—as a factor that shapes the work regimes that workers experience. Though the link between state politics and the nature of work and employment was acknowledged in earlier American scholarship, as in Sabel's (1982) study of Emilia-Romagna and in Burawoy's (1985) theory of factory regimes, an appreciation

of the capital/state link has tended to vanish from more recent American accounts. Thus the recent literature on precarious labour has largely focused on the
power that capital itself enjoys, as if political structures could safely be ignored.
This is true of Ho's ethnography of Wall Street (2009), Lin and Tomaskovic-
Devey's study of financialization (2013), Western and Rosenfeld's study of
deunionization (2011), and much work on the hyper-mobility of capital as well
(Bronfenbrenner and Luce 2004; Collins 2003). The danger here is that scholars
begin to accept what Polanyi viewed as the myth of the self-regulating market, in
effect turning a blind eye towards the myriad ways in which state policy under-
girds capital's power and preferences. For this reason, the emphasis that Doellgast,
Lillie, and Pulignano place on the role of the state will be an especially welcome
intervention for US-based sociologists in particular.

Yet the argument can be made that their treatment of the state accords
too much emphasis to its material side and too little to the symbolic or cultural
struggles in which the state is often engaged. Arguably, their model stands in need
of a more fully elaborated conception of the political, acknowledging the social
and ideological influence that the state can exert—influence that may at times
overwhelm and condition the possibility of worker solidarity. Involved here is the
question of boundaries—that is, whether it is fruitful to adopt an employment-
centred approach towards solidarity and strategy, or whether a more embedded
approach seems necessary.

The meaning of this point can be illustrated using an important yet often
overlooked episode in the American debate over the contours of the welfare
state. During the early 1990s, downsizing and outsourcing exploded on to the
national scene, and white-collar groups began to face levels of job insecurity that
only manual workers had previously endured. A deep recession occurred in
1990–1, hammering home the fact of labour market uncertainty and costing the
first Bush administration its chances at re-election. It was against this background
that there arose a wide-ranging debate concerning the 'urban underclass', whose
members were widely portrayed as exhibiting morally dubious qualities. Key
to this implicitly racialized debate was its portrayal of the underclass as refusing
to satisfy conditions deemed necessary for inclusion within civil society—
specifically, the willingness to perform wage labour. This episode amounted to
a public degradation ritual (Handler 1995), orchestrated by national political
leaders from both parties, that served at least four important functions. First, it
justified a stripping away of the institutional conditions that poor and working
people had won during an earlier period. Second, it infused a punitive quality into
national labour policy, in which 'workfare' came to resemble a criminal penalty
(Wacquant 2009). Third, it served to reaffirm an ideological discourse that had
begun to fray, involving the 'work ethic' as a binding moral obligation on all
Americans. And fourth, by framing the underclass as 'others', it provided symbolic compensation for workers at a moment when the value of paid employment
was beginning to erode.

My point is that the Doellgast–Lillie–Pulignano model in its current form may
need to accord greater space to these kinds of cultural struggles at the macro-social
level, which often shape the institutional conditions that workers are likely to
encounter. It may be true (as the editors might reply) that racial divisions in the
United States have long impeded working-class solidarity, placing severe limits

on the inclusiveness of the welfare state (Quadagno 1994). This is undeniable. But what is missing in such a view is an acknowledgement of the political-ideological functions that the state commonly performs, and that can provide discursive frames that can overwhelm solidarity-based mobilizations at the firm or field level.[2] Unless we acknowledge the importance of such ideological struggles, and of the state's role in conducting them, it may be difficult to address the challenge of ensuring that 'local-level successes . . . can feed back up to the national level', as Grimshaw et al. conclude in Chapter 2.

11.5. DISCUSSION AND CONCLUSION

Quantitatively oriented readers of this volume may already be envisioning the possibility of multi-level modelling strategies that might test some of the many propositions these chapters contain. Such exercises will surely be fruitful, as will additional qualitative efforts that extend this volume's analytical reach into domains that are as yet unexplored. Yet it seems safe to suggest that the chapters assembled here have already contributed to our knowledge in multiple ways. Using qualitative, case study methods, these chapters have sensitized us to the structural and cultural conditions that shape labour market outcomes in ways that have not previously been noted. What emerges is an image of work regimes as malleable constructs—that is, as socially negotiated outcomes that reflect the actions and orientations of the respective combatants. Here we begin to see the volume's theoretical contribution—an effort to outline a causal matrix whose elements are at least partly subject to human control.

These are major achievements. But building on them will take much additional thinking and research. I want to use these concluding remarks to address an issue that this volume has broached, if obliquely so: the broader goal or purpose in defence of which workers can unite. At one level this is an empirical question, and one that future research can usefully address. What are the moral and cultural features exhibited by movements that achieve strong forms of worker solidarity? What discourses have emerged that enable regular and temporary workers—or for that matter, native-born and migrant workers—to form common cause? Here qualitative work on the moral economies that foster worker solidarity constitutes a much-needed area for future research.

Alongside these questions, however, lies a different set of issues that are both theoretical and strategic at one and the same time. What are the 'ends' towards which worker solidarity aspires? Is the workers' movement engaged in a Polanyian double movement—that is, simply a refusal of market-driven instability and a demand for the right to secure, full-time work? Or must workers, labour activists, and policymakers begin to anticipate something different and more challenging, stemming from what Beck (2000) once called a crisis of the 'work society'?

---

[2] A parallel narrative might be constructed with respect to the infamous Hartz reforms that began in Germany just after the turn of the new millennium.

It is worth recalling Beck's views on these questions. Invoking classical themes drawn from Max Weber's studies on the Protestant ethic, Beck argued that secularization did not simply banish the sacred from everyday life. Rather, it displaced the pursuit of salvation into the sphere of wage labour:

> Having lost their faith in God, [actors] believe instead in the godlike powers of work to provide everything sacred to them: prosperity, social position, personality, meaning in life, democracy, political cohesion. Just name any value of modernity and I will show that it assumes the very thing about which it is silent: participation in paid work.
>
> (Beck 2000: 63)

The problem was that having invested work with sacred meaning, the further development of modernity actively undermined the institutional supports on which such beliefs could rest. As capital has demanded ever more flexibility from its workforce, what has emerged is a '*risk-fraught system of flexible, pluralized, decentralized underemployment*' (Beck 1992: 142, his emphasis) that can no longer support the meanings that workers attach to their careers. What resulted, he believed, would be a proliferation of crisis tendencies as a chronic feature of late modernity. A society that has historically obligated its citizens to ground their identities in the performance of wage labour, and which imbued work with the trappings of a civil religion, itself becomes precarious when its institutional provisions for work have been emptied of their former stability.

If Beck's reasoning bears scrutiny, then the landscape that worker solidarity must confront will face many challenges indeed. For example, Davis (2013) foresees an erosion of the dominant position that large corporations have held within capitalist societies, pointing out that the most highly capitalized firms today—Google, Amazon, Facebook, etc.—have little apparent need for human workers on anything approaching the scale that was previously required. Business schools and governmental circles have increasingly suggested that digital technologies, the Internet, robotics, and artificial intelligence all argue powerfully on behalf of Work 4.0—a work regime unlike anything previously known (European Political Strategy Centre 2016). Wrapped up in these shifts, however implicitly, are subtle and not so subtle issues of gender, as the centrality of work in men's lives undergoes especially wrenching change. These disruptions arguably fuel at least some of the populist movements that have been roiling civil society in recent years.

It is the great virtue of this volume to suggest that economic liberalization has had far-reaching consequences that cannot be left to the designs generated by economic policy elites. Active labour market policies and the rhetoric of flexicurity cannot suffice as responses to what may well be a far-reaching structural upheaval whose effects have perhaps only begun to make themselves felt. Needed is an equally far-reaching effort that conjoins the orientations of workers labouring under heterogeneous circumstances yet facing the same issues of uncertainty, instability, and risk. The question is whether worker solidarity and labour organization, together with kindred social movements, will prove equal to the task, fashioning proactive visions of work that expand its boundaries beyond the 'value imperialism' the market has enjoyed thus far. This may well be the challenge that worker solidarity and union strategy will need to confront in the coming years.

REFERENCES

Alvesson, M. and Willmott, H. 2002. 'Identity Regulation as Organizational Control: Producing the Appropriate Individual'. *Journal of Management Studies*, 39: 619–44.

Appelbaum, Eileen, Bailey, Thomas, Berg, Peter, and Kalleberg, Arne L. 2000. *Manufacturing Advantage: Why High-Performance Work Systems Pay Off*. Ithaca, NY: Cornell University Press.

Bauman, Zygmunt. 2000. *Liquid Modernity*. Cambridge: Blackwell.

Beck, Ulrich. 1992. *The Risk Society: Toward a New Modernity*. London: Sage.

Beck, Ulrich. 2000. *The Brave New World of Work*. Cambridge: Polity.

Beck, Ulrich. 2007. 'Beyond Class and Nation: Reframing Social Inequalities in a Globalizing World'. *British Journal of Sociology*, 58(4): 679–705.

Bendix, Reinhardt. 1956. *Work and Authority in Industry: Ideologies of Management in the Course of Industrialization*. New York: Wiley.

Bonacich, Edna. 1976. 'Advanced Capitalism and Black/White Race Relations in the United States: A Split Labor Market Interpretation'. *American Sociological Review*, 41(1): 34–51.

Bourdieu, Pierre. 1998. *Acts of Resistance: Against the Tyranny of the Market*. New York: New Press.

Bronfenbrenner, K. and Luce, S. 2004. *The Changing Nature of Corporate Global Restructuring: The Impact of Production Shifts on Jobs in the US, China, and around the Globe*. Washington, DC: US–China Economic and Security Review Commission.

Burawoy, Michael. 1985. *The Politics of Production: Factory Regimes under Capitalism and Socialism*. London: Verso.

Collins, Jane L. 2003. *Threads: Gender, Labor, and Power in the Global Apparel Industry*. Chicago: University of Chicago Press.

Davis, Gerald F. 2013. 'After the Corporation'. *Politics and Society*, 4(2): 283–308.

DiMaggio, Paul and Powell, Walter W. 1983. 'The Iron Cage Revisited: Institutional Isomorphism and Collective Rationality in Organizational Fields'. *American Sociological Review*, 48: 147.

du Gay, Paul. 1996. *Consumption and Identity at Work*. Thousand Oaks, CA: Sage.

du Gay, P. and Salaman, G. 1992. 'The Cult(ure) of the Customer'. *Journal of Management Studies*, 29(5): 615.

Emirbeyer, Mustafa and Johnson, Victoria. 2008. 'Bourdieu and Organizational Analysis'. *Theory and Society*, 37 :1–44.

European Political Strategy Centre. 2016. 'The Future of Work: Skills and Resilience for a World of Change'. *EPSC Strategic Notes*, 13 (10 June). Available at: <http://ec.europa.eu/epsc/sites/epsc/files/strategic_note_issue_13.pdfs>.

Fleming, Peter and Sturdy, Andrew. 2011. 'Being Yourself in the Electronic Sweatshop: New Forms of Normative Control'. *Human Relations*, 64: 177–200.

Fligstein, Neil. 1987. 'The Intraorganizational Power Struggle: Rise of Finance Personnel to Top Leadership in Large Corporations, 1919–1979'. *American Sociological Review*, 52(1): 44–58.

Fligstein, Neil. 1990. *The Transformation of Corporate Control*. Cambridge, MA: Harvard University Press.

Fligstein, Neil and McAdam, Douglas. 2011. 'Toward a General Theory of Strategic Action Fields'. *Sociological Theory*, 29(1): 1–25.

Fligstein, Neil and McAdam, Douglas. 2012. *A Theory of Fields*. New York: Oxford.

Gallie, Duncan. 1978. *In Search of the New Working Class: Automation and Social Integration within the Capitalist Enterprise*. Cambridge: Cambridge University Press.

Giddens, Anthony. 1991. *Modernity and Self-Identity: Self and Society in the Late Modern Age*. Palo Alto, CA: Stanford University Press.

Handler, Joel. 1995. *The Poverty of Welfare Reform*. New Haven, CT: Yale University Press.

238   *Reconstructing Solidarity*

Harvey, David. 2005. *A Brief History of Neo-liberalism*. Oxford: Oxford University Press.

Hatton, Erin. 2011. *The Temp Economy: From Kelly Girls to Permatemps in Postwar America*. Philadelphia: Temple University Press.

Hirschman, Albert O. 1970. *Exit, Voice and Loyalty*. Cambridge, MA: Harvard University Press.

Ho, Karen Zouwen. 2009. *Liquidated: An Ethnography of Wall Street*. Durham, NC: Duke University Press.

Kalleberg, Arne L. 2011. *Good Jobs, Bad Jobs: The Rise of Polarized and Precarious Employment Systems in the United States, 1970s to 2000s*. New York: Russell Sage Foundation Publications.

Kunda, Gideon. 1992. *Engineering Culture*. Cambridge, MA: MIT Press.

Lin, Ken-Hou and Tomaskovic-Devey, Donald. 2013. 'Financialization and U.S. Income Inequality, 1970–2008'. *American Journal of Sociology*, 118(5): 1284–329.

Padavic, Irene. 2005. 'Laboring under Uncertainty: Identity Renegotiation among Contingent Workers'. *Symbolic Interaction*, 28(1): 111–34.

Palier, Bruno and Thelen, Kathleen. 2010. 'Institutionalizing Dualism: Complementarities and Change in France and Germany'. *Politics and Society*, 38(1): 119–48.

Piore, M. and Sabel, C. 1984. *The Second Industrial Divide*. New York: Basic Books.

Quadagno, Jill. 1994. *The Color of Welfare: How Racism Undermined the War on Poverty*. London: Oxford.

Reich, Adam. 2016. 'Contesting Authority in a Moralized Market: The Case of a Catholic Hospital Unionization Campaign'. In *The SAGE Handbook of Resistance*, edited by David Courpasson and Steven P. Vallas. London: Sage.

Rueda, David. 2007. *Social Democracy Inside Out: Partisanship and Labor Market Policy in Advanced Industrialized Democracies*. New York: Oxford University Press.

Sabel, Charles F. 1982. *Work and Politics: The Division of Labor in Industry*. Cambridge: Cambridge University Press.

Sallaz, Jeffrey J. 2009. *The Labor of Luck: Casino Capitalism in the United States and South Africa*. Berkeley: University of California Press.

Saxenian, Anna Lee. 1994. *Regional Advantage: Culture and Competition in Silicon Valley and Route 128*. Cambridge, MA: Harvard University Press.

Scott, William Richard and Meyer, John. 1983. 'The Organization of Societal Sectors'. In *Organizational Environments: Ritual and Rationality*, edited by John W. Meyer and W. Richard Scott. Beverly Hills, CA: Sage.

Sharone, Ofer. 2014. *Flawed System, Flawed Self: Job Searching and Unemployment Experiences*. Chicago: University of Chicago Press.

Smith, Vicki. 2001. *Crossing the Great Divide: Worker Risk and Opportunity in the New Economy*. Ithaca, NY: Cornell University/ILR Press.

Standing, Guy. 2011. *The Precariat. The New Dangerous Class*. London: Bloomsbury Academic.

Thelen, Kathleen. 2012. 'Varieties of Capitalism: Trajectories of Liberalization and the New Politics of Social Solidarity'. *Annual Review of Political Science*, 15: 137–59.

Tilly, Charles. 1998. *Durable Inequality*. Berkeley: University of California Press.

Vallas, Steven P. 2003. 'The Adventures of Managerial Hegemony: Teamwork, Ideology, and Worker Resistance'. *Social Problems*, 50(2): 204–25.

Vallas, Steven P. 2016. 'Working Class Heroes or Working Stiffs? Domination and Resistance in Business Organizations'. *Research in the Sociology of Work*, 28: 101–26.

Wacquant, Loic. 2009. *Punishing the Poor: The Neo-liberal Government of Social Insecurity*. Durham NC: Duke University Press.

Western, Bruce and Rosenfeld, Jake. 2011. 'Unions, Norms, and the Rise in U.S. Wage Inequality'. *American Sociological Review*, 76(4): 513–37.

Zuboff, Shoshana. 1988. *In the Age of the Smart Machine*. New York: Basic Books.

Index

Note: entries pertaining specifically to individual chapters can be found as sub-entries under the relevant chapter headings but general entries pertaining to numerous chapters are listed as main headings with the chapter as a sub-heading.

Printed and bound by CPI Group (UK) Ltd, Croydon, CR0 4YY